Music in Fascist Italy

ALSO BY HARVEY SACHS:

Toscanini (1978)
Virtuoso: The Life and Art of Nine Instrumentalists,
from Paganini to Glenn Gould (1982)

MUSIC IN FASCIST ITALY

Harvey Sachs

W· W· NORTON & COMPANY
New York   London

First American Edition, 1988
All rights reserved

ISBN 0–393–02563–2

W. W. Norton & Company, Inc.,
500 Fifth Avenue, New York NY 10110
W. W. Norton & Company, Ltd.,
37 Great Russell Street, London WC1B 3NU

Printed in Great Britain

1 2 3 4 5 6 7 8 9 0

. . . A state, is called the coldest of all cold monsters. Coldly lieth it also; and this lie creepeth from its mouth: 'I, the state, am the people.' . . . Everything will it give *you*, if *ye* worship it, the new idol: thus it purchaseth the lustre of your virtue, and the glance of your proud eyes. . . . See them clamber, these nimble apes! They clamber over one another, and thus scuffle into the mud and the abyss. . . . My brethren, will ye suffocate in the fumes of their maws and appetites? Better break the windows and jump into the open air! . . . There, where the state ceaseth . . . there commenceth the song of the necessary ones, the single and irreplaceable melody. . . .

Friedrich Nietzsche, *Also sprach Zarathustra* (trans. Thomas Common)

Contents

Acknowledgements   ix

Introduction   1

CHAPTER I: The Terrain   5

CHAPTER II: Institutions   33

      Musical Education   33

      Interview with Massimo Mila   47

      Opera Houses   55

      Concert Societies   87

      Festivals   89

      Competitions   96

      Performance Sites   98

CHAPTER III: Composers   101

      Puccini, Mascagni and Contemporaries   101

      The 'Generation of 1880'   121

      Interview with Goffredo Petrassi   139

CHAPTER IV: Performers   148

      Interview with Gianandrea Gavazzeni   157

CHAPTER V: Foreigners, Alliances, Racism and War   166

CHAPTER VI: The Toscanini Case   207

Epilogue   241

Notes   244

Bibliography   255

Index   258

Acknowledgements

This book was made possible by a grant from the John Simon Guggenheim Memorial Foundation, to whose administrators I offer my gratitude. My particular thanks also go to the following individuals and institutions: Clara and Lorenzo Castelnuovo-Tedesco, Elena Cesari Silva, Fiorenzo Copertini, Gianandrea Gavazzeni, Peter Heyworth, Denis Mack Smith, Massimo Mila, Fiamma Nicolodi, Goffredo Petrassi, Bruno Pizzetti, Barbara Sachs and Philip Wults; Mario Serio, Dottoressa Giannetto, Giulia Barrera and other staff members at the Archivio centrale dello stato, Rome; Maria Adelaide Bacherini and staff at the Sala musica of the Biblioteca nazionale centrale, Florence; Agostina Zecca Laterza and staff at the library of the Conservatorio di musica 'G. Verdi', Milan; Thor Wood and staff at the Research Division of the Library and Museum of the Performing Arts, New York; Pierluigi Petrobelli and staff at the Istituto di studi verdiani, Parma; Stefano Bagnoli of the Fondo Respighi at the Fondazione Giorgio Cini, Venice. My work was also facilitated by the staffs of the Music Division of the Library of Congress and the National Archive, Washington, and of the Reading Room of the British Library, London. Finally, thanks to Juliet Gardiner, Linden Lawson and colleagues at Weidenfeld and Nicolson for their patience and co-operation.

Introduction

In the mid-1970s, while working on a biography of Arturo Toscanini,[1] I examined many documents that concerned the evolution of his resistance to fascism in his native Italy. They made me wonder about other well-known Italian musicians of the period. Did they not understand what was happening in their country? Did any of them protest, and if so, with what consequences? These questions inevitably led to others. To what extent was the fascist government concerned with Italian musical life? Were opera houses, conservatories, and other musical institutions made to comply with directives from Rome? Which ministries and individuals were responsible for musical policy, and how did that policy change during the twenty-one years of fascist rule? What was the official attitude towards foreign music and musicians? Was racism an important element in the story of music under fascism? How did the alliance with Nazi Germany affect Italian musical life?

I discovered that although some of these issues had been dealt with individually in short studies or had been touched upon in monographs on certain twentieth-century Italian composers, performers and musical institutions, there was no single book that attempted to achieve an overview of the subject. Why, in the more than thirty years that had already passed since Mussolini's downfall, had no full-length study of Italian music under fascism been published? The most obvious answer was that too many of the period's musical protagonists were still alive and active during the 1950s, 1960s and 1970s, and that awaiting natural attrition was the easiest form of prudence. But the Outs under fascism had every reason to treat the Ins summarily and pitilessly at war's end, and, in many cases, anti-fascism was more, rather than less, ferocious in the early post-fascist period. Collective trauma, then? No. Open, public discussion of fascism and its adherents has been a constant feature of Italian life from July 1943 to the present, although some of the talk has inevitably demonstrated foggy thinking or bad faith.

The answer probably lies more in the nature of music than in that of the Italian nation or of fascism and its sympathizers. The neo-imperial architectural style encouraged by the fascist regime can be seen – indeed cannot be avoided – by anyone who visits Rome's EUR district, the Piazza della Vittoria in Brescia, or any of the hundreds of other surviving examples. The limited subject-matter and inflated, xenophobic tenor of fascist-inspired literary-oratorical buffooneries are embarrassingly obvious to anyone who has had to plough through them. Films touching in any way upon fascist crimes, government corruption and other delicate subjects would not have been tolerated by the regime, and therefore were not produced in Italy. But how can pro- or anti-fascist intentions in a piece of music be pinpointed, unless that music accompanies a tendentious text? Were there composers, performers or musical administrators who did as they were told out of fear, or in order to advance their careers, or because they truly believed in Mussolini? Were musicians able to ignore the political situation and to go on living and working exactly as they would have done under any other system?

These issues fascinated me, and I began to collect material for this project in 1980. I was not, however, the only person at work in the field. In 1984, a highly informative monograph on the same subject was published by Fiamma Nicolodi of the University of Florence.[2] Nicolodi is a specialist in twentieth-century Italian music, and a substantial portion of her book is devoted to compositional currents in Italy prior to the fascist period. In this and many other structural respects, our studies have little in common. Nevertheless, her lucid and well-documented exposition of many aspects of musical activity under Mussolini's regime stimulated me to reconsider the material I had already gathered. Although there is some unavoidable overlapping, my choice of material usually differs from hers. Our points of view, too, vary greatly, even in cases where our conclusions are similar. I am indebted, however, to Nicolodi's book and to the other help she has generously given me.

The objective of this book is to examine and interpret evidence, not to accuse or sit in judgment. But all authors have, or ought to have, points of view on the subjects they write about, and however fair one attempts to be in handling one's material, the very act of selecting that material, let alone deciding how to treat it, inevitably comprises some degree of tendentious-ness and manipulation. Once I had gathered the bulk of the 'facts' – and had arranged and cut and sifted them – I saw my own view emerging. To balance that view, or perhaps to verify it, I arranged to speak with a few musicians who were active during the fascist period. I was not primarily interested in additional information, but in how they now view the events of fifty years ago, especially in regard to the regime's influence on music. I did not originally plan to publish these interviews as such, but simply to incorporate into the text any useful impressions or ideas gathered from them. But Massimo Mila, Goffredo Petrassi and Gianandrea Gavazzeni are all intelligent men with strong personalities. What each of them had to say seemed worth repeating in its entirety, as a counterfoil to the statements of an author who was born after the Second World War and who grew up far from the Italian cultural milieu. I therefore decided to transcribe the tapes of our conversations, rather than simply making notes from them; the transcripts were then submitted to each of the people concerned, and all consented to publication of the interviews, with no changes of substance.

Those interviewed – a writer on music, a composer and a conductor – were able to talk about different aspects of musical life. Each was differently situated in relation to the regime: Mila – the youngest – was a militant anti-fascist who paid a high price for his convictions; Petrassi was active, albeit in a limited way, in the musical bureaucracy; and Gavazzeni was, by family background and cultural formation, opposed to fascism, but went along with its outward forms and 'did not assume heroic attitudes', as he himself says. There is a minor conclusion to be drawn about the nature of musical life under fascism from the fact that all three were good friends at the time, despite their political differences, and have remained so ever since.

This is neither a history of fascist Italy nor a history of Italian music during the second quarter of the twentieth century. Those seeking further information on, say, Futurist music, or on the lives and works of specific Italian composers, are referred to Nicolodi's book and to the excellent bibliographies accompanying J. C. G. Waterhouse's fine entries on twentieth-century Italian musicians in *The New Grove*. This is a study of how certain musical institutions changed and of how certain musicians fared and acted during more than twenty years of fascist rule.

Harvey Sachs
Loro Ciuffenna, September 1986

CHAPTER I

The Terrain

The story of Italian music in the twentieth century begins with a death: Giuseppe Verdi died in Milan on 27 January 1901, at the age of eighty-seven. Born when Napoleon's armies still dominated much of Italy, Verdi grew up under the Austrian hegemony and reached maturity at the climax of the Italian reunification movement, which he wholeheartedly supported. In the popular imagination, his intense, characterful music and his straightforward personality synthesized the best elements of the epoch of Mazzini, Garibaldi and Cavour. Verdi was the last of the great Risorgimento figures. In Milan, tens of thousands of Italians participated in his funeral procession, and his death was officially commemorated in hundreds of Italian towns. At Forlì in the Romagna, a memorial speech was improvised at the local theatre by a seventeen-year-old student with a talent for oratory: Benito Mussolini.

In 1901 only the most pessimistic of prophets would have predicted that within twenty-five years the Italian operatic repertoire would be stagnating, or that Verdi's passing prefigured the death of opera as a refined art form with mass appeal. Although a hundred and fifty years had elapsed since the musical primacy of Europe had passed from Italy to the Germanic states, the steady succession of capable, popular and influential Italian composers showed no sign of coming to an end. During the 1890s – the decade in which Verdi had given the world his last masterpiece, *Falstaff* – several composers half a century his junior had achieved their first major triumphs. A network of theatres extending from New York to St Petersburg and from Stockholm to Buenos Aires absorbed into their repertoires Pietro Mascagni's *Cavalleria rusticana* (first performed in 1890), Ruggero Leoncavallo's *I pagliacci* (1892), Giacomo Puccini's *Manon Lescaut* (1893) and *La bohème* (1896), and Umberto Giordano's *Andrea Chénier* (1896) as readily as, earlier in the century, they had assimilated the works of Rossini, Donizetti, Bellini and Verdi. Great publishing houses – the Milanese firms of Ricordi and Sanzogno, above all – sought to discover and encourage the composers and compositional trends most likely to attract huge audiences at home and abroad. Well-trained performers were required so that new and old works could be heard to best effect. Even a short list of Italian singers active between 1890 and 1910 is extraordinarily impressive: Mattia Battistini, Gemma Bellincioni, Alessandro Bonci, Giuseppe Borgatti, Enrico Caruso, Lina Cavalieri, Giuseppe De Luca, Fernando De Lucia, Antonio Pini Corsi, Titta Ruffo, Antonio Scotti, Rosina Storchio, Francesco Tamagno, Luisa Tetrazzini and Giovanni Zenatello. Young Arturo Toscanini was well on his way to becoming the most influential conductor of his time. Other Italian conductors – Luigi Mancinelli, Edoardo Mascheroni, Leopoldo Mugnone, Cleofonte Campanini, Tullio Serafin – were then in their prime and were developing important international careers. Symphonic and chamber music, which had for many decades been in the background of Italian musical life, was slowly beginning to arouse interest again as a result of the efforts of composer-performers such as Giuseppe Martucci, Giovanni Sgambati, Marco Enrico Bossi and, most important, Ferruccio Busoni. Although Busoni spent most of his adult life outside Italy, his cultural ties to his native country remained strong. His compositions never achieved mass popularity, but his career as a pianist was so successful that he must be considered, after Paganini, the most important Italian instrumentalist of the last two hundred years.

Italy was well-provided with beautiful opera houses and with institutions for educating young musicians. Milan, Turin, Naples, Venice, Bologna, Rome, Parma, Florence and Palermo all had major theatres and front-ranking conservatories, and smaller music academies existed throughout the country. The training they provided was reactionary but solid. Nearly every town had at least a month-long opera season every winter, and the larger cities usually had several opera theatres whose seasons lasted one to six months each. The lyric repertoire was adventurous, or at least up to date. Like today's public for cinema or musical comedy, opera audiences a century ago were generally more interested in new works than in the classics of the genre. Opera composers wrote in a slowly but continuously evolving musical language; a reasonably open, attentive listener had little trouble keeping pace. By the turn of the century, the works of such foreign composers as Wagner, Bizet, and Massenet were being presented with success at major Italian theatres; soon after, operas by Tchaikovsky, Mussorgsky, Richard Strauss and Debussy began to be heard.

By 1915, when Italy entered the First World War, several new trends among young Italian musicians were becoming evident. The first was an inevitable reaction against opera's stranglehold on the nation's musical life – a much sharper and less conciliatory reaction than in the previous generation. Rebellious youngsters like composers Alfredo Casella and Gian Francesco Malipiero and musicologist Fausto Torrefranca made sweeping accusations against nineteenth-century melodrama and called for a new aesthetic in the theatre and a great stride forward in the production of 'pure' instrumental music. Many years later, Massimo Mila, the music historian and critic, dubbed Casella and Malipiero, along with the less radical Ildebrando Pizzetti, Ottorino Respighi, Franco Alfano and Riccardo Zandonai, *la generazione dell'ottanta* – the 1880 generation. All of them were born between 1875 and 1885, but their talents and points of view were very dissimilar, often even clashing.

Francesco Balilla Pratella and Luigi Russolo belonged, chronologically, to the *generazione dell'ottanta*, but, as the musical sub-deacons of Filippo Tommaso Marinetti's controversial Futurist movement, they made a different attack against what they declared to be the complacency of the Italian musical scene. They were iconoclasts, experimentalists and, to a great extent, sensationalists, whose diatribes helped to awaken a few dormant musical minds, but whose works quickly proved to be inconsequential. They eventually exerted some influence on Edgard Varèse and on the *musique concrète* movement, but their own compositions were too ephemeral to become classics in any genre. From roughly 1910 to 1935, the Futurists were the oddest creatures in Italy's musical menagerie.

This, then, in very broad outline, was the Italian musical terrain immediately prior to Benito Mussolini's arrival at the centre of Italian political life – an arrival whose background is extremely complicated. Italy was a constitutional monarchy headed by the House of Savoy – former kings of Sardinia, whose capital had been at Turin in Piedmont. The nation had existed as a political entity only since 1860; parts of it, including Venice and Rome, were annexed later, and the Trent and Trieste regions were not taken away from Austria until the end of the First World War. At the turn of the century, the country was beset by a variety of ills. There were vast economic disparities between the agrarian south and the mercantile, increasingly industrialized north. Massive unemployment was creating great waves of emigration, and working-class unrest was connected with the assassination, by an anarchist, of King Umberto I in July 1900. An ambiguous Constitution coupled with an exceptionally faction-ridden parliament weighed upon legislative procedures, and the ruling classes were bitter over Italy's military defeat in Ethiopia (1896), at the end of an unsuccessful attempt to become a colonial power. Francesco Crispi, prime minster from 1887 to 1891 and from 1893 to 1896, had favoured ultra-nationalistic and socially repressive policies that were in some respects proto-fascistic; but Giovanni Giolitti – five times prime minster between 1892 and 1921, and the canniest figure in Italian politics between Crispi and Mussolini – preferred a skilful combination of liberalism, corruption and strategic inaction to overt repression.

A brief war with Libya in 1911–12 gave the country a colony, but the First

World War proved to be a long-term disaster for Italy, as for the rest of Europe. In May 1915, she gave up her neutrality, forswore the Triple Alliance with Germany and Austria, and entered what was expected to be a quick, decisive set-to on the side of Britain and France. When the war ended three and a half years later, the cost of Italy's territorial gains was calculated at approximately 600,000 dead and 148,000,000,000 lire – double the sum of all government expenditures in the previous half-century of the nation's existence.[1] The resulting economic and social upheaval was the worst the country had known. By 1919, Giolittian liberalism was opposed by three major groups: the socialists, the centrist Catholic *popolari* and the newly founded fascists, who were initially ultra-nationalists with bolshevik-like domestic policies. The elections of November 1919 returned 100 *popolari* and 156 socialists to the 535-seat parliament; no fascists were elected. But the *popolari* were internally divided and the socialists more so. 'The only constant factor among the socialists', according to historian Denis Mack Smith, 'was their association of violent language with a timid uncertainty in deed.'[2]

> Only when these elections showed the folly of competing with the official socialists for working-class support did Mussolini reveal his true colours as those of pure opportunism and change to the conservative side. His only consistency was in the use of violent means for the pursuit of power, and the agrarian disorders of Emilia and the Po Valley soon gave him the chance to launch a civil war against the socialists who in 1914 had thrown him out of their party [. . .]. Gangsterism came out on top once electoral failure had turned him not only against socialism but against the parliamentary system itself.[3]

Mussolini and his supporters were favoured by the disarray of the other parties, the legitimate anger of young veterans who had to face massive unemployment while witnessing the well-being of war profiteers, and the nationalistic exploits of poet Gabriele D'Annunzio, who illegally, but with government connivance, occupied the disputed Istrian city of Fiume (1919–20) with a band of demobilized soldiers and malcontents. Government after government failed to resolve pressing problems and resorted to stop-gap measures that invariably aroused antagonism among large sectors of the nation. Labour unrest and strikes also played a part in the general disorder, but these conditions existed in other countries without disastrous effects. There is no proof that a subversive master-plan lay behind the labour problems.[4]

Increasing lawlessness led landowners and other people with interests to protect to engage paramilitary gangs, which ranged over parts of the country, meting out summary justice as they saw fit. Governmental authority as well as individuals were attacked, and the resulting anarchic conditions made many people long for authoritarian government. Although the socialists were responsible for some of the violence, the bands became the nucleus of the fascist *squadre*. The fascists were 'better organized, better armed, and had more money; their raids were more numerous, more widely felt, and infinitely more successful'.[5]

By October 1922 the Italian government, headed by Luigi Facta, was reduced to impotence, and the fascists made it known that if they did not participate in the formation of a new government they would start a revolution. Militarily, they were still a minor force; any concrete action by the government could have called their bluff. Facta, however, indicated his readiness to concede to the fascists a part in the new government; when the fascists escalated demands and called for the government to resign, Facta decided to decree martial law and to arrest the fascist leaders. King Victor Emmanuel III, probably fearing a demand for his abdication, refused to ratify the order. The public authorities believed that the government would do nothing to stop the fascists and 'adjusted their loyalties [. . .]. Mussolini now knew that the king, having once yielded to a threat, would always do so again, for he had been made an accomplice [. . .]'.[6]

Mussolini had remained in Milan during the wavering and bargaining, ready to escape to Switzerland if his bluff were called. He insisted on an official telegram from the king, asking him to form a government, and when that reached him on 29 October, he 'marched on Rome' in a sleeping car. 'In the meantime,' wrote historian Gaetano Salvemini,

> after the revocation of martial law, on the afternoon of October 28th and throughout the day and night of the 29th, thousands of fascists had 'marched on Rome', joining those who had 'marched' on the night of the 27th and the morning of the 28th. Some of them, like the Duce, 'marched' in a sleeping car; the majority 'marched' in trains they had taken by force [. . .]. Finally, on the afternoon of October 31st, when all was ready, this ridiculous demonstration took place. Fifty thousand [*sic*] men paraded through the streets of Rome to celebrate their victory, after a 'march on Rome' that had never taken place. [. . .] Fascist historiography calls this comic opera a 'revolution'.[7]

Italian political and social history during the twenty-one Mussolini-dominated years that followed proved to be comic opera-like only in outward aspect. Like other totalitarian or would-be totalitarian governments, the fascist regime gradually attempted to gain control of all aspects of society. (The Duce sometimes referred to 'his' Italy as a 'corporative state'. He and many of his principal supporters, however, also had a pronounced weakness for the word 'totalitarian' and for the behaviour it implied.) But despite the eventual alliance and claims of kinship between Mussolini's Italy and Hitler's Germany, the two societies and their leaders were very dissimilar in most respects. Hitler had a fundamental belief – the supremacy of the so-called Aryan race – and a precise goal – German domination of as much of the world as possible. He persuaded a large number of Germans that they had specific, identifiable enemies – Jews, communists, cosmopolites – whose disappearance was a prerequisite to their nation's triumph; and he saw himself as the anointed saviour and leader of his people. By contrast, Mussolini's deepest belief was in his own genius for ruling. Italy happened to be the tool by which he could achieve his own manifest destiny. The motto he handed down to his people was of telegraphic brevity: 'Believe, obey, fight'; he might have added: 'Details to follow at unspecified date', since his policies on nearly every issue fluctuated violently. In Mussolini's view, Italy's enemies were the unenlightened or evil people who opposed his infallible leadership; their origins and convictions in other areas meant little to him, at least during his early years in power. His real talent, the facts demonstrate, was not for governing, but rather for persuading people, including himself, that he had such a talent.

Hitler was consistent in his delusion; Mussolini was chameleon-like. His short-term strength and long-term weakness lay precisely in his ability to adapt his act to the audience of the moment. To the bloodthirsty he was a sabre-rattler; to the cultured he was a sensitive soul who played the violin and appeared to favour government assistance to the arts; to farmers he was the man who stood bare-chested, helping to thresh wheat during the harvest season; to sports enthusiasts he was a horseman; to believers in the myth of the Latin lover he was an unregenerate seducer of women; to practising Catholics he was the moving force in the creation of the Lateran Accord with the Vatican, which ended seventy years of Church–State hostility; to archaeologists he was the man who wished to bring to the surface Italy's buried glories of the past; to modernists he was the man who was unafraid to destroy vast tracts of Rome's historic centre in order to monumentalize fascism's achievements. The lack of enduring conviction behind any of these poses proved disastrous for the millions of Italians who were to pay dearly for what proved to have been an extraordinarily ephemeral illusion.

Most Italian musicians lived through the twenty-year fraud in much the same way as other citizens, by trying to carry on their daily lives without becoming involved in the pros and cons of the regime. Study of Italian music under fascism reveals a picture of workaday infighting and intrigue in abundance, much grotesque opportunism, occasional examples of naïve good faith in the government, and very little real political opposition. Through it all, there flowed an endless torrent of fluctuating government directives on musical education, the management of opera houses, the formation of innumerable musicians' unions, corporations, councils and committees, and the organization of festivals, congresses, competitions and musical showcases – all brainchildren of various party Excellencies or of musical personalities who had ingratiated themselves with the fascists. Some of the ideas were good, others absurd; all but a few remained partly or wholly unrealized.

An understanding of musical life in fascist Italy requires knowledge of the country's musical super- and sub-structures at the time of Mussolini's takeover and their augmentation and transformation under the regime. This, in turn, requires familiarity with the people who determined the music bureaucracy's policies by interpreting generic government directives according to their own ideas, temperaments and instincts for political survival.

At the very top, claiming godlike omniscience in the field of music as in other areas, was the Duce. By all accounts, public and private, contemporary and post-mortem, Mussolini seems to have had a genuine liking for music. Guesses as to the extent of his musical knowledge vary widely, but his desire to turn music to his political advantage cannot be doubted. From the moment he came to power, Italian music journals watched for opportunities to thank him for having received this or that musician at Palazzo Venezia, for having given his approval to one musical undertaking or another, and for his professions of interest in the nation's opera houses, conservatories and musicians' unions. Mussolini encouraged the press to describe and praise his polyhedric personality, and he enjoyed – especially during his early years in power – playing the role of the sensitive music lover who, despite the immeasurable problems and labours that his daily work imposed upon him, managed to find time for the finer things in life.

In 1927 the Library of Fascist Propaganda commissioned Raffaello De Rensis, a well-known musical journalist, to write a booklet entitled *Mussolini musicista* (*Mussolini the Musician*), twenty-fifth instalment in a series ('Mussolinia') whose purpose was to inflate and praise every aspect of the great man's life. Mussolini loved obsequiousness – the more insipid the better – and De Rensis's pamphlet demonstrates exactly how the dictator wished to have his musical background and tastes represented.

> Little Benito diligently frequented the church [in his native village, Predappio] to hear the dragging cantilenas of the faithful and the organ's harmonious sounds, which perturbed him in a strange, indefinable way. When the gay, noisy Romagnole bands arrived for religious holidays, he was among the most assiduous listeners; he often followed them as they marched through the streets of the village, and the dry, bold rhythm stirred his instinctively war-like spirit. He harboured a special sympathy for birds and listened with curiosity, in the solitude of the woods, to their tweeting, their chirping and their screeching, as if their language revealed profound mysteries.[8]

Following further ornithological musings, the author attempts to upholster as thickly as possible the skeletal information Mussolini had given about his scant musical training.

> There was even a little music-making in the shop of his father, Signor

> Alessandro, whose helper was a village violinist. It is probable that Benito, who also worked in his father's shop, was possessed of the desire to study the violin precisely through contact with this blacksmith-musician. [. . .] During his [general] studies, he was inseparable from his faithful violin [. . .][9]

In describing the dictator's troubled early years – during which 'he gathered in his breast all the heroic upheaval of humanity' – De Rensis mentions a day in 1902, in Lausanne, when the nineteen-year-old 'lacked any means for food and lodging'. He quotes Mussolini directly:

> An infinite melancholy assailed me, and I asked myself, on the pier in Lake Leman, if living another day was worth the effort [. . .]. But a harmony as sweet as the song of a mother over her baby's cradle deviated the course of my thoughts. I turned around. Forty orchestra musicians were playing in front of the grandiose Hotel Beau Rivage. I leaned against the garden gates, looked at the dark green leaves of the fir trees, lent an ear and listened. The music consoled my brain and my stomach.[10]

Mussolini, records De Rensis, resumed his study of the violin at Forlì in 1909, this time under the supervision of one Archimede Montanelli, 'who was surprised by his strange pupil's "extraordinary" progress.'[11] (A few months after De Rensis's booklet appeared, *Musica d'oggi* (*Today's Music*), a journal published by the Ricordi company – always adept at looking after its political interests – printed the momentous news that Montanelli had celebrated his eightieth birthday at the Victor Emmanuel rest home in Forlì.) In a conversation with his illegitimate son, Yvon de Begnac, in 1940, Mussolini called Montanelli 'an excellent teacher'. During the same period, while employed as editor of a new but short-lived local socialist weekly, *La lotta di classe* (*Class Struggle*), the future dictator attended the opera season 'from the gallery of the [Teatro] *Comunale*, paying [for admission] in order to be able to write what I thought. Music criticism was entirely in my hands and grew out of my conversations with Montanelli.'[12] Examination of the four-page newspaper shows that Mussolini reviewed a total of two or possibly three performances and that he was not completely ignorant of music. 'We shall not discuss the repertoire presented at Forlì, which, thanks to its most unfortunate theatre, must nearly always make do with operas that are real musical exhumations', says an unsigned article of 2 April 1910.

> We get nothing, or almost nothing, modern. The citizen of Forlì who wants to hear Wagner must head for Cesena or Ravenna. From the point of view of musical culture, this is lamentable. Thus, we would have preferred two modern operas instead of the *Barber of Seville* and *I Puritani*. [. . .] [About the performance of the *Barber*:] The queen of the production is [. . .] the soprano Saffo Michelini. [. . .] Her voice is clear and powerful. [. . .] The other artists neither add to nor detract from the ensemble. [. . .] Maestro *Manno*, the

conductor, gets all that is humanly possible to get out of that simulacrum of an orchestra. [. . .] The chorus was off rhythm.

The following week's review states that 'the performance of Bellini's I *puritani* was infinitely superior to that of the *Barber of Seville*'. The baritone role in this 'first-class production' was sung by the twenty-two-year-old Mariano Stabile – 'a secure artist'. His official début was still a year in the future, but he was to become one of the most famous protagonists of Verdi's *Falstaff* in the work's history.

De Rensis, in order to add something resembling first-hand testimony to his inventions about the importance of music in the young Mussolini's life, quotes Antonio Beltramelli, a novelist who grew up in Mussolini's native region and who later became an ardent supporter and protégé of the fascist government. 'In his darkest hours', says Beltramelli of the future dictator's Forlì days,

> he took refuge in music, which led him far away, to the divine world of the spirit, where unreality dwells. He would go off with his violin, and he would forget that he was poor, alone, oppressed, [. . .] in a peaceful world of impoverished spirits – a world led by people with no culture, no enthusiasm, no idealism, no strength for action, no pride and no conscience.[13]

Mussolini gave up the violin for a while; but he told de Begnac that 'in 1918, at the time of my illness following my war wounds, I resumed with "a few" studies by Dankle [*sic*, for Dancla] and Pist [Pixis?]'.[14] The construction of a new, violent political movement and the struggle to achieve power left him little time for music during the next few years. De Rensis resumes his boot-licking, however, by assuring his readers that on one of the first days after 'this gigantic and many-sided man' had made his 'epic entrance into Rome', people who worked in the palace that housed the prime minister's offices were amazed to hear the 'timorous, sonorous voice of his violin. "This man", they said, "does everything and knows everything. He even understands music and the secrets of an instrument that is not easy to play." '[15]

In a propagandistic volume (*Mussolini: The Man of Destiny*, published in 1928), Vittorio E. De Fiori wrote: 'Music is the best medium of expression for great minds, and Mussolini's favourite pieces were great symphonies and triumphal marches, the prelude, as it were, to his march on Rome.'[16] Long after Mussolini's death, his butler stated, more simply, that the Duce had enjoyed listening to the radio and records at Palazzo Venezia and that he had 'a strong dislike for dance music and so-called light music'. De Rensis, however, was determined to demonstrate a more serious musical commit-ment on Mussolini's part. Plagiarizing from Margherita Sarfatti's *Dux*, a biography of the dictator, he said: 'At whatever hour he returns home, from whatever harassing cares, he throws himself at the violin with voracious anger, and the angrier he is the better he plays – especially if the music is new to him.' De Rensis adds, in his own words, that 'among Corelli's works, [Mussolini] favours *La follia*; he plays some Beethoven sonatas, a great many compositions by Veracini, Vivaldi, Bach and, among the moderns, Granados, Fauré, and Virgilio Ranzato's *Barcarola*'.[17]

But *how* did he play them? Sarfatti, who had known the dictator since his socialist days and had been his lover, did not allow Mussolini the Musician to evade a dose of criticism, however small:

> He has the [right] tone and expression, but he is domineering even with music. He respects neither style nor balance. Whether it be Tannhäuser's aria for evenings when the moon is full [n.b.: presumably 'O du mein holder Abendstern'] or Corelli or Beethoven, he plays everything in his own way; and as he unleashes the melody, his frowning face is smoothed into an intimate, victorious cheerfulness.[18]

De Rensis, however, had 'not yet been allowed the great honour' of hearing Mussolini play, and could therefore assume that

> Sarfatti must have expressed herself incompletely and with slight exaggeration. No doubt the Duce plays in his own fashion. His terrifying individuality and extremely vast spirituality certainly permit him a characteristic and personal type of interpretation, but it is not possible to believe that he does not respect style and balance, especially in dealing with eminently architectonic composers. [...][19]

Emil Ludwig queried the dictator in 1932 about the amount of time he dedicated to the violin. 'If I play for half an hour, it soothes me, but in an hour I get excited and tired. It's like a poisonous drug, which may be useful in very small doses, and deadly in large ones.'[20] Mussolini later told de Begnac:

> I haven't played in many years. I have to laugh at those old photographs from 1922 that show me in a morning-coat while I play the violin. That was the time of my earliest innocence. But even that caused a fuss. Hostile critics took advantage of the incident. After all, I wasn't playing the emigrants' harmonica or the beggars' barrel-organ. [...] I wasn't an ace, but I didn't do too badly for a mediocre amateur.[21]

But De Rensis insisted that although

> Mussolini is certainly not a musician in the strictly technical sense, or a virtuoso violinist, he is something more and better: he is an instinctive musician. [...] I arrived at this conclusion by having attended several musical events next to Him, at his home in Via Rasella, in the strictest privacy. (This honour was permitted me, and it will constitute the proudest and most ineradicable memory of my life.)[22]

De Rensis's description of Mussolini listening to a Hungarian string quartet playing Beethoven's Opus 95 would have made a fine scene in Chaplin's *The Great Dictator*.

The Duce had listened with religious attention, inhaling the perfume of a carnation; he had visibly welcomed into his great soul the magical, divine, revelatory word of the giant of Bonn, experiencing indescribable emotion. At the back of his bright, motionless, dilated pupils, as at the bottom of the sea, one distinguished a wealth of goodness, gentleness and sweet melancholy. He declared to the stalwart interpreters – who seemed charged with an unusual, unforeseen exaltation – all his satisfaction, and he pointed out to them the pessimistic, universal meaning of this poem of Beethoven's.[23]

Beethoven was Mussolini's favourite composer – or the composer whom he wished people to think was his favourite. On the centenary of Beethoven's birth, he made a fulsome declaration to the *Hamburger Nachrichten*:

I adore Beethoven as the greatest chanter of terrestrial symphonies and harmonies. The joy he gives to the spirit is so high and superhuman that it is often crossed by a subtle, almost anguished, shiver. In fact, only lofty peaks convey a fear of the absolute and the unknown. Beethoven's music detaches man from his moral humanity. It is the miracle of the saints guided by God.[24]

His remarks on the subject to Emil Ludwig were less inflated: 'For us moderns, Beethoven still remains the greatest of all composers, especially as author of the *Sixth Symphony*, the *Ninth Symphony*, and the last of his quartettes [sic].' Ludwig asked him whether he liked Wagner. 'I can't stand *Parsifal*,' he said, 'but I am fond of the third act of *Tristan*; and also of the earlier, more melodious works of Wagner – *Tannhäuser* and *Lohengrin*.' (Mussolini's sons, Vittorio and Bruno, often had to screen their sleeping father from public view during performances of Wagner's operas.) 'Still,' the Duce told Ludwig, in a successful attempt at one upmanship, 'Palestrina and his school are more congenial to me [. . .].'[25] This profession of love for a composer whose music was even less played fifty years ago than it is today was probably made for purposes of nationalistic and personal propaganda; but Mussolini's subordinates in the party hierarchy, always ready to enlarge upon his already exaggerated statements, were soon demonstrating that their leader stood in the vanguard of the proto-revivalists of early Italian music. In a book entitled *L'arte e il Duce*, Francesco Sapori wrote:

This insatiable and incomparable achiever is determined to reawaken the art of polyphony. In the ethereal tone-world, his favourites are named Palestrina and Monteverdi among vocal composers, Frescobaldi among organ composers, Galuppi and Scarlatti among harpsichord composers, Corelli and Vivaldi among symphonic [sic] composers.[26]

Mussolini also wanted to be viewed as a modernist. Towards the end of the dictator's life, one hanger-on asked him about his favourite contemporary Italian composers. He replied:

Among opera composers of the popular, national category, Puccini and Mascagni; among [other] composers, Pizzetti, although he has an opportunistic and vulgar soul. Malipiero's efforts seem to me exemplary, although his opponents never fail to upbraid me |for this opinion|. | . . . | Of the very youngest, we can expect good things from |Luigi| Dalla Piccola |sic| and |Annibale| Bizzelli, for example. I heard an opera |by Bizzelli|, I don't remember whether in the theatre or on the radio, and it was full of delectable and intelligent things.[27]

De Rensis portrayed Mussolini as an adherent of Mazzini's ideas about art and its 'highest humanitarian and political mission', and supported his opinion with one of his hero's typically clumsy, rhetorical, ambiguous statements:

Today, when all the conditions most looked forward to by the great Italians – unity first and foremost – have been realized, a great art can be developed in our land, an art that comprises within itself all of life's manifestations and at the same time shapes them, an art that must be traditional and at the same time modern, that must look towards the past and at the same time towards the future. We must not remain meditators, we must not take advantage of the heritage of the past; we must create a new heritage to set alongside the ancient one, we must create a new art, an art that is of our times, a fascist art.[28]

De Rensis's apologia is lengthy, vacuous and overblown – and it is merely one example of the deification of Mussolini to which people connected with music, like their counterparts in other fields, were expected to contribute. Again, the Italian music journals of the period bear witness. *Musica d'oggi*, April 1927, reported that Mussolini had bestowed his patronage upon the new 'G. Rossini' Music Academy of Pesaro – the composer's native town – and had 'consented' to having the library of its sister organization, the Musical High School, take his name. A few months later, the same magazine informed readers that Mussolini had become patron of the Scarlatti Orchestra of Naples and that he had received a delegation of musicians and politicians who had presented him with the first reconstructed edition of music 'drawn from the precious collection that came to light in a village of the Monferrato region'.[29] The issue of February 1929 says that the king and Mussolini had been given copies of Ricordi's new publication, *Musical Soul of the Nation*, which contained music dating from 1796 to the march on Rome. 'The August Sovereign and the Duce examined the two volumes at length, declaring their satisfaction to the editor and the publisher' – who happened also to publish *Musica d'oggi*. Both *Musica d'oggi* and the much more serious and independent *Rassegna musicale* found it prudent to announce, in the autumn of 1933, that Mussolini had approved the programme of the following year's International Music Festival in Venice. The August–September 1937 issue of *Musica d'oggi* states: 'The Duce expressed his satisfaction with the positive outcome of the *open-air opera performances* and has decided that in the summer of Year XVI |1938| such events will be further developed and strengthened, setting up towards that end – from this moment – a precise and ample plan.'

In contrast to all these tea-party niceties, however, stood Mussolini's determination to transform Italians into a harsh, spartan, militaristic people and to rid the country once and for all of its agrarian–artistic image. In 1931, the Duce – the man who 'took refuge in music', in the 'divine world of the spirit', who 'adored Beethoven', and in whom one could distinguish 'a wealth of goodness, gentleness and sweet melancholy' while he listened to string quartets – sent the following secret circular to all Italian diplomatic and consular representatives in foreign countries:

> I prescribe that from now on, no favour be shown in any way to [Italian] musical initiatives – operas, vocal [recitals], concerts or musical evenings – [and] that they be treated icily. Exceptions will be made for symphony orchestras, whose performances also give an idea of collective group discipline. All the rest must be ignored. It is high time that the world – that is, hundreds of millions of men – get to know a different type of Italian from that of yesterday – the eternal tenor and mandolinist [who exist] for others' diversion. Caruso and the like were or are [representatives of] the old Italy. Mussolini.[30]

Under the regime of this sensitive soul, Rome's outstanding concert hall, the Augusteum, was torn down and never replaced; racially and nationally 'undesirable' composers and performers were eventually banned from Italian musical life, and some of them were subjected to great suffering; and the few Italian musicians who openly opposed fascism were attacked, forced into exile or imprisoned.

Directly below Mussolini, the top echelon of power within the Fascist Party consisted in large part of violent men, limited in intelligence, next to whom the Duce would necessarily look impressive. Their contacts with music and the other arts were purely ceremonial or peripheral. Achille Starace, party secretary for many years, was, according to Mack Smith, 'unintelligent, humourless, [and] utterly obedient' to Mussolini, who 'knew that his police dossier contained accusations of involvement in prostitution, drugs, peculation, rape and pederasty'.[31] Starace's views on culture were summarized in some of his directives to provincial party bosses. 'It must be decided', he wrote, 'to sweep away little cultural circles and the like, in which residues of afascism, if not downright anti-fascism, are sheltered.'[32] In the political jargon of the day, 'afascists' were people who, without being openly antagonistic to the regime, did not demonstrate enthusiasm for it. On another occasion he wrote: 'For some time now, "Saturdays" of every kind – artistic, musical, and springtime "Saturdays", etc. – are being invented. I remind you that there is only the "Fascist Saturday".'[33] To Starace, any endeavour that did not in some way contribute to the glory of the regime was suspect. Nevertheless, in an earlier phase of his career (1925), he was the man to whom Mussolini had given the honour of presenting a bill that eventually led to the nationalization of Rome's main opera house, the Teatro Costanzi.[34]

The following dialogue is not an excerpt from a pulp novel: it is a transcript of a telephone conversation between Roberto Farinacci, one of the most ruthless and uncouth of the Duce's immediate inferiors, and the mezzo-soprano Gianna Pederzini, a famous Carmen of the 1930s, celebrated for both her voice and her beauty. Their relationship was probably Farinacci's closest approach to the world of music – although he often took credit for musical events in his home town, Cremona, which he ran as a fief. The transcript exists because Mussolini, like other absolute rulers, trusted no one and was always careful to obtain precise information on the public and private activities of his underlings for use if any of them ever disputed his supremacy.

> F: Must I throw myself at your feet to see you again?
> P: Yes.
> F: If I do that, I'll make myself even more ridiculous . . . So only if I prostrate myself will you do it . . .
> P: The fact is that we get along on one point only: the one created by Mother Nature. There it's divine, perfect. But there is no other area.
> F: And I thought I'd found a soul, not just a body! But I'll make you pay for this. I'm the one who's suffering today, but tomorrow . . .
> P: Phoning you was a mistake.
> F: You humiliate me every time you talk to me, you slap me, and you don't justify yourself for what you've done to me.
> P: I don't have to justify anything.
> F: What? You've led me by the nose countless times! Everybody knows it now. And this torments me, it distresses me. My God, how you make me suffer! No one would dare to do to me what you've done to me.
> P: I haven't done anything to you.
> F: Drop dead, you miserable wretch.[35]

Other party bosses managed to associate their names with the world of music by attending special events as official representatives of the government. The press duly noted, for example, the presence of Costanzo Ciano – Minister of Communications, head of one of the most rapacious families in the fascist hierarchy and father of Mussolini's future son-in-law – at the reinterment of Luigi Boccherini, who had died in Madrid in 1805, but whose remains were transferred in 1927 to his native town of Lucca.[36] The joint attempt of Ciano and Leandro Arpinati, Under-secretary of the Interior, to make their official presence felt at a special concert conducted by Toscanini in Bologna in 1931 was to trigger the most embarrassing event in the story of fascism's relationship to the arts.

But if most of Mussolini's immediate subordinates – the people who helped him to achieve and maintain power – were fools, criminals or barbarians, the administrative ranks directly below them included several intelligent men, highly competent in their respective fields. Some of them were involved in directing the Ministry of Public Education and, later, the Ministry of Popular Culture, each of which had a measure of authority over certain aspects of Italian musical life.

The various national conservatories and music schools fell under the jurisdiction of the Education Ministry, and Mussolini's first choice to head the department was the well-known philosopher Giovanni Gentile. Gentile, the principal intellectual apologist of fascism, was a fundamentally inde-pendent-minded man. Although he did not hesitate to engage 'afascist' or anti-fascist intellectuals for jobs he felt they were exceptionally qualified to carry out, he was also willing to rationalize some of the party's more questionable methods of proselytization. During an election speech in Palermo in 1924, for instance, to excuse the bludgeonings and assassinations perpetrated by the fascists during the campaign, the Minister made some odd remarks about those who differentiated between moral and material force:

> [These are] naïve distinctions, if they are made in good faith! All force is moral force, because it is always addressed to the will; and whatever form of persuasion is adopted – from the sermon to the truncheon – its efficacy can only be that which in the end urges man internally and persuades him to consent. What the nature of this form of persuasion ought to be is not a subject for abstract discussion.[37]

Having left the Ministry to assume other high government positions (president of the committee to study 'constitutional reform' – that is, the gradual legalization of dictatorship; president of the High Council on Public Education; member of the Grand Council of Fascism; founder and president of the National Fascist Institute of Culture; director of the monumental and generally excellent *Enciclopedia Italiana*), Gentile rationalized the dismissal of subordinates who had refused to take the oath of loyalty to the Fascist Party. He also swallowed Mussolini's increasingly jingoistic policies and put up with the officialization of racism. Shortly before the Allied liberation of central Italy in 1944, he was assassinated in Florence by partisans who apparently favoured material forms of persuasion over moral ones.

As Minister of Education, Gentile initiated a much-needed programme of school reforms. Many of these changes, however, were regarded by most fascists as too élitist in nature and were blocked by Gentile's successors at the Ministry, the name of which was changed in 1929 from Ministero della Pubblica Istruzione to Ministero dell' Educazione Nazionale.[38] (*Istruzione* is roughly equivalent to the English word education, in its contemporary sense, whereas *educazione* refers to the overall formation of individuals, rather like the

German *Bildung*.) Most of these successors were lightweights*; although teachers and educational administrators were increasingly pushed by the government to make public avowals of faith in and enthusiasm for fascism, there were few changes in the teaching of traditional subjects. Early in 1935, however, Mussolini appointed Cesare Maria De Vecchi, a comrade from fascism's early days, to head the Ministry. Mack Smith calls De Vecchi 'one of the more brutal and foolish fascists' and says that the appointment 'seemed deliberately designed to humiliate the teaching profession. Some thought that De Vecchi was chosen merely because he had the reputation of bringing good luck [. . .]. Mussolini was superstitious [. . .].'[39] As Minister, De Vecchi emphasized the importance of religious instruction at primary and secondary school levels and introduced 'military culture' as a required subject at the latter and during the first two years of university studies.[40]

Giuseppe Bottai, the last significant personality to hold the Education portfolio under fascism, is generally regarded today as having been one of the more intelligent and less sordid of Mussolini's henchmen. But Bottai helped to found the Roman *fascio di combattimento* in 1919 and then became a leader of proto-fascist thuggery in and around the capital. Soon after the party came to power, he founded the review, *Critica fascista*, and later held positions as Under-secretary and Minister of the Corporations (1926–32), and as President of the National Fascist Institute of Social Insurance (1932–5). He was a key figure in what would today be called the public relations campaign to apotheosize the Duce. No figure in history, he said, could compare with Mussolini.[41] As Minister of National Education (1936–43), Bottai came closer than any of his predecessors to completing the fascistization of Italian educational and cultural organizations. The 'character-building powers' of music and the other arts, he said, 'must be usefully employed and controlled by the State itself'.[42] Although much less powerful and visible than Mussolini, Bottai was almost as consummate a politician as his master: he succeeded in persuading industrialists that fascism was less radical than they feared, in convincing intellectuals that it was less conservative than they feared, and in reassuring Mussolini that despite his (Bottai's) expressed qualms regarding some of the Duce's decisions, he would always stand by him. Bottai was one of the members of the Fascist Grand Council who signed the order divesting the Duce of power in July 1943.

During the regime's last eight years, the Ministry of the Press and Propaganda, whose name was changed in 1937 to Ministry of Popular Culture,

---

* Holders of the portfolio under fascism were: Gentile, 1922–4; Count Alessandro Casati, 1924–5; Pietro Fedele, 1925–8; Giuseppe Belluzzo, 1928–9; Balbino Giuliano, 1929–32; Francesco Ercole, 1932–5; Cesare Maria De Vecchi, 1935–6; Giuseppe Bottai, 1936–43; and Carlo Alberto Biggini, 1943.

exercised more influence on Italian musical life than any other official agency.* Nicola De Pirro, whose ideas on music carried the most weight, headed the ministry's General Theatre Administration. Like Bottai, he must be classed among the more intelligent and competent of top-level fascist bureaucrats. De Pirro had fought in the First World War; he later obtained a law degree and, like Bottai, was an early supporter of fascist *squadrismo* in the Rome area. He served the regime as director-general of the National Fascist Entertainment Association, president of the Opera Consortium, member of the National Council of Corporations, editor-in-chief of *Critica fascista*, and founder-editor of a theatre magazine, *Scenario*.

In the fascists' sub-ministerial musical bureaucracy, three names appear more frequently than any others: Adriano Lualdi, Giuseppe Mulè and Alceo Toni.

Lualdi, a solidly trained composer of decidedly conservative stamp as well as a conductor and writer on musical subjects, ardently supported the regime from its early years and, in 1929, entered the completely fascisticized, evirated Chamber of Deputies as representative of the Fascist Union of Musicians. His official activities later extended to representing the artistic and professional category on the governing board of the Corporation of the Performing Arts, which entitled him to serve as a national councillor in the Chamber of Fasces and Corporations. These high-ranking political positions gave him a great deal of clout within the Italian musical world: he founded and organized government-subsidized festivals, and he participated – or interfered – in the administration of many important cultural organizations and enterprises. Lualdi directed the Naples Conservatory from 1936 to 1944, arranged important national and foreign tours for himself and managed to have his works performed by the most important ensembles in the country.

Throughout the 1930s, Lualdi used the party's increasingly xenophobic political line to support his own provincial aesthetic philosophy. As Italy's representative to the First Congress (1934) of the Corporation of German Composers, presided over by Richard Strauss in Hitler's Berlin, he made a speech about 'the work achieved by the fascist regime on behalf of music, of which Benito Mussolini is a great connoisseur and to which he is a great friend'.[43] Two years later, at the time of Italy's brutal conquest of Ethiopia, many Italian newspapers commented enthusiastically on Lualdi's new 'colonial rhapsody', entitled *Africa*.[44] There were to be more serious examples of his meddlesomeness.

At war's end, Mussolini's private files yielded numerous letters and

---

* This portfolio was held by Galeazzo Ciano, 1935–6; Dino Alfieri, 1936–9; Alessandro Pavolini, 1939–43; and Gaetano Polverelli, 1943.

telegrams from musicians, celebrated and obscure. These documents make for sad reading, and none of them more so than Lualdi's communications, which are replete with grotesque flattery and grovelling. Typical is this invitation to the Duce (9 April 1930):

> Your Excellency,
>
> I am taking the liberty of reminding you of the great hope you gave me, months ago, that you would attend the |Roman| premiere of my |opera| Il diavolo nel campanile |The Devil in the Belfry|, which will open on the 12th of this month at the Royal Opera Theatre.
>
> I am enclosing the libretto, which may interest you. I wrote it in 1919: it is a satire and caricature of the world of little white lies, false order and spiritual decrepitude in the midst of which all of us lived (even you, until you took possession of the belfry of the 'old' Italy). It is the forewarning of indispensable revolution.
>
> I beg you a thousand times, Your Excellency: come to the theatre Saturday evening. It may be that you will be attending a battle, because the spirit of the opera (not the *quality* of the music, which is very clear and melodic) is combative; but I promise you here and now that my *grotesque* piece will make you smile more than once, and that it won't leave you time to be bored.
>
> I thank you and I beg your pardon for my persistence. Yours very faithfully | ... |.[45]

On preparing to board ship or train for lengthy foreign tours, Lualdi would send Mussolini telegrams: 'Genoa, 21 April 1932. I address my affectionate thoughts, my fervid, deferential greetings, to Your Excellency, before departing for South America, where I go to serve |with| my modest powers |the| cause of fascist Italy's art and culture. Devotedly | ... |.'[46] Lualdi also bombarded the dictator with copies of his writings and phonograph recordings – some of them with dedications such as the one on his January 1941 address in memory of Verdi: 'To the Duce, the "Man" hoped for by Verdi, with devotion and ever stronger faith. | ... |'.[47]

The tenor of these communications would seem so silly, so Little-Jack-Horner-like, as to make them unworthy of attention. But Mussolini's government nourished itself almost entirely on Lualdi-style protestations of fidelity. Although the amount of damage that could be done by even the most powerful musician was relatively small, Italy as a whole was nearly destroyed by people who shared Lualdi's opportunistic attitude.

The career of Giuseppe Mulè in many respects parallelled Lualdi's. Both were born in 1885, both came from economically depressed regions in the south, both were composers whose tastes lagged a generation behind those of their more original contemporaries, and both rose to positions of prestige under fascism. Like Lualdi, Mulè directed important state-supported conservatories – that of Palermo from 1922 to 1925, and thence, until the regime fell in 1943, Rome's prestigious Santa Cecilia Conservatory. Like Lualdi, he became a parliamentary deputy in 1929. Mulè also served as National Secretary of the Fascist Union of Musicians, as a member of the governing boards of the Corporations and of the Italian Society of Authors and Publishers, and as president of the Fourth Section of the Upper Council for Antiquities and Fine Arts, which was under the jurisdiction of the Ministry of National Education.

By most accounts, Mulè was a gentler soul than Lualdi, less eager to trounce musicians whose aesthetic points of view differed from his own. He, too, however, occasionally wrote to Mussolini to thank him for a show of favour, to tell him of a forthcoming radio broadcast of one of his works ('for me, it would be a joy to know that you, an authoritative listener and judge, were [tuned in]')[48] or to iron out a minor misunderstanding.

Alceo Toni was a northerner, born in Mussolini's native Romagna in 1884. Music critic for the fascists' Il popolo d'Italia throughout the regime's existence and president of the Milan Conservatory from 1936 to 1940, Toni was also a conductor, arranger and composer of retrograde tastes and great pretensions. His political functions under fascism included a period as secretary of the Province of Milan's Musicians' Union and, later, membership in the National Directorate of the Fascist Union of Musicians.

Toni's letters in Mussolini's file demonstrate that he was a more ardent believer in the movement than Mulè, at least to all appearances – and appearances were what counted most – but less full of hot air than Lualdi. Like the others, he knew how to ingratiate himself. In 1933, for instance, he wrote to his editor-in-chief at Il popolo d'Italia, asking him to intercede in arranging for him to meet with the Duce, in order to give him copies of 'two of my new scores that have just been published and the Three Psalms', written in memory of Mussolini's nephew. 'My only aim in this is to present a token of my endless efforts on behalf of the Man of whom not just we in particular but the whole world thinks with utmost dedication.' Toni also wanted to discuss his idea of forming a permanent orchestra and chorus in Milan, and added: 'although I shall have to refer to the musical situation in Italy, and have hopes that putting the project into effect would create for me, too, an artistic position of a sort that I take the liberty of believing I deserve, I have neither personal goals to reach nor jeremiads to launch into'.[49] Mussolini received him. What issues were raised at that meeting is not recorded, but jeremiads were a Toni speciality. One of them, made public less than a year earlier, had stirred up a great deal of trouble in the Italian musical world. It testifies to the depth of the schism within the Italian musical world in those days.

On 17 December 1932, three of the country's most important newspapers – Il popolo d'Italia (Rome), Il Corriere della sera (Milan) and La Stampa (Turin) – printed 'A Manifesto of Italian Musicians for the Tradition of Nineteenth-

Century Romantic Art', framed by Toni and signed by Respighi, Mulè, Pizzetti, Zandonai, the critic Alberto Gasco, Toni, Riccardo Pick-Mangiagalli (composer and pianist, later director of the Milan Conservatory), the composers Guido Guerrini (director of the Florence Conservatory) and Gennaro Napoli (assistant director of the Naples Conservatory), and Guido Zuffellato, a member of the Venetian branch of the musicians' union. The poorly written document set forth the beliefs and apprehensions of the more conservative exponents of contemporary Italian music, and mirrored a way of thinking that is usually termed 'xenophobic' in political matters and 'provincial' in artistic ones. Franco Alfano and Mario Castelnuovo-Tedesco, two other important conservative composers of the day, refused to sign the manifesto.

Beginning inauspiciously with a protestation of innocence, the signatories declared that 'it is not their custom to create factions and splinter groups with this or that aesthetic end, or to form artistic co-operatives for mutual flattery'. Under the circumstances, however, they could not sit idly by without demonstrating their 'collective faith'.

> [...] All the aesthetic creeds that were going to subvert traditional laws have been set forth and put into practice.
>
> Our world has been hit, so to speak, by all the squalls of the most reckless futuristic* concepts. As it grew more furious, the password [sic] truly aimed at the destruction of every old and ancient artistic ideal. [...] Everything was good so long as it was [previously] unthought and unthinkable.
>
> What have we gained from this?
>
> Atonal and polytonal honking. And what has been achieved by objectivism and expressionism? What is left of them?
>
> [...] We are still at the stage of 'tendencies' and 'experiments', and we do not know what definitive statements and safe roads these may lead to.
>
> The public [...] no longer knows which voice to listen to or which road to follow. [...]
>
> [...] A sense of facile rebellion against the centuries-old, fundamental laws of art has infiltrated the spirit of young musicians [...].
>
> The future of Italian music seems safe [according to the modernists] only at the tail-end of all the different types of foreign music. [...] There are [also] those who wish to re-chew the cud of our distant musical past. Above all, however, the last century's romanticism is being opposed and combatted.

All this, say the signatories, is an error on the part of young musicians and bad for the public. All our artistic past, from the Gabrielis through Verdi and Puccini, is worthwhile.

> We are against so-called objective music which, as such, can only represent sound in itself, without the living expression caused by the animating breath

---

* The word *avveniristici* was carefully used instead of *futuristici*, to avoid any specific reference to the Futurist movement.

that creates it. We are against this art, which does not wish to have and does not have any human content [...].

We Italians of today [...] – in the midst of a [political] revolution that is revealing, once again, the immortality of Italian genius, and that is strengthening every one of our virtues – feel the beauty of the times in which we live and wish to sing of them, in their tragic moments as well as in their ardent days of glory.

Yesterday's romanticism [...] will also be tomorrow's romanticism [...].[50]

That musicians of conservative tendencies should have been disgruntled by the avant-garde during that critical period in the history of the art is not in the least surprising; that such gifted and intelligent men among them as Respighi, Pizzetti and Zandonai could have allowed themselves to be represented in a public forum by Toni's superficial notions, botched historical résumés and specious arguments is shocking. The document opens with a vague description of 'collective faith', but only at the end is it stated that that faith has been placed in 'romantic values'. The signatories undoubtedly defined these values in a variety of ways. To Respighi, Pizzetti and Zandonai, 'romanticism' was a catch-all term for a moral and expressive aesthetic that could be applied to a wide range of musical languages; to Toni, Mulè and some of the others, it represented the linguistic immobility of which they approved. No matter how the values were defined, the manifesto was an attack on such progressive composers as Casella and Malipiero – a gratuitous attack, because these two had as hard a time getting their works performed as most of the signatories, and a harder time than some. The jealousy of Toni, Guerrini, Napoli and the like for the various *succès d'estime* of Casella and company can be understood; but what possible interest could Respighi and Zandonai, whose works were played all over the world, or Pizzetti, whose success within Italy was at least as great as that of any of his contemporaries, have had in breaking lances on their colleagues' heads?

The manifesto, declared Andrea Della Corte, *La Stampa's* conservative but fair-minded music critic, was a 'psychological outlet' for its framers, and an example of 'the pain of doubt that fills the spirits of all contemporary musicians with anxiety'.[51] In an editorial printed immediately below their declaration, he upbraided the manifesto's perpetrators, pointing out that the non-specialized public knew little or nothing of modern music, whatever the tendencies of its creators: 'The public's critical capacity derives from its cultural level and guides it towards making distinctions, towards choosing artistic values. To impose limits on the range of its awareness is to lead it to the most narrow-minded provincialism and to somnolence.'

Few others in the field took Della Corte's measured, Olympian view. Toni had touched a sensitive nerve, and the Italian musical world was soon divided into pro and contra camps and sub-factions. Reactions were fairly predictable. The youngsters subscribed, for the most part, to critic Fedele D'Amico's remark that the document ought to have been called 'The Manifesto of Triteness'. Casella expressed his hurt feelings to Pizzetti; Pizzetti replied defensively and with disingenuous astonishment. Progressive writers such as Luigi Pirandello and Massimo Bontempelli publicly declared their solidarity with Casella and Malipiero; the conservative writer Giovanni Papini was delighted with the document. The upper echelons of government wisely refrained from taking a public stand on the matter. Pizzetti and some of his colleagues may have signed the declaration more as a polite bow towards Toni, Mulè and the regime's other officialized musicians than for any particularly strong feelings on the subject, and it is easy to imagine their dismay at being counter-attacked by musicians – no less enthusiastic than Toni about Mussolini and fascism – who reminded them that the regime was revolutionary, youthful, energetic and dynamic: the antithesis of the romantic mentality.[52] Looking back on the episode some years later, Casella remarked:

> The only novel aspect of the manifesto lay in the fact that all previous artistic documents of this type – from the famous romantic proclamations to Marinetti's [Futurist Manifesto] – had always been real appeals to insurrection, inspired by a revolutionary and even iconoclastic spirit. They had their sights set on the future of art and humanity. Never before had such a manifesto as that of 'The Ten' appeared, publicly announcing the urgent need to retreat. In this sense the manifesto was indeed unprecedented, and it is to be hoped, for the good name of our land, that it will have no successor.[53]

The combat soon ended, but some of the wounds continued to fester. 'Please, let's not talk about the Manifesto – please, please don't talk about it', wrote Malipiero to Pizzetti more than a year later, and then proceeded to talk about it.

> I know Toni's methods perfectly well. I'll just tell you this one thing: Toni is indebted to me for a favour I did him. Why he behaves in so undignified a way towards me will always be a mystery. [...]
>
> I know: you people didn't think that the Manifesto would achieve the opposite effect to what you were after, nor that the Duce did not approve of it.* If some had known, they wouldn't have signed. And what of that? The Manifesto was against you, against Respighi, against all those composers who aren't extremely popular, and you should all [...] realize that this exaggerated *material* love for the composers of the nineteenth century will destroy the art of music if it isn't stopped. Because despite all the Beniamino Giglis and all the Toti Dal Montes, the public will soon tire of this. In fact, it is already showing signs of weariness. [...] All the composers are tearing each other to pieces, and when two parties are in litigation, the third party wins. In

---

* Nor did the Duce particularly disapprove of it. His philosophy in such cases was to side with all parties.

other words, we're witnessing the likes of a Toni concocting manifestos and, with the help of some hooligans, trying to carry out systematic demolition [...].[54]

Mario Labroca was not given space in Mussolini's files. The Rome-born composer and organizer, who had studied with Respighi and Malipiero, served as secretary of the Corporation of New Music from its inception in 1923. He seems to have been a true-believing fascist but a man of complete honesty who never debased himself in his dealings with the government. Labroca was well liked by a wide range of musicians whose work he encouraged by every means at his disposal. He held a number of important positions within the fascist musical bureaucracy. He was chosen in 1930 to direct the Opera Consortium, and five years later he became chief of the music section of the General Entertainment Administration under the Ministry for the Press and Propaganda. As director of Florence's Teatro Comunale and Maggio Musicale (1936–44), he was responsible for the first performances of many Italian works – some specially commissioned – as well as the Italian premières of many important foreign works and the revival of many forgotten pieces. His personal record under fascism was clean. Casella wrote of him:

> [He is] a rare type of man, of many, varied and transposable energies: a composer of authentic and unmistakable personality, a writer and journalist of great authority, [and] an organizer [...] of exceptional ability [...]. His greatest strength lies in his pure morality [...]. He is one of the few examples of an artist who has been able to ascend [professionally] without ever lowering himself [personally ...]. In this respect [...] he is capable of rekindling faith even among those who doubt the present possibility of [achieving] artistic integrity.[55]

A plethora of corporations, unions, committees and departments, were considered necessary to regularize and govern the country's musical activities. Their decisions and directives, constantly fluctuating and frequently conflicting, were the steadiest feature of musical administration under the regime.

As early as 1924, Italian music journals began to make pompous announcements of fascist cures for musical ailments. The first of these solutions was the establishment of an Italian musicians' union under the jurisdiction of the National Corporation for the Theatre. Its ranks were to be filled by composers, librettists, performers, teachers and lecturers, and its goals based upon 'the principles of fascist unionism [... :] the moral edification of its members and the protection of their legitimate interests within the limits dictated by national exigencies'. The conditions comprised in the term 'national exigencies' were not specified, although the fact that the governing board was entirely made up of people friendly to the regime, including Toni, leaves little doubt that here as elsewhere, the country's needs and the needs of the Fascist Party were to be equated. And since the government would soon be undertaking more and more responsibility for the financing of major musical institutions while carrying out the fascistization of the unions, it was in effect proposing itself as champion of both employers and employees. The union's first widely publicized act was, significantly, a call for the establishment of a national opera company in Rome – to create a government-funded theatre where, up to that time, a private profit-and-loss operation had attempted to fill the capital's operatic needs.[56] A fascist-dominated union was asking a fascist government to put musicians on its payroll and to defend those musicians' rights as workers.

In 1926 – a fertile year for musical bureaucracy – the Association of Theatrical Agents was constituted, then absorbed into the National Fascist Confederation of Businessmen; members of the Association of Theatrical Proprietors 'voted unanimously' to change their organization's name to the Association of the Theatres of Italy and to annex themselves to the General Fascist Confederation of Industry, which was also joined by the Musical and Theatrical Publishers' Association;[57] and the National Fascist Union of Musicians urged its provincial cadres to organize concerts whose earnings would be invested in government bonds that would constitute 'the first assets of our pension funds'.[58] The following year brought more changes: seven professional groups joined to form the National Fascist Federation of Theatrical, Cinematic and Related Industries, under the authority of the General Fascist Confederation of Italian Industry. Its components were the 'National Groups' of Musical and Theatrical Publishers; Cinematic Film Producers; Theatre Proprietors; Cinema Proprietors; Radio Industries and Musical Appliances; Operatic, Prose, Operetta and Vaudeville Productions; and Industries Related to the Theatre and Cinema – i.e. suppliers. The seven were augmented by the National Concert Union and the newly formed National Association of Autonomous Theatre Societies. At the same time, the Group of Operatic, Prose and Operetta Impresarios was formed within the General Fascist Confederation of Industry.[59]

Nomenclature began to sound more threatening in 1928, when the 'Political Group of Artists of the Milan *Fascio*' was formed, with the intention of 'incorporating fascist artistic forces into the Party'.[60] Next came the Commission for Intellectual Co-operation, whose musical representatives were Respighi and Mascagni.[61] By the end of the year, the bureaucratic gnomes had again reshuffled the components of the National Fascist Federation of Theatrical Industries. The seven groups became ten: theatrical proprietors; cinema proprietors; opera companies; prose theatre companies; operetta, vaudeville and revue companies; cinema producers and processors; film leasers and vendors; cinema-related industries; music and theatre pub-

lishers; and radio and musical appliance industries.[62] The National Fascist
Federation of Theatrical Industries changed its name in the autumn of 1930 to
the National Fascist Federation of Entertainment Industries.[63] A few months
later it was again reconstituted, this time as the Corporation of Entertainment.

The national organizations had lower-level affiliates, each split into
committees and sub-committees. Meetings were legion, and no doubt the
honour of representing one's provincial cell at inter-provincial, regional or
national meetings was an incentive for some members to rise through the
ranks. Late in 1931, for example, both the Directorate of the Corporation of
Entertainment and the Executive Council of the National Union of Musicians,
including Respighi, Lualdi, Alfano and Bernardino Molinari, met in Rome in
the presence of Bottai, who was then Minister for the Corporations, and who,
after listening to summaries of all the work his minions had accomplished,
duly congratulated one and all on the splendid job they were doing and sent
them home.[64] A few months later, representatives of the provincial unions
met in Rome to discuss the absorption of bandmasters and private music
teachers into the organization, the regulation of professional activities, union
representation within musical organizations, union sponsorship of demons-
tration-performances, and the national social insurance fund.[65]

In 1935, the Ministry of Popular Culture was founded, superseding the Press
and Propaganda Ministry. The MinCulPop, as it was commonly known, then
gave birth to a Theatre Inspectorate, the name of which was changed five years
later to the General Administration for Theatres and Music. A statement
issued at the time of that change proclaimed that although 'this does not
signify an alteration in this important office's jurisdiction [...] it does
constitute a further, concrete sign of the Regime's interest in music [...]'.[66]

What was expected of these organizations? The National Fascist Union of
Musicians – according to its constitution – claimed jurisdiction throughout
the Kingdom of Italy. It was made up of 'the interprovincial musicians' unions'
and 'the societies and institutes for [musicians'] social assistance'. Its goals
were to upgrade musicians' activities; to protect members 'moral and
material interests' and to ensure that their 'activities and abilities' were put to
good use; to co-ordinate educational programmes and establish a form of
social insurance; to 'promote the development and support the application of
current labour laws'; and to 'nominate, through the Confederation, its own
representatives to the political, administrative and technical organs of the
State'. In cases of conflict between union and corporate decisions, the
Corporation was granted higher authority. The national union had the right to
intervene in and change decisions made by lower-level unions.[67]

The national union was run by an executive council, a directorate and a secretary. The council, convened at least once a year, was presided over by the national secretary and consisted of the secretaries and two members of the directorates of all the provincial chapters. Its duties were to make top-level economic decisions, elect members of the national directorate, elect three national overseers and make constitutional changes – which, however, were subject to government approval. The directorate, which was convened once every two months, ran the union on a day-to-day basis. There were nine members, elected for four-year renewable terms; eight were chosen by the national council from among members of the provincial branches and one was appointed by the Association of War Invalids and Cripples. From that number the national secretary was elected. The directorate executed the decisions made by the council, pronounced upon decisions contested within a given affiliate, passed orders down to the affiliates, designated its representatives to the various national associations to which it belonged, and upheld the regulations of higher organizations and the laws of the State. The national secretary represented and was responsible for the actions of the national union. He functioned as president of both the council and the directorate and watched over all their activities and decisions.

Budget provisions were similar to those of any such organization under any type of government, except that the category of permissible expenditures for 'assistance' to members included 'moral, religious and national education' in addition to economic, social and cultural aid. In the bureaucratic jargon of the regime, this meant funding of fascist-approved programmes.

In 1940, the list of officers in the National Fascist Union of Musicians consisted of many important names in contemporary Italian music. Mulè was national secretary, and the directorate included Giuseppe Blanc, dear to the regime as composer of 'Giovinezza' and other party anthems, Toni, Giordano, Malipiero, Zandonai and the conductor Gino Marinuzzi. The union's representatives to related corporations were Alfano, Lualdi, Molinari and Pizzetti. Its executive council included the composers Ettore Desderi, Franco Casavola, Adone Zecchi, Vito Frazzi, Mario Barbieri, Gaspare Scuderi, Franco Vittadini, Giovanni Spezzaferri, Alfano and Malipiero; conductor Renato Fasano, who later founded I Virtuosi di Roma; musicologist Guglielmo Barblan; organists Ernesto Berio, father of Luciano, and Luigi Ferrari Trecate; and the celebrated voice teacher Ettore Campogalliani. All 105 names on the list are male, despite the active presence of many fine female musicians in Italian musical life. This does not mean that women were less enthusiastic about fascism than their male counterparts: it is simply one among many examples of the contempt with which women's intellectual and organizational capacities were regarded by the regime.

The national union's constitution gave provincial affiliates the right to expel individual members who did not adhere to established regulations.

Expelled members could, however, appeal to the national union and, if so inclined, even to the President of the Confederation or to the Minister for the Corporations. The national union had the right to inspect, audit and censure provincial branches.

Although the provincial unions carried out direct negotiations with local employers on behalf of their members, the national union was allowed to counsel its affiliates. In cases where national contracts for an entire sector of the profession were to be formulated, the national union was to undertake the negotiations.

The Inter-provincial Fascist Union of Musicians had its own constitution, which contained similar provisions at a lower level and stipulated that membership was open only to those who 'normally and as their principal activity practise the art of music as composers, concert artists, bandmasters, or private teachers of music or other analogous artistic activities'. Their 'moral and political behaviour, from a national point of view' had to be 'good' (i.e. they had at least to appear to be well-disposed towards the regime and not obstreperously opposed to the Church); their dossiers could not show expulsions from other unions; they had to reside within the jurisdictional territory of the union; and they had to possess all the documentation required by the State and by the regulations of the national association. Foreigners resident in Italy for at least ten years and meeting all the other requirements could be admitted to the union but were ineligible for elected office.

A National Aid Fund, constituted under the jurisdiction of the national union, 'gives temporary allowances to its members and their families, and intends, depending upon the means at its disposal, to: a) provide for the establishment of scholarships for musicians' children; b) give other forms of assistance, if possible, and in keeping with the regulations'. An amendment to its statutes stated that the Fund would give child allowances, provide special donations to particularly needy widows and children of deceased members, and lend money to help members meet professional expenses such as the purchase of instruments and required formal dress. Although the system was not a pension fund, the amendments provided for the future possibility of 'annual payments in cases of permanent need owing to complete invalidity for professional activity, deriving from old age, illness or mishap', for members who had paid into the fund for at least five years.

Finally, the Corporation of Entertainment was established 'by decree of the Head of Government, 23 June 1934–XII*.' Its governing council comprised a president and thirty-four members: three representatives of the National Fascist Party; twenty-eight employers' and employees' representatives covering the categories described in the National Fascist Federation of

---

* i.e., twelfth year of the 'Fascist Era', which began with the march on Rome.

Theatrical Industries; and the presidents of the Italian Society of Authors and Publishers, the LUCE (national film society) and the National Institute of Workmen's Clubs. The Minister for the Corporations was automatically its president; other ministers and under-secretaries as well as the Head of Government's press secretary had the right to attend the corporation's meetings.

These were the people and the structures set up to govern Italian musical life. In theory, membership in the regime's musical bureaucracy required few compromises by rank-and-file musicians who were not convinced fascists. By the mid-1930s, those who refused to find a *modus vivendi* within the bureaucracy's jurisdiction could expect to lose their jobs.

CHAPTER II

Institutions

Mussolini's first speech to the Italian parliament in 1922 contained few specific legislative proposals, but it demonstrated the generally illiberal, anti-democratic nature of his political thinking. His declarations pleased some and alarmed others. Even among the alarmed, however, there were those who believed that certain beneficial ends might be reached more quickly through the new administration than under the old system. In the musical field as in any other, some decided to wait and see, while others preferred to act immediately, to try to turn the government's attention towards their individual pet projects. Since artistic organizations are always, under every political system, short of funds, beset by institutional difficulties, submerged in internecine rivalries and overrun with theoreticians who disagree among themselves, the desire to have someone strong put things in order, one way or another, often lurks beneath the surface.

At the time of the march on Rome, Italy was abundantly supplied with musical organizations of all kinds, at every level of quality; fascism had an effect on the workings of all musical institutions: music schools, opera companies, concert societies, festivals, competitions, and performance sites. Music publishers and journals, which were also affected by the regime, are here considered only in passing, since studies of the publishing industry and of journalism under fascism already exist.

The *Annuario musicale italiano* for 1923, which contains information gathered just before the fascists took control of the government, lists over 150 institutions of musical education in more than a hundred Italian cities and towns. These schools included State-subsidized conservatories, Church-run music schools, municipal *licei musicali* (musical high schools), schools of choral singing and private schools specializing in voice or in one or more instruments. The most important of these organizations – and the only ones that were potentially subject to large-scale State interference – were the six royally chartered conservatories, institutes of music and musical high schools and ten non-chartered, major schools. The first group consisted of the Regio (Royal) Conservatorio di Musica 'G. Verdi', Milan; Regio Conservatorio di Musica 'Arrigo Boito', Parma; Regio Istituto Musicale 'Luigi Cherubini', Florence; Regio Liceo Musicale di 'Santa Cecilia', Rome; Regio Conservatorio di Musica 'San Pietro a Maiella', Naples; and Regio Conservatorio di Musica 'V. Bellini', Palermo. Of the ten schools without royal charters, two were in Trieste and one each in Turin, Genoa, Venice, Padua, Bologna, Pesaro, Rome and Naples. The faculties of all these institutions included major Italian musicians of the day – among them the composers Alfano, Marco Enrico Bossi, Casella, Cilea, Giuseppe Gallignani, Antonio Illersberg, Malipiero, Mulè, Napoli, Cesare Nordio, Giulio Cesare Paribeni, Pizzetti, Respighi, Giacomo Setaccioli, Antonio Smareglia, Amilcare Zanella and Guglielmo Zuelli. Well-known professors of piano or organ included Attilio Brugnoli, Ernesto Consolo, Luigi Ferrari Trecate, and Alessandro Longo; of violin: Enrico Polo and Remy Principe; of violoncello: Arturo Bonucci, Gilberto Crepax and Luigi Forino; of singing: Fernando De Lucia; and of music history: Domenico Alaleona, Arnaldo Bonaventura, Gaetano Cesari, Guido Gasperini, Ferdinando Liuzzi, Guido Pannain and Giusto Zampieri.

During the regime's early months in power, government functionaries had little time for examining the needs of the music education system. The fascisticized Ministry of Public Education, under Gentile's leadership, made its first noteworthy intervention in the area in December 1923 – an embarrassingly clumsy operation that involved the seventy-two-year-old Giuseppe Gallignani, who had directed the Milan Conservatory since 1897. In earlier years, Gallignani had been highly regarded as an administrator and was given the Milan position with Verdi's blessing. Some reports say that he had since become disorganized and authoritarian and that, in any case, the time had come for him to retire. In addition, he had not shown any enthusiasm for the fascists. The ministry decided to replace him, and Under-secretary Arduino Colasanti sent a highly confidential letter to Pizzetti – who was then director of the Florence Conservatory and already one of the best-known composers of the day – to ask whether he would be interested in leaving Florence for the more prestigious Milanese position. Before Pizzetti had had time to reply, Gallignani received a brusque ministerial telegram announcing his dismissal. Whatever the reasons for his firing, the way in which it was carried out was abrupt and inhumane. Upon receiving the news, Gallignani committed suicide.

An obituary in the January 1924 issue of *Musica d'oggi* praises Gallignani generically but criticizes his severity and single-mindedness. Neither the fact that he had been fired nor the cause of his death is mentioned – a prototypical example of how ingratiating journalistic self-censorship gradually allowed Mussolini to gain nearly complete control of the press. But Milanese musicians soon learned the real story. Gentile, who was just making his first, tentative pronouncements about 'regulating the study of music in Italian schools',[1] may well have been shocked to receive a brutally frank telegram from the nation's most celebrated performing musician: 'Maestro Gallignani, who did what no Minister or Director-General has been capable of doing for our Conservatory, has committed suicide. Gentlemen of the Ministry of Public Education, Minister and Directors-General: I tell you that this suicide will weigh upon your consciences forever. Arturo Toscanini.'[2]

Toscanini and other leading Milanese personages attended Gallignani's funeral, arrangements for which had been supervised by Gaetano Cesari – musicologist, critic, and director of the Conservatory's library. When Cesari noticed a huge wreath from Gentile that was to be placed on the hearse! he exclaimed to the attendants: 'He makes people kill themselves and then expects to have his wreath attached to the hearse! Put it wherever you like, but not here.'[3] His words reached Rome, and not many days later the Ministry asked Cesari to resign his post at the Conservatory. He informed Toscanini, who wrote to Mussolini:

> I feel it necessary to call your attention to the sudden and groundless firing of Prof. Cesari from the position of librarian of the Milan Conservatory.
>
> His Excellency, Minister Gentile, is evidently unaware of Cesari's worth. I consider him the very, very best of Italy's musicologists and I know that Sen. Mangiagalli, Prof. Scherillo and Count Casati [future Minister of Education] have made a protest in this regard to the Minister. I beg Your Excellency with great fervour to have the provision revoked. It will be a true act of justice towards an artist.
>
> With unchangeable devotion and affection [...].*

Cesari was given back his position, Pizzetti took over the direction of the Conservatory, and the Gallignani episode remained an isolated case. Although ministries are always run by political appointees who will do everything in their power to give the jobs within their jurisdictions to their supporters, and although the ousting of an ageing administrator from his post was not so unusual an event, the nonchalant brutality with which Gallignani was fired was new. Yet instead of alerting music administrators to the dangers of fascism, it augmented their awareness of the precariousness of their positions. During the remaining twenty years of fascist rule, those conservatory directors who were not convinced fascists were at least careful to pay lip-service to the regime and to praise its magnanimity towards the arts.

Programmes for the reform of musical education abounded in fascist Italy, and one of the first to enter the fray was the progressive composer, Casella. He described the state of instruction (1925) as generally confused and ascribed the problem, in part, to massive emigration, which had drained off a great deal

---

* A different version of this story was given in my biography of Toscanini. My information has since been corrected by Cesari's widow, Elena Cesari Silva, who owns the original draft of Toscanini's letter to Mussolini.

of potential energy and, presumably, talent – a strange theory, since at that time most emigrants were from impoverished areas of the rural south. Had they remained in Italy, they would not likely have been sending their children to conservatories. 'This condition', said Casella, 'in the field of music as in all others, will be corrected gradually by the present national development and constantly growing national well-being' – thanks, of course, to the regime. He also believed that the six national conservatories should be reduced to three, as there were few good students or competent teachers, and that the one in Rome should function as a 'musical university'. This, he expected, would be hard to achieve, 'especially in a European country with a powerful bureaucracy', and for that reason there should be more private support and less government interference.

> Today the state would do well to detach itself from almost everything that has to do with art, even the teaching of art. | . . . | I believe that private schools, administered according to modern methods and free to choose their professors and to dismiss them | . . . |, would be infinitely superior in their output to these state schools, which are survivors of a past age.

Only the state, however, should be allowed to grant final diplomas, said Casella. And he concluded:

> One must hope that the Italian Government, which is in a privileged situation as compared with other European nations, except Russia, as regards liberty of |n.b.: clearly a mistranslation; should read: 'freedom from'| parliamentary action, will realize at last that the teaching of music by an incompetent person is quite as reprehensible as the selling of boots with paper soles | . . . |.[4]

In asking the state to control the conservatories without running them, Casella was making a distinction that would have been too subtle even for a more enlightened regime than Mussolini's. He was, however, only one among a legion of educators who pressed the fascist government to adopt their ideas for the transformation of the conservatory system. Many of these musicians, like their counterparts in other areas, adopted fascist rhetoric in the hopes of furthering their own aims, generous or otherwise. They seem to have assumed, too, that their chances for success would grow if the reforms they propounded smacked in any way of nationalism. Luigi Perrachio, a composer, pedagogue and critic, used this technique in a plan he published in the *Rassegna musicale* in 1929: 'The Courses of Study in Our Conservatories: Open Letter to Maestro Giuseppe Mulè, Member of Parliament'.[5] Perrachio was known for his collections of Piedmontese folk music, his writings on the keyboard works of Bach and Debussy and his harmony and composition textbooks. Like any good teacher of composition, he knew how to set the right sort of introduction before his main theme: speaking of his many attempts to revise the conservatory syllabus, he complained that the officials to whom he had applied 'have never deigned [. . .] to give me a yes or a no'.

> It would be easy to clarify the obvious and less obvious reasons for their contempt, to put it bluntly. But in order to do this I would have to re-prosecute an outmoded regime, irrevocably liquidated classes and castes, and a miserably mediocre and bourgeois mentality. I shall not do this. It has already been done too often, and to re-do that which has already been done is boring and in bad taste. And it is only basic decency to refrain from speaking ill of the dead.
>
> Instead, I shall express my admiration for the new regime for having re-created an environment in which open debate – which always clarifies things – is possible and desirable. Because by putting the values upon which the philosophy and the life of the nation are based back at a properly high level, [the regime] has granted music its proper importance and has welcomed it into the Corporative Chamber – through you, illustrious Maestro, and through Adriano Lualdi: valorous creators and vigilant guardians of our art and our ascent. A national treasure.

Flattery of this sort was *de rigueur* under the regime; Perrachio used it to lead into his thesis.

> [. . .] Our Conservatories are not Italian schools, much less schools of Italian-ness. [. . .] Italian schools ought not to be the *longae manus* of the Jadassohns, the Riemanns, the Dubois, the Ševčiks and the Pischnas [n.b.: foreign theoreticians whose texts were then in general use in Italian conservatories]. We have books in Italy. And above all, we have music . . . I am not saying that we should show Bach and Beethoven the door! These are heresies with which I believe no one wishes to sully himself. But alongside Bach and Beethoven there should be not only Scarlatti and Clementi but also Monteverdi and Michelangelo Rossi, Azzolino della Ciaia and Durante, Porpora and Locatelli and Leonardo Leo. . . .
>
> [. . .] How are we to put our old Italians and – why not? – some more recent ones like Martucci, noble in life and in deed, back in their proper places? Very simple: by making them obligatory. Everyone knows that there are required pieces in the examination schedule for instrumentalists – Bach, Clementi, Paganini, Liszt. The others should be made obligatory along with these.
>
> Next to the six or twenty-four [required] fugues of Bach, room should be made for three chosen from the long period that stretches from Frescobaldi to Clementi. [. . .]

For students of composition, Perrachio recommended

> written analysis of at least ten works by Italian composers, chosen from various periods [. . .] including the most recent – and from all types of music – from Palestrina's motets to Marenzio's madrigals, from Pasquini's *tastate* to della Ciaia's fugues – [. . .] including, say, one of Verdi's recitatives – the most beautiful ever conceived. [. . .]

Maestro |Mulè|: the Duce has begun to fight, with the greatest vigour, a battle to elevate Italians, or to keep them at the level of the great nation that Italy is. From farm production to sports, from the army to the family, from work time to relaxation time, from the prohibition of smoking to the obligation to spread the use of books, from road-building to educational reform, from social security to the restoration of religion to its former splendour, there is no element of national life that escapes his watchfulness and his most fervid care. It is as intensive a treatment as possible: every seed must produce the biggest possible fruit; nothing must be wasted; development must be grandiose, magnificent, enormous – expansion carried to the breaking point.

But I have the unmistakable sensation that our conservatories are following an altogether opposite path: diminution rather than expansion, malnutrition rather than nutrition, coercion approaching suffocation rather than development and increase and growth.

Perrachio believed that the course of study was hopelessly conservative, and that teaching only archaic compositional techniques was the equivalent of teaching only Latin, to the exclusion of modern languages and literature.

| . . . | When my pupils have become accustomed to scholastic counterpoint, I familiarize them with modern counterpoint. I replace the *cantus firmus* with a theme by Strauss or Debussy or Bloch or Hindemith and let them embroider on it in complete freedom. What joy, what voluptuousness in being able to range freely, to leap, to fly without weights attached. | . . . |

Strauss, Debussy, Bloch, Hindemith . . . Perrachio, despite his flag-waving, did not put the name of a single contemporary Italian composer on his list.

Perrachio closed by pointing out that the study of sonata-form composition was almost as over-emphasized as that of fugue; that, logically, instrumentalists should be taught to sight-read on their instruments, and not only with their voices; that voice students ought to be taught harmony; and that students of conducting or music history should not be forced to take as exhaustive a composition course as is required of composition students. And he signed his letter to Mulè 'with greatest fascistic respect'.

Within a few months of the publication of Perrachio's article, a booklet by Luigi Forino on the same subject – *Come si studia nei Conservatori di musica. Considerazioni e proposte* (How One Studies in the Conservatories of Music: Thoughts and Proposals) – appeared in print, with an introduction by De Rensis. Forino, a well-known cellist who had written a five-volume practical treatise on the instrument, had already been teaching nearly thirty years at Rome's Santa Cecilia Academy when this pamphlet was issued.

Italian conservatories, Forino said, were for the most part staffed and directed by talented, dedicated teacher-musicians. Despite this, the yield of first-rate young professionals was not very high.

People complain of deficiencies, especially in the instrumental classes; and they repeat that not only do our conservatories not produce great concert artists, but [. . .] not even the players needed to fill the ranks of our orchestras. [. . .] Gone are the days when great Italian instrumentalists brought glory to Italian instrumental art throughout the world. Today, there is a definite *commercial deficit*, as they say in financial jargon.[6]

Forino quoted and commented on Pizzetti's declaration that as a result of the rules then in force,

'at least a third of the total number of students admitted and kept in our musical institutions have a musical aptitude in no way superior to that of any shop employee or barber's errand-boy who happens to be an amateur mandolin-player [. . .].' It seems to me that those pupils whose aptitude is insufficent are in the majority; those who have some aptitude are few, and those with marked aptitude are very rare – at least as far as the string instrument classes are concerned.

Why was this the case? Forino's diagnosis matches Casella's: 'The bureaucratic spirit with which we in Italy are all imbued – some more than others – has a pernicious influence on artistic institutions and does great harm, especially to the many young people who, despite deficiencies in other subjects, show real aptitude for their instrument.' Since children at the very outset of their studies may show greater aptitude for one aspect of musical training than another, says Forino, 'to pigeonhole and regiment so many disparate aptitudes through uniform regulations, just as is done in non-artistic disciplines, seems a serious error'. Forino was convinced that music schools 'should have only administrative and disciplinary regulations, never artistic ones'.

Regarding admission, Forino again quoted Pizzetti, who had said that the examination requirements then in force not only impeded ' "the separation of the apt from the inept [. . .], but actually favour the admission of the inept and perhaps even of imbeciles" ', with the result that ' "every year our musical Institutes produce many graduates who are absolutely unworthy of the title of 'Maestro' in even the most modest sense of the word [i.e. elementary school teacher]" '. Forino suggested that instead of giving children an aptitude test before they have had a chance to do any preliminary study and a 'confirming examination' at the end of the first year, there should be a preliminary one-year course, open to all as an optional supplement to their regular school courses, in which they might try out their instruments under the observation of expert teachers before being subjected to the admission examination.

Forino's ideas on required subjects coincided with Perrachio's: although the ability to sight-sing in all the clefs was useful, it was over-emphasized; supplementary courses in harmony and music history, as organized at the time, were too superficial to do instrumental students any good; and there was something wrong with schools in which failure to remember systems and statistics learned by rote could lead to having to repeat a whole year.

> We know that in order to accomplish something on our instruments [. . .] we need to practise assiduously five or six hours a day; but what with sight-singing, supplementary subjects, Italian, national history, choir practice, chamber music sessions, orchestra rehearsals for end-of-year concerts and so forth, the young people in our conservatories spend nearly the whole day at school and in trips back and forth. [. . .]
>
> In my opinion, it is better to produce capable players, even if they are not highly cultivated, than to have our institutes graduate students who [. . .] cannot earn a living, and who are forced to play in *cinemas* and *cafés* [. . .].

Casella, Perrachio and Forino all wished to revivify a moribund educational system; they were all ignored by the people in power. Professional debate over the functions and organization of music schools cooled somewhat during the 1930s: among musicians, those who believed in fascism must have realized as clearly as those who did not that the government was not sufficiently interested in music to undertake major reforms of musical education. Even had it been more deeply committed, it could not have brought off the miracle – and an undesirable miracle at that – of uniting musicians' opinions on what ought to be done. While Perrachio and Forino, for example, were lamenting the scarcity of decent musicians in the country, Count Enrico di San Martino, head of the Santa Cecilia Academy, stated that there were too many musicians in Italy and that conservatory examinations ought to be more severe.[7] High echelon office-holders seem to have decided that the ills they were being asked to cure were, by their very nature, incurable, and that any attempt to act upon one faction's advice would inevitably antagonize several others. Proposals for reform were therefore made through an increasingly elaborate bureaucratic structure whose employees listened to almost everything and acted upon almost nothing.

What did interest the regime, as usual, was lip-service. A Royal Decree signed by the king, Mussolini, De Vecchi and others in October 1936 set forth new norms governing the hiring of music-school teachers and orchestra players throughout the country. In addition to providing birth and citizenship certificates, diplomas, and other unremarkable bureaucratic papers, all current and aspiring practitioners of these professions had to certify – through the police – their 'good moral, civic and political conduct' and prove that they were members of the National Fascist Party. Political clearance was, therefore, a prerequisite to receiving official professional qualification, which, in turn, was necessary in order to secure steady employment. Applications for official qualification were examined by commissions nominated by the Minister of National Education; these panels, headed by the Director of one or another of the royal conservatories, comprised two conservatory professors, two experts designated by the Musicians' Union but subject to confirmation by the Ministry for the Corporations, one representative of the Theatre Inspectorate and a 'Level-A functionary of the Ministry of National Education, who has an advisory vote and who also exercises the duties of secretary'. The professors and others who sat on these commissions varied according to the examination category – keyboard, string, woodwind or brass instruments, composition. Decisions were made by majority vote, and further examinations could be demanded of candidates whose credentials did not warrant a clear-cut decision. The commission could also make arbitrary changes: a musician who asked, for instance, to be deemed suitable to play in symphony and opera orchestras could be restricted to playing in operetta orchestras.

The same Royal Decree states that 'currently existing [private] Schools and Institutes of musical education, even if they have obtained official recognition in the past, may not pursue their activities if they do not request and obtain proper authorization from the Minister of National Education'. The heads of these schools had to provide – for themselves, their faculties and all other employees – the same documentation required of applicants in the above categories, with one rather odd difference: war invalids or amputees did not have to be members of the Fascist Party in order to work for private institutions.

One of fascism's goals had been realized: the Party's membership card had become a meal-ticket for millions of Italians. This also meant, however, that the card had lost its original significance. In music as in many other fields, it was necessary to become a party member in order to keep a decent job; protest resulted in harassment at the least, and possibly imprisonment or exile to a remote part of the country. Only the staunchest anti-fascists were willing to take such a risk. And so, along with all the true-believing fascists, cunning opportunists and naïve camp followers, the party now began to enrol vast numbers of Italians who were apathetic or even silently hostile to the regime, thus encouraging hypocrisy towards itself.

By 1939, nation-wide enrolment in Italian conservatories and equivalent-rated music schools was distributed as follows: piano, 650; violin, 350; viola, 40; cello, 70; double-bass, 50; flute, 30; oboe, 50; clarinet, 60; bassoon, 40; horn, 50; trumpet, 60; trombone, 40; and harp, 60.* More than half the pianists, violinists and harpists were female. As to quality, a list of only the best-known musicians who were mainly or entirely educated in Italy between 1922 and 1943 is sufficient to demonstrate that fascism did not suffocate musical education.

* Figures for non-instrumental categories are not available.

Composers: Luigi Dallapiccola, Bruno Maderna, Riccardo Malipiero, Goffredo Petrassi. *Conductors*: Guido Cantelli, Franco Ferrara, Gianandrea Gavazzeni, Carlo Maria Giulini, Fernando Previtali, Nino Sanzogno. *Instrumentalists*: Arturo Benedetti Michelangeli, Aldo Ciccolini, Pietro Scarpini (piano); Riccardo Brengola, Pina Carmirelli, Cesare Ferraresi, Franco Gulli, Arrigo Pelliccia (violin); Dino Asciolla (viola); Severino Gazzelloni (flute).

Chamber ensembles formed during or shortly after the fascist period and made up primarily of musicians trained under the regime: Quartetto Italiano (Paolo Borciani, Elisa Pegreffi, Piero Farulli, Franco Rossi); Trio di Trieste (Dario De Rosa, Renato Zanettovich, Libero Lana [later replaced by Amadeo Baldovino]); Trio di Bolzano (Nunzio Montanari, Giannino Carpi, Antonio Valisi [later replaced by Sante Amadori]); I Virtuosi di Roma; I Musici.

Singers: Iris Adami Corradetti, Licia Albanese, Fedora Barbieri, Gino Bechi, Carlo Bergonzi, Sesto Bruscantini, Maria Caniglia, Margherita Carosio, Franco Corelli, Mario Del Monaco, Giuseppe Di Stefano, Tito Gobbi, Magda Olivero, Rolando Panerai, Clara Petrella, Giacinto Prandelli, Cesare Siepi, Giulietta Simionato, Giuseppe Taddei, Ferruccio Tagliavini, Italo Tajo, Pia Tassinari, Renata Tebaldi, Giuseppe Valdengo, Cesare Valletti.

Musicologists: Guglielmo Barblan, Fedele D'Amico, Massimo Mila, Nino Pirrotta, Luigi Rognoni, Claudio Sartori, Giampiero Tintori.

Despite the policies of all the ministries and other bureaucratic agencies whose authority extended in any way to the conservatories, fascism's existence made very little difference to most students' professional training. Although autarchy (the regime's policy of national self-sufficiency in all fields, initiated when Britain and France adopted anti-Italian sanctions following Italy's invasion of Ethiopia in 1935, and increasingly encouraged thereafter) and anti-semitism affected certain aspects of the system, the admission of students continued to be determined by the eternal, universal mixture of objective criteria and luck; certain instructors and courses of study succeeded with some students and failed with others, just as they did and do throughout the world; and the graduating classes produced a small number of outstanding or good musicians and a large number of mediocre or poor ones, just as they always have everywhere. There is no excuse for the regime's politicization of the field and demands for fidelity, but in the vast majority of instances its pronouncements consisted of nothing worse than empty rhetoric.

Outside the conservatories, or loosely connected with them, several special courses in music were organized during the fascist period. Under the auspices of the Ministry of Public Education, a summer course apparently intended mainly for American students, along the lines of the American Conservatory programme at Fontainebleau in France, was initiated at Tivoli in 1925;

instructors included Respighi (composition), Consolo (piano) and Mario Corti (violin).[8] The following year, a new School of Singing and the Stage was opened in Milan by the SIFAL (Fascist Italian Union of Lyric Artists). The school, connected with the 'M. E. Bossi' Music Academy, was free to successful applicants who could 'present documents attesting to absolute poverty' and was open to students from all countries – unlike the state conservatories, whose extra-musical requirements made non-Italian-speakers virtually ineligible for enrolment.[9]

The June 1932 issue of *Musica d'oggi* announced a new undertaking that proved to be of major importance: 'On the initiative of Count [Guido] Chigi-Saracini, and with the Government's approval, an Advanced School of Music will be founded in Siena under the auspices of the Italian Inter-University Institute, with its headquarters at Count Chigi's palace.' Courses ran from July to September, and the original faculty included Vito Frazzi (composition), Arrigo Serato (violin), Arturo Bonucci (cello), Ada Sassoli (harp), Gemma Bellincioni (dramatic arts), Giulia Boccabati and Adolfo Barutidella (voice), Fernando Germani (organ) and Claudio Gonvierre (piano). The Count, a generous music-lover, was the last of a family that had been in the forefront of Italian finance and culture since the Renaissance. He continued to support the school until his death in 1965, and he left his palace – one of the most beautiful buildings in Siena – to the organization. Many of the finest musicians in the world have received part of their training in master courses at the Accademia Musicale Chigiana during the past half-century.

In 1935 the government announced that a new Fascist Music Academy in Rome would select twenty-five members of two fascist youth movements – the Balilla and Avanguardisti – for free training, including room, board and uniforms, at the Santa Cecilia Conservatory.[10]

Throughout the fascist period, there was much talk about promoting musical awareness in the national school system. Gentile appointed a commission in 1923 to examine the problem,[11] and in 1926 the Ministry of Public Education organized a committee to observe the progress of the new programmes, which consisted mainly of the teaching of choral singing in elementary schools.[12] Within a few months, two of the prime movers of the choral singing plan – the pedagogue Achille Schinelli and the musicologist Domenico Alaleona – presented recommendations to the minister: that 'musician-inspectors' be required to oversee the programme; that teachers be prepared for the task through special courses, lectures and pamphlets; that children be able to attend concerts and possibly to hear recorded and broadcast music; that there be at least two music lessons per week in the schools rather than only one, even if the total amount of time remained the same; that songs and texts be carefully chosen and regulated; that pupils' music notebooks contain some useful information, in addition to blank music staves; that the children be given an additional booklet containing the most important religious and political songs; and that every school make essential materials, including blackboards with musical staves, available to music instructors.[13]

Late in 1927 the ministry urged secondary school principals to organize concerts in their schools, in order to expose students to music – above all, 'to our glorious musical art from 1500 to 1800' – which meant works from outside the familiar nineteenth-century operatic repertoire.[14] Shortly thereafter, the *Rassegna musicale* took the matter up in an unsigned editorial in the style of its editor, Guido Maria Gatti. For Italians, it said, music was no longer 'empirical, spontaneous and popular', as had been the case in the previous century, but neither was it 'scientific and organized', as in modern Germany. The usual response to such problems was to request government intervention; but although 'a wise and enlightened Government can do a great deal', co-operation is required. 'In Italy today, intellectuals understand nothing about music. [. . .] An intelligent clause in Gentile's law [on education] established the option of studying a musical instrument in Teachers' High Schools, and the Superintendents of Education in some cities felt duty-bound to interpret "option" as meaning "don't do anything".'[15]

The government was to some extent hampered by the usual dissension among musicians as to what ought to be done. Some thought choral singing a waste of time, others believed instrumental lessons in the schools to be useless, and still others were interested in experimenting with more controversial methods. A Turin-based association, for example, with Alfano and other leading musicians among its members, favoured the use of Jaques-Dalcroze's eurhythmic method in Italian primary and secondary schools.[16] But the ministry plodded on with what was basically Schinelli's choral singing plan.

The noble cause of music education often served as an excuse for yet more flag-waving. Writing in the *Rassegna Musicale* of September 1929, musicologist Gino Roncaglia was slightly critical of the government's previous musical interventions, but his comments also illustrate precisely the sort of narrowly nationalistic point of view that allowed fascism to remain in power so long. The whole piece is a maddening mixture of confused theorizing, nostalgia for an idealized past that never existed, and useful practical observations.

> [. . .] The art of music, of which we were once the glorious teachers for the entire world, must be diffused among the masses, must become a necessity, an instinct, a daily habit among them, if it is to flourish again.
> [. . .] It is unacceptable that people who know the names and works of Dante, Michelangelo, Raphael, etc., are ignorant of the names and works of Palestrina, Monteverdi, etc. These are the varied expressions of a single spiritual world [. . .]. The infiltration of various types of exoticism, of all the

musical eccentricities that have passed through the cerebral alembics of modern foreign composers and that have unfortunately been welcomed, with little sense of Italian-ness and of art, by too many fashion-conscious Italian composers, have altered the original physiognomy of our art and threaten to sweep it into degradation. To reawaken, therefore, the sense of *melody*, of simplicity and of naturalness through concerts of classical music and lessons in music history (which is mainly *our* history), it is necessary to lead public taste, which has lost its way, back to the correct path. [. . .] Led astray by the vulgarity of popular songs and feeble operettas, or by the intellectualizations of modernistic eccentricities, [the public] is no longer capable even of distinguishing between what is spontaneous and what is artificial, between what is beautiful and what is not.

In order to eliminate these serious improprieties, the Government has opportunely revived and broadened the teaching of music in general and of choral singing in particular in the Royal Teachers' Training Institutes. And the celebration of 'St Cecilia's Day' is highly useful for observing year-by-year progress. [. . .] In the other schools, the establishment of 'Classical music concerts' ought to have familiarized youngsters with this type of high and difficult art, opening their souls to musical beauty. After two years' experience, it is now legitimate and necessary to say that the results have not been entirely comforting.

The reasons for this failure, said Roncaglia, were to be found in the negative attitudes of some of the students, who were often unprepared to listen to complicated polyphonic works or to chamber music, and in the lack of enthusiasm of many school principals. This was not surprising, he admitted, given that many of the educators were products of schools 'in which musical instruction was *zero*' and of a society in which music meant nothing more than relaxation.

Roncaglia suggested that grammar-school pupils be taught choral singing and that they listen to relatively uncomplicated pieces from the standard repertoire. Older students ought to be exposed to longer programmes after having been provided with appropriate historical and aesthetic background information.

Where and how are we to find performers capable of effectively illustrating such lessons? For pity's sake, let's not discuss those who come *recommended* by high authorities! A self-proclaimed and very highly recommended singer made the rounds of various Italian schools this year, initiating certain conversations about whose educational nature the less said the better! [. . .] My suggestion is [to use] the *phonograph*. [. . .] It is perfectly adequate as a scholastic apparatus – altogether comparable to [. . .] slide, opaque and film projectors. [. . .] It is possible to play and replay pieces several times, to stop, and to repeat the most important themes and their developments [. . .].

According to Roncaglia, the commission set up in Rome to deal with this problem was 'certainly highly competent, but too centralized'. Instead of depending upon this group's reports, the ministry ought to have based its decisions upon 'more practical and efficacious suggestions' from people in a position to observe 'how things are going in provincial cities and smaller centres [. . .]'.

> Useful general directives can then emanate from Rome, as long as they take into account that the art of music, more than any other discipline, requires free initiative and must be able to breathe freely, if it is to take root and develop.
>   The moment will then come when we shall ask that the Universities, too – the Faculties of Arts and Letters – establish chairs of music history and musical aesthetics, as other Nations have done.

By 1934, Schinelli seemed reasonably happy with the progress that had been made. In an article in *Regime fascista* he summarized the directives then in effect: obligatory teaching of choral singing in the elementary schools, music listening sessions in all junior high schools, and the establishment of choral music departments in the royal conservatories. He suggested that the teaching of music be extended to the classical and technical high schools; and he expressed confidence in fascism's ability to 'perfect' during its second decade in power the reforms it had initiated during the first.[17] Andrea Della Corte contradicted this rosy view a few months later in an article in the *Rassegna musicale*. Having duly paid homage to the policies that 'the fascist Government, with fresh and exquisite sensitivity, has since 1927 brought to the attention of the superintendents, principals and educational directors of every type of school', he pointed out – as the *Rassegna*'s editorialist had done six years earlier – that since the directives were not obligatory, the situation was fundamentally unchanged.[18]

Late in 1935, the musicians' union urged the Ministry to introduce compulsory music courses in primary, secondary and superior schools and to create free evening and Sunday schools of singing – which means that, contrary to Schinelli's implication, music courses were not yet obligatory.[19] A year later, Roncaglia praised Bottai, who was then Education Minister, for having made the 'elements of music history' part of the high school course of study, but noted that few of the literature professors who were required to teach this new subject had sufficient musical background.[20]

As the bureaucracy expanded, the directives – including those on musical education – increased. *Musica d'oggi* reported in the spring of 1937:

> The Ministry of National Education has sent out a circular to the principals of junior, classical, scientific, pedagogic and technical educational Institutes, concerning musical education for junior high school students. For the coming academic year, 1937–38, principals must scrupulously keep to the following seven prototype programmes, all included in the circular: (1) illustrated

lecture on Greek, Hellenic, liturgical and troubador music; (2) fifteenth-century *villotte* and music of the sixteenth century; (3) music of the seventeenth century; (4) music of the eighteenth century; (5) music of the nineteenth century; (6) and (7) Italian and foreign symphonic music from the eighteenth century to our day.[21]

A musicians' convention was held in Venice from 11 to 13 September 1938 to determine 'the aspirations and needs of Italian musical art in the school sector'. Among those present were Mulè, Nordio, Pannain, Pizzetti, Labroca, Mascagni, Corti, Toni, Lualdi, Schinelli, Casella, Torrefranca, Della Corte, Giordano, Marinuzzi, Guerrini, the composer Ennio Porrino, the musicologist Monsignor Raffaele Casimiri, the drama critic Silvio D'Amico and the journalist Ugo Ojetti. Marino Lazzari, president of the General Arts Administration within the Ministry of National Education, gave an address in which he praised fascism's deeds in the field of musical culture and education and generically encouraged bigger and better achievements for the future. And Bottai, who opened and closed the convention, stated that 'Imperial Italy expects Italian composers to give it an art worthy of the present historical moment – an art representing the most unadulterated virtues of the race'.[22] The words 'unadulterated' and 'race' had taken on new political meanings a few days earlier, when Mussolini had made anti-semitism official government policy; consequently, the faculties and student bodies of Italy's educational institutions were about to undergo some changes in accordance with the directives of the half-Jewish Bottai.

*   *   *

Massimo Mila was born in Turin on 14 August 1910, and graduated from the University of Turin in 1931 with a dissertation on Verdi. Mila was among the first to apply Croce's aesthetic principles to music history and criticism. He was part of a circle of outstanding Turin intellectuals who opposed fascism, and he spent two months in 1929 and then five years (1935–40) in prison for activities against the regime – following which he became a leader in the Resistance movement (1943–5). Mila taught music history at the Turin Conservatory from 1953 to 1973 and at the University of Turin from 1960. He has published many books, including fundamental studies of Verdi and Mozart, *Cent'anni di musica moderna*, the highly successful *Breve storia della musica*, 'readings' of Beethoven's Ninth Symphony and *The Marriage of Figaro*, *L'esperienza musicale e l'estetica* and *Maderna musicista europeo*, as well as thousands of essays and articles – the latter as critic, at various times, for *L'unità*, *L'espresso* and, since 1968, *La stampa*. Mila has also translated Goethe, Schiller, Hesse and others, and has written literary criticism and articles on mountain-climbing. His writings on music are pungent but not gratuitously polemical, erudite but intensely communicative. As writer and teacher, he is the most influential Italian critic and musicologist of his generation, and he is in a particularly good position to sum up the story of musical education under the fascist regime.

HARVEY SACHS: Professor Mila, your education was carried out during the fascist period. Were there, to your knowledge, government directives regarding musical education in the universities or conservatories?

MASSIMO MILA: It was out of the question at the universities, for the simple reason that there were no university music courses. They did not exist at all. Perhaps [Fausto] Torrefranca already had his chair in Florence,* which for many years was the only university chair of music history, and which was abolished on Salvemini's initiative after the liberation.

HS: Why?

MM: He got rid of it in order to replace it with another of the many history chairs, but it was later re-established.

HS: And the conservatories?

MM: I don't believe there were any [specifically] fascist directives, although it was under fascism – in 1934, I think – that the dreadful, infernal conservatory courses of study came out.

HS: Dreadful in what sense?

MM: As far as the music history courses are concerned – and those are the ones I was familiar with – one can't even say that they were done in accordance with an incorrect methodology. There was no method to them! They rigidly followed positivistic categories of musical forms and types irrespective of chronology and history. Since opera was studied before instrumental music, the kids had to study Wagner and Debussy before Frescobaldi or Couperin. All conservatory students did two years of music history, but students of composition did a third year, pompously entitled 'musical aesthetics' – and not even five years of study would have been enough to carry that course out properly. I discovered, however, that the conservatory courses were based upon the so-called 'Hoepli Manuals'.† These were very good for certain disciplines – for technical subjects and even for some musical ones, as in the cases of Gasperini's manual of musical notation and Tacchinardi's of rhythm. But they were not at all good for music history. Yet the 1934 conservatory courses used the Hoepli manuals as their foundation and framework – as if no other musical literature existed. I don't believe, however, that this fact was a result of specifically fascist orders from on high, mainly because there was a total lack of competence. The Hoepli manuals were convenient – they were already at hand.

* Only from 1941.

† Hoepli is a Milanese publishing firm; its manuals are condensed outlines of the subjects under study, crammed with data – and useful for that reason – but not put together with any critical overview.

HS: How did your opposition to fascism develop during your student years?

MM: I didn't become an anti-fascist by choice or by an act of will. There came a moment when one found oneself forced to take sides. When I was nineteen, in 1929, I knew nothing of politics. I had no opinions on the subject. I had, however, signed that famous letter from the students at the University of Turin to Benedetto Croce.* I was discovering Croce at that time; for me he was the author of *Aesthetics*, and I venerated him and held him in high esteem. I was not even aware that I had made a political gesture. But for that signature alone I was imprisoned for eighteen days, then admonished – as they used to call it – and above all cut off from all subsequent activity. I could no longer be a teacher, which was my profession; nor could I be a journalist, since I couldn't become a party member – nor, I must say, did I want to. So there came a point at which one found oneself on a certain side, without having willed it. Once I found myself on that side, I tried to do my best.

HS: How did you manage to earn a living?

MM: I managed through what Senator Luigi Einaudi so beautifully described as the 'economic anchoretism of the anti-fascists': I did some supply teaching in the junior high schools as long as I could – but only as a substitute, never in a regular position. I also gave some private lessons: I was tutor to Giovanni Nasi, a boy from the Agnelli household,† who is still one of the company's big guns. Another refuge for sinners was the UTET publishing firm which, with all its encyclopaedias and manuals, employed a great many people who had no other job options. As a result, the administrators were able to claim to be protectors of anti-fascists while securing for themselves – for the price of a crust of bread – contributors who were often very fine; because it must be said that most of those who faced that situation for an ideal were clearly people with their heads on their shoulders. I worked for a few years on the UTET encyclopaedias, and that was always a help.

HS: You also contributed to the *Rassegna musicale*, which seems to have been a rather open-minded review.

MM: When I was very young, I had my very first things published in *Il Baretti*, the last survivor among Gobetti's journals.‡ It was kept alive – with great difficulty, what with confiscations and other problems – for a year or two after his death, by a group of professors [n.b.: the 'Liberal Revolution Groups'] that

* In a speech to the senate, Croce had criticized the Church–State Concordat; the police were ordered to read his mail, and several students from Turin, including Mila, were questioned and arrested for their joint letter of support.

† The Agnellis founded, owned and ran the Fiat automobile corporation in Turin, and were therefore the city's most powerful industrialists – as they still are today.

‡ Turin-born Piero Gobetti (1901–26) was a political scientist and journalist whose work greatly influenced the entire anti-fascist movement, despite his untimely death in exile. He founded *Il Baretti*, a Turin-based cultural journal (1924–8) of liberal-idealistic stamp, frowned upon by the fascist regime; its contributors included Croce, Salvemini, Einaudi, Gobetti and the young poet Eugenio Montale (Nobel Prize for literature, 1975).

included my teacher, Augusto Monti.* I had written a short, ridiculous, puerile article on Clementi, and another article that wasn't too bad, after all, on Ravel. Following my arrest and release in 1929, I spent the summer at the Einaudis' house in the hills at Dogliani, where I gave lessons to the future publisher Giulio Einaudi.† That autumn, back in town, I was sent for by Guido Maria Gatti, the director-general of the Teatro di Torino. Gatti was a highly cultivated, extraordinary man, who, a few years earlier, had founded the journal that later became the *Rassegna musicale* [n.b.: originally called *Il pianoforte*]. He had read my article on Ravel and wanted to know whether I wished to work for the *Rassegna*. You can imagine my reaction! At that time the magazine was still rather well-off. For a year I drew a small salary, but afterwards I worked for nothing, out of affection and dedication.

HS: Gatti obviously had a real flair too. The *Rassegna* was in the vanguard in those days: it published substantial articles on the most important Italian and foreign composers of the day and also on forgotten seventeenth- and eighteenth-century Italian composers. How was it regarded by the more reactionary segment of the Italian musical scene?

MM: Lualdi, in his book *L'arte di dirigere l'orchestra* (*The Art of Conducting*), attacked the *Rassegna musicale* very violently. It was an attack that could have been taken to court. He said that these people should be silenced.

HS: Was this only because he didn't share the aesthetic point of view or also for explicitly political reasons?

MM: For nationalistic reasons. He said that we were the spokesmen for what was then called the 'demo-plutocratic-Jewish-Masonic' plot.

HS: In any case, between one job and another, you were able to survive for a few years.

MM: Yes, and then from 1935 to '40 I had no economic problems, because in prison they used to bring a big bowl of soup to my cell every day.

HS: How did your arrest come about?

MM: Turin was one of the operational bases of the '*Giustizia e Libertà*' movement that was led from Paris by Rosselli, Tarchiani and Lussu. The movement's strength lay in maintaining continuous contact with Italy, in having fresh information and contributions for its weekly newspaper. While the communist exiles were completely cut off from the country – and they did sometimes make blunders because they were no longer in touch with what was happening here – 'Giustizia e Libertà' was always able to keep up direct communication, thanks above all to us, in Turin. Ours was the strongest

---

* Augusto Monti was a Piedmontese writer and influential teacher, whose pupils included Gobetti, Pavese and Mila.

† The Liberal economist and senator Luigi Einaudi was an opponent of fascism; after the war he became president of the Italian Republic. His son, Giulio, founded the Einaudi publishing house in 1933.

nucleus. The leader was Leone Ginzburg, and when he was put in the clink there was Vittorio Foa who, after the war, became a great union leader. Foa had myself and others working with him. I used to go back and forth between Turin and France – rarely Paris, more often border towns like Modane, Chambéry and Lyons. I brought fresh contributions from Italy to a man who came down from Paris, and I took away packs with printed matter, which I brought back here. All this went very well until a spy infiltrated among us. This was a certain Pitigrilli [n.b.: pseudonym of Dino Segre], a widely-read author of pornographic novelettes with titles like *Cocaine* – that sort of thing. He was a distant relation of Foa, and he had said to him: 'Why go on with these expeditions on foot across the mountains just to pick up thirty or forty copies of the paper? I can bring you suitcases full of them every time I come back from Paris. I'm very well known at the border; the customs officials know my books, they ask for my autograph. . .'. And that's how he infiltrated. He was then able to betray us by discovering our only weak spot: besides my direct contacts with people from the other side of the Alps, we also had a secret correspondence in invisible ink. One of our number was old Professor Giua, a great and celebrated chemist of the day, who had created a sort of [anti-fascist] network. Since I was a music critic, I already had a bit of correspondence with foreign countries; and from the Paris headquarters of 'Giustizia e Libertà' they sent me sheets of music paper – popular songs, dance music and so on – where messages were written in invisible ink. That pig of a Pitigrilli explained all this to the police, to the OVRA [Mussolini's secret police], and they used a quartz lamp to decipher what was written, taking note of everything. One fine day a hundred or a hundred and fifty of us were arrested in Turin. Many were then released and others were sent to the internal exile commission. Nine of us were put on trial – two were acquitted and seven sentenced. Vittorio Foa and old Professor Giua got fifteen years each; our friend and comrade Cavallera got eight, I got seven, and Perelli and Augusto Monti each got five.

HS: Were you already married at the time of your sentence?

MM: I was about to get married, and my future wife, good woman that she was, waited for me, although I sent to tell her to look after her own life. We were married a few months after I was released.

HS: Were other people economically dependent upon you?

MM: No, I was still living at home with my mother at the time. I wasn't earning much. The business about dependents was a propagandistic invention of Rosselli in *Giustizia e Libertà*: when we were arrested, he printed biographies of us, and he said of me that I had maintained my whole family by my work.

HS: You did not serve your whole sentence.

MM: No, I was pardoned after five years, on the occasion of the birth of an heir to the Prince of Piedmont or some such thing. I got out in March 1940, and

Italy entered the war three months later. Naturally, I wasn't able to do anything relating to music. At first, I went back to work half-days for UTET. After a few months I transferred to Einaudi, full time.

HS: So your work was editorial.

MM: Yes. It was a nice job – Cesare Pavese was on the staff and there were other interesting people, too. In prison I had learned German, and during the war translations of English and French books were not allowed; in practice, the only foreign books that could be published were German. So I actually became a valuable consultant, working as a reader of foreign manuscripts and books, not only for Einaudi but also for Frassinelli, another Turin publisher. I then did a year of military service, from 1942 to '43, but nothing heavy. After three months' duty away from Turin, I came back. In the end, I was able to continue working half-days for Einaudi. Then, on 10 September 1943, my wife and I escaped by bicycle [into the mountains of Piedmont]. We hid up in the Canavese, where she had family, and we set ourselves up in a farmhouse. I made contact with the men who were not yet partisans but simply disbanded soldiers returning from France. We got them together and helped them; and little by little, units were formed.

HS: So you became involved in the Resistance.

MM: Oh, I became a big gun – I ended up as commissioner of war for the Third Region, 'Canavese–Val di Lanzo' – the highest position next to that of military commandant. The war commissioner was the political authority who guided the military commandant. But I didn't do anything heroic. Our region consisted more of people who were on the defensive than of attackers, and we often had to flee in great numbers. It was our good fortune to know the terrain and the villages well. Many of our men did, however, carry out some useful attacks. And then, during the night of 25–6 April 1945, leaving 800 in the hills, 1,600 men went down to Turin, where they wiped out the military barracks one by one in three or four days of very hard fighting. I stayed halfway back in the Region and arrived in Turin during the night of the 28th–9th.

HS: Gavazzeni says that apart from Riccardo Malipiero, you were the only active anti-fascist musician known to him who stayed in Italy. Did you know any others?

MM: As Fiamma Nicolodi's book demonstrates, the situation was terrible: you can find every last one of them in it, involved in some way. In my review of the book, I ended by expressing compassion for the Duce, because he had all those puffed-up musicians coming around, imploring and supplicating. In a democratic state those matters are passed along to the right people; the Head of Government doesn't have to bother with musicians' intrigues. Well, he wanted to be a dictator – nobody made him do it. . . . The worse the musicians were – and above all, the older and more forgotten they were – the more often they insisted on claiming their just deserts. The only composer who isn't implicated in Fiamma's book is old Leone Sinigaglia of Turin, the man who collected so many Piedmontese folksongs.

HS: He was Jewish, wasn't he?

MM: Yes, and in fact he died tragically. They didn't kill him, but he virtually died of heart failure, from fear, when his house was searched.

HS: And Gui's anti-fascism?

MM: I really don't believe Gui ever begged [the regime] for anything, and he was truly anti-fascist in his sympathies. Perhaps he wasn't totally unsusceptible to nationalism and patriotism: he had fought in the First World War – certainly not with pleasure, but with great dedication; so he had a certain foundation of nationalistic conviction.

HS: Did you have anything to do with Casella?

MM: Yes. Until the time of the racial laws, Casella was a fascist – not an evil one, but full of enthusiasm. But I saw him later, during the war, in 1940 or '41, and he was undergoing a complete change. He was beginning to understand. In any case, he had behaved admirably to me when I was arrested in 1935: my mother didn't know which way to turn, and she approached him, among others. Casella was very good about it – he wasn't scandalized or indignant. He said, 'I'll take care of it, it's nothing'; and he was very optimistic. He believed that by saying a word to the right person. . . . Poor man, he was deluding himself, as always. Still, he spoke with Federzoni [president of the Accademia d'Italia] and did whatever he could. He was very kind and very affectionate.

HS: And the other composers? Pizzetti? Malipiero?

MM: Well, Malipiero was moody and fickle; and where Casella was a good European, Pizzetti was provincial. On the other hand, one person who was very important during the whole fascist period and whose activities had a salutary effect was Mario Labroca. He was a fascist – a true-believing fascist, I think, with black shirt and all the rest – but he always did good, musically speaking. His outlook was broad and he was an honest person, incapable of harming his neighbour.

HS: And the scholars, critics and musicologists?

MM: Oh, they were all rather . . . in line. Torrefranca was a fascist. Good old Della Corte didn't prostrate himself, but he wasn't anti-fascist. The same for Pannain.

HS: All in all, do you believe fascism had an important influence on the country's musical life?

MM: No. You have only to look at the fact that the fascists gave a little bit of support to everybody, modernists and reactionaries alike. They had no real awareness of or competence in the matter. There was, however, some harm done by those people who thrust themselves in and tried to turn fascism to their advantage. I'm talking about the petty musical bosses – the Tonis, the

Lualdis, the Mulès – who were always hovering around the regime. During the great purges in Russia in 1935,* when Zhdanov was driving poor Shostakovich and Prokofiev crazy, I understood perfectly well what was happening there. It wasn't that Zhdanov had clear-cut musical ideas or that he wanted one thing rather than another: he was surrounded by a little clique of musicians who were hostile to and jealous of those two and who mounted a cabal against modern music. It was the same here, but fortunately we had powerful enough people on both sides. In opposition to the Lualdis and the Tonis there was a group of political leaders who were rather open to modern requirements. Bottai was one of them, and probably also De Pirro. Perhaps musical activities could have been better directed, better financed, but I don't believe that the regime had a real musical policy – for the simple reason that the regime was inferior. It wasn't capable of determining such things, either to the right or to the left. It wasn't up to dealing with these problems.

POSTSCRIPT TO THE MILA INTERVIEW

The following information and quotations are taken from File No. 3281.32455, 'Mila, Massimo', in the *Casellario politico centrale* (central political police files) of the Ministry of the Interior. The documents originated with the Royal Prefecture of Turin.

10 August 1929 | . . . | Mila's period of admonition |i.e. probation|, reduced to two months, ended on 31 July. | . . . | He is being kept under surveillance.

30 June 1935 | . . . | |Mila was| arrested on 15 May for belonging to the *Giustizia e Libertà* movement. He was transferred to Rome on the 5th of this month and is at the disposal of the Ministry of the Interior.

3 August 1935 | . . . | He was denounced before the Special Tribunal for the Defence of the State for the crime of political conspiracy through association, to attack the powers of the State. . . .

Same date | . . . | Mila's activity, closely linked to that of Vittorio Foa and Michele Giua, also arrested, has emerged through the investigations that have been carried out and the admissions he made during the interrogations to which he was subjected. He was the recipient of clandestine correspondence originating at the movement's Paris headquarters, and he had assumed the pseudonym 'Pallotta' within the secret organization.

30 September 1936 | . . . | The Special Tribunal for the Defence of the State condemned him on 28 February 1936 to seven years' imprisonment, to the joint and several payment of court costs and of |the costs| of his preventive custody as well as those of his |pre-trial| release on bail, for the crimes referred to in Art. 305 |etc.|.

* *sic*; 1948

Throughout his five years at the Regina Coeli prison in Rome, Mila had to apply to the Ministry of the Interior every time he wished to have books or periodicals sent to him and every time he wished to initiate a correspondence – despite the fact that all incoming and outgoing letters were thoroughly censored. His file is filled with such applications: could he have permission to read Croce's book on Dante, D'Annunzio's *Laudi*, the newspaper *Il meridiano di Roma*, works by Mario Soldati, Sinclair Lewis, Schopenhauer, Carlo Pisacane ... ? The list was endless, and the answer, though long in coming, was usually positive. (The 'Nos' were for the most part applied to such long-shot possibilities as a volume of works by Soviet writers.) Mila was allowed to correspond with his mother and his fiancée. He also requested permission to correspond with his old school friend, Cesare Pavese, who, after the war, would emerge as one of the foremost Italian writers of his generation. The Ministry asked the Turin Prefecture for advice; after investigating the matter, the Prefect replied that Pavese, 'formerly confined to internal exile, is friendly with the political convict Massimo Mila. Considering the bad political background of both of them, our opinion is negative.' (2 September 1936.)

Mila was released from prison on 6 March 1940, but had to report regularly to the police and was kept under surveillance – until his escape into 'the bush'.

*   *   *

Three types of administration existed among Italian opera houses when fascism came to power: the impresario system, the general managership and the *enti antonomi*. By far the most prevalent of these was the first system, which had been in use throughout the previous century. In general, each city and town, as a public entity, owned its most important theatre, but aristocratic and other powerful families owned their individual boxes. Every year the city council and a box-holders' committee jointly licensed an impresario to organize the opera season and undertook to cover basic expenses in the event of an operating loss. The impresario's job was to schedule repertoire and provide casts, conductors and sets that would attract the largest possible public. Orchestras and choruses were generally made up of local musicians and singers; in smaller towns, extras were brought in to fill out the ranks. The more tickets the impresario sold, the more money he earned.

During the nineteenth century, the system usually worked well, artistically as well as economically. The audiences of the day, for whom opera was high quality popular entertainment, wanted to hear the most recent works by the most successful composers. Although a few thirty- to fifty-year-old classics were generally performed each season, the repertoire was constantly renewed. By the beginning of the twentieth century, however, the classics had begun to predominate. The linguistic innovations of foreign masters such as Debussy, Richard Strauss and, later, Schoenberg and his school, left most of the Italian theatre-going public far behind – and the theatre, during the previous hundred years, had been understood as a place where even the most serious concepts were purveyed to as heterogeneous a public as possible. If an Italian impresario in 1852 – seventy years before the march on Rome – had decided to produce only operas written within the previous fifteen or sixteen years, he would have been able to choose among several of Donizetti's works, including La fille du régiment, La favorita and Don Pasquale; well over a dozen Verdi operas, including Nabucco, Ernani, Macbeth and Rigoletto; Meyerbeer's Les Huguenots and Le Prophète; and many now-forgotten works, highly popular at the time, by Mercadante, Petrella, Halévy, Auber, the young Gounod and a legion of others. (Operas written during the same decade by Wagner, Berlioz, Glinka and Schumann were then virtually unknown in Italy.) In 1922, an impresario who looked back over the previous decade and a half, searching for operas that had had enormous popular success in Italy, could not find even one. Such works as Puccini's La fanciulla del West, the Trittico and La rondine, Zandonai's Francesca da Rimini and Giulietta e Romeo, Giordano's Madame Sans-Gêne, Montemezzi's L'amore dei tre re, Mascagni's Il piccolo Marat and Wolf-Ferrari's L'amore medico had obtained a measure of public approval; but the Italian and foreign operas that today's music historians consider to have been the most important creations of those years – Busoni's Turandot, Arlecchino and Doktor Faust; Strauss's Der Rosenkavalier, Ariadne auf Naxos and Die Frau ohne Schatten; Stravinsky's The Nightingale and Mavra; Berg's Wozzeck; and Schoenberg's Die glückliche Hand – were then of no interest to the vast majority of Italian audiences. The passion for new works had metamorphosed into a passion for new interpretations of nineteenth-century works, and so it has remained.

The gradual transformation of opera from a living organism into an audio-visual objet d'art brought many shifts in attitude. The word 'culture' was heard with increasing frequency, and the notion began to circulate that the works of Rossini, Donizetti, Bellini and Verdi, and perhaps even of earlier, largely forgotten masters like Monteverdi, Pergolesi and Cimarosa, were national treasures, cultural monuments worth perpetuating as such – at public expense, if necessary. At the same time, some Italian musicians and critics, blinded by recent developments in German and French music, began to feel embarrassed about Verdi and company, and positively cringed at the mention of such contemporary lions of the stage as Puccini and Mascagni. They looked for and found Italian ancestry for transalpine symphonism, and declared that centuries of concentration on music for the theatre had been a betrayal of the true mission of Italian music, which was instrumental and therefore 'pure'.

The theoretical debates had little immediate effect on the public, but several other problems made a much greater impact. Home-grown Italian star singers – Caruso, Tetrazzini and many dozens of others – had discovered that theatres in the boom towns of the western hemisphere, especially New York and Buenos Aires, were willing and able to pay much higher fees than even the most celebrated Italian houses could afford. This situation was exacerbated by Italy's precarious economic circumstances following the First World War. The big talents spent less and less time at home. Meanwhile, the effect of Wagner's half-century-old ideas concerning the unity of voice, action, scenography and orchestra, and Verdi's less overtly polemical efforts in the same direction, had begun to make themselves felt in some of the major Italian houses. The realization of these reforms, however, required major mechanical overhauling of the old theatres: construction or deepening of orchestra pits, updating of lighting systems and improvement of facilities for creating and installing sets. Performers needed longer rehearsal periods to prepare each aspect of a production and put the parts together. Faced with the diminishing availability of star singers, how could an impresario also confront the mounting costs resulting from the demand for more refined productions?

The impresario system began to break down. The bigger the theatre, the more these problems pressed; nowhere, therefore, did they hurt so much as at La Scala, the largest and most prestigious house in the nation. As early as 1897, the Milanese theatre's financial embarrassments had caused the cancellation of an entire season; and when La Scala reopened in December 1898, it was no longer run by an impresario. Instead, its fortunes were entrusted to a principal conductor, who functioned as what would today be called artistic director, and a general manager; both were salaried employees of an administrative council. This board, presided by a nobleman-boxholder and made up of leading figures from the city's aristocratic, financial and artistic circles, was responsible for guiding and advising the conductor and manager and for soliciting funds from three sectors: the boxholders' society, a new association of shareholders, and the City of Milan. The impresario's function at La Scala was reduced to that of an agent who leased singers from his 'stable' and took a percentage of their earnings.

The system functioned reasonably well at the top of the pyramid, but the majority of Italian opera houses never adopted it. Most of them did not sense a need for organizational reform until after the First Word War, by which time La Scala was making another, more drastic and more attractive leap forward. Toscanini, supported by the liberal senator Luigi Albertini, editor of the *Corriere della sera*, and Emilio Caldara, Milan's socialist mayor, formulated a plan for reconstituting the theatre as an *ente autonomo* – a self-governing, non-profit society. The old societies of boxholders and shareholders were dissolved; proprietorship of the theatre's boxes was gradually taken away from the families who had occupied them, and seats in them were eventually made available to the general public; and the city relinquished its titular ownership of the theatre, although the mayor continued, and continues to this day, to assume the presidency of the administrative council. Financing was carried out in a variety of ways: an annual contribution from the city, public subscription, private donation, and the levying of a two per cent surtax on the admission prices of all other theatres, cinemas and places of public entertainment in Milan and its *provincia*. La Scala, which had been forced for economic reasons to shut its doors in 1917, was able to reopen them at the end of 1921 as a result of the new administrative system – a model of combined public and private responsibility in a city whose strong theatrical tradition touched every echelon of society.[23]

At the time of the march on Rome, numerous Italian lyric theatres were still run on the age-old *impresa* system and a few were mixed-system houses based upon the 1898 Scala arrangement. La Scala was an isolated showcase of enlightened theatrical administration. Although the existence of the *ente autonomo* in Milan aroused the curiosity of other theatres, it did nothing to ease their many immediate difficulties. Fascism seemed to bring out the most meddlesome qualities in everyone who had a hypothetical solution to offer or an axe to grind. One of the first to jump into the lyric theatre organizational battle was Cornelio Di Marzio, a journalist who later headed the Fascist Confederation of Artists and Professionals. In the first issue (January 1924) of the Sonzogno music publishing company's short-lived magazine, *Musica e scena* (music and stage), Di Marzio published an article, 'The National Theatre Council', in which he outlined the 'highly varied causes' of the 'ever-growing crisis' that was 'eliciting sounds of discontent on every side'. He blamed the 'fabulously high fees requested by the few listenable singers and the scarcity of |singers| capable of representing our art', as well as 'the selfish opportunism and apathetic incompetence of the productions' organizers', who purveyed 'seasons based upon rancid and uninteresting programmes | . . . |.' Although these complaints could be printed in any current music journal without appearing dated, Di Marzio's proposed solutions could not – nor, one hopes, could his prose, which is a model of the bombastic, goading, toadying, and often nearly incomprehensible style so beloved of the men who rose to high positions within the fascist bureaucracy:

> To the breath of new life that has rejuvenated our national energies, we now feel the absolute necessity of bringing a cure for the gangrene that has attacked this worn-out theatrical organism. | . . . | Through the iron idealism of fascist discipline, the Corporation of the Theatre is being created. It has received the personal attention of His Excellency the President of the Council of Ministers |Mussolini|, who recently received |members of| the Commission. The Duce recognized that the lyric theatre constitutes an important means of aesthetic education within the country and of expansion and national propaganda in foreign countries, and that its smooth functioning can

be an inexhaustible source of economic activity for the nation; and he placed his highest confidence in the Commission, so that they will make legislative proposals of a general nature with the intention of disciplining, encouraging and defending the renewal and the values of Italian lyric art.

The President gave the task of formulating concrete proposals for the solution of the most urgent problems and for organizing actions aimed at protecting and improving. [n.b.: Di Marzio does not specify what is to be protected and improved.] He also examined the question of establishing *enti autonomi*.

The first meeting [of the Council . . .] led to the conviction that in order to proceed towards a practical realization of the corporations, it will be necessary to establish a national society that will examine the administration of monies taken by the State as a royalty on works in the public domain (Giacomo Puccini will be among the [society's] patrons), and that will study and initiate theatrical administrations, announce competitions, and over-come difficulties through practical, measured and decisive proposals.

As with all the manifestations of energy and faith that have guided the fascist victory, this flame, which [. . .] is brightening up the areas of theatrical art, is truly beautiful. [. . .]

The one piece of useful information that emerges from Di Marzio's harangue is the attention being given to La Scala's *ente autonomo* system. Within two years *enti autonomi* on the Scala model were set up at Bologna's Teatro Comunale, Florence's Teatro della Pergola, Genoa's Teatro Carlo Felice and Turin's Teatro Regio, and representatives of all four attended a congress of the Federation of Italian Lyric Theatres in Bologna in the spring of 1926. Conspicuous by its absence, however – and not even referred to in the report – was La Scala. Its dictator, Toscanini, was by that time at daggers drawn with the nation's dictator. Nevertheless, several decisions were made at this meeting of 'the principal theatres of Italy': to create *enti autonomi* where they did not already exist; to form a National Federative Consortium of those *enti* already in existence; to resolve the problem of a national opera theatre for Rome; and to transform the administrative structures of Italian theatres. Plans for this transformation bore a striking resemblance to the Scala system.[24] That summer the Teatro San Carlo of Naples was converted into an *ente autonomo*, and a commission began to plan the company's reorganiz-ation.[25]

By encouraging the creation of *enti* and by sponsoring the federations, confederations, commissions and consortia to which they belonged, the government soon found itself directly involved in the opera business, which had always been left to individual cities and towns. Next came subsidization: a five per cent surtax on gross box-office earnings at all performances of 'operatic, dramatic and mime works, Italian and foreign, given in theatres, institutes, recreation circles, associations, etc.' went into effect on 15

November 1926. Some of the money was recycled into subsidies for the *enti autonomi*.[26] There is, of course, no perfect system for financing artistic organizations, and state subsidization has as obvious a set of drawbacks as most other methods – especially when the state involved is run on blatantly anti- democratic principles. Before long, newly created or reorganized government organs began to establish norms and policies for the *enti autonomi* – whose 'autonomy' was therefore born dead.

Political appointees who naïvely accepted what they assumed would be easy, music-related bureaucratic jobs must have been shocked to realize that dealing with opera companies requires the executive abilities of a prime minister, the diplomatic skills of a foreign secretary and the arsenal of threats of a minister of war. Imagine, for instance, a neophyte fascist bureaucrat awaiting his first opportunity to impose the will of the government on old-fashioned bourgeois impresarios. One day, a committee of those extra-ordinary ladies and gentlemen accosts him and *demands* that the regime pass regulations regarding the administration of theatres not strictly under state jurisdiction. Why? Because they, the impresarios, want the government to make recalcitrant aristocrats pay their long overdue box rental fees! What – the impresarios ask – are the fascists going to do about this deplorable situation? Is this a self-respecting dictatorship or isn't it? The matter had to be passed up the line, until a cabinet decree-in-council (1928) declared that 'in the municipal theatres of all cities, those boxholders who do not intend to help cover the production expenses must cede the use of their boxes to the managing *impresa* for the duration of the season'.[27]

The sanctification and officialization of opera and its transformation into High Culture grew year by year. In Turin in 1927, the Fascist Union for the Theatre created an Experimental Lyric Theatre, supervised by Alfano, Gui and other important musicians; an orchestra and chorus, reinforced when necessary by 'the best professionals', were to be made available. Although 'experimental' implied support for new artistic tendencies, the organization was really intended to be a master course for singers, conductors, dancers, scenographers and make-up artists who had already completed regular study programmes – to preserve and develop performing techniques that would for the most part be applied to the traditional repertoire.[28]

Three years later, a similar, more elaborate project was initiated in Rome at the prompting of a committee of artists and financiers. The Accademia e Teatro Nazionale dell'Arte was meant to 'participate – through multiple and continuous productions, in harmony with the Regime's directives – in the rebirth of Italian art, especially as regards music and musical theatre. This will give an openly Italian direction to our art.'[29] Mascagni was made director-general of the new body; Aldo Aytano, whose setting of a text by Horace had been approved by Mussolini in 1927, was president of the administrative council, and De Rensis was its secretary. None of these gentlemen was a flaming radical. Yet the institution's declared intentions were to organize productions and concerts as well as competitions for operas and instrumental works, and to encourage young composers and performers by giving them a chance to have their works performed, albeit under sterile conditions. Another experimental lyric theatre was created for the purpose, 'thanks to the initiative of the Hon. Giuseppe Mulè, general secretary of the National Musicians' Union'.[30] The majority of musicians sincerely concerned with the broadening of young artists' musical horizons found the new measures insufficient and ineffective. Not until 1935 was a government agency given enough power to change the situation to any perceptible degree.

The question of government financial aid to opera houses was taken up by the Chamber of Deputies on 13 February 1931. An Under-secretary of State for the Economy reported that 'the provision for handing over the proceeds accruing from taxation rights and public rights received for productions given under La Scala's supervision [...] was rendered advisable by the necessity of State intervention in [La Scala's] definitive financial structure'. The government was recycling tax monies received from La Scala back into the theatre, as part of a subsidy plan. The measure had been applied to Florence's Politeama the previous July, 'in order to make life possible for a newly created *ente*, the lack of which was strongly felt in such an eminently artistic centre'. Although he paid tribute to the good work of other theatres, such as those of Rome, Naples, Turin and Genoa, the Under-secretary, Casalini, said that the budget did not allow for further extensions of the plan. A bill would, however, be presented with the intention of removing the current ten per cent tax on donations received by those theatres that were public *enti*.

Lualdi, representing the Fascist Union of Musicians, took the floor to thank the government for its efforts and to plead for more help. He believed that the same sort of assistance given to the Milanese and Florentine *enti* ought to be extended to the other four. Although the cost of living was slowly going down and many artists were unemployed – two reasons why performers ought, in theory, to have been available at lower fees – production costs had risen by as much as twenty-five per cent between 1921 and 1929. Besides, said Lualdi, state intervention was good 'for moral reasons': the government could protect the *enti* from speculators by establishing a code that might eventually be extended even to provincial theatres. This would only be achieved if everyone obeyed

the password that has been launched by the Head of Government, and if those who [...] have created one of the principal causes of the lyric theatre's present hardships are persuaded that the days of getting something for

nothing and of profiteering are over. [...] Fascist discipline demands this;
today's way of life demands it; and the present and future greatness of our art
demands it.[31]

Lualdi's line eventually prevailed: subsidization became the accepted
method for coping with increasingly large segments of the major opera
houses' deficits. A transformed Italian Opera Consortium, created within the
Corporation for Entertainment under Labroca's direction, announced a rather
vague goal: 'the total execution of obligations taken on by member
theatres',[32] which included the principal opera houses of Milan, Rome,
Naples and Genoa. In mid-December 1931, the Entertainment Council –
under the joint presidency of Mulè, De Pirro and Melchiorre Melchiori,
General Secretary of the National Federation of Fascist Entertainment Unions
– approved subsidies to many minor theatres, with the proviso that these
houses conform to 'precise regulations' not further specified.[33] A year later
the Corporation for Entertainment granted a total of 1,300,000 lire to fifty-four
small-town opera houses. The average sum was trifling even for those days;
but a precedent had been established.

Perhaps Lualdi was naïve enough to believe that government intervention
would eliminate corruption and profiteering. No doubt the fact that he and a
handful of other musicians who enthusiastically supported the regime were
eternally being appointed to positions of authority did not strike him as a
form of corruption. But there must have been others in the Italian musical-
theatrical world who had grave misgivings about teaching opera companies
to depend upon the presumed benevolence of a dictatorial government. Few
dissenting opinions were voiced. The only gesture resembling a protest was
Toscanini's departure from La Scala in 1929, although this was as much
motivated by personal considerations as by the increasing politicization of
Italian musical life. Significantly, however, once his decision to go was
officially announced, the government approved a vastly increased annual
grant to La Scala.[34]

Toscanini's fears in regard to fascism were generally those of a convinced
liberal; but part of his opposition to the corporate system stemmed from
mistrust of union participation in executive decisions. In this, if not in other
respects, he was seconded by many other administrators. Guido Boni, general
secretary of the National Fascist Association of Enti and Concert Societies,
commented shortly after the parliamentary 'debate' on assistance that artists
should be kept off the executive councils of artistic organizations, 'in order to
avoid corruption in the allotment of work'. Instead, he said, the unions and
the councils, presumably incorruptible without the musicians' pernicious
influence, should resolve their problems jointly.[35]

Labroca set forth some worthwhile proposals, in 1931, for preserving and even raising operatic standards. The Corporation for Entertainment, he said, intended to attack the theatre crisis at its roots. Its first task would be the elimination of 'incompetent and ignorant singing teachers who are responsible for ruining so many voices'. A government-controlled registry of teachers would be set up, and it would include only those furnished with conservatory diplomas or possessing demonstrable pedagogic talents. In addition, the Corporation would oversee mutually beneficial exchanges of information among the various enti autonomi and would replace 'corrupt', privately run agencies with official labour exchanges,[36] whose tools would include an orchestra musicians' registry similar to the one intended for voice teachers.[37] But how and to whom were voice teachers to demonstrate their pedagogic talents? Were all private agencies for musicians corrupt? Who could guarantee that the government-supported exchanges would be incorruptible? Such questions were not answered, and perhaps not even addressed.

The real roots of the theatre crisis were to be found elsewhere – in the degeneration of opera as a popular art form and in the rapidly increasing competition posed by the cinema. As early as 1927, the mayor of Thiene in the Veneto had proclaimed that local cinemas were to remain closed on days when operas were being given – a futile and presumably short-lived measure.[38] When Italy began to produce sound films in 1930, the crisis worsened: the great opera companies of the major cities faced reductions in their activities, and second-, third- and fourth-rate provincial companies soon found themselves struggling for sheer survival. In places where few other forms of entertainment had formerly been available, people could now see and hear famous actors and actresses – Vittorio De Sica, Emma and Irma Gramatica, and Eduardo, Peppino and Titina De Filippo – in skilfully-executed films. In 1931 traditional summer opera seasons were cancelled in fourteen towns, including such sizable centres as Rimini and Pesaro.[39]

To counteract this near-catastrophic situation, Labroca announced the government-funded 'Mulè Project', to create small, touring opera companies that would provide professional training for their members, 'first-rate performances' for small centres and popular opera seasons for larger cities following the big winter seasons. At about the same time the Carro di Tespi (Thespis's Wagon) was created: the mobile outdoor theatre, equipped to seat 3,000–6,000 spectators, gave seasonal work to 500 performers, stagehands and administrators. In 1932, for example, the Carro – under the artistic direction of Giovacchino Forzano, a well-known playwright and stage director – toured the provinces with four standard operas: Rigoletto, La bohème, I pagliacci and Cavalleria rusticana. Like Forzano, the Carro conductor (Edoardo Vitale) and many of the singers (Giannina Arangi Lombardi, Florica Cristoforeanu, Mafalda Favero, Hina Spani and Benvenuto Franci) were Scala veterans. Ticket prices were kept low, and, to squeeze every possible drop of pro-fascist publicity from the enterprise, the whole operation was linked to the government-sponsored National Workers' Recreation Association (*Dopolavoro nazionale*). Starace, the party secretary, who was as innocent of artistic aspirations as a new-born babe, even took some of the credit for having ordered technical improvements for the following year's productions.[40] But rehearsal conditions were primitive, the company was constantly on the road, and the *Carro*'s acoustics were poor. Marinuzzi, who was persuaded to conduct a single performance, complained: 'What happens to art [. . .]? It's only a job . . . I feel sorry for all the participants [. . .]. How did poor old Vitale stand it?'[41]

The theatre crisis worsened. In 1936 Italians spent nearly as much on opera tickets (25,000,000 lire for 2,223 performances) as on admission to sports events (26,000,000) or to the spoken theatre (31,000,000); but the cinemas took in 439,000,000 lire – more than five and a half times the combined total of the other entertainments.[42] Government intervention, however inadequate, seemed the only solution to the emergency situation. Florence's Politeama and the EIAR (government-controlled national radio network) joined the Consortium of Opera Houses in the spring of 1932, and the organization continued to expand. Administrators from the member theatres met from time to time in an attempt to find joint solutions to their companies' economic woes; before long, the Consortium had become the sole agency through which those theatres engaged artists.[43] Later that year, management and labour representatives signed a national collective work contract for orchestra players employed by either the new *enti* or the old-fashioned *imprese*. This agreement established fundamental job qualifications and categories of payment, depending upon the instrument one played and one's position within the section. It also determined the maximum number of compulsory services (two rehearsals or one rehearsal plus one performance per day, six days a week), the length of rehearsals (not longer than three and a half hours each, but extended to four and a half hours for dress rehearsals, with a ten-minute break, and not more than five and a half hours, total, on any given day), and scheduling of rehearsals (not to begin before ten a.m. or to end after midnight). Norms regarding overtime payments and extra payments for broadcast performances, regulations regarding the fining and firing of musicians, and qualifications for holiday and sickness pay all fell within the confines of the contract. Membership in the Fascist Party was not obligatory.[44]

As the *enti* grew in number, many independent opera organizers felt threatened. The more clever ones, however, soon realized that they could take advantage of government handouts. Walter Mocchi, last in a long line of powerful and frequently unscrupulous impresarios, decided in 1932 to form the Associated Lyric Artists' Society, 'with the aim of running opera houses in Italy' – more precisely, with the aim of continuing to run as many Italian opera houses as were willing to remain faithful to the old system. Mocchi's board members included the well-known singers Carlo Galeffi and Ernesto Badini.[45] Although the efforts of Mocchi and a few other impresarios succeeded in the short run, official bureaucratic machinery eventually overwhelmed them.

The UNAT, or National Union of Theatre Art, established in 1934 under government supervision, declared itself to be the 'sole office for regulating commercial relations among [independent] theatre, cinema and vaudeville house proprietors'. Under the General Directorship of Remigio Paone, who was also General Director of the National Office for Dramatic Art, the UNAT proclaimed its responsibility for 'assigning operatic or concert seasons to [specific] *imprese* or syndicated firms, favouring a rational distribution [. . .] in accordance with the importance of each season in question and with the theatre's location'. The UNAT also meant to regulate business negotiations between theatre owners and impresarios and to facilitate the transportation of companies and their production properties from one town to another, in order to avoid the expense of contracting and creating new productions in each town. But 'the Consortium's activities absolutely exclude the direct running of theatres and companies as well as everything that concerns relations between [. . .] impresarios and the artists under contract with them'. Representatives of theatre owners as well as impresarios sat on the association's board; their names had to be approved by the National Fascist Federation of Businessmen, whose president would automatically be president of the UNAT. Opera houses and impresarios in the category under the UNAT's jurisdiction were to contribute two per cent of their gross earnings for its operating expenses.[46]

No doubt Labroca and other honest fascists saw the UNAT and its sister organizations as elements in a concerted effort to clean up the corrupt world of musical performance. Many of those who worked in the field, however, simply developed a new style of corruption in keeping with the operational methods of the new system; and the maze of agencies with overlapping jurisdictions often created great confusion. When Marinuzzi, for instance, was arranging to conduct at both the Rome Opera and La Scala during the 1932–3 season – previously a fairly straightforward contractual operation – he wrote to a friend that 'a lot of effort was required before they reached an agreement. What with the Theatre Consortium, [Performing] Artists' Consortium, Unions, etc., no one can figure anything out!'[47]

Inevitably, those people whose musical ignorance was equalled by their political arrogance began putting their minds to solving opera's eternal problems. A Catania-based lawyer named Marchi with a lifelong interest in music sent his friend Marinuzzi a colourful report of how an opera orchestra was put together for the Sicilian city's theatre.

[. . .] The local union boss produced a circular according to which the *imprese* were supposed to hire unemployed [musicians]. Thus, the creation of an artistic organism is treated like the organization of any old work squad. The circular decrees that no one who has a regular salary or a pension may be engaged. Consequently, [. . .] the best players must be eliminated and those who aren't even good enough for the down-at-the-heel little neighbourhood revue houses must be taken on. [. . .] But never fear! Write elsewhere, [the theatre's management was told,] and have some good players sent by the labour exchange offices beyond the Straits of Messina [i.e. outside Sicily]. [They] will choose as they please. (Once, when the late, lamented [Michele] Bianchi [a high fascist official] was secretary of the orchestra musicians' union in Milan, he sent an unemployed bassoonist instead of the cellist that had been requested!) The jerks arrive, the conductor protests, the rehearsals grind to a halt, fees skyrocket and the *impresa* goes bankrupt! The image is discouraging and the theatre won't open. [. . .] The Theatre Inspectorate has tried to alleviate the bitterness [caused by] the circular by allowing people whose salaries or pensions do not amount to more than 500 lire ([a negligible amount] these days!) to be engaged. I think the time has come to make these incompetent blockheads understand that the criterion to be adopted is the one stated by the King's Procurator in Palermo [: . . .] an opera orchestra must purely and simply obey its artistic exigencies.[48]

The Theatre Inspectorate to which Marchi refers was the most important agency created by the regime for dealing with opera companies' ills. Constituted in 1935 within the Under-secretariat (later transformed into a full-fledged Ministry) for the Press and Propaganda, the Inspectorate had its name changed to the General Administration for Theatre and Music when the MPP was redubbed Ministry of Popular Culture. According to the terms of the Royal Decree (1 April 1935) by which it was created, the Inspectorate was meant to deal with all the questions formerly shared among the Ministries of the Interior, of the Corporations and of National Education 'touching upon the subject of theatre censorship, government vigilance, and directives relating to all forms of theatrical and musical activity'. Financing for the Inspectorate was to come from radio tax monies diverted from the now obsolescent branches of the three ministries. The Under-secretariat – and the Inspectorate, as its agent – could determine whether works proposed by theatres were 'detrimental to public order, morality or decency'.

Another Royal Decree issued the same day predetermined for the Inspectorate the measures governing the responsibilities of the *enti autonomi*, which were to look after

(a) the running of the theatre or theatres whose management has been entrusted to them, by organizing opera productions and concerts;
(b) the possibility of organizing productions and events outside their headquarters, by taking advantage, normally, of personnel already under

contract for the |regular| seasons.

The *enti*'s activities must not be directed towards financial gain; they must rather be prompted by artistic criteria, and with the intention, above all, of educating the people about music and the theatre. The *enti* must therefore manage the theatres directly and may not in any way cede |management| to persons or to other societies, however the latter may be constituted.

| ... | The funds needed for running the *enti* consist of:

(a) proceeds from the opera and concert seasons and from the special events they organize, |said funds| to be made up of subscription sales, ticket sales, boxholders' contributions in theatres that are condominial, and all other proceeds deriving from their artistic activity;

(b) |national| subsidies and contributions from municipalities whose budgets already provide for this | ... |;

(c) any contributions forthcoming from the provinces, provincial economic councils and any other public or private society;

(d) | ... | private donations, offers and legacies.*

The *enti*, according to the decree, were to be directed by a president (the mayor of the city), a *sovrintendente* (general manager) nominated by the president, three municipal representatives, one representative of the regional branch of the Musicians' Union, one representative of the National Fascist Federation of Entertainment Industries, and one representative of the National Fascist Federation of Entertainment Industry Workers. All nominations to these positions, except that of president, in all the *enti* were subject to confirmation by the Ministry, and all appointments lasted two years, renewable any number of times. The mayor and the union and business representatives had to be members of the Fascist Party; only the *sovrintendente* could possibly have been a non-fascist, but this was unlikely, since he had to be *persona grata* to the Ministry.

The *sovrintendente* was charged with submitting complete programmes for each season at least four months before the opening date to the Theatre Inspectorate; the programmes were subject to the Ministry's approval. Furthermore,

| ... | the theatre inspector has the option of modifying the season's programme | ... | within the limits set by the *ente*'s budget estimate. Should the *ente* find the proposed modifications unacceptable, the *ente*'s president has the right to appeal to the Minister | ... |, who will pass final judgement on the appeal.

---

* Lest anyone think that the man who supposedly made the trains run on time managed to get subsidy funds to the theatres on time, there exists in the lawbooks another Royal Decree (16 June 1938) that recognizes the 'urgent and absolute necessity of hastening the delivery of said subsidies, thus eliminating the causes of employees' hesitation to observe with rigour the directives contained in the Royal Decree | ... |'. Payment of artists' fees has probably been delayed under every form of government in every country on earth since the dawn of history.

| ... | The Theatre Inspectorate | ... | may appoint young singers who have successfully passed certain practical tests; these singers are to be employed by the individual *enti*. The procedures for and programmes of said practical tests will be determined by the Ministry | ... | in accordance with proposals to be set forth by the National Fascist Federation of Entertainment Employers and the National Fascist Federation of Entertainment Workers | ... |.

In every town with an *ente*, three auditors were to be appointed by the provincial prefect and the mayor, for examining the theatre's books, and the results were to be communicated to the Ministry.[49]

This constitution, as established by the decree, presented many possibilities for corruption. Most of the personal accounts of that period show that both De Pirro, who directed the Inspectorate, and Labroca, who was responsible for specifically musical concerns, acted in good faith and were not corrupt. Their moral influence did not, however, reach down to every individual administrator and artist under their command. 'We have learned only too well', the conductor, Gui, wrote after the war, 'that the General Administration for the Theatre | ... | *was mother to many evils*, despite some good initiatives every once in a while and – above all – despite the constantly open tap that poured forth more or less excessive subsidies | ... |.'[50] Gui and others have testified that many theatres, major and minor, began to employ unnecessary individuals merely because they were politically well-connected and therefore potentially useful.

Never had such an orgy of incompetence and arrogance been seen to equal the one that accompanied the first |government| nominations |in the theatres|. | ... | The carnival of 'introductions' and 'commands' reached incredible proportions; the theatres' administrative offices were flooded with ministerial telegrams | ... |. We saw some astonishing ones, in which such-and-such a minister ordered that contracts be given to virtually unknown conductors | ... |. Was it really necessary to employ thirty-six people – thirty-six! – in the administration of a theatre that had formerly been run by three? And when there were |only| three, the artistic productions reached a level never again achieved. (I am talking of things I myself experienced.)[51]

De Pirro, even if not corrupt, was blindly loyal to the regime. He intended to 'fascisticize' the lyric theatre's 'way of life, | ... | to bring it back to the level of importance from which it has fallen under the blows of middlemen | ... |'. And he wished 'to free it of that jot of parliamentary behaviour that still impedes its action here and there | ... |'.[52] One way to ensure that government directives could not be ignored was to force the people responsible for determining artistic policy in individual theatres to submit to the decisions made by the regime's corporative structures. As of 1 January 1936, for example, all Italian conductors who wished to work in the nation's theatres, even for a single engagement, were required to join the Fascist Confederation of Professionals and Artists – although a few exceptions were later made.[53]

The nature of De Pirro's declared goals was simultaneously populist – inexpensive theatre tickets for the masses – and Cultural – encouragement of young composers. Nicolodi has pointed out the difficulty inherent in the attempt to 'reconcile the ideal of "theatre for the people"' with the plans of the more original composers of the day, who were 'intentionally moving away from the products packaged by [. . .] the *verismo* composers so dear to the masses'.[54] By making itself the official defender of living Italian composers, the regime invited an army of ambitious and in some cases paranoid and hungry musicians, authentic and self-proclaimed, to plague government agencies with their requests, pleas and letters of recommendation.

The bureaucrats should have foreseen the problem. As early as 1926 a congress of opera composers had declared that state-subsidized theatres had the duty to perform more new Italian works.[55] Six years later an editorial in *La nuova Italia musicale* had reported Respighi's and Zandonai's doubts about the new *enti autonomi*: although neither of these composers would have criticized the regime outright, each complained that the subsidized theatres often announced productions of new works but rarely realized their plans.[56] Nearly everyone in the field agreed that something had to be done to promote contemporary opera, but what action was to be taken, and by and for whom, was a complicated matter. A few projects were half-heartedly initiated before the creation of the Theatre Inspectorate. The association that ran Verona's outdoor summer opera season in the Roman arena, reconstituted as an *ente autonomo* in 1934, established a competition whose aim was to build a repertoire of new Italian operas suitable for open-air performance and reflecting 'the spirit and emotions of the fascist revolutionary epos'.[57] And from time to time the national governing board of the musicians' union urged generically that 'more space be given to the most appropriate contemporary works', without specifying by what criteria appropriateness was to be judged.[58]

One of the Theatre Inspectorate's solutions to the dilemma of producing contemporary works was the establishment of experimental opera theatres 'where young singers and opera composers can gain experience'.[59] The first was set up in Rieti in 1935; another, the Teatro delle Novità (Theatre of New Works), was founded in Bergamo two years later, and Nicolodi describes it as a 'ghetto institution'.[60] A permanent committee for the examination of new opera scores was created in 1936.[61] In the spring of 1938, the MinCulPop decreed that as of the following season, the *enti autonomi* were to devote half or more of their repertoire to twentieth-century works, at least half of which had to have had their first performances not more than twenty years earlier.[62] Administrators whose theatres were not *enti autonomi* were told to use the same figures as guidelines 'to the greatest extent possible'.[63] In order to set a good example both before and after the publication of this declaration, the Ministry commissioned ten operas by well-known Italian composers. Six of those selected (Alfano, Lualdi, Mulè, Pick-Mangiagalli, Wolf-Ferrari and Zandonai) were of distinctly conservative musical tendencies; three (Casella, Giorgio Ghedini and Malipiero) were at the opposite end of the spectrum; and one (Lodovico Rocca) was in the middle. At about the same time, seven *enti* (Genoa, Milan, Naples, Palermo, Rome, Trieste and Venice) each commissioned an opera. None of the composers chosen – Carlo Jachino, Jacopo Napoli, Mario Peragallo, Mario Persico, Giuseppe Savagnone, Giulio Cesare Sonzogno and Antonio Veretti – has survived the test of time.[64]

Nicolodi's book contains a chart of living Italian composers whose operas and ballets were performed between 1935 and 1943, during the regular seasons of the *enti* and at three important festivals: Florence's Maggio Musicale, and the Contemporary Opera Cycles in Milan and Rome. Fifty-eight names appear on the chart. Of these, however, only thirteen had any work or combination of works produced more than five times: Mascagni (42), Giordano (33), Respighi (27), Zandonai (21), Cilea (19), Wolf-Ferrari (19), Pizzetti (15), Alfano (12), Mulè (12), Casella (11), Pick-Mangiagalli (10), Rocca (8), and Lualdi (7). All the people on this shorter list except Casella were musical conservatives in varying degrees; and decidedly inferior but well-placed composers such as Mulè and Lualdi managed to have their works performed more often than those of the less conservative Malipiero, Ghedini and the young but already highly regarded Dallapiccola.[65]

During the eight years of the Theatre Inspectorate/General Administration's existence (1935–43), the *enti* and special seasons and festivals presented a slightly larger number of productions by living Italian composers (320) than by dead ones (315). But the living composers' music was not necessarily given more performances or attended by a larger public. The opposite is more likely true: at La Scala, for instance, the average attendance during the 1938–9 season was only about seventy-five per cent of capacity,[66] and it dropped further in following seasons.[67] Since La Scala never ceased to be packed when the company's stars performed Donizetti, Verdi and Puccini, the house must have been very sparsely populated on contemporary opera evenings. Theatres that were not *enti autonomi* – and the *enti* themselves, during their extra or popular seasons – no doubt gave very little attention to living composers other than the surviving *veristi*. Still, the roughly fifty–fifty production proportion suggests that the agency's policies, however artificial, had some effect. There is comfort in the knowledge that a few young composers of merit managed to have their works performed with the backing of the MinCulPop, but it is sobering to recall that the operas of Giuseppe Mulè were produced as often as Bellini's and more often than those of Busoni, Cimarosa, Monteverdi, Ponchielli or even the ever-popular Leoncavallo.[68]

The selection criteria under the fascist bureaucracy cannot have been objective or free from political considerations.

An isolated episode in the history of the regime's dealings with the lyric theatre was the creation of a national opera house in Rome. La Scala, glorious but intractable – at least throughout the 1920s – was located too far from the capital to be of use as a showcase for impressing visiting dignitaries; and Mussolini was determined to establish a company in Rome that would equal and, if possible, overtake the Milanese *sanctum sanctorum*.

As early as September 1924, authoritative sources revealed that the cornerstone of a new national opera theatre would be laid next to Queen Margherita's palace in the Via Veneto the following month, on the second anniversary of the march on Rome. Marcello Piacentini, one of the leading architects who served the regime, was to head the project; his design, in compliance with one of fascism's principal fixations, was in the neo-Roman-imperial style – especially its amphitheatre-like outside. More important, the new theatre was to be equipped with the most up-to-date facilities. The anniversary came and went, and nothing further was heard until the following spring, when party secretary Starace, that devout acolyte of Euterpe, presented a bill in the Chamber of Deputies that outlined the transformation of the Teatro Costanzi into a national opera house. Since its inauguration in 1880 the 2,200-seat Costanzi had been the city's main lyric theatre; the world premières of *Cavalleria rusticana* and *Tosca* were among the many noteworthy events to have taken place there. In 1925, the Costanzi was still run on the *impresa* system, under the joint direction of its owners, the soprano Emma Carelli, who had retired from the stage a decade earlier, and her husband, Walter Mocchi. (At the turn of the century, young Mocchi, accused of 'socialist agitation', had a file with the Italian political police. He changed his ways, made a fortune as a banana merchant in South America, branched out into the opera business, and eventually assumed control of Buenos Aires's prestigious Teatro Colón and several important Italian theatres. Mocchi joined the Fascist Party in 1926.)[69] Part of the property contiguous to the Costanzi, needed for the planned expansion, belonged to the Postal Minstry, and this complicated purchase procedures. But by the summer of 1926 the government had taken over, the modernization of the house was underway, and the reopening was planned for the autumn of 1927.[70]

In a report to the Boston-based *Christian Science Monitor*, Alfredo Casella declared that the Costanzi project demonstrated how 'the unique regime which at the moment presides over the destinies of the nation often permits of a solution of problems which seemed insoluble before 1922'. It exemplified 'the advantages of this new "liberty of movement" ' that had 'for some time been very numerous and salutary. . . '.

> One must be grateful to Mussolini's government for having tackled with such boldness and breadth of vision one of the most difficult problems of the national musical life. One must again hope that this theatre may escape as long as possible from the 'bureaucratization' which almost inevitably ensnares all state enterprises [...].[71]

Renovating the Costanzi proved more time consuming than anticipated: the utter filth and dinginess caused by continuous use and poor maintenance during the Mocchi–Carelli reign had to be remedied, and decisions and plans had to be made. The main entrance was to be moved to the Via del Viminale side of the building, and there would be a piazza with garden in front of it. The interior décor was to be redone and each tier of boxes was to have its own foyer. The pit had to be lowered and both it and the stage enlarged and modernized. Rehearsal rooms were to be added.[72] The plans were good and were largely realized.

The company's structure, oddly, did not initially follow the pattern of the *enti autonomi*, or even of the Scala managerial system of 1898: this new jewel in the fascist diadem was entrusted to Ottavio Scotto, an old-fashioned Italo-American impresario, presumably because he had the wherewithal to entice to Rome such darlings of the American public as Claudia Muzio.[73] Unlike La Scala or the Florentine Politeama, for example, whose metamorphoses, stability and artistic growth depended largely upon the control exercised by their principal conductors (Toscanini and Gui, respectively), the Royal Opera did not even bother to engage a principal conductor until two and a half months before the opening performance. The position was given to Marinuzzi who, although gifted, found himself restricted by Scotto's nonchalant behaviour. 'Had I been able to imagine your sudden departure for America,' wrote the stunned conductor to his superior only six weeks before the scheduled first night,

> I would have rushed to Milan [...]. But I would not have believed that after having promised me you would come to Turin [n.b., where Marinuzzi was then working] [...], and with so many problems to be resolved in Rome, you would suddenly drop everything and catch a ship to New York ... Instead, I have received your brief letter from Paris, in which you let me know that you have made some changes in the [season's] programme, adding some new works – without bearing in mind those already decided upon – and that you have deleted *Fidelio*, which I wanted very badly to do ... I must emphasize that there are too many new works, and that we will not be able to do them all, or in any case do them well. Sixty pre-established performances in so short a season [two months] fit too tightly, and I conclude that it is imprudent not to wish to take into account the artistic and practical experience of someone who has been working in the theatre for twenty years. You were looking for a real partner, not an employee, and the contractual article of agreement between

us is a guarantee for you, too, in regard to choosing and realizing the
programme. Why don't you begin by respecting it? . . .[74]

Marinuzzi went on to complain about the production cuts unilaterally
decided upon by Scotto, and ended by saying that 'coming to the [Teatro]
Reale is a great aspiration for me, but [also] a sacrifice, and you know it. If I am
to stay, it is necessary that my artistic aspirations be respected absolutely, for
the sake of our dignity and for that of the theatre. . . .'[75]

Despite less than ideal conditions, preparations for the season proceeded.
A fine Latin plaque was set in place at the house – not in a modest corner of
the lobby, but directly over the proscenium arch: 'Victorio Emanuele III Rege
/Benito Mussolini Duce / Ludovicus Spada Potenziani Romae Gubernator /
Restituit /MCMXXVIII / A. VI' – i.e. Year Six of the Fascist Era. Mussolini, his
government and fascist party officials attended the dress rehearsal. All was
ready for opening night, 28 February 1928: the Rome première of Boito's
Nerone, attended by the king and queen.[76]

Scotto was fired without appeal after the second season. The Royal Opera
was placed under the direct control of an administrative council similar to La
Scala's, under the jurisdiction of the Governor of Rome. Marinuzzi became
artistic director, and the company's story began to parallel that of the *enti
autonomi*.

The international prestige of La Scala far outdistanced that of every other
Italian performing organization when the fascists came to power. La Scala was
an important part of the nation: no wonder the documents in Mussolini's
office file on the great house cover the entire period of his tenure as head of
government. The first, dated 3 January 1923, is a letter inviting the new prime
minister to become an honorary president of the recently approved lottery in
support of La Scala, in the hopes that Mussolini's name will 'make the appeal
more formal and authoritative [. . .] for the Citizenry and for all of Lombardy
[. . .]'.[77] He accepted with such alacrity and enthusiasm ('I applaud your work
[. . .] to keep La Scala at the high level of its marvellous artistic traditions in
Italy and throughout the world')[78] that the people responsible for La Scala's
finances immediately asked him to see what he could do to help the company
out of its difficulties. Mussolini apparently thought that a short note to the
Minister of Finance, Alberto De Stefani, would do the trick.

> [. . .] The Committee FOR THE TEATRO ALLA SCALA wishes to obtain concessions
> regarding taxes on the tickets and posters needed for the Lottery, which was
> granted through a prefectural decree.
> I have accepted the honorary Presidency of said lottery.
> If the matter won't cause excessive damage to the Exchequer, I see no
> problem in your granting the request.[79]

But De Stefani was a professional economist who had recently been instructed by Mussolini to cut government spending. His reply was curt and slightly sarcastic:

> [...] I do not have the authority to grant any of the things asked of me.
> Nor could I intend to promote legislative orders for immunity of this sort at the very moment when I am waiting to be able to withdraw exemptions, [...] in every field, that do not coincide with the direct and exclusive interests of the State. On this point we are already very much in agreement.
> I should therefore have to reply in the negative to the communication about La Scala's lottery that Your Excellency has brought to my attention with exquisite delicacy. [...][80]

Mussolini repeated the attempt two months later, this time leaning heavily on the imperatives:

> Dear De Stefani
> I am passing on to you a memorandum sent me by the *Ente autonomo* of La Scala in Milan, which requests a few concessions. I am in favour of all of them. Examine the requests, decide quickly upon the method to be adopted, and see to answering the interested parties.
> Cordial greetings.[81]

This time, De Stefani wrote to Mussolini's office chief, Alessandro Chiavolini, to point out that, 'as I have already had occasion to tell His Excellency the Prime Minister', the conditions necessary for such concessions did not obtain.[82] To this note he attached a detailed account of the considerations that had caused him to make his decision – a document that demonstrates his unwillingness to distinguish between the financial structure of an opera house and that of a racetrack.[83] The matter was closed.

Senator Borletti, a member of La Scala's administrative council and board president of the newspaper *Il secolo*, informed Mussolini one day in November 1923 that he and Toscanini would 'arrive in Rome on the 7 p.m. train from Milan', and that it was 'indispensable' that the prime minister receive the conductor and himself 'this very evening. [Toscanini] must discuss the very serious Scala question [...] and wishes to depart this very evening at 11, so as not to delay the beginning of the season.'[84] Their conversation concerned the way La Scala was being run and the way it was to be run in the future: Toscanini was displeased with the government's corporative plans and wished his theatre to remain unpoliticized.

Franco Ciarlantini, who was one of the City of Milan's representatives on the Scala board, wrote a lengthy memorandum to Mussolini about La Scala some weeks later. Like the Duce, Ciarlantini had begun his political career as a socialist and had become an interventionist on the eve of the First World War. He had joined the fascist movement in its embryonic stage, was a member of the National Party Directorate and, from 1923, of the Grand Council of Fascism. Journalist and cultural board-sitter, Ciarlantini later helped to found Venice's Biennale art festival and to organize a notorious convention, in Bologna, of fascist intellectuals. He disapproved of the national press agency's news release on Toscanini's visit to Mussolini, and claimed that the 'few sheets of paper' Toscanini and Borletti had shown the prime minister as an alternative to the plans laid by the Corporation for the Theatre – with which he was connected – had convinced people that 'my criticisms [. . .] were virtually unfounded, or at least so superficial as not to have aroused even the slightest concern among those who have the interests of the Greatest Theatre of Italian Operatic Art at heart'. But, he said, 'one has only to compare the last two [annual] budgets of the Ente in order [. . .] to have the greatest hesitation regarding the administrative methods currently held in esteem there'. The cost of individual performances during the ente's second season had risen above those of the first, while average ticket sales had gone down. Ciarlantini did not indicate how these statistics had been calculated (i.e. whether they included special expenses, such as the cost of technical improvements being made in the theatre), but instead plunged immediately into an explanation.

> In my opinion, the causes of administrative upheaval are:
> (1) the *real* deficit of the establishment which, as of 30 June 1923, was approximately *five million* [lire];
> (2) the burden of passive interest on the said deficit and on other debts inherent in the company's various requirements;
> (3) the weight of the excessive value set upon the [theatre's] boxes: about seven million, with a consequent interest of 280,000 lire to be paid by the boxholders;
> (4) the lack of any liquid reserves [. . .];
> (5) the fact of having combined and confused administrative tasks with technical-artistic ones, thus putting a variety of often incompatible jobs in the hands of one functionary [Angelo Scandiani, the Director-General], and leaving board members [. . .] with the [sole] job of putting their signatures to plans that have already been carried out;
> (6) La Scala's excessively *autonomous* attitude which, if necessary artistically, is not so in all other respects [. . .].[85]

Ciarlantini's goal was to bring La Scala into the fold – the Corporation for the Theatre – in order 'to synchronize [it] with other theatres' and to bring an 'indispensable industrial character' to its operating procedures.[86] But Scandiani, Toscanini and others must have realized that there were several good reasons for keeping La Scala independent. A year after the march on Rome Mussolini's desire to consolidate power in the hands of the National Fascist Party could not be doubted. The corporations were a fascist project, partisan from their inception and obviously destined to become increasingly so. La Scala's directors knew that if they wished to keep their company out of the political quagmire, they would have to avoid the Corporation for the Theatre. They also knew that joining the Corporation could as easily bring their theatre down to the level of the others as pull the others up.* Toscanini – the company's focal point throughout the 1920s – though interested in efficiency as a tool for keeping his ensemble in good shape, would have been appalled at the notion of giving the organization an 'industrial character'.

Milan was Italy's economic capital and La Scala was a symbol of Milan's accomplishments; Mussolini could not simply refuse to have anything further to do with this issue. As a not yet fully fledged dictator trying to prove his ability to control all facets of society, he had to cope with the Scala case. For advice, he wisely turned to the elderly Senator Luigi Mangiagalli, a famed gynaecologist who was then mayor of Milan and, as such, president of La Scala. Mangiagalli appears to have been respected by all the political parties, and his remarks to Mussolini were outspoken but well considered:

> As I was so invited, I shall engage Your Excellency on the Scala question, which may seem small but is not so, and which could seriously damage the structure of the Municipal Administration. | ... | La Scala now has world-wide prestige and fame, thanks to Toscanini. Astronomic distances separate him from other conductors. | ... | La Scala is his passion; it is the temple of art, and he does not want it profaned by selfish interests or party passions.
>
> The point of departure for the quarrel that is hampering the Adminis- tration's normal functions is the Ciarlantini episode. The Honorable Ciarlantini showed himself, in the end, to be incompatible |with other members of the board|. He said so himself. His behaviour was certainly not consistent. I put him on |La Scala's| Financial Committee as a representative of the Municipal- ity; he never commented on the budget – not even at Board meetings – but later, he did not approve the budget. He would like to see a Managing Director appointed, but the Board's constitution does not allow it. If he were one of the Municipal Representatives, he would misrepresent the Muncipal- ity | ... |; and one cannot say that he belongs among the Boxholders or the donors. How, then, can a place be found for him on the Financial Committee, which has one representative from each group|?|
>
> The fascist party wishes to have three fascist municipal representatives |on

* La Scala has never been looked upon with fondness or pride by opera administrators in other Italian cities. From the time of Italian reunification to the present day, it has always been a privileged sister whose siblings sometimes grant grudging admiration but more often express their vituperation. Paolo Grassi, La Scala's *sovrintendente* in the mid-1970s, stated the case for a special law for financing his theatre by pointing out that just as Milan could never contest Rome's archaeological primacy, so Rome and other Italian cities ought not to call Milan's operatic primacy into question. His argument was attacked by the *sovrintendenti* of all the other state-subsidized theatres, exactly as La Scala's special status in the 1920s had been opposed by those responsible for the other houses.

the Scala board|; but besides disrupting the harmony among the various political groups, this would give Toscanini the impression of a political act. He won't hear of it. Can we allow Toscanini to leave and La Scala to lose its prestige? I cannot agree with the fascist party in its |attitude of| not caring a rap, and I would propose a solution that seems to me equitable. Some fascists would come on to |the board|, but not three of them; and the Administration would be given a solid foundation. | . . . |[87]

Mangiagalli's solution was to allow one fascist party member and one fascist sympathizer – people Toscanini would trust as individuals – on to the Scala board. He concluded his letter by declaring his belief that Mussolini's intervention in the affair would be 'useful, or rather necessary'.[88]

The affair provides an excellent example of the basic technical problem – moral problems aside – inherent in the fascist system: the regime paralysed the decision-making process at sub-executive levels. Lower- and middle-level bureaucrats were afraid to proceed with plans, however inoffensive, unless they were sure that the Duce would not disapprove, but local fascist deacons like Ciarlantini could do a great deal of damage by throwing their weight around at random unless and until someone at the highest echelon brought them to order.

If Mussolini needed to save face for not fascisticizing the Scala administration, he could always point out that the *ente autonomo* had been devised as a nine-year experiment, that that experiment had been initiated two years before the march on Rome, and that it was only fair to allow it to run its course. He followed Mangiagalli's advice, and La Scala's activities continued as before – until the experimental period ended and Toscanini departed.

The Scala administration sent a memorandum to Mussolini's office in the summer of 1929, six weeks after Toscanini's resignation, assessing the company's economic conditions.

> During the Ente Autonomo's nine experimental years, eight opera seasons were carried out. The first six ended with a total cash surplus of approximately 6,600,000 lire; the seventh, on the other hand, left a deficit of L.373,000; and the last | . . . | a deficit of about L.2,000,000.
>
> The previous surpluses were used to cover, in part, house |restoration| expenses amounting to more than L.13,000,000. In addition, theatre materials (costumes, sets, footwear etc.) costing about L.10,000,000, completely amortized, were acquired during the nine years. Property worth about L.2,000,000 was also acquired.
>
> It is believed that the deficit of recent years is a result of:
> (1) general economic conditions;
> (2) decreased movement of foreigners |i.e. tourism|;
> (3) the theatre crisis, which concerns both operas and performers;
> (4) the orientation of public taste towards other forms of entertainment (sports, cinema etc.);

(5) the excessive [monetary] demands of singers;

(6) the burdensome working conditions of the orchestra, chorus etc.

In such a situation, which is non-transitory in nature, it is obvious that even given the most optimistic forecast, the resources that the Ente Autonomo can count upon cannot suffice to cover the theatre's production requirements, carried out and understood in accordance with truly superior artistic criteria.

Calculating the average expense of a performance at L.85,000 (excluding materials), based upon the reduced number of 120 performances (the average for the eight seasons was 140 performances), the cost would be L.10,200,000; plus materials (about L.1,200,000) = L.12,000,000 [sic].

On the other hand, calculating the average intake per performance at L.60,000, plus subscription sales, we arrive at L.7,200,000; plus earnings from supplementary taxes, roughly predictable at L.2,300,000; plus the municipal contribution of L.312,000, after taxes; plus other income at L.200,000 = L.10,012,000.

This rounds out to L.10,000,000; thus, if the season should come off as predicted, roughly two million lire would be lacking to cover expenses.

For information's sake, it should be kept in mind that in foreign countries the State gives very large subsidies to Theatres. In Germany, for example, the State allocates 40,000,000 marks (more than 180,000,000 Italian lire) for opera houses [etc. . . .].

[. . .] Rome's Teatro Reale dell'Opera, whose season is considerably shorter than La Scala's receives a fixed [government] contribution of L.2,000,000. In addition, the Governorship [of Rome – financed by the national government] pays all the staging costs (sets, costumes, props etc.) for nine operas; this represents an additional subsidy of at least two million. In addition, such expenses as electricity, heating, bill-posting and fire attendants are not paid by the management.

As has been suggested, every possible attempt will be made to limit expenses; and the agreement just concluded between La Scala [. . .] and the Teatro Reale [. . .] will contribute to that end. Besides providing for the exchange of several productions, this agreement will help to eliminate a sort of competition in engaging artists, which served only to raise their demands [. . .].

But in order to insure La Scala's existence [. . .] and to avoid the danger of having to close this theatre (whose seasons are a source of revenue for the city) or of its artistic degeneration, with obvious damage to national traditions and culture, Government aid is necessary. We must ask [that the government], in addition to maintaining [current provisions] and some fiscal relief [. . .], give up entirely its tax on the theatre's performances – considering, too, that the State earns this money only because the Scala season takes place.[89]

La Scala's changed circumstances – financial crisis, end of the nine-year experiment, Toscanini's departure – caused a flurry of letters, wires and meetings between Mussolini and some of the people closest to the theatre – primarily Sen. Borletti, who had been named Royal Commissioner-Extraordinary for the temporary management of the *ente autonomo*. *Il popolo d'Italia* published an interview with Borletti, worth citing at length not only for its overview of the theatre's situation, but also because the views expressed were undoubtedly approved by Mussolini.

[...] 'My duty', Sen. Borletti began, 'is to stitch together the nine-year experimental period and the definitive shape of the Ente, which will have to assume not only a predominant artistic function, but also, and to a considerable extent, an economic [one ...]. So there is no crisis, but simply the shortest possible transition period [...] for the transfer of power from the old Board – which was a manifestation of a temporary system – to a Board that will represent, constitutionally, the new, permanent judicial status of the Ente. [...] My judgement of the nine-year experiment [...]: a grandiose artistic success and a considerable economic success. [...] It may now truly be stated that a repertoire Theatre has been established [...]. In eight seasons there were well over 800 performances [...]; the repertoire consisted of fifty-six operas [... including] five operas new to Italy, six new to Milan and sixteen world premières. There were also five ballets.

'To accuse La Scala of not having opened its doors to new achievements is patently unjust. Apart from the figures just mentioned, La Scala cannot [...] welcome every new work – especially those that [...] do not always awaken the interest, let alone the sympathies, of the Scala public.

'La Scala is a University, not a junior high school. [...] Who, for that matter, can name another theatre in Italy or the rest of the world where such revelations or confirmations have taken place, the absence of which at La Scala is deplored? [...]

'[...] La Scala has not limited itself to welcoming already famous or nearly famous singers; it has also brought in youngsters who, after musical and artistic training, have begun their brilliant careers [there]. [...]

'Angelo Scandiani, [...] who has carried out his not easy task in the most admirable and noble way these past nine years, will remain Director. This is in keeping with the wishes of the Head of Government, who invited him, through Sen. De Capitani [mayor of Milan], to keep his position of responsibility, despite [Scandiani's] reluctance.

'[...] An opera house like La Scala cannot live on its own earnings, and not even the supplementary tax granted for its benefit was enough to eliminate the inevitable deficit. This is a chronic, incurable disease: the lyric theatre – understood not as a profit-making organization, but as [a creator of] artistic criteria – has always needed the support of benefactors or societies. [...]

'His Excellency the Head of Government, with his quick and profound instinct and [...] his love for Milan, has grasped with admirable readiness the whole artistic and economic problem connected with La Scala's existence, and he has granted everything I asked of him. Not only that: the Duce has also promised to exert influence upon [lower-level] governments so that they, in turn, will look after further necessities. I have already had proof of this in the passionate and effective involvement of His Excellency the Prefect [of Milan].

The Province and the Economic Council have already contributed, and the citizenry ought to be very grateful to them. [. . .] I am sure that the formal promises made by the mayor [. . .] for increased municipal contributions, will be kept by his successor [Visconti di Modrone], who must have inherited a love for our greatest opera house from his illustrious father [the president of the Scala board thirty years earlier].

'[. . .] Increasing the stability of the orchestra and chorus means enabling them to work under La Scala's auspices for the entire year. Thus a problem that is eminently economic could, if resolved, bring about undeniable artistic and cultural results. [. . .] As long ago as the late, lamented Sen. Mangiagalli's time [as mayor], and at the express desire of Maestro Toscanini, the possibility of ensuring a permanent orchestra and chorus for La Scala was actively under study. [. . .]

'No one can fail to recognize that the replacement of Arturo Toscanini has created a difficult and worrisome problem. The great Maestro undeniably represented the centre of attraction in past seasons. He ended up by enjoying exceptional prestige and an exceptional personal position. It was therefore necessary to formulate a programme that would satisfy the public through the variety of its operas or interpreters. [. . .]

'It is not up to the Commissioner, for the time being, to *foresee putting a long-term artistic policy into action*, as some have claimed. Art is the manifestation of beauty that has already been achieved, and not simply the planting of hope. La Scala has never refused to open its doors to new art, too – if it is art – nor will it do so in the future; and it will open them all the more widely if [that art] is in tune with the spirit of the fascist State. [. . .]'[90]

Scandiani died a few months later and Borletti invited Toscanini's former administrative assistant, Anita Colombo, to assume the direction of La Scala. 'I think I should tell you', the prefect of Milan wired to the Ministry of the Interior, 'that the news has not made a good impression in various circles.'[91] He referred to the Milanese fascists, who had looked upon Toscanini's departure and Scandiani's death as miracles that opened their way to untroubled domination of La Scala. 'Signorina Colombo', wrote Bottini, Milan's Federal Fascist Secretary, in a letter to Chiavolini, 'is not only Maestro Toscanini's ex-secretary, but the person who is said to have received an explicit mandate from Toscanini himself to run La Scala according to his orders.'[92] Although Toscanini was not issuing orders as such, his former assistant was indeed determined to follow his artistic advice whenever possible and to remain faithful to his policy of non- or minimal politicization of the theatre, and apart from her administrative experience, Colombo had sufficiently high fascist connections to enable her to qualify for the job.

The Colombo appointment was the cause of repeated complaints from Carlo Peverelli, a Milanese fascist parliamentary deputy. Chiavolini received an anonymous letter from someone who claimed to be a good friend and who had several axes to grind. The correspondent declared that 'fascism and its Duce have alienated the sympathies of a good fifty per cent of the Milanese' by putting La Scala in the hands of Borletti (a 'gaming- house keeper'), Commendatore Ferone – another board member (a 'Masonic thief [. . .], monopolizer and strangler of the whole Italian operatic field') and Colombo ('a whore'). 'Everyone is saying that as long as Comm. Ferone enjoys Bottai's support, nothing can be done, because this pimp supplies him with the best call-girls! [. . .] Open the Duce's eyes; there's still time, but do it without delay.'[93] Chiavolini duly passed this priceless document on to Mussolini, who loved such titbits and who read it without comment.

Anita Colombo was dismissed after one season: besides the many factional complaints, a woman at the helm of so important an organization had been an anomaly under fascism. The Scala administration then became a battleground for muncipal–provincial rivalries within the bosom of the Fascist Party. Colombo's successor, Erardo Trentinaglia, was a minor composer who seems to have been a pawn of Jenner Mataloni, President of the Province of Milan, who sat on the Scala board. The theatre critic Ulderico Tegani later described Trentinaglia as 'a good, cultivated person [. . .] an authentic gentleman – perhaps too much so to be capable of plunging into the heterogeneous and somewhat cantankerous world of the theatre'.[94]

The minutes of the Scala board meeting of 6 April 1932 demonstrate that the season then ending had had more than its share of difficulties. Mataloni blamed Trentinaglia's advisors – the composers Giordano and Pick-Mangiagalli, the publisher Tito Ricordi and the conductor Ettore Panizza (one of the few survivors from the Toscanini era) – for the much criticized programming choices and took care to state that he (Mataloni) had been responsible 'for exclusively administrative procedures', such as changing the personnel in keeping with the requirements of the *stagione* system now being adopted by La Scala. (The administration was abandoning the high-productivity repertoire system achieved by great effort during the 1920s.) Mataloni also declared that the public now seemed to be more interested in gossiping about behind-the-scenes goings-on at La Scala than in attending performances.[95]

Mataloni, shortly after the board meeting, reported to Mussolini's office chief that 'La Scala's central problem' was the incompatibility of the members of the board – a problem that *'damages* the management of the Ente'. Mussolini seems not to have replied and Mataloni took his silence as a go-ahead for a *coup de théâtre.* He secretly lined up sufficient internal political support on the Scala board, outflanked his opponents, and had himself elected director of the theatre, thus replacing his protégé, Trentinaglia. Important board members such as Giordano and Pick-Mangiagalli were indignant; with Gino Rocca, another musician on the council, they protested to Mussolini:

Out of pure love of truth, the undersigned hold it their duty to inform Your Excellency that at the meeting of 23 June |i.e. five days earlier| the board of the Ente Autonomo of the Teatro alla Scala was dissolved in a surprise move. This board had never been given a chance to function.

Unaware of what was happening in the Theatre's Offices, they |i.e. the signatories| were assembled to discuss normal administrative matters. They were never told about the repeated resignations of the Director, Maestro Trentinaglia, or of the changes in the 1932–33 programme, or of other arbitrary decisions.

They believe that Your Excellency should know the truth of the matter in order that their moral responsibility and their desire to act properly on behalf of La Scala's artistic fortunes not be compromised by the laconic communiqué |regarding Mataloni's accession|, which could give rise to the most unflattering comments. And they declare themselves ready to furnish more detailed information that will confirm this exact and loyal statement on their part.[96]

Mataloni's takeover must not have displeased Mussolini, for the provincial president kept his additional job ten years. Theatre critic Tegani said, shortly after the war, that Mataloni quite possibly did not know how to read a note of music and 'was at any rate no musician'. He had had nothing to do with theatre administration, 'of which he knew nothing', before his appointment to the Scala board. But he was accustomed to political struggle and was 'well furnished with the talents necessary for steering a course through any | . . . | set of circumstances. Pliable, versatile, quick, relatively young, resolute, | . . . | he succeeded in manning the breach.'[97] Thus, within three years of Toscanini's departure La Scala found itself completely submerged in the political swamp, where it remains to this day.

The rest of the Scala documentation in Mussolini's files merits attention precisely because of its triviality: it bears witness to the often bizarre preoccupations of a monomaniacal dictator. Take, for instance, the matter of the special concert marking the tenth anniversary of the 'march on Rome': Mussolini was to attend the event, and he had Mataloni and conductor Victor De Sabata submit a tentative programme for his approval. The first piece would be either Verdi's overture to I *vespri siciliani* or Rossini's overture to *Semiramide;* Mussolini chose the Verdi. Possibilities for the next number included Debussy's *Prélude à l'après-midi d'un faune*, Strauss's *Don Juan*, and a coupling of Borodin's *In the Steppes of Central Asia* with Liadov's *Kikimora;* Mussolini initialled the Debussy piece. Wagner would conclude the first half of the programme, and Mussolini selected the 'Ride of the Valkyries' instead of the prelude to *Die Meistersinger* or the Prelude and *Liebestod* from *Tristan*.[98] The second half was to consist of various arias and choruses from operas, to be chosen by the performers. Not even so inconsequential an operation as this, however, could be kept outside the ring of intra-party warfare. A few days before the concert, an agent of Mussolini's *servizio speciale* presented his boss with the transcript of a telephone conversation between Alceo Toni, then music critic for the fascist Il *popolo d'Italia*, and the composer Nino Cattozzo, who was then on La Scala's musical staff. (Italics indicate phrases underlined by Mussolini.)

> AT: Hi, Cattozzo. I wanted to talk to Mataloni, but I'll talk with you and you'll tell him what I've said. T*he concert has made a really disastrous impression*. People are saying that what's really missing, for the tenth anniversary of the Italian Revolution, is contemporary Italian music. The public says that Italian symphonic music, which has found a place for itself all over the world, isn't on the programme of the concert. These protests really aren't very nice, and you have to tell Mataloni about them. I wouldn't have said anything, but since these protests have come from my colleagues, from friends – and some of them have been quite bitter – I'm forced to talk. Now, I'm not only echoing other people's ideas, but I want |Mataloni| to know that there is someone very close to the Duce who will echo these complaints. If |the problem| is a result of an oversight on your part, resolve it if there's time.
>
> NC: It might have been a matter of |limited| time |for planning or rehearsing|.
>
> AT: Respighi can't be left out and Pizzetti can't be left out. Respighi has been made an Academician |for his work| as a composer of concert music, and you can't show him the door. Just ask the Authors' Society what he earns in royalties abroad. And besides what the public might say . . .
>
> NC: Allow me to observe that the evening is in Mussolini's honour and that no one is going to worry about the programme. Let's not fool ourselves: all eyes will be fixed on the Duce.
>
> AT: But *the programme will be made known abroad! And there are Italian composers who will rebel against Mussolini, because they'll say:* 'Mussolini *organized the evening, Mussolini made up the programme.'* These things will all be incorrect, but they're damaging. Talk to Mataloni about it, surely. For the Victory concert we can't leave Italian composers out. You've got to get Respighi in. See to it in time. B*etter to see to it in advance than to get a comment from the Duce – you know how he gives them – or to have him look after it.*
>
> NC: *All right, I'll talk to Mataloni about it.*[99]

Toni's aim was to place composers from his conservative faction on the programme of this event. Mataloni, however, did not bite the bait: he no doubt understood that to choose one faction over the others would have created a much more difficult situation than choosing none at all. The Milan Prefecture communicated to Mussolini's office that the programme 'can no longer undergo changes'. The concert concluded with pieces by two Grand Old Men among Italian composers: the 'Hymn to the Sun' from Mascagni's Iris and the 'Hymn for the Tenth Anniversary' by Giordano.[100] Mussolini 'paid' for his ticket by having the government give 5,000 lire to the president of La Scala 'for charitable works in Milan'.[101]

Six months later, Mataloni sent Chiavolini a summary of his first year's management.

> La Scala closes tomorrow with an already sold-out performance for the Municipal Employees' Recreation Association. I am therefore able to provide precise information. Please be so kind as to show the following facts to His Excellency the Head of Government:
>
> The Year XI [Fascist Era; i.e. 1932–3] Season has had eighty performances as against eighty-three in Year X.
>
> All the opening dates announced for the twenty operas included in the Programme were scrupulously respected.
>
> The Season has cost 1,500,000 *less* than the previous season (10,500,000 against 9,000,000) and had an increase of more than 900,000 lire in single ticket and subscription sales (4,214,000 against 3,310,000).
>
> On the average, each performance had 417 more attendances than in the previous season; 277 more than during the Colombo Season; only 129 fewer than during the last Scandiani Season. (Per-performance attendance Yr. XI – 1783; Yr. X – 1321; Yr. IX – 1461; Yr. VIII – 1867).
>
> Of eighty performances, *twenty-seven were completely sold out.*
>
> Total expenses for the period 1 July 1932 to 30 June 1933 (estimate of final account) will be 13.8% less than that of the previous [annual] period and 21.5% less than that of the 1930–31 period [. . .].
>
> *The results will allow us:*
>
> 1 – *not* to ask for the further subsidy of L.500,000 for this Season, as promised by H. E. the Head of Government;
>
> 2 – to set aside L.300,000 to pay the debt contracted for the previous season's deficit of 3,000,000;
>
> 3 – to distribute forty-seven Prizes (total amount L.30,000) for discipline and efficiency among the Theatre's Personnel, who had to undergo a salary reduction;
>
> 4 – to establish the maximum requirements for normal annual Scala seasons at L.9,500,000, against the average of 13,200,000 represented by the cost of the last decade's Seasons and the 12,000,000 cost of the three-year period 1930–31–32;
>
> 5 – to request that a definitive provision of L.1,000,000 be established as the State's tax contribution to La Scala's opera seasons. [. . .][102]

Mussolini was too clever not to have noticed that Mataloni's statistics conveniently referred back only as far as 'the last Scandiani season' and not to the previous Toscanini–Scandiani seasons. In those years nearly twice as many performances were given at only twenty per cent greater total cost; average attendance even on evenings when Toscanini did not conduct was much higher than in any of the succeeding seasons; orchestra, chorus and house singers enjoyed fuller employment without salary cutbacks; and, above all, the artistic results made an international impact. But the Duce wired the prefect of Milan: 'Communicate [Provincial] President Mataloni my satisfaction for results management Teatro alla Scala in Year XI.'[103] Mataloni had done what he could, had not asked the government for more money, and was not complaining.

One of Mussolini's police organizations sent him a report later that year 'regarding the high figures that [artists] have to pay Maestro Fabbroni of the Scala [staff] in order to get an engagement'. The Duce referred the matter to a Milanese subaltern: by the regime's standards, this was an exceedingly paltry form of corruption.[104] More interestingly, when the Ministry of Education had to nominate a representative to the Scala board, which was being re-constituted in March 1934, two possible choices were sent to Mussolini, who made the final decision. He scrawled a large 'No' over the name of Prof. Ettore Modigliani, head of the ministry's Milanese Office for Medieval and Modern Art, and a Jew. The other name was that of Mataloni, whose position was therefore consolidated: he now represented both the national and provincial governments on the board of the theatre that employed him to direct its operations.[105]

If Mataloni's reign pleased the government's budget-balancers, it had undeniably negative effects on the house's artistic activities. In 1935, for example, the management eliminated the spring symphonic series that had traditionally followed the opera season, and the desperate orchestra enlisted Pizzetti to defend its interests. 'The Scala Orchestra', wrote the composer in a special report to Sandro Giuliani, Editor-in-Chief of Il popolo d'Italia, '[. . .] was at one time employed for nine full months of the year. Today it can only count upon work for about five and a half months.'

> In addition to the economic factor, it is necessary that the orchestra stay together as long as possible to maintain its high artistic level, thus also allowing a continuation of the old Milanese tradition of a serious, artistic season of symphonic concerts.
>
> [. . .] The season we are planning will necessarily be short this year; there will be only seven concerts. Three will be conducted by Italians (Maestri Ferrero, Marinuzzi and [Antonino] Votto) and four by foreigners (a Frenchman, a Belgian, a Russian and a Dutchman). Renowned soloists will take part in nearly all the concerts, and among these [artists], too, the choice has fallen mainly upon Italians (Maria Caniglia, [Zino] Francescatti [sic; a Frenchman], [Enrico] Mainardi and [Carlo] Zecchi). Foreign guests will be [Vladimir] Horowitz and Lotte Lehmann.
>
> The Committee has also ruled that at least one work by a living Italian composer will be played on every concert.[106]

Financial support for the series came from the municipality and province of Milan, the Corriere della sera, the music publishers Ricordi and Carisch, several individuals and La Scala itself. But the 149,000 lire that had so far been raised was insufficient, and Pizzetti invited Il popolo d'Italia to make a contribution.

Giuliani would not commit himself without consulting Mussolini[107] who, according to his office chief, 'will not block the donation if the newspaper wishes to make one'.[108]

Most of the remaining documents in the file contain little of interest, but a few of them allow glimpses of La Scala's true situation. In 1939 Mussolini's office received a letter from a group of singers at La Scala (no individual signatures); the artists complained of the house's musical degeneration and of 'unheard of goings-on. Now we have the experiments of the new *Toscaninis*. How many conductors with unknown first and last names?! MOLA – POLZINETTI – NEGRELLI – SIMONATO, etc. Given this state of affairs, how can we hope for a better future? Everyone is talking about it: the subscribers, the public – all repeat together, "Poor Scala!"'.[109] And a newspaper cutting, presumably sent along with the letter, made essentially the same point in relation to a performance of I *pagliacci* conducted by 'the nice, well-intentioned Maestro Dagoberto Polzinetti'.

> [...] the idea that old repertoire operas can be conducted by anyone at all may not be condoned; for the old repertoire ought to have a distinguished character at La Scala. Some may object to this observation by saying that there have always been second-class conductors at La Scala. Very true; but there was a conductor there for the whole season who assumed the entire responsibility, and who watched over everyone and everything. Today, however, every conductor is left to fend for himself. And since we're moving from second- to third-class conductors, what will happen to La Scala?[110]

But by 1939, most of the world's best conductors either could not or would not perform in Italy, and those few who both could and would were in great demand throughout the fascist-dominated countries. La Scala had to make do, much of the time, with 'anyone at all'.

One of Mussolini's last acts on La Scala's behalf was to intervene in favour of the theatre's orchestra, stage musicians, chorus and *corps de ballet* in a dispute about overtime payments during the 1940–1 season. He received a message of 'gratitude and devotion' from the 'exultant' victors.[111]

In 1942 the musicologist and composer Carlo Gatti replaced Mataloni as La Scala's *sovrintendente*. On 5 June 1943, at the end of his first season, Gatti was received by Mussolini. In a letter written immediately afterwards to Mussolini's office chief, Gatti spoke of the Duce's 'benevolence', of 'the great consolation of hearing Him speak words of full approval' for La Scala's activities, and of his 'enlightened understanding' of the company's situation.[112] But Gatti returned to Milan shaken and haunted by the meeting: the Duce, he told a few trusted friends, appeared to be completely out of his wits.[113] Twenty days later, Mussolini was removed from office; and by mid-August, La Scala had entered the bleakest period in its 165-year existence.

*   *   *

When the fascists came to power, over 350 Italian cities, towns and villages had officially chartered non-operatic music societies. Most were amateur bands, mandolin ensembles and choral groups; much rarer were concert societies that backed permanent professional orchestras or chamber ensembles, or that sponsored regular seasons of concerts given by visiting professional artists. Rome appears to have had four such societies; Milan, Turin, Venice and Bologna three each; Florence and Naples two each; and Padua, Treviso, Udine, Verona, Vicenza, Trieste, Ferrara, Genoa, Parma, Reggio Emilia, Leghorn, Siena, Ancona, Pesaro, Perugia, Bari, Palermo and the occupied town of Fiume one each, for a total of thirty-nine. Although Italian concert life had grown remarkably during the first quarter of the twentieth century, it continued, under the regime, to attract a much smaller public than did opera. In 1936, the year in which Italians spent seventeen times as much on cinema admissions as on opera tickets, operas outsold concerts eight to one.[114] And despite the fact that there were approximately 500,000 paid concert attendances a year in Italy during that period, the government appears to have acted on the probably correct assumption that massive intervention would not have yielded much political glory.

As a result, Italian concert societies were realistically treated as the less-loved stepsisters of the opera companies. Their directors no doubt felt badly done by at the time, but in the long run the organizations benefited from being ignored. Although they were usually required to belong to the same corporations, confederations and consortia as the lyric theatres, or to similar ones, and although Italian concert artists and symphony orchestra members had to belong to the National Fascist Union of Musicians, the guidelines that concerned concert life seem always to have been after-thoughts. Prior to the introduction of the racial laws, which banned Jewish music and musicians, there was only one widely mentioned, high-level directive regarding concert programming: issued by the General Theatre Administration of the Ministry of the Press and Propaganda at the end of 1936, this document recommended that Italian concert societies 'give much more space to soloists in pro-grammes of symphonic music, in order to obtain greater variety [. . .], to encourage Italian soloists, and to make familiar many unknown or rarely played compositions of the past'.[115] The Ministry suggested specifically that administrators include at least one soloist on every symphonic programme.[116]

The most important symphonic institution in Italy at the time of fascism's accession to power was the orchestra of the Augusteum in Rome, and so it remained throughout the following two decades. Bernardino Molinari, the ensemble's artistic director and principal conductor from 1912 – four years after its founding – to 1943, was a gifted musician whose abilities as an orchestra trainer earned him the praise of Debussy, Richard Strauss,

Stravinsky and Toscanini. He brought a great deal of new home-grown and foreign music to the attention of the Italian public. His enthusiasm for the regime was helpful to his orchestra, which received government funding for such prestigious projects as a 1937 tour of Nazi Germany.

Milan, for all its justifiable claims to Italian musical primacy, had no permanent symphonic institution of high professional calibre at the time of the march on Rome, except the Scala orchestra, which usually gave concerts at the end of each opera season. In 1924, the Ente concerti orchestrali (ECO) was founded in an attempt to fill the gap. The ensemble was made up mainly of members of the Scala orchestra, who thus managed to extend their earning season by a few weeks in the spring, when most of the ECO's concerts took place. The organization's sponsors included numerous private benefactors, the Teatro del Popolo – formerly a socialist institution – the already fascist-dominated Musicians' Union and the Symphonic Concert Society. The ECO's artistic director was Vittorio Gui and its governing board included Count Giovanni Ascanio Cicogna; Carla Toscanini, the conductor's wife; Cesare Albertini, technical director of La Scala; Luigi Ansbacher, a lawyer deeply interested in the city's musical life; Guido Carisch, music publisher; Carlo Clausetti, co-director of the Ricordi Company; and Carlo Gatti.

According to a history of the ECO published a few years later, a decision was made in 1925

> to combine efforts by making use of the Scala orchestra [now labelled as such] for the ECO's concerts and by offering the players a longer season: nine months instead of seven. At the same time, the annual activities of the ECO were to be split into two periods: one in the autumn, just before the opera season, and the other in the spring, immediately afterwards. Maestro Toscanini declared himself in favour of such an arrangement, which enabled his orchestral team to stay together for a longer period; moreover, he agreed to conduct some of its concerts. The participation of so eminent an artist, the economic advantage deriving from the reduction in the orchestra's expenses, and the use of the theatre gratis (excluding expenses, of course) [...] all favoured the conclusion of such an agreement.[117]

Many of the concerts were repeated at the Teatro del Popolo, with ticket prices greatly reduced; and even at La Scala, blocks of seats were often reserved at low rates for workers.

In organizing this venture, as in so many other enterprises, Milan was far ahead of most of the rest of the country. The only other major orchestral undertaking to be initiated during the fascist period was the Florentine Orchestral Repertory Ensemble, founded by Gui in 1928, which later spawned the Maggio Musicale festival.

During the first fifteen years of fascist rule, Italian chamber music associations – often known as 'Friends of Music Societies' or 'Quartet

Societies' – drew upon native and foreign musicians in much the same way as did their counterparts in other countries. Programme content was in no way limited by government interference. But with the banishment of Jews from the national musical scene in 1938 and the gradual application of other politically induced limitations thereafter, the situation changed dramatically.

*   *   *

Italy's most and least enduring music festivals were born during the fascist period. Even more obviously than the lyric theatre's *enti autonomi*, these showcases grew out of such non-political phenomena as the trend towards enshrining cultural masterpieces of the past and the need to protect significant works of the present that were not independently obtaining a popular following. The regime, however, was able to use such festivals, as Nicolodi says, in order to demonstrate its 'magnanimous, watchful openness'.[118] The most important of these periodic events were the *Festival internazionale di musica* in Venice and the *Maggio Musicale* in Florence. Both cities were centres of international tourism, for which reason the regime may have had particular interest in presenting a more cosmopolitan image than served its purposes elsewhere.

The first Venice festival, held in early September 1930 in conjunction with the city's already celebrated *Biennale* art festival, was presided over by Lualdi, with Casella as vice-president and such luminaries as Labroca and Malipiero on the executive committee. Mussolini, fearing that the event would prove unpopular, withheld his official patronage; but Lualdi stated – clearly with approval – that the festival was being held 'under the aegis' of the Duce, who had contributed 'moral and material assistance'.[119] Anticipating attacks from the extreme musical right, Lualdi also wrote in the festival programme that 'despite its international character, [. . . the event] is an unadulteratedly Italian and unadulteratedly fascist institution. [. . .] Certain artistic poisons and drugs that have wreaked havoc beyond the Alps' – an obvious reference to the Schoenbergians – were being excluded.[120]

The first festival included the Italian premières of a wide range of non-Italian works: Bartók's Fourth String Quartet, Milhaud's *La Création du monde*, and pieces by Walton, Kodály, Roussel, Bloch, Szymanowski, Hindemith and Křenek. There were also world premières of music by many native composers, including Alfano, Castelnuovo-Tedesco, Lualdi, Renzo Massarani, Pick-Mangiagalli, Francesco Santoliquido and Vincenzo Tommasini, and performances of rarely heard music by Stravinsky, Prokofiev, Falla, Honegger, Respighi, Casella, Turina, Tansman, Malipiero, Pizzetti, Zandonai and the ubiquitous Mulè. The Augusteum and Milan Radio orchestras performed under the direction of Molinari, Serafin and Votto, and soloists included the soprano Mafalda Favero, Casella as pianist and Hindemith as violist. The first festival was reasonably successful with the public, and income slightly exceeded expenses. 'Many people', says Nicolodi, 'considered it the only testing bench then extant in Italy for taking modern music out of the realm of indifference, of ghettoized specialization or of open ostracism.'[121]

But success brought other problems to the organizers: everyone now wanted to be included in the programme of the second festival, planned for early September 1932. 'Please inform those responsible', wrote Toni to festival secretary Aldo Finzi, 'that I am the composer of numerous works, many of which have been performed – albeit not booed or barely tolerated or accepted with resignation' – the implication being, of course, that most of the works chosen for the festival were by composers less popular than himself. 'Let me add that I shall make this known when and as I think best, in public and in private.'[122] Lualdi parried Toni's thrust by having Finzi send a copy of the letter to the editor-in-chief of Il popolo d'Italia, of which Toni was music critic. Other Italian composers – Cesare Nordio and Guido Guerrini, for example – also wrote to complain about being excluded from the programme, and Casella thought it unfortunate that 'all our best youngsters ([Vittorio] Rieti, [Virgilio] Mortari, [Mario] Pilati etc.)' had been kept out.[123] Despite complaints and attempts at interference, the festival turned out well. Small orchestras conducted by Désiré Defauw, Fritz Busch, Fritz Reiner and Lualdi performed, respectively, concerts of contemporary French, German, North American and South American music by such composers as Roussel, Poulenc, Ibert, Toch, Hindemith, Graener, Sowerby, Eichheim, Saminsky, Achron, and Gershwin. Works by three distinctly pro-regime Italian composers – Franco Casavola (L'alba di Don Giovanni), Casella (La favola di Orfeo) and Lualdi (La Grançèola) – were specially commissioned; Malipiero's Pantea received its world première; Falla's El Retablo de Maese Pedro was heard for the first time in Italy; and Respighi's Maria Egiziaca had its first staged performance.

Mussolini personally approved plans for the 1934 festival when a committee of the Biennale's administrators visited him at Palazzo Venezia. In an article celebrating the festival's opening, Lualdi said that the atmosphere of the Duce's quarters was more like that of 'the study of an art enthusiast, of a patron', than of the office of a statesman 'who, for twelve years, has been guiding a Nation's destinies with most humane firmness and with an incomparable sense of responsibility [. . .] – so great were the interest, the understanding, the magnificent, always well-balanced quickness of judgment and argumentation that Benito Mussolini evinced, whether the subject was music, architecture or painting'. The dictator approved the inclusion of orchestral and choral music as well as chamber works in the festival's programme. '[He is] the Leader,' said Lualdi, 'even in the arts, even in the specific field of music.'[124]

The 1934 festival, held from 8 to 16 September, gave more space to young Italian composers, including Dallapiccola, Rieti and Antonio Veretti, but left plenty of room to the more celebrated musicians of the day. At one imaginatively conceived concert, Constant Lambert, Milhaud, Pizzetti and Stravinsky each conducted one of his own works and Hermann Scherchen conducted Berg's *Der Wein* in the composer's presence. The statistics are impressive: twenty-eight works, each by a different composer, were performed; sixteen were world premières. Three orchestras, five choruses, two ballet companies, fourteen conductors and thirty-four vocal and instrumental soloists took part in the proceedings. But the inclusion of the Verdi *Requiem*, with such stars of the moment as De Sabata and Beniamino Gigli, a concert by the Vienna Philharmonic under Weingartner and guest performances of *Così fan tutte* and *Die Frau ohne Schatten* by the Vienna State Opera ensemble under Clemens Krauss led the young composer and conductor Gianandrea Gavazzeni to criticize the 'decorative, official appearance that [the festival] is taking on'.[125]

The pattern, however, had been established, and the Venice festivals continued at two-year intervals, with an extra one added in 1937. Some trouble was caused in the early 1930s by the founders of Florence's *Maggio Musicale*, who seem at first to have regarded their Venetian counterparts as competitors rather than as fellow combatants against artistic provincialism. But the friction quickly gave way to reasonably peaceful coexistence. The wartime (1942) Eighth International Music Festival in Venice contained – apart from one retrospective concert of works by Malipiero, Honegger, Ravel, Stravinsky, Richard Strauss and Falla – little of interest, especially in comparison with previous years. Then, after twelve years' existence, the festival temporarily collapsed.

The Florentine festival began as an offshoot of the *Stabile Orchestrale Fiorentina* (Florentine Orchestral Repertory Ensemble), which had been founded in 1928 under Gui's artistic direction. Gui, who was not enthusiastic about the regime, was counterbalanced by what Leonardo Pinzauti, in his history of the Maggio, calls the 'politically reassuring' presidency of Carlo Delcroix.[126] Delcroix, a Florentine writer who had lost his sight and both hands during the First World War, became a well-known political figure under fascism and served as president of various associations for veterans and handicapped people. Gui's orchestra could thus immediately be considered a 'fascist initiative'.[127] So successful was the first season that the Ministry of Education elevated the orchestra's status to that of an officially recognized non-profit organization. The number of players rose from 83 to 100, a 3,000-pipe organ was built, and the EIAR agreed to broadcast some of the concerts. According to Pinzauti, the orchestra's development was facilitated by a conjunction of interests among those who were truly interested in a musical rebirth for Florence, others whose ambitions were merely 'parochial or political', and a group of socialites responding to 'the promptings of fashion'.[128]

The orchestra developed so well that local politicians began to think of it as a possible showcase – an example of how the performing arts were flourishing under fascism. A decision was made to associate the orchestra with the city's main opera house, and to call the reconstituted organization the *Ente autonomo* of the Royal Florentine Politeama Vittorio Emanuele. According to the *Gazzetta ufficiale* of 1 October 1931, the new ensemble 'will be run on a non-profit basis, in accordance with pure artistic criteria, with the aim of fostering the growth of musical education and culture among the people'.[129] Delcroix admitted in an interview that – 'sad to say' – most of the financial backing was being provided by Florence's foreign colony,[130] but this did not prevent local fascists from gathering whatever crumbs of the undertaking's glory fell in their laps. In this, however, they were merely behaving as politicians, and not specifically as fascists.

Official recognition of the orchestra emboldened Florentine musicians, political bosses and aristocrats to plan a triennial music festival – the *Maggio Musicale* – and their idea was looked upon with favour by Mussolini, who allocated 100,000 lire for a trial run in May 1933. Along with some traditional repertoire, the first festival included such stage rarities, for those days, as Verdi's *Nabucco*, Rossini's *La Cenerentola*, Spontini's *La vestale*, and Pizzetti's *La rappresentazione di Santa Uliva*. One concert was dedicated to Busoni's music, and in another programme the Kolisch Quartet played works of Bartók, Schoenberg and Vito Frazzi. In conjunction with the performances, an International Music Congress was held in the Palazzo Vecchio between 30 April and 4 May, presided over by the well-known journalist and academician Ugo Ojetti, with the participation of such luminaries as Alban Berg, Casella, Edward J. Dent, Henry Prunières, Paul Stefan, Emile Vuillermoz, Hans Rosbaud, Aloys Mooser, Lualdi, Basil Maine, Roger Sessions, Carl Ebert, Andrea Della Corte, Ferruccio Bonavia, Paul Bekker, Alfred Einstein, Guido Maria Gatti, Cesari, Mila and Gavazzeni. The papers delivered covered four broad areas: music criticism; tendencies in contemporary opera; the relationship of radio, film and the gramophone to music; and the connection between the spread of musical culture and international cultural exchanges.[131] Mila, who at twenty-three was becoming an important figure among Italian musicologists, reported in the *Rassegna musicale*:

> It was comforting to observe, in this showcase of the forces operating in the field of music criticism in all countries, that the Italians demonstrated incomparable depth and solidity of preparation, which the best of them have achieved through a broad philosophical awareness drunk at the fount of idealism [...].[132]

Mila had cleverly made an obeisance to nationalistic pride while pointing out

– without naming the forbidden name – that the best people in the field owed their intellectual training to the idealistic aesthetic of the anti-fascist Croce.

The *Maggio* as a whole succeeded so well that Mussolini immediately approved a plan to make it biennial rather than triennial. And even during the 'off' spring of 1934, the Duce lent his patronage to the Twelfth Festival of the International Society of Contemporary Music, which was held in Florence. Dent presided, and participants included Nadia Boulanger, Křenek, Hilding Rosenberg and Vladimir Vogel. Compositions by Malipiero, Casella, Mulè, Castelnuovo-Tedesco, Riccardo Nielsen, Gino Gorini, Dallapiccola, Labroca, Pizzetti, Alfano, Berg ('the "Lyric Suite" for string quartet was especially well liked | . . . | the second movement had to be repeated'),[133] Jean Françaix, Arthur Honegger, Ravel, Bartók, Igor Markevitch, the twenty-one-year-old Benjamin Britten and Hans Apostel were performed, representing most of the important trends of the day. Conductors included Gui, Fernando Previtali and Hermann Scherchen.[134]

Narrow-minded fascist musicians – invariably those whose works were not included in the *Maggio's* programmes – complained that too many foreign composers were performed at the festival, but Mussolini approved the plans for the 1935 event and tripled the government's financial backing.[135] It was a small price to pay for helping the regime look good to the outside world, especially in comparison with the increasingly xenophobic, racist follies of Hitler's Nazis. Most Florentine fascists happily seconded Mussolini: the festival showed their city – whose economy even then was dependent to a significant extent upon tourism – in an excellent light. The *Maggio Musicale*, said the newspaper *Bargello*, 'is assuming a unique aspect and importance in the fascist life of Florence and of Italy'.[136] The 1935 festival included the world premières of Pizzetti's opera *Orsèolo* and Castelnuovo-Tedesco's incidental music to Rino Alessi's *Savonarola*, and revivals of Rossini's *Mosè*, Rameau's *Castor et Pollux* and Gluck's *Alceste*. Bruno Walter conducted an Italian version of *The Abduction from the Seraglio*, and Felix Weingartner appeared at the head of the Vienna Philharmonic.

For the 1937 festival, 'the |Florentine| prefect, the mayor, the local fascist boss and the |festival's| general director, Labroca, went to Mussolini to present the programme. | . . . | It was approved, but not without "some modifications", as the newspapers tell us.'[137] The nature of those modifications is not known, but the Duce simultaneously approved a proposal to make the Maggio an annual event.[138] Once again, the list of events was varied and interesting, containing the world première of Casella's *Il deserto tentato*, the Italian première of Berg's Violin Concerto, the first staged performance in Italy of Stravinsky's *Oedipus Rex*, the first Florentine production of Malipiero's *La Passione*, and revivals of Monteverdi's *L'incoronazione di Poppea* (transcribed by Giacomo Benvenuti), Rossini's *Il signor Bruschino* and Verdi's *Luisa Miller*. The presence at many events of Maria José of Piedmont, consort of Crown Prince Umberto, helped fill portions of the theatre with socialites who might not otherwise have dreamt of entering it. (But the princess was musically accomplished and highly intelligent – unlike, it was said, most of the members of the family into which she had married.) The anti-fascist Gui did not hesitate to conduct the Royal March and the fascist party hymn, 'Giovinezza', as required at all performances attended by Maria José or other representatives of the crown or the government.[139]

A second International Music Congress, again held in conjunction with the festival and again presided over by Ojetti (with G. M. Gatti as secretary), was addressed by a cosmopolitan group of artists and scholars: Křenek, Conrad Beck, Markevitch, Casella, Malipiero, Petrassi, Hindemith, Egon Wellesz, Dallapiccola, Pannain, Vuillermoz, Willi Reich (who had translated Mussolini's speeches into German and was very enthusiastic about the Duce), Luigi Ronga, Piero Coppola, Mooser, Della Corte, Torrefranca, Sebastiano Arturo Luciani, Veretti, Darius Milhaud, Roland Manuel, Maurice Emmanuel, Francesco Vatielli, and the writers Arturo Loria and Giacomo Debenedetti.[140] This was the last truly open musical event in Florence for a long time. The orchestra's tour of Nazi Germany in April 1938, and the presence at the following month's Maggio Musicale of Hitler, Ribbentrop, Hess, Mussolini, Ciano, Alfieri and Bottai, symbolized what was happening not just to the festival but to Italy.

'All the boxes', reported La Nazione proudly, 'were decorated with bouquets of flowers bearing swastikas and the colours of the Third Reich combined with the Italian colours.'[141] Gui behaved rather oddly, for a convinced anti-fascist, in conducting for such an audience a special performance of excerpts from Simon Boccanegra with a cast that included Alexander Sved, Tancredi Pasero and Maria Caniglia. Although the Maggio's programme of novelties and rarities was still rich (world première of Malipiero's Antonio e Cleopatra; Italian premières of Kodály's The Spinning Room and Haydn's L'isola disabitata, Florentine première of Respighi's La fiamma, revival of Orazio Vecchi's L'Amfiparnasso), the new, not yet official anti-semitic campaign altered the list of performers. Otto Klemperer and Ida Rubinstein, both of whom had originally been scheduled to participate in the 1938 Maggio, did not attend. Instead, there were two guest concerts by the Berlin Philharmonic under Wilhelm Furtwängler. Rome granted Bruno Walter special permission to conduct a performance of Brahms's Deutsches Requiem that revealed, according to one critic, 'a high sense of noble spiritual elevation'.[142] But Pinzauti's statement that the exceptionally warm reception given Walter was 'one of the most impressive pieces of evidence of a spontaneous, undisputed atmosphere of tacitly shared anti-fascism'[143] is not convincing. More likely, it showed solidarity with an artist who had suffered at the hands of what many

Italians apparently felt was a stupid and barbaric policy of anti-semitism on Germany's part. The 1938 *Maggio* also included a production of *The Tales of Hoffmann* – a work that had been banned in Germany because of Offenbach's 'racial' origins – while the parallel Third International Music Congress included a lecture by one Oskar Walleck on the staging of 'Aryan' operas. A programme planner with a sense of humour sandwiched Walleck's talk between lectures by the Jewish composer Darius Milhaud and the Jewish director Herbert Graf.[144]

These equivocations had come to an end by the time of the 1939 *Maggio*, which was Jew-less and parochial, despite such worthwhile events as performances of the *St Matthew Passion* by the Berlin Philharmonic under Furtwängler, the Italian première of Hindemith's *Nobilissima Visione*, and revivals of the Tasso–Gluck *Aminta*, Cimarosa's *Le astuzie femminili*, and Rossini's *William Tell*. The parallel international congresses of former years were replaced by a showcase of contemporary Italian music, whose programmes contained works by composers now forgotten even within Italy, excepting Malipiero, Mortari and Nino Rota.[145] Successive festivals were purely Axis affairs, although the programming continued for a while to be unusually interesting. The 1940 festival, for instance, included the world première of Dallapiccola's *Volo di notte*, the Italian première of Busoni's *Turandot*, a production of Mussorgsky's original edition of *Boris Godunov*, and revivals of Purcell's *Dido and Aeneas*, Handel's *Acis and Galatea*, and Rossini's *Semiramide*. The following year's schedule contained the first performances in Florence of Gluck's *Armida* and Schumann's *Paradise and the Peri*, a revival of Rossini's *L'italiana in Algeri*, and concerts by the acceptably Aryan Edwin Fischer and Herbert von Karajan. By 1942, the festival's worthwhile novelties were limited to the Italian première of Busoni's *Doktor Faust* and a revival of Monteverdi's *Il ritorno di Ulisse in patria*. Karajan and Fischer appeared again, and there were guest performances of *Fidelio* and *Der Rosenkavalier* by the Dresden Staatsoper under its Kapellmeister Karl Böhm, who had happily replaced the anti-Nazi Fritz Busch in that job in 1934. Wartime circumstances forced cancellation of the 1943 *Maggio Musicale*, and after a severely reduced series of events in 1944, the history of the festival under fascism came to an end.

In addition to the Venetian and Florentine festivals, such regular exhibitions as Perugia's *Sagra musicale umbra* (Umbrian music festival) dedicated to religious music, and Siena's *Settimane musicali* (musical weeks), conceived as a forum for the revival of forgotten early Italian music, were relatively un-politicized (until 1938) products of the fascist era that outlasted fascism. All four series are still in existence half a century and more after their founding. Other special musical undertakings proved to be less durable – in some cases because of their political orientation, in others simply because the public did not find them sufficiently attractive.

The regime sponsored a series of events designed to give a hearing to contemporary Italian music. These strictly national festivals – held sporadically and infrequently – often changed name and venue. The first of them was the *Mostra del Novecento Musicale Italiano* (Exhibition of Twentieth-Century Italian Music), held in Bologna from 31 March to 12 April 1927 under the honorary presidency of Mussolini, who sent Ciarlantini to represent him.[146] Works of fifty-five Italian composers were performed by four orchestras, three chamber ensembles and one choir; not one of the pieces on the programme was specifically fascist in inspiration.[147] A similar festival – the First National Exhibition of Contemporary Music – took place in Rome during the last week of May 1930. Reviewing the event in *Musica d'oggi*, the composer Renzo Massarani spoke enthusiastically of works by Casella, Respighi, Mortari, Pilati, Mulè, Rieti and Labroca, but disliked pieces by Ettore Desderi, Spartaco Copertini, Carlo Jachino and Rota. He also lamented the absence of compositions by such important figures of the day as Malipiero, Pizzetti, De Sabata, Toni, Veretti, Frazzi and Enzo Masetti. Although Massarani was at that time an ardent fascist, he openly mocked the artistic nationalism of a Bolognese critic who had proclaimed Respighi's superiority to Stravinsky.[148]

Massarani and Mulè were responsible for the Fascist Musicians' Union's National Exhibition, held in Rome in April 1933. These concerts were presented by the Augusteum Orchestra and performers from the Santa Cecilia Academy. Forty-eight Italian composers of all ages and degrees of celebrity were represented. Other national exhibitions in this series took place in later years.

Miscellaneous events included inter-provincial exhibitions of contemporary music and the music sections of the *Littorali della cultura*, which were fascist-orientated festivals. Some of these, however, straddled the fence separating festivals from competitions, with more emphasis on the latter.

*   *   *

Many fascist cultural organizations sponsored competitions from time to time to encourage writers, painters and musicians to glorify the regime, its achievements and its anniversaries. A representative sampling shows the ways in which musical contests were either set up by political groups or had political ends.

1928: the journal L'*arte fascista* (Palermo) announced a competition 'for a symphonic poem for large orchestra, on the subject of "The March on Rome". First prize, 500 lire; performance in an important theatre and publication in the Journal (for the first three prize-winners). [. . .] Participation is limited to members of the "Fascist Art Groups".'[149]

Adriatico nostro, a magazine intended to encourage imperialistic thinking, held a competition for a political anthem, but none of the entries was deemed satisfactory.[150]

The Political Group of Artists of the *Fascio* (Milan) offered a prize of 40,000 lire for an opera, 15,000 lire for an operetta, and 3,000 lire for a short symphonic composition, but no political significance was required.[151]

1930: Milan's Università Popolare offered a 1,000-lira prize for 'an anthem whose subject will be the battle for wheat production; the text has already been written'.[152]

1931: 'On the occasion of *the Duce's Third Health Camp* next August, a choral singing competition will be held for the Avanguardista [fascist youth corps] legions, who will perform *Giovinezza* [fascist party hymn] and *Balilla* [youth corps hymn].'[153]

1934: The Fascist University Group of Milan organized a competition for young music critics. One of the required essay subjects was: 'the position of the fascist generation of Italian musicians in relation to the previous, so-called revolutionary, international generation'. The judges were Pizzetti, Cesari, Toni and the critic Ferdinando Ballo.[154]

1936: The Fascist Recreation Association of Naples held a competition for 'a song or military march', and the panel of judges – headed by Lualdi – assigned a first prize of 1,500 lire to Damiano Cortopassi for his song, '*L'ha detto Mussolini'* ('Mussolini Said It'), and a second prize of 1,000 lire to Pina Carmirelli (later well known as a violinist) for her song, '*Casetta abissina*' ('Little Abyssinian Cottage').[155] From the National Fascist Union of Musicians: 'On the occasion of the fourth exhibition of contemporary music, which will take place in Rome in the spring of 1937–XV, the following competitions are announced: (a) a Composition for large Orchestra, of a heroic nature, intended to celebrate the foundation of the Empire [. . .]; (b) a Composition for Orchestra, in several movements [. . .], of a Mediterranean nature (that is, luminous, constructive, agile, dynamic, free from every Nordic and impressionistic influence) [. . .].'[156] The prize in the first category (3,000 lire) was won by Barbara Giuranna, a fairly well-known composer, for her *Tenth Legion*; that in the second (same amount) was won by Giovanni Bianchi for his *Triptych*.[157] 'To celebrate the foundation of the Empire, the EIAR announces a national competition for all musicians, for a composition that glorifies the events of Year XIV [1935–6] – epoch-making events, and blazing material capable of awakening high and violent inspiration.'[158]

1937: The *Littorali della Cultura*, held in Naples, included a 'competition for a symphonic or choral composition of a *heroic nature*', as well as performance competitions whose participants were allowed to play only Italian music.[159] The National Recreation Association's competition for an opera by an Italian composer 'has had negative results. Of the twenty-five operas presented, not one seemed worth the consideration of the Judging Panel, made up of Maestri

Alfano, Pizzetti, Mascagni, Zandonai, Mulè, Vitale and Labroca.'[160]
1938: The *Littorali della cultura*'s music section – whose theme that year was
'Continuity and development of an Italian musical art as the interpreter of
renewed national sensitivity' – sponsored a composition competition.
President of the section: Adriano Lualdi; president of the competition:
Giuseppe Mulè.
1939: 'The "Cristofori" Association of the Royal Academy of Florence's "L.
Cherubini" Conservatory announces a competition, open to Italian [piano-]
builders, for the construction of a piano "that will be as suitable as possible
for transportation to the Colony [i.e. Ethiopia] and the dominions of the new
Italian Empire" [. . .].'[161]

Great claims were made for the demonstration of 'fascist faith' on the part
of the artists (and artisans) who entered these competitions. But since most
artists under any regime are notoriously ignorant, politically, and since they
usually enter competitions because they have faith in themselves, all that is
politically discernible from their participation in fascist-run contests is that
they were to be numbered among the millions of Italians who did not openly
rebel against fascism. If orthodox *fede fascista* existed at all in this area, it was
more likely to have been found among the people who conceived and ran the
competitions than among those who won and lost them.

*   *   *

Fascism's record in the construction and restoration of auditoria for
musical performance was more abysmal than in any other area of its musical
dealings. Although in 1922 Italy was already graced with more fine opera
houses than any other country in the world, many of them required
maintenance and modernization. Not much help was forthcoming from the
regime. The transformation of the capital's Teatro Costanzi into the Teatro
Reale dell'Opera was the government's one noteworthy achievement in the
field – and it was a come-down from the original intention of building a new
house equipped with the most up-to-date facilities. Italy was insufficiently
provided with concert halls when Mussolini came to power, and the situation
was worse by the time the regime collapsed. The haphazard official attitude
towards these problems can be shown in a few representative examples.
1926: The City of Milan, with the national government's approval, bought the
historic Teatro Lirico (formerly Teatro della Canobbiana) for 9,100,000 lire,
with the intention of demolishing it in order to build new municipal offices on
the site; but the Lirico is still standing and very much in use.[162]
1936: Rome's Augusteum, a large concert hall with outstanding acoustics,
constructed within the ruins of Augustus's mausoleum and the site of many
important musical events (especially Bernardino Molinari's concerts with the
Augusteum Orchestra), was demolished by Mussolini's order. One aspect of
the Duce's neo-imperial obsession was to make the capital's ancient

monuments more visible by isolating them from surrounding buildings, at whatever cost to the people who lived in the city. In the spring of 1934, the inauguration of the hall intended to replace the Augusteum was announced – 'by will of the Duce' – for the spring of 1936. 'The new building, which will be located at the bottom of the Aventine hill, will have a great auditorium large enough to seat 10,000 people, several smaller halls, and all the accessories necessary for equipping a modern concert structure.'[163] The dream hall had not been begun when the Augusteum was torn down, and Molinari and his ensemble were moved – temporarily, it was said – to the smaller and much inferior Teatro Adriano; nor was the new auditorium any further along when the regime fell. The hall destroyed by the fascists has never been replaced.

1936: A fire on the night of 8–9 February destroyed Turin's historic Teatro Regio, 'which, however, by will of the Government and of the City, will soon be re-born on the same site'.[164] A new Teatro Regio was not completed until 1973.

1936: The Teatro Dal Verme – an historic Milanese theatre that had fallen on bad times – was to be torn down and replaced by a 5,000-seat auditorium.[165] The Dal Verme still stands, after many years' service as a cinema, and the national radio and television network is still talking about converting it into a concert hall.

1937: Plans were announced for the building of a 'large new theatre' at the Tre Fontane in Rome, for the International Exposition of 1941.[166] The war put an end to that project.

1938: A 4,000-seat theatre was to be built in Bologna on the site of the Arena del Sole; under the management of 'a fascist organization', it was to provide two opera seasons and one prose theatre season 'at very modest prices'.[167] But the old Arena del Sole, built as a popular theatre in 1810, was never destroyed; it is used today as a cinema.

1938: According to Musica d'oggi,

> a new government measure for the improvement and development of municipal theatre construction and for the equipping of theatres for the masses has just become effective. The municipalities that intend to build or restore structures to be used as theatres will be permitted to request loans on favourable terms |or| accessible mortgage guarantees | ... |. The State will participate to the extent of two and a half to four per cent in the amortization of the loan, for a maximum of twenty-five yearly instalments.

But the war soon put an end to the expansion and restoration of opera houses and concert halls. Many theatres and auditoriums were damaged or destroyed during the war years, and the regime fell long before any of its assistance plans could be put to the test.

Does Mussolini's government deserve criticism for its failure to provide funds for cultural buildings when Italy was beset by so many other, more pressing economic needs? The regime spent vast amounts of public monies on internal and foreign propaganda and subversion, on ephemeral colonial adventures, on assisting Francisco Franco, on monitoring its political opponents and maintaining them in prison, and on many other projects that were often ill-planned and always reprehensible from any humane point of view. Rome's Augusteum and Turin's Regio could have been replaced through the allocation of a microscopic fraction of the funds fascism misspent in any one of these other areas. Mussolini and his henchmen were constantly bragging of the regime's grandiose plans for halls and theatres, few if any of which were ever realized. The combination of self-praise and nearly total inaction makes the regime look especially poor – and most Italian musicians were afraid to offer the regime anything but praise in return for its non-efforts.

CHAPTER III

Composers

[. . .] my parents got their two-room apartment – for us an incredible dream of luxury – as a reward [from the government] for my winning the first prize in [the] Brussels [music competition]. [. . .] By pointing out that one has done something which was of use to the State and by implying that more could follow if only the conditions of work were improved, one stands some chance of success.[1]

Vladimir Ashkenazy's description of the way in which celebrated Soviet musicians lend the glory of their names to the regime in order to obtain special favours from it may be transferred with no difficulty to the otherwise quite different world of fascist Italy. Although the best-known Italian composers of the fascist period already had their 'two-room apartments' by 1922, they all cohabitated quite readily with the regime, which granted them certain advantages in exchange for the propagandistic benefits to be reaped from their enthusiastic or silent collusion. The story is miserable and petty, depressing rather than enraging. Though set in a country known for colour, it is a grey tale – a tale of dozens of Peer Gynts dutifully scratching their corneas, hoping that the trolls will look beautiful to them. To do justice to all these composers' stories would require an entire book, as Nicolodi's fine volume has demonstrated. This chapter deals with only a few of the more important ones, chosen for their vastly different intellectual capacities, character traits and cultural backgrounds. Nearly all of them assisted their dictatorial government in its struggle towards self-legitimization in the esteem of the outside world.

When Mussolini came to power in 1922, the most celebrated composers in Italy's musical establishment were those whose reputations had been forged before the turn of the century: Puccini, Mascagni and, to a lesser extent, Giordano and Cilea. None was politically astute, and all were happy, as they reached their declining years, to accept as many official honours as their native country offered them. By the mid-1930s the regime had obligingly beatified them all, dead or alive, as well as several of their somewhat less prominent younger colleagues, by placing them in a fascist pantheon from whose niches they faced each other rather uncomfortably.

Giacomo Puccini was and remains the only Italian composer since Verdi to have contributed a whole body of works to the popular international operatic repertoire. At the time of the march on Rome, his *Manon Lescaut* (1893), *La bohème*(1896), *Tosca* (1900), *Madama Butterfly* (1904), *La fanciulla del West* (1910), *La rondine* (1917), and the *Trittico* (1918) were being produced every night on stages throughout the world, and he was working on his last opera, *Turandot*. More than any other individual in 1922, Puccini represented musical Italy to the world. He lived through only the first two years of fascist rule, and his responses to it were uninformed and, as far as his work was concerned, insignificant. They were, however, symptomatic of the times, as had been his reactions to the political events of earlier years.

In 1898, Puccini had expressed his attitude towards politics in a letter to a childhood friend who had requested his support for the political candidacy of a mutual acquaintance in their home district:

> [. . .] I don't want to hear about election demonstrations *et similia*. [. . .] I would abolish Chamber and deputies – that's how much these eternal manufacturers of chatter annoy me. If I were in charge I'd happily go back to the days of that good soul, 'Carlo Dolovio'.* Let them elect Mundo or Felice the lifeguard at Viareggio, it's all the same to me. [. . .][2]

In the summer of 1914, on the eve of the First World War, when Puccini and his family went to the sea at Viareggio with the Toscanini family, the two musicians often discussed politics. 'Puccini was pro-German,' Toscanini's daughter, Wally, later recalled, 'while Papà hated the Germans [. . .]. Their arguments became very animated. One day, Puccini complained that everything was going badly in Italy: there was no order, everyone cheated, the authorities acted in their own interests and the poor always got the worst of it. He ended his speech by saying, "Let's hope the Germans come to put things in order." ' Toscanini was outraged, but the composer did not retract his statement.[3]

Once the war had begun, Puccini certainly did not wish to see his country defeated; on several occasions, however, he was accused of philo-Germanism. In the spring of 1919, a few months after the armistice, he wrote – under pressure from his friend Prospero Colonna, who was then mayor of Rome – a 'Hymn to Rome', as if to clear himself of all charges. The piece, intended for use on the national holiday, 21 April, that honoured the Birth of Rome, was a setting of a text written expressly for the occasion by the Roman poet Fausto Salvatori:

* Popular corruption of Carlo Lodovico, Bourbon duke of Lucca (Puccini's native town) from 1824 to 1847.

Divine Rome, to you on the Capitol,
where the sacred laurel is eternally green,
to you, our strength and our pride,
    the chorus rises up.

Hail, Goddess Rome! Sparkling before your brow
stands the sun that is born with the new History.
Resplendent in arms, at the last horizon
    Victory stands.

Sun, rising free and joyful
on our hill, tame your horses:
you will not see anything in the world
    greater than Rome.

Puccini referred to his hymn as 'a real piece of trash', but its bombastic nationalism and implicit imperialism appealed to fascist leaders when they assumed power – so much so that Mussolini eventually made the anthem part of the patriotic hymnal to be learned by school children throughout the country. In 1936, when the dictator proclaimed the birth of the Italian Empire, Puccini's hymn became a sort of third national anthem, after the Royal March and 'Giovinezza'.[4]

Prior to the fascist takeover, however, Puccini was still privately professing his admiration for traditional German orderliness and conservatism and declaring his increasing disillusionment with Italy, the hymn notwithstanding. In letters to Riccardo Schnabl Rossi, a close friend then living abroad, he often referred disparagingly and uncomprehendingly to his country, which was entering its darkest period of post-war upheaval:

[9 July 1920] [. . .] the world is disgusting – you're very right to stay away [from Italy]. But I still have faith in Giolitti, and it seems that the *uprisings* were repressed with an iron hand.* One learns how things really are by word of mouth and not from the newspapers – so let's hope for the best. But to come here from London, where everything is orderly, clean and polite, would certainly not be very pleasant. There is an atmosphere of banality that distresses me. [. . .][5]

[Early September 1920 . . .] Have you heard about the workers taking possession of industries? I've always thought and said that Italy is basically an agricultural and artistic country. Let's cultivate and create. Let's leave industry to those who have no agriculture and little genius. But the government should help art in general and the cultivation of the fields, so that we'll be able to live well and with fewer upheavals, which ruin everything. [. . .][6]

[11 December 1920] [. . .] You're right – here in Italy life is miserable. A hundred times better in defeated Vienna than in victorious Milan?!! [. . .][7]

* Giovanni Giolitti's last term as prime minister (June 1920–June 1921) was beset by strikes and violent unrest, but the rumour referred to by Puccini was unfounded.

[7 June 1921] [. . .] my country disgusts me [. . .] but France isn't the place for us, either – better beyond the Rhine! [. . .][8]
[July(?) 1921] [. . .] You're right about our Italy. It's totally reduced to filth! [. . .][9]
[28 September 1922] [. . .] Italy! Italy! Fascists . . . Taxes, high prices, filth, disorder, bad taste, an Eldorado of horrors, all in all. [. . .][10]
[4 October 1922] [. . .] here you can't even speak of music: it's a luxury. It's a continuous affront. And who's interested any more? Fox trot and Giovinezza, Giovinezza! [. . .][11]
[Mid-October(?) 1922] [. . .] Here, as you know, the fascists want power. We'll see whether they succeed in bringing order to this beautiful and great country of ours, but I doubt it [. . .].[12]

Shortly after the march on Rome, Puccini wrote to his librettist Giuseppe Adami: 'And Mussolini? Welcome to him, if he'll rejuvenate the country and bring it a bit of peace.' He was voicing a sentiment that had become commonplace. The country had been racing towards ungovernability since the end of the war, and many astute politicians completely unsympathetic to fascism believed they could first use Mussolini to restore order and then defeat him in parliament. Small wonder, then, that the far less politically canny Puccini, who was contemptuous not only of party politics but also of democratic government, began to think that Mussolini might indeed be the man Italy needed. The new prime minister's actions apparently pleased him, because his musicologist friend Guido Marotti reported a statement made by the composer in 1924, which, though it cannot be accepted as a verbatim quote, has the ring of authenticity.

[. . .] I favour a strong state. Men like [former prime minsters] Depretis, Crispi and Giolitti were to my taste because they gave orders instead of taking them. Now Mussolini has prevented Italy from falling to pieces! [. . .] Germany was the best-governed state and ought to have been a model to others. I don't believe in democracy because I don't believe in the possibility of educating the masses. It's like trying to hold water in a wicker basket! Without a strong government headed by a man with an iron fist, like Bismarck in Germany in the past and like Mussolini in Italy now, there is always the danger that the people, who construe freedom as mere licence, will become undisciplined and wreck everything. That's why I'm a fascist: because I hope that fascism will achieve in Italy, for the good of the country, the pre-war German national model.[13]

In November 1923, Puccini met Mussolini 'to set forth' – as the composer later told Marotti – 'certain ideas I have about the National Lyric Theatre to be built in Rome'. The specific ideas are not known; Mussolini, however, barely listened to them and repeated emphatically that there was no money for the project. Puccini had wanted to suggest that the Italian government sponsor a national opera tour of foreign countries, but under the circumstances he kept the notion to himself.[14]

Two months before his death Puccini was made a Senator of the Kingdom, 'for exceptional services towards the fatherland'. He made a joke of signing letters to friends as *Sonatore* (instrument-player) rather than *Senatore*, but was proud of belonging to the upper, unelected house of the Italian parliament. His death in a Brussels clinic, of throat cancer, on 29 November 1924 was announced to the Chamber of Deputies by Mussolini, who mentioned that 'some months ago, this eminent musician asked to become a member of the National Fascist Party. By this gesture he wished to show his solidarity with a movement that is much argued about and arguable, but that is also the only living thing in Italy today.'[15] According to other sources, Puccini had merely accepted honorary membership in the party rather than soliciting it – although he could have refused the 'honour', just as he had always previously refused to have anything to do with partisan politics. That he acted as he did is not surprising: his views on Italian political life represented a certain upper-middle-class professional perspective that was not uncommon at the time. Of the composer's political attitudes in his last years, the musicologist Giampiero Tintori has written:

> Puccini was essentially the child of an immature and arrogant Italy that had won a war through a tragic game of human lives [. . .] and that thought it could continue to live as if nothing had happened, simply by dedicating a few plaques and monuments to the fallen, and even accepting fascism in order to avoid confronting problems that history was posing ever more unpostponably.[16]

Did Puccini's political opinions influence his work as a composer? Some have called his operas proto-fascistic because they exhibited characteristics typical of fascism. Fascism was violent, and many of the plots Puccini chose contain sadistic elements. Fascism proclaimed that motherhood and domestic chores were the only fully normal, healthy occupations for women, and the female protagonists of Puccini's operas – rarely home-and-hearth types – generally meet with retribution. But fascism was certainly not the only politically violent movement, nor the only one to define women as child-bearing house cleaners; and Puccini was merely one of a legion of composers whose operas' plots are sometimes brutal and whose fallen women end badly.

The anti-democratic nature of fascism was clear by 1924, and had been so long before the movement came to power; but the extent to which its aims were totalitarian was not entirely obvious within Puccini's lifetime – nor was he sufficiently interested in political developments to have given the matter much thought. Whether he would in time have awakened to the evils and dangers of the regime is doubtful. As a highly intelligent musician who had quickly recognized the virtues of Debussy and even of Schoenberg, and as a cosmopolite whose friendships cut through all national and religious barriers, he certainly would have found absurd the provincial anti-European-ism and racism of the later, imperial brand of fascism. Given his love of law and order, however – concepts so often extolled by Mussolini – and of strong, even repressive, government, he would most likely have allowed himself to become one of the regime's sacred cows.

Pietro Mascagni and Puccini were born only five years and twenty-five miles apart, but their personalities were nearly opposite. Puccini – elegant, urbane, a Don Juan – usually maintained a degree of aloofness in his private and professional relations; Mascagni embodied the stereotype of the astute Tuscan merchant who can never be pinned down, who makes everyone and everything work to his advantage, and who – despite treading on a few toes now and again – remains, at worst, a lovable rascal in the Gianni Schicchi mould.

Unfortunately, he was also an *imbroglione*, a born trickster, who couldn't help sowing trouble even when there was no personal benefit to be reaped. In addition, Mascagni was hot-headed, so that in moments of anger he sometimes overthrew his own carefully laid schemes. He thrived on backstage rough-and-tumble, and his motto might have been 'I came, I saw, I enraged' – for wherever he conducted, supervised or merely observed productions of his works, he drove impresarios, theatre administrators, house conductors, musical assistants and scenographers to apoplexy. As with many irascible people, Mascagni was capable of spontaneous acts of generosity, some of which caused him more trouble than his bad behaviour.

The extremes in his personality were exaggerated by a singular circum-stance: on 17 May 1890, the première of his opera *Cavalleria rusticana* at Rome's Teatro Costanzi brought instantaneous world-wide fame to the twenty-seven-year-old musician, who had been eking out a living as bandmaster in a small Apulian town. From that moment on, however, his career was a long, slow *decrescendo*. A few of the dozen operas he wrote after *Cavalleria* were popular in their day, but Mascagni never again, in the remaining fifty-five years of his life, came close to repeating the success of his first mature work. He could neither understand nor accept this state of affairs. Like so many artists who do not find the public they believe their works deserve, he attributed his woes to the machinations and cabbalas of large numbers of enemies, visible and invisible.

All these factors had their part in determining Mascagni's naïve, irresponsible and opportunistic acceptance of fascism. But in order to ingratiate himself with the regime he had to live down his slight, almost accidental political past. At the turn of the century, Mascagni had been friendly with the radical poet Felice Cavallotti and with various socialist leaders, including Andrea Costa and Enrico Ferri. When he refused to declare himself publicly for the socialists in an election campaign, they attacked him, and they renewed their offensive in 1909 when, at the invitation of the king, he conducted a concert for the visiting tsar, who conferred upon him the Order of St Ann. Early in September 1920, however, at the height of postwar turmoil, he appeared to be supporting the left again. The Orlando Shipyard workers in the port of Leghorn, Mascagni's native town, occupied offices and harbour facilities and persuaded the composer and his wife, who were the most celebrated local residents, to participate in the launching ceremonies for the destroyer *San Martino*. Lina Mascagni became the ship's 'godmother', and her husband – his heart occupying its usual position on his sleeve – made a speech that was quoted in the newspapers:

> You want to be productive, to be craftsmen. May victory smile upon you! I wish it with all my heart. My heart breathes [sic] with the people; it was yours at my birth, it is yours in art and in mentality [sic . . .]. As a free man, in the most complete sense of the term, I express my sincere good wishes for the workers of the Orlando company – stalwart men who have all my admiration and affection.[17]

Although Mascagni went on to recommend orderly behaviour and to state that his interest was in justice rather than in socialism, his words of encouragement to the rebels were enough to earn him the vituperation of the right-wing press, which lampooned him as an opportunist and a half-baked socialist. Mussolini's newspaper, Il popolo d'Italia, attacked 'Mascagnian Bolshevism, which has sprung up like a mushroom'; and even the more measuredly conservative Giuseppe Prezzolini wrote contemptuously, in E*poca*, of the composer's politics.[18]

Eight months later, at the première of his new opera, Il piccolo Marat, at the Costanzi, socialist and fascist factions both cheered Mascagni. The fascists even gave him a laurel wreath adorned with red, white and green ribbons – the colours of the Italian flag.[19]. The shrieks of 'Viva Mascagni! Viva l'Italia!' from both right and left were no doubt provoked in part by Giovacchino Forzano's libretto, in which, notes Nicolodi, 'revolution and reaction are continually changing places against the backdrop of an unspecified political horizon'.[20] The composer told a friend that his opera had 'muscles of iron. Its power lies in its voice; it doen't speak, it doesn't sing: it *shouts, shouts, shouts!* I wrote the opera with my fists clenched, like my soul! [sic . . .] It's my conscience's hymn.'[21]

No sooner were the fascists in power than Mascagni asked to be received by Mussolini. Their first meeting, early in 1923, was intended purely as a formality, but the composer launched into a tirade about the impresario Walter Mocchi and his associates who, he said, had mistreated him during his recent engagement at the Teatro Colón in Buenos Aires. Mascagni, however, declared that these 'enemies and destroyers of Italian art', these traitorous purveyors of Germanic music, had been put in their place when the box-office success of his *Marat* had outdistanced that of *Parsifal*.[22] At a meeting of musicians, impresarios, union leaders, journalists and theatre owners, held in the foyer of Rome's Teatro Argentina a few months later, Mascagni reiterated his accusations against Mocchi; but the impresario – as hot-headed as his adversary – punched the composer in the face.[23]

When the government announced its plans to transform the Costanzi into a national opera house, some thought Mascagni would become artistic director. An article, 'Let the Ostracism of Pietro Mascagni Come to an End', immediately appeared in *Roma fascista*, defending the composer from charges of 'bolshevism'; and the Sonzogno company's journal, *Musica e scena*, reprinted it (June–July 1926) along with an item on the same subject taken from G. Orsini's newly published *Vangelo d'un mascagnano* (*Gospel of a Mascagnian*).[24] Mascagni had earlier suggested to Mussolini that the opera industry in Italy be run by the state – not a terribly original idea at the time. Now he took the offensive by sending the Duce a lengthy, emotive, fulsome letter with some concrete proposals on how the Costanzi ought to function.

> [...] I hoped that all Rome's artistic and musical activities would be concentrated once and for all in the hands of the State, which would no doubt have been able to find a brain to lead it and an *Ente* to manage it.
>
> For that matter, I confess that State handling of the music industry is an idea fixed in my mind from the moment of my artistic birth in this divine Rome and in the Teatro Costanzi, as dear to me as the memory of my mother.
>
> From that moment, with the Eternal City before me, I dreamt of a theatre worthy of Imperial Rome. But my dream remained dormant, like all dreams. Why? ... Why? ... Because Rome slept, and our Country slept.
>
> Where was the man who could understand my idea? ...
>
> Where was the man who could realize my dream? ...
>
> And my dream continued to hammer futilely in my head for many, many years. But in these last years, it seemed to me that my poor dream was indirectly becoming gigantic: day by day, I felt, growing steadily within me, the sensation that my dream could become reality ...
>
> The Man who could understand me had arisen: the Man who, like myself, more than myself, better than myself, had dreamt of Italy's grandeur, the grandeur of Rome! And with a sure and powerful arm, he knocked down every obstacle and cleared the road upon which he proudly travelled, bringing His own dreams to glorious reality. A Man of profound thoughts and decisive actions.
>
> Oh, I do not doubt that Your Excellency has dreamt all this, that he has

dreamt the whole grandiose work of reconstruction and regeneration that he is carrying out before the astonished eyes of the civilized world.

And I cannot express my soul's strong emotion of recent years, as I watch the brilliant rebirth of the Country [and] the joyous reawakening of the Italian people. This emotion is still greater at this moment, when my dream has become a hope. A hope for the welfare of Art, for the greater glory of our Nation.

My plans regarding the future of the Teatro Costanzi are very simple.

The theatre crisis is not caused, as is generally believed, by the public, but rather by the productions offered: the public, thirsty as it is for the divine enjoyment that the language of tones can give the soul, always rushes to a production of a true work of art. The cause of bad or mediocre productions may be found above all in the now common system of allowing theatres to be used by inept, makeshift impresarios who [...] receive noteworthy subsidies or gifts of hundreds upon hundreds of thousands of lire; for if modern impresarios [...] are artistically incompetent and negligent, they have shown themselves to be past masters at profiteering.

Another cause of our lyric theatre's decay is the exaggerated number of operas piled one on top of another in a single season, which creates overly hasty preparation [...].

[...] The artistic direction of the Teatro Costanzi must be placed in the hands of the person who enjoys everyone's confidence – a confidence that must be founded upon his artistic authority, his personal honesty, the steadiness of his mental balance and, above all, the ascertainable proofs of his competence for the general management of a supremely important theatre.[25]

Mascagni – who no doubt thought he was describing himself, though few others would have agreed – went on to propose a financial plan similar to the one devised for La Scala six years earlier, although he did not mention La Scala by name. As to the restoration of the Costanzi, he said:

Repairs are needed inside, and a great clean-up is needed more than anything else. It is not a matter, with the Costanzi, of giving Rome the great State theatre, the superb National opera house, the monumental Imperial theatre of my dreams (and perhaps also of yours, Your Excellency): it is simply a matter of making decent [...] the only theatre in the Capital suitable for opera productions. [...] The Teatro Costanzi will have the glory [...] of having prepared and progressively continued the proud ascent towards the glorification of that divine Art which has rendered the holy name of Italy great and sacred throughout the world.

And the glorification will be celebrated by the Man who governs the Destiny of our Country.

May God protect Him who protects Italy![26]

For all his love of obsequiousness, Mussolini was no fool: Mascagni's transparent mixture of self-interested calculation and visionary ecstasy, delicately seasoned with axe-grindings, clearly was not the best recipe for a national opera company. The composer was not asked to direct it. The following year, however, he did his patriotic duty by writing an anthem for the Corporations (the so-called 'Work Hymn') to a text by Libero Bovio and Edmondo Rossoni.[27] He then collaborated with the playwright and drama critic Renato Simoni on a hymn for the fascist youth movements, and decided that all proceeds from the piece would go towards the Leghorn Provincial Committee.[28]

There certainly was no further talk of Mascagni the bolshevik. On the contrary: during a concert in Paris conducted by the sixty-five-year-old composer in 1928, a young Italian exile threw anti-fascist leaflets around the theatre.[29] For those opposed to the regime, Mascagni was now a member – however politically insignificant – of the Establishment. And as if to confirm this fact, Mussolini chose Mascagni and Giordano as the two charter members representing music in his *Accademia Reale d'Italia* (Royal Italian Academy), founded in 1929. Original members in other fields included such luminaries as Marconi, Pirandello and Marinetti. Nicolodi has aptly described this instituion as fascism's mausoleum for artists and intellectuals; it was used for 'drawing them into the political arena and fossilizing their productive capacities, which were diverted to the mere bureaucratic management and supervision of "Italic" culture'.[30] There were exceptions: the young Enrico Fermi, for instance, became an academician while at the height of his career, and many other members delivered themselves of important works notwithstanding their honorary duties. But for the most part, when these gentlemen paraded in review before the Duce, in their gold-braided uniforms and two-cornered hats, they resembled nothing so much as a corps of paunchy, superannuated drum majors.

Some academicians accepted membership simply as a welcome form of recognition and an extra source of income; others, including Mascagni, splashed around happily in the little puddles of power now available to them. As early as October 1929, Lina Mascagni was complaining to friends of her husband's new duties.

> [...] He has had [to attend meetings of] the Authors' Society, the Radio, others for folk songs, still others with singers, again regarding the folk business ... which is a real bother, and a waste of time that makes him irritable and nothing more. Then he has had various interviews, or meetings, at the Governor [of Rome's] offices [... where they tried to persuade him] to conduct some performances of his opera Isabeau – to which he replied decisively no. [...] He has also had various procedural meetings for the Academy, as the grand inauguration will take place on Monday the 28th at the Capitol. [...][31]

Mascagni readily proclaimed his opinions regarding the elevation of other musicians to the Academy. In 1930, for instance, he proposed the name of Lorenzo Perosi, a composer-priest whose well-written works had enjoyed considerable popularity at the turn of the century. Like Cilea and Respighi, who were also candidates that year, Perosi was a musical conservative. Perosi, however, held an additional card: in the wake of the Lateran Accord, the appointment of a priest to the new Italian Parnassus could appear as a further conciliatory gesture towards the Vatican. As Mussolini, who made the final decisions, explained in a telegram to D'Annunzio, the Academy's president:

> Maestro Mascagni made apologia Maestro Perosi, praised Cilea and stated many reservations about Respighi the Italian-ness of whose inspiration he questioned Stop After making the necessary distinctions my choice fell on Perosi Stop Cilea in fact has produced nothing for many years having stopped at *Adriana Lecouvreur* and as to Respighi whose symphonic talent I greatly appreciate he can wait Stop[32]

During the same period, Pius xi received Mascagni at the Vatican and invited him to write an official papal hymn.

For the celebrations in Leghorn honouring the fortieth anniversary of *Cavalleria rusticana*'s première, the Duce wired his congratulations: 'In honouring you, the good citizens of Leghorn are interpreting the spirit of all those Italians who are grateful to you for everything new and great that you have created in the realm of pure beauty and divine harmony. I, too, count myself among those Italians.'[33] Giovanni Orsini, a journalist friendly towards Mascagni, wrote: 'Today we have a Leader who loves Pietro Mascagni's art. Need one fear any longer?'[34] And as if this weren't preposterous enough, Orsini also claimed that the members of the New York Philharmonic, after their concerts in Milan in 1930, had heard Mascagni conduct his *L'amico Fritz* at La Scala and had 'understood the difference between metronome-orchestras and Italian orchestras [. . .]'.[35] The grotesque chauvinism is even more appalling than the artistic judgment, especially since roughly twenty per cent of the Philharmonic's players, including its concertmaster and principal oboe, were Italian – not to speak of its conductor, Toscanini.

Since Toscanini, whose celebrity had for decades been a thorn in Mascagni's flesh, had by then given up La Scala, the composer-academician now initiated an all-out effort to put himself in a position of power at Italy's greatest theatre. He even wrote to Mussolini's office chief, G. Beer, to say that the four most important members of La Scala's administration, including the mayor of Milan, had decided to offer him (Mascagni) a post on the board, and that the mayor 'has formally stated that if he receives the necessary authorization from the Head of Government, he is ready to remove a name from the previously compiled list of board members, replacing it with mine.'[36] But when Beer, no doubt on Mussolini's orders, investigated the matter, the prefect of Milan informed him that there was 'no truth in what was said in P. Mascagni's letter | . . . | regarding either the presumed meeting of the four | . . . | or the Mayor's intention to change the composition' of the board.[37] Mascagni's attempt to embroil even the Duce in his machinations had failed, and the matter appears to have been dropped.

Within three weeks the composer was charging at a different windmill. In a letter of 4 July 1931, he told Mussolini that although he had 'never wanted to cause Your Highly Illustrious Excellency any disturbance' and would prefer even now to 'spare you that of having to read the following', he could no longer allow others to 'take advantage of your good faith through conversations and reports that hide and falsify the real truth'; therefore:

> Allow me to intervene, not at all out of self-interest, but purely for the sake of Art and Country.
>
> The Italian Lyric Theatre is going from bad to worse, and always for the same reason: the incompetence of its administrators | . . . |.
>
> The Minister for the Corporations |Bottai| is largely responsible in this matter since, even after your explicit and spontaneous statement confirming the exclusion of a certain person |Gino Pierantoni| from the Council of the Corporation for Entertainment, he elected that very person President of the Council.
>
> Such an election is to be deplored, and all the more so in as much as I had shown the Minister for the Corporations, at his request, the reasons for excluding that person from the matter. These were | . . . | complete incompetence, supine dependence upon influential personalities who must keep themselves hidden, and | . . . | motives regarding personal morality.
>
> Today, in the authoritative presence of the Minister for the Corporations, the President of the Corporation for Entertainment was allowed to illustrate to Your Excellency what has so far been done for the national lyric theatre.
>
> Words, Excellency, nothing but words: the Corporation for Entertainment has so far done nothing positive | . . . |.
>
> A Consortium of Italian lyric theatres has been instituted: this Consortium has been able to unite only four theatres. There were several very important basic proposals | . . . |; but at the first meeting the impossibility of activating even one | . . . | was recognized | . . . |.
>
> Nice outcome!
>
> The second point to which the Corporation for Entertainment turned its attention is of exceptional gravity | . . . |.
>
> It is a matter, Excellency, of obtaining the modification of an article of the Law regarding Authors' royalties – that Law created by Your Excellency's loving care and profound intellect, that Law which is the pride of the new Italy and which is regarded with envy by the intellectuals of all civilized Countries. | . . . |
>
> This Law | . . . | was never swallowed by the profiteers of intellectual creativity who | . . . | today have found |their representative| in the person of

the President of the Corporation for Entertainment. This person, the obedient servant of every base interest and secret speculation, has agreed to have the Corporation over which he presides vote for the reform of that |law . . . |.

Feeling somewhat uneasy, however, he has asked help of the President of the Italian Society of Authors and Publishers in obtaining a similar vote from the Tax Collection Agency | . . . |.

The President of the Italian Society of Authors and Publishers |*n.b.*: Roberto Forges-Davanzati; Mascagni himself was vice-president| has not hesitated to insert a proposal in this sense into the Order of business of the next meeting of the Society's Board | . . . |.

And I have been sorrowfully surprised to see a Man devoted to the Duce, a tried and true fascist from the beginning, a former General Secretary of the Party that governs Italy, putting the Society | . . . | at the disposal of so unworthy an action | . . . |.

| . . . | All this is well known to the Minister for the Corporations, who continues to give his approval, support and assistance |to Pierantoni|. | . . . |

Thank God, I have no |official| responsibilities, nor do I wish to have any; but I weep over the ruins of our Glory and over the disaster of our Tradition. | . . . |[38]

At the top of Mascagni's letter, Mussolini scrawled 'Copy to H|is| E|xcellency| Bottai'. Bottai immediately telephoned Mussolini's secretary to say that he was 'ready to kick Maestro Mascagni in the arse'.[39] He then wrote to Mussolini to defend himself from Mascagni's

false statements and grave accusations, in regard to which it is indispensable that |he| be specific and precise | . . . |.

It is false that His Excellency Maestro Mascagni specified at my request the reasons for which, in his opinion, the Hon. Pierantoni ought to have been excluded not only from the Presidency of the Board of the Corporation for Entertainment, but also from any position on the Board itself.

Maestro Mascagni, in the defamatory outburst of which he is so proud, limited himself to generalizing about Pierantoni's incompetence. If | . . . | he had had accusations to make against him, it would have been his duty to state them immediately, in writing | . . . |. For more than three years, Pierantoni has presided over the Artistic Commission of the Higher Radio Broadcast Control Committee, of which H. E. Maestro Mascagni is a member, and the latter has never had occasion to complain in any way about Pierantoni's work. | . . . |[40]

According to Bottai, Pierantoni was a practising lawyer who, for the previous six years, had been involved in various official arts- and recreation-related activities, and who

has received nothing but praise for his disinterestedness and for the fidelity with which he has always carried out his work. No question has ever been raised regarding his character.

| . . . | This Consortium is only a few months old, and given the extremely

serious difficulties in the area, it has already achieved satisfactory results, such as the exchange of artists and productions. The Consortium has its own President and its own Board. Pierantoni is neither President nor even a Board member.

And so we come to the subject that probably occasioned H. E. Maestro Mascagni's declaration: the proposal to modify Article 44 of the law on authors' royalties. [. . .][41]

Pierantoni, said Bottai, did not act unilaterally, but rather called a joint meeting with numerous artists' and employers' representatives and government officials, in order to resolve matters mainly pertaining to retroactivity and similar technicalities. In any case, nothing would be decided until all the appropriate experts and departments had given their opinions.[42]

The rights and wrongs of the matter are hard to determine at this distance and with so many missing details. Quite possibly, Mascagni was more right than wrong in this case. But the exchange demonstrates his incapacity to refrain from rumour-mongering, his thoughtless meddling, his deep-seated need to embroil others in his schemes. One day he was tearing La Scala down; the next he was trying to sweet-talk his way into its administration. One month (July 1931) he was insulting Forges-Davanzati for having agreed to convene a meeting requested by Pierantoni; the next he was sending Forges-Davanzati a respectful letter, insisting that he 'immediately suspend' the General Director of the Italian Society of Authors and Publishers (ISAP), Francesco Fedele, asserting that the latter's secretary is 'widely suspected' of having broken into the Society's accounting office and of exerting – together with others in the office – 'systematic pressure [. . .] upon the female personnel for illicit ends'.[43] Four days later, he took it upon himself to inform Mussolini that

the greatest responsibility for the disorganization and impoverishment of the Society actually falls upon President Forges Davanzati who, owing to absenteeism or weakness or incompetence, has left the Society in the hands of the General Director, a man of no ability and no conscience, guided only by the anxiety to look out, selfishly, for his personal interests, without a care for the sacrosanct rights of the Members, whom he has always treated as pests.[44]

Attached to this last note is a twenty-page document in Mascagni's hand, addressed to Mussolini, in which the composer outlines the alleged abuses of the ISAP. He claims, for instance, that from late in 1928 to the end of 1930, the society's liquid assets fell from 10,800,000 to 3,700,000 lire, although he admits that property had been acquired with a substantial part of the difference. Annual earnings, wrote Mascagni, had dropped from 68,100,000 lire in the first half of 1928 to 58,800,000 in the first half of 1931. Personnel at the society's headquarters and Rome office had numbered 246 and had cost 3,000,000 lire for all of 1928, while the number of employees had now risen to

377 at a cost of 2,100,000 for only the first half of the current year (he does not mention that this was a slightly lower per capita expenditure); several relations or mistresses of the society's officers drew regular salaries without having to perform specific duties connected with the society; general discontent among staff members who really did their work was 'detrimental to the interests of the Authors'; and representatives employed abroad by the society were paid too much.

> The conclusion is very sad. In only two years, the current President's administration has managed to turn the Society [. . .] upside down, materially and morally.
> The figures I have presented in this Report are more than convincing in their eloquence: millions have disappeared; and little by little the abundant earnings are also disappearing. On the other hand, expenses are increasing at a dizzying rate [. . .].
> As to morality, I have not wanted to go deeply into the subject; but a strict inquest might reveal unsuspected facts . . .
> The current President's responsibility is enormous, towards the State and towards Italians whose work is intellectual.[45]

Mascagni's exposé was a mixture of tendentiously presented facts, *ad hominem* attacks and unsupported insinuations. A great deal of the corruption he describes was undoubtedly real: fascism, to an even greater extent than most other systems, owed its survival to nepotism, favouritism and other friend-buying methods. But the composer's attack was as obviously provoked by his own interests as the abuses were created by the interests of others. Mussolini apparently took no action, and Mascagni soon resigned the vice-presidency of the ISAP. A few weeks after the resignation, the composer let Mussolini know that he was in Rome and available for a consultation, presumably on the same matter. The Duce refused to receive him.[46]

Mascagni's next and last major campaign to obtain favours was connected with the première of his last opera, *Nerone* (Nero), completed in 1934. The septuagenarian Maestro, dressed in full battle regalia for the offensive, made use of every weapon at his disposal: string-pulling, self-advertisement, below-the-belt swipes at adversaries (real and imagined), tear-jerking, public and semi-public lamentations, threats, flattery, cajolery and calculated outspokenness. Mussolini's secret police had by then tightened their methods of control, and an informer intercepted a tirade sent by Mascagni on 23 June 1934 to his faithful apologist, the journalist Orsini. The letter is a magnificent example of Mascagnian whimsy, unconscious self-mockery and political parrying and thrusting.

> [. . .] I must thank you for your continuing thoughtfulness towards me. I read your always valuable articles with great interest and profound emotion.
> I should like to bring you up to date on the ups and downs that have

hitherto blocked the performance of *Nerone*, but the story is too sad for me and too shameful for our Country.

The operas of Malipiero, Capozzo [*sic*: pun on (Nino) Cattozzo, composer; a *capozzo* is a numbskull], Mulè, Catella [*sic*: pun on Casella; a *catella* is a female puppy] etc., are performed in Italy, at the most important theatres, and millions of lire are spent on these operas; but an opera composed by Pietro Mascagni at the age of seventy, with the sacrosanct goal of putting a bit of life into our lyric Theatre, which seems to be in its death-throes, cannot be performed. And they prepare and carry out every unspeakable trick so that the Italian people be kept from hearing my soul's outcry, which invokes peace and addresses the Country, as I sing my last song and weep my last tears (pardon my plagiarism).

Added to the infamy I have had to suffer (and who knows how much longer I shall have to stand it, with Christian resignation?) there is the tragic boycott that has put my person and my artistic output on the Index of every theatre in Italy.

And now, the excuse that I am not a Fascist [party member] no longer exists, because I have been a Fascist for two years. But before that, it was a spontaneous impulse that brought me close, spiritually, to the Man whom I admired and continue to admire; and everyone knows that before becoming a Fascist, I served the Regime with enthusiasm because of my love for the Chief. Now I feel humiliated, because I am commanded to feel an enthusiasm that no longer has its original freshness (I confess this in discouragement).

The first International Music Congress was held in Italy, in Florence, the capital of Tuscany. But there was no place in that congress for me, a Tuscan to the core and a musician still in active service.

For two years in a row, in Florence itself, the Florentine 'Maggio' has been held, with operatic [. . .] seasons for which millions and millions have been spent or thrown away; but not the slightest need was felt for my personal participation or my artistic *œuvre*.

The centenary of the birth of Amilcare Ponchielli, my great teacher, occurs this year. Two years ago, I corresponded [. . .] with the Mayor of Cremona, who wrote to invite me to take on the direction of a worthy musical ceremony in 1934. I drafted a programme [. . .].

But meanwhile, there is a new Mayor of Cremona. This year, the Hon. Farinacci [n.b.: Farinacci, who was from Cremona, ran the city as his private fief], together with Miss Colombo and Maestro Serafin, formulated a new programme (without ever asking my opinion), and everything was set up for the Ponchielli commemoration, whose programme includes two works by Ponchielli and one by Bizet: *Carmen*. But for God's sake! Must we put up with such profanations? A foreign opera to commemorate so Italian a Master? And no one protested! . . . My God, how shameful! And I, who was Ponchielli's pupil (his favourite pupil, if I do say so myself), have been excluded from the ceremony! [. . .][47]

Mascagni had conveniently forgotten that his relations with Ponchielli had not always been rosy, and that he had been dismissed from the Milan Conservatory, where the composer of *La Gioconda* had been his teacher. His complaints about the boycott of his works in Italy were completely unjustified: 'Capozzo', 'Catella' and the others would gladly have traded places, in that respect, with Mascagni, whose operas were then and for the rest of his life performed far more frequently than those of any other living Italian composer.

But statistical and historical exactitude had never been matters of importance to Mascagni, whose single-minded goal for nearly half a century had been to make his operas succeed, no matter what principles or people had to be steam-rollered in the attempt. *Nerone* had been written, *ergo Nerone* had to be performed – and in the most splendid possible setting. There was talk of giving the première outdoors, in the Colosseum, for the twelfth anniversary of the march on Rome, and when that idea was abandoned Mascagni set his sights on La Scala. Mussolini favoured the Rome Opera, but the composer – if his own testimony is to be believed – told him that the capital's theatre was too disorganized and that seven members of its administration were incompetent. At that, boasted Mascagni, the Duce had fired the culprits and had assured *Nerone*'s author that he could schedule the première wherever he pleased.[48] Under pressure from Mussolini's office, La Scala agreed to present *Nerone* in a splendid production.

Mario Morini, an expert in Mascagnian matters, has claimed, logically enough, that Mussolini's interest in the project grew out of his political acumen, his skill at turning everything to his own account.[49] Once it had become clear that the undertaking had been approved On High, the press got to work – rather too zealously, according to an informer's note to Mussolini's office on 16 January 1935, the day of the première.

> Concerning *Nerone* and Mascagni, I must report that the public is complaining about the great publicity being given the event. For some time now, one reads and hears of nothing in Milan except *Nerone*.
>
> Mascagni's public talk on his opera [at the Milan Conservatory three days earlier] has also caused much comment: in the first place because, it is said, a composer never talks about his work before [it has been heard], and secondly because the rather outspoken talk contained several points that were considered remarkable. [...]
>
> (1) Speaking of the Roman-ness of his opera, Mascagni added that it was made known to him that he was to have it performed in Rome, in homage to this Roman-ness. 'I went to bed at night and got up in the morning with the thought that my opera was Roman.' All this was stated with a facetiousness that pleased no one. Then, still on the subject of the work's Roman-ness [...], he told the story of how it had come not to be performed [in Rome, for its première], citing with many quotations his conversations on the subject with the Duce. [...]

(2) Talking, next, about power, in relation to Nero, he said | . . . |: 'What would be the point of power if it could not be abused?' This sentence created much comment afterwards; at the moment when it was uttered, it caused many murmurs among the crowd.

(3) Referring to the scenographer |Edoardo| Marchioro's sketches for the opera | . . . |, he | . . . | managed to attack modern architecture and art, adding that the architects who were competing to build the Palazzo Littorio ought to bear these sketches in mind.

All of this caused much surprise, especially among the young people who, for instance, criticized the Minister |Giuseppe| De Capitani d'Arzago. At every one of Mascagni's anti-modernist *boutades*, he shook himself enthusiastically in his chair and applauded nervously.[50]

Mascagni had not failed to invite Mussolini to attend the première, since, as he put it:

> Your Excellency's presence at the baptism of my new opera would be a great symbol of recognition for this work. It was inspired by the resurrection of Imperial Rome which, thanks to the Duce, is again illuminating the World with the light of its Greatness and Civilization. For me, personally, Y. E.'s presence would be an immense support and would represent the most sought-after reward for my efforts which, however miserable they may be, were carried out as a dutiful contribution to be offered to Art and Country.[51]

Mussolini noted on the invitation: 'I'll see it after the première (he is advertising himself too much).'[52] Mascagni then tried to persuade Francesco Ercole, the Minister of National Education, to attend; but Mussolini told this subordinate: 'Galeazzo |Ciano| is going. That's enough – especially since the outcome is dubious.'[53]

Aristocrats, industrialists, party bosses and important members of the musical establishment crowded the flower-bedecked theatre on opening night. The great tenor, Aureliano Pertile, sang the title role. On the podium was the seventy-one-year-old composer – 'the old *imbroglione*', according to Gavazzeni's eye-witness description – 'who glistened with make-up and hair dye, like a circus performer under the beams of the floodlights'.[54] During an intermission Ciano received a telephone call from Mussolini, who wanted 'to learn the outcome of the noble battle, and how many curtain calls there had been'. When the Minister told this to the Maestro, 'Pietro Mascagni's face beamed with the sweetest emotion'.[55]

Ten days later, Mascagni wrote to Mussolini – first to pat himself on the back ('I have done my duty as an Italian and a Fascist: I have made my modest but vibrant contribution to my Art and my Country. The Milanese public has given its affectionately favourable vote to my effort; the world press has taken a lively interest in Italian Art'), and then to complain about the lukewarm reviews he had received from some Italian critics, who had treated him in a 'cowardly' manner, 'forgetting my whole artistic past and all the love I have always nurtured in my breast for the preservation of the Italian artistic tradition'. He thanked Mussolini for his help in getting *Nerone* produced and asked him to accept copies of the libretto and vocal score of the opera. After making some small, miscellaneous complaints, Mascagni reminded the Duce, once again, that his opera 'was inspired by Y. E.'s grandiose work' for the 'miracle' of Imperial Rome's rebirth, which was 'on the verge' of taking place.[56]

Within a few weeks, however, a paid informer reported to Farinacci that at a recent reception, Mascagni — 'swollen with pride because of his recent success [. . .] and because he had been received by the Duce' — had openly insulted both Farinacci and Mussolini. Using 'an irreverent phrase', the composer had bragged of 'having succeeded in getting *Nerone* performed despite [the Duce]'.[57] The phrase in question, reported elsewhere, was: 'I shoved *Nerone* up the Duce's arse!'[58] 'There are people', continued the informer, 'now serving time for less serious faults; and nothing could be less suitable than such statements when pronounced in the presence of outsiders and foreigners by a Member of the Accademia d'Italia at the current delicate political moment.'[59]

The moment's delicacy was created by Italy's increasingly belligerent attitude towards Ethiopia, justly but hypocritically opposed by such colonial powers as Britain and France. The military campaign that followed taught Mascagni the cruellest of lessons about the dangers of a regime he had thought would always work to his advantage: in the spring of 1936, his son Edoardo, a lieutenant in the Corps of Engineers, died of an infection contracted in a military hospital in East Africa. From that time on, Mascagni's ambitions and favour-seeking diminished.

He did not, however, altogether cease to ask favours of the government. Mascagni had never made provision for an inactive old age; as he began to decline he found himself in straitened economic circumstances. The MinCulPop put him on its list of artists, writers and journalists to be subsidized from its secret funds, and before the regime collapsed in 1943, Mascagni had received the very substantial sum of 1,290,000 lire in monthly and occasional payments — more money than any other individual received, and nine times the amount paid to any other musician. In buying power, it was roughly equivalent to US $700,000 in 1987.* 'I am old,' he told Mussolini in 1938, in a letter concocted with the usual

* Other musicians on the payroll were, in descending order: Alceo Toni, 144,000 lire; Bianca Bellincioni Stagno, singer, 109,500; Bruno Barilli, critic, 100,600; Gino Rocca, opera administrator, 100,000; Alberto Ghislanzoni, composer and critic, 75,000; Arturo Lancellotti, journalist, 44,500; Alfredo Casella, 40,000; Francesco Santoliquido, composer, 22,700; Barbara Giuranna, composer, 18,500; Antonio Guarnieri, conductor, 15,000; Franco Ferrara, conductor, 10,000; Leopoldo Mugnone, conductor, 10,000; Fausto Torrefranca, musicologist, 10,000; Raffaello De Rensis, 7,000; Maria Caniglia, singer, 5,000; Tito Aprea, pianist, 3,250. Non-musicians on the list whose names appear in this book were: Vincenzo Cardarelli, 132,000; Yvon de Begnac, 124,000; F. T. Marinetti, 55,000; Remigio Paone, 50,000; Rino Alessi, 20,000; Alessandro Bonsanti, 5,000; Arturo Martini, 3,000. Not everyone on this list, however, is automatically to be considered a fascist sympathizer, and at least one — Bonsanti — was actively anti-fascist. It is possible, although not demonstrable, that some of the recipients of small sums received the money as payment for professional activities and may even have been unaware of the funds' source.

mixture of gratitude, complaints and swaggering,

> but Divine Providence has kept me in perfect health, and ever young and robust at heart. This allows me to be able to work, still, without signs of weariness. And seeing myself constantly excluded from every artistic event had mortified my morale and oppressed me physically. Your gesture, Excellency, has today reanimated my spirit. Your words [. . .] give new light to my soul, into which the intimate understanding of Y. E.'s supreme goodness has penetrated. Through the superhuman providence that Y. E. distributes with such good sense and such heart to all of Humanity, you have found a way to bring relief to a poor citizen, the work of whose long existence was insufficient to assure him the most modest tranquillity in his old age.[61]

'Neither the Pact of Steel with Germany [. . .] nor the Second World War seems to have shaken [Mascagni's] faith in the regime or in its "chief" ', says Nicolodi.

> [. . .] On 26 May 1939, shortly after the annexation of Albania and the alliance with the Nazis, he repeated [in a letter] to the Duce his 'sincere enthusiasm and profound recognition, as an Italian, for the great conquests that will ensure peace in Europe and spread the reborn civilization of eternal Rome through the world.' [And] in a letter of 7 November 1941 he begged high party officials to convey 'to the leader of all Italians my feelings of admiration, affection and recognition for His grandiose work of justice and civilization.'[62]

If, in the end, Mascagni never quite managed to become the Father of the Gods in fascist Italy's musical pantheon, the explanation most likely lies in the too-close-for-comfort resemblance between certain aspects of his personality and some of fascism's more striking characteristics. A readiness to stoop to low tactics in order to realize plans that had not been well thought out, and a desperate need for flattery, however patently insincere, distinguished both. An ageing composer's silly efforts to nourish his vanity cannot seriously be compared with the self-aggrandizement of a violently repressive political regime; but a similarity undeniably existed between Mascagni's choleric, intolerant, dishonest behaviour and the paranoiac self-righteousness of Mussolini's government. The subtly opportunistic Bottai and the cynically egocentric Farinacci may have detested Mascagni because when they looked at him they saw themselves in a distorting mirror: grotesque, toothless images of their colder ambition.

Like Mascagni, Umberto Giordano was a child of the 1860s who achieved a stunning success with an early work. *Andrea Chénier* (1896) has maintained a place in the lyric repertoire for nearly a century, while its younger siblings have fallen into virtual oblivion from the fairly high level of popularity they enjoyed as late as the 1930s. Unlike Mascagni, however, the Apulian Giordano was not given to hysteria, buffoonery or gross attempts to manipulate others. And although he, too, became an academician and a Grand Old Man under the regime, his relations with fascism were less intense, less significant and less blatantly opportunistic than Mascagni's. Mussolini's file of communications to, from or about Giordano is roughly one-tenth the size of the Mascagni file and consists almost entirely of harmless or silly items. There are notes accompanying scores with dedications, and details regarding Giordano's 'Hymn to Italy', whose name Mussolini changed to 'Hymn for the Tenth Anniversary' – of the march on Rome, naturally. The file also contains the composer's comments on his 'Imperial Hymn', 'inspired' – he wrote to the Duce – 'by your historic words: "Greet the Empire that is reappearing on Rome's fateful hills".[63] With Mussolini's approval Giordano was made a member of the national radio network's governing board in 1934;[64] and five years later the composer wrote incidental music to Giovacchino Forzano's drama, *Cesare* (Caesar), which Mussolini claimed to have helped to write.[65]

Francesco Cilea's relations with the regime were minimal. The composer of *Adriana Lecouvreur* was already director of the Naples Conservatory when the fascists came to power, and there he remained until his retirement in 1936. He was admitted to the Accademia d'Italia but does not appear to have abused his position. Cilea's notes to the Duce are as insignificant as Giordano's, with the exception of one whining plea (1934) for help in having his opera *Gloria* performed at Rome's Teatro Reale. The letter was passed to the company's commissioner, who promptly informed Mussolini's secretary that the work would be inserted into the following season's programme, 'which still has a few gaps'.[66]

*　　　*　　　*

Four days after the march on Rome, Ildebrando Pizzetti began work on a Requiem Mass. Not that he had even the most minimally malicious intention of referring to the event that had just taken place or to its consequences; but the gift of such divinations is sometimes bestowed upon artists, and transcends their capacity for judgement. – Massimo Mila[67]

Although Puccini, Mascagni, Giordano and Cilea – all born in the 1850s and 1860s – were the most frequently performed contemporary composers of the fascist period, they had passed their creative peaks well before the regime came to power. Pizzetti, Casella, Malipiero and Respighi – children of the late 1870s and early 1880s – were in their prime in 1922. They were somewhat less worried than their seniors about immortal glory and somewhat more preoccupied with work and survival. Among the composers of the '1880 Generation', Pizzetti probably reaped the most benefits from the new system. He neither understood nor attempted to understand more than his colleagues about fascism's fundamental nature, nor was he more selfish or more short-sighted than they. Most of the others were simply happy to stoop to gather whatever honours were flung in their direction, but Pizzetti seems to have been arrogantly calculating. His seething ambition was only partly concealed under the guise – probably sincere – of ascetic religiousness.

There is good reason to question talented artists' protestations of asceticism and purity. Pizzetti was a highly skilled composer, an inspiring teacher, a perceptive critic and a reliable administrator; but he was also one of those creative people whose instinct for protecting and furthering their work dominates every other aspect of their natures. The end, they sense, always justifies the means, where their talent is concerned; and the nineteenth-century Cult of Genius, still very much alive in the early decades of this century, provided that instinct with a rationale: 'What I have to say is so unique and so overwhelmingly important that I must do whatever is necessary in order to make my contribution to humanity.' This is strikingly similar to, though less dangerous than, the attitude of many politicians and political theorists who, in their zeal to do good for humanity as an abstract concept, are willing to increase the misery of individual human beings. Pizzetti's protectiveness towards his work and his thirst for honours would hardly have been worthy of notice under ordinary conditions. But the degree of moral compromise fundamental to fascism was exceptional, as were the temptations extended by the regime to ambitious people willing to grace it with the aura of their names. By giving in to those temptations, Pizzetti participated in the compromise.

Musically, Pizzetti was a radical conservative – a contradiction that grew directly out of his background. He was born in Parma, the capital of Verdi's native *provincia* and the most celebratedly opera-minded town in Italy, and he received his musical training at that city's conservatory, which has bred many notables of the lyric theatre. Although Giovanni Tebaldini, the teacher who most influenced him, was one of the earliest champions of the revival of pre-classical Italian music, especially sacred music, Pizzetti's first job was as coach and assistant conductor at Parma's Teatro Regio – which meant that he was nurtured on the traditional and contemporary operatic repertoires. He was committed to the revitalization of Italian music, which he thought could best be achieved by eliminating the excesses of *verismo* and by assimilating the forgotten musical languages of important fifteenth- to eighteenth-century Italian composers; but his works descended directly from the grand tradition of nineteenth-century Italian melodrama. Pizzetti never developed more than a half-hearted, basically hostile interest in contemporary musical developments outside Italy.

If, as a student, Pizzetti was influenced by the religious purity of Palestrina and the emotionally supercharged operas popular at the turn of the century, a formidable third influence soon made itself felt: the decadent eclecticism of Gabriele D'Annunzio. Soon after they met in 1905, the virtually unknown, twenty-five-year-old composer set to work writing incidental music to the celebrated poet's play, La nave (The Ship, written 1905–7). Next, he wrote an opera, Fedra (Phaedra, 1909–12), based on a libretto by D'Annunzio. Pizzetti emerged from the collaboration deeply committed to the theatre, determined to eschew bombastic effect in favour of 'purified' melodic construction harking back to the early seventeenth-century operisti, and preoccupied with larger-than-life protagonists and emotions.

The Florence Conservatory was his operational base from 1908 to 1924 – the first nine years as an instructor, the remaining seven as director. The early portion of his sojourn in the city coincided with the most fertile period in the life of La Voce (The Voice), an influential political–cultural journal of liberal–idealistic stamp whose contributors included some of the most important writers and thinkers of the day: Giuseppe Prezzolini, Giovanni Papini, Benedetto Croce, Giovanni Gentile, Gaetano Salvemini, Giovanni Amendola, Ardengo Soffici and Giuseppe De Robertis. A broad range of opinion in almost all areas was represented in La Voce, and Pizzetti, who was drawn into its circle and who wrote articles for the journal, was among the group's more conservative members. By the time Mussolini came to power La Voce had long since ceased publication, and its contributors assumed widely divergent attitudes towards fascism. Three openly opposed the movement: Croce, the philosopher, was old enough, famous enough and harmless enough to be left in peace; Salvemini, the historian, was imprisoned for a time and then spent twenty years in exile – more than half of it as a professor at Harvard University; and Amendola, the radical-liberal leader whom Mack Smith has called 'one of the finer minds and more attractive characters in recent Italian parliamentary history',[68] was murdered by fascist thugs. The writers De Robertis, Soffici and Prezzolini were fence-straddlers. Papini, who was also a writer, became an ardent supporter of fascism, especially in its virulently nationalistic and racist phase – so much so that some of the more intelligent party bosses found him an embarrassment.

Gentile, as Mussolini's first Minister of Public Education and the regime's semi-official theorist, appears to have been Pizzetti's main contact in the government during its early years in power. One of Gentile's under-secretaries initiated the bureaucratic procedure that led to Pizzetti's becoming director of the Milan Conservatory in 1924, following the suicide of Giuseppe Gallignani. In February 1925 Gentile – no longer a cabinet minister – invited the composer to take charge of the music section of the Enciclopedia Italiana, which was being prepared under his direction. The monumental project was one of the most positive cultural achievements of the fascist period. Although, as Salvemini wrote, its thirty-six volumes were published between 1929 and 1939, under Mussolini, [. . .] they were not written by children born and raised since 1922, under Mussolini's influence. The Enciclopedia was the work of Italian scholars who had been educated during the previous fifty years in the schools of a free Italy. Fascism made its presence felt in the Enciclopedia in only a few fields, such as modern history, political science, history of religion, and history of the Catholic church, and in all these cases its influence was deleterious.[69]

Pizzetti accepted Gentile's offer and wrote several generally fine music entries for the Enciclopedia.

Given the favours he had accepted from the regime through Gentile, it was no coincidence that on 21 April 1925 Pizzetti's name appeared among the signatories of the so-called 'Gentile manifesto' of fascist intellectuals. The document had been conceived at a convention held in Bologna the previous month, at which Pizzetti and the critic Bruno Barilli had been the only important personalities from the world of music. In it, fascism's origins were falsified: squadrismo and the other forms of violence by which the movement had achieved power were idealized and history was rewritten in an attempt to make fascism appear to have been, from birth, the defender of monarchy, religion, the armed forces and traditional discipline. The manifesto described the fascist government's 'transformation of legislation [. . .] in keeping with social currents and with the spiritual requirements of the Italian people', and sought to demonstrate that 'perfect public order under an austere financial system' had brought the post-war economy back to normal, despite the 'oscillations of public opinion, violently agitated by the press' – which, however, had virtually been muzzled by 1925. For fascists, 'the Nation' was 'a school for subordinating that which is small and inferior to that which is universal and immortal; respect for law and discipline; [. . .] freedom to conquer in accordance with the law, which is established through the renunciation of all small, arbitrary acts and irrational, wasteful fantasies'. The manifesto's authors sought to defend the regime from accusations of illiberalism and anti-labour policies: 'Fascism is the spirit of progress and propulsion behind all the nation's forces.' Opposition to the regime was made up of the 'democratic, reactionary, radical, masonic waste products of old-fashioned Italian politics', and was therefore doomed to wither and die in the face of fascist vitality. 'Thus, the present Italian spiritual crisis will be overcome. Thus, in the very bosom of fascist and fascisticized Italy, new ideas, new programmes and new political parties will slowly ripen and will eventually come to light.'[70]

Pizzetti and some two hundred and fifty other Italian artists and scholars, including Pirandello and Marinetti, signed the generic, empty document. Perhaps the composer did not really share the opinions expressed by Gentile and the others who had framed the manifesto; perhaps his interest in politics was practically nil and he did not read the document. If signing it was a *pro-forma* act, however, it was all the more reprehensible. If done in ignorance, it was the act of an assenting know-nothing – who did know, however, not to bite the hand that feeds.

Eleven days after publication of the manifesto, *Il Mondo* – one of the few remaining opposition newspapers in the country – published 'A Reply by Italian Writers, Professors and Journalists to the Manifesto of Fascist Intellectuals'. This rebuttal, later known familiarly as the 'Croce Counter-manifesto', in reference to the philosopher who framed it, demonstrates that many of the country's respected thinkers were still refusing to be blinkered by the regime. (The only musician who signed it was Vittorio Gui.) The document's signatories did not 'pretend to represent, much less monopolize, the category of anti-fascist intellectuals, who have not been and never will be called to a congress, to take part ostentatiously in an artificial line-up'. It was, rather, 'a reaction against a method that intends to bend intellectuals to the tasks of an *instrumentum regni*' and a 'protest raised by some free minds against the version and interpretation of things Italian that fascist intellectuals have wished to spread beyond Italy's borders'.

The counter-manifesto accused the signatories of Gentile's document of lending their support to 'deplorable violence and arrogance and to the repression of freedom of the press'.

> One cannot tell from the words of this verbose manifesto what the new gospel comprises; [. . . it] demonstrates to the unprejudiced observer an incoherent, bizarre mixture of appeals to authority and of demagoguery, of declared respect for law and of violation of laws, of ultra-modern concepts and mouldy old rubbish, of absolutist attitudes and bolshevik tendencies, of non-belief and flirtation with the Catholic Church, of abhorrence of culture and of the sterile efforts of a culture lacking a foundation, of mystical languor and cynicism. And even if a few plausible provisions have been effected or initiated by the present government, there is nothing in them that can boast of so original an imprint as to warrant the title of new political system, as fascism calls itself. [. . .]
>
> [. . .] The current political struggle in Italy will serve [. . .] to revive the value of liberal systems and methods and to make our people understand them more deeply and love them with more conscious affection. Perhaps some day, when people look calmly at the past, they will judge that the test we are now undergoing – so bitter and sorrowful to us – was a stage through which Italy had to pass in order to revitalize our national way of life, to complete our political education and to feel more seriously our duties as a civilized people.[71]

The noble intentions and embarrassing inadequacies of the counter-manifesto are evident even from these very brief excerpts. The critique of the fascist manifesto was pungent, but no serious political alternative to

Mussolini was offered. Italians, the document seemed to say, will not lose their indifference to the evils of fascism until they become good liberals, and they cannot become good liberals until they cease to be indifferent to the evils of fascism. But the liberal–conservative and conservative–liberal coalitions of 1919 to 1922 had neither solved the country's ills nor prevented a gang of violent opportunists from taking control of the country. Why should anyone have believed that such a coalition would have been more effective in 1925? Signing the Croce counter-manifesto may have been morally uplifting, but it had no more impact against the regime than a mild breeze against a brick wall. A nation that had recently swallowed – albeit with difficulty – the murder of socialist party leader Giacomo Matteotti was not likely to rally round a faded flag raised by an elderly philosopher. Mussolini cannot have been pleased by the declaration, but his attitude towards most of its signatories was to fold his arms and wait. And indeed, when the going got rough most of them repented their apostasy, or at least made a show of so doing, and were admitted to the fold.

The rewards for being on the right side were not long in coming to Pizzetti. Mussolini soon asked for a private concert of his works, and the press duly reported the December 1925 event, performed by the violinist Arrigo Serato and the cellist Enrico Mainardi, with the composer at the piano.[72] The event seems to have made a great impression on Pizzetti, who wrote to Mussolini in 1932:

> The long conversation you allowed me to have with you nearly seven years ago is one of my best memories. [...] It is my hope that the gift of your penetrating and thoroughly comprehending attention will again be granted me. Not so that I may boast of it among others, but because I know the value of every moment lived near great men, and the good they can do those who understand how to listen to them.[73]

In 1931, largely as a result of writer Ugo Ojetti's machinations, the Royal Italian Academy awarded Pizzetti's opera *Débora e Jaèle* the 'Mussolini Prize' of 50,000 lire, donated by the *Corriere della sera*.[74] Pizzetti wrote to Mussolini to tell him 'how proud I felt' to have the name of his work associated with 'the name – so fateful for every Italian – of Benito Mussolini'.[75]

Being a good fascist, or at least doing a good job of looking like one, could, however, be inconvenient on occasion, and Mussolini's patronage twice proved irksome to Pizzetti in connection with his opera *Orsèolo*. In 1932 the composer sent the libretto, which he had just finished writing, to the Duce, who actually took the trouble to read it. When Mussolini came to the following passage, he baulked: '*Doge e voi pur vestitevi a gramaglie: / che per i cittadini di San Marco / Giustizia e Libertà son presso a morte*' ('You, too, Doge, dress yourself in mourning, because for St Mark's citizens, Justice and Liberty are near death'). Pizzetti's political ignorance was apparently so deep that he was unaware that 'Giustizia e Libertà' was the name of the strongest anti-fascist underground organization; and since *doge* and *duce* are variants of the same word, Mussolini was not pleased with the implications of this stanza. He underlined the three dirty words in pencil and sent the libretto back to Pizzetti, who promptly castrated the offending passage.[76] Then, in 1934, the directors of Florence's *Maggio Musicale* asked Pizzetti's permission to give the world première of the still-unfinished *Orsèolo* the following year. The composer at first replied brusquely that several other theatres had already requested that right. None of his operas had been performed in Florence for fifteen years, he complained, so why not give the locals a chance, at last, to see *Débora e Jaèle*, which had been making the rounds of the world's opera houses since 1922? But the *Maggio* administrators wanted the prestige of a première, and turned to Mussolini for help. The Duce immediately wired the composer: 'THE COMMITTEE FOR THE MAGGIO MUSICALE FIORENTINO AWAITS ORSEOLO AND HAS ANNOUNCED IT STOP I AM SURE THAT ORSEOLO WILL BE READY FOR THE 1935 MAGGIO AND ITS PERFORMANCE WILL BE A HAPPY EVENT FOR ITALIAN OPERA — MUSSOLINI'.[77]

The fascist motto was 'Believe, obey, fight', and Pizzetti promptly came around to the Duce's point of view: 'I AM PROFOUNDLY GRATEFUL TO YOU FOR YOUR INVIGORATING WORDS WHICH INSPIRE ME TO MAKE EVERY EFFORT OF WILL AND OF ENERGY AS A DUTY IN ORDER TO BE AND TO SHOW MYSELF TO BE WORTHY OF YOUR FAITH PLEASE BELIEVE ME TO BE WHAT I AM YOUR MOST DEVOTED ILDEBRANDO PIZZETTI'.[78] *Orsèolo* was given its world première under the baton of Tullio Serafin at the 1935 *Maggio*, after Ciano, Minister of the Press and Propaganda, had assured the president of Florence's Teatro Comunale that 'I have advised the most important dailies to give broad coverage' to the event.[79] Ciano had previously invited Pizzetti to represent the National Fascist Union of Musicians on La Scala's governing board,[80] and a few weeks after the *Orsèolo* première the composer took part in a short-wave broadcast, beamed to the United States, about his work – again at Ciano's request.

By this time, Pizzetti was aiming at membership in the Accademia d'Italia, and he certainly was not averse to scratching the backs of those who counted in the process. Quoting Mussolini became a constant feature of Pizzetti's public statements – as in his 'Open Letter by an Italian Composer of 1936' published in the *Rassegna musicale*:

[. . .] words that remain firmly implanted in my mind and heart are these, by Mussolini: 'Works for the theatre' – and of course this is to be applied to art in general – 'must excite great collective passions, must be inspired by a sense of lively, profound humanity, and must bring things that really count in the life of the spirit and in human affairs on to the stage.'[81]

Respighi died on 18 April 1936, and within days of his death his old friends Pizzetti and Malipiero had both – unbeknownst to each other – asked to be given his chair of advanced composition at the Santa Cecilia Conservatory. Malipiero had gone right to the top by informing Mussolini that he was '*the only one* in Italy, apart from Respighi, who has for many years guided most of our young [musicians]'.[82] Pizzetti, on the other hand, had written to De Vecchi, the Minister of Education, to point out that he had 'pedagogic qualifications such as absolutely no other Italian musician can show for himself'.[83] Pizzetti got the job, left the Milan Conservatory and moved to the capital. According to his son, Rome was 'a city [Pizzetti] never came to love and in fact hated in the last years of his life. But in 1936 he was certain that his presence in Rome would be an "express train" for arriving at the Accademia d'Italia, as he so ardently wished – and events proved him right.'[84]

Pizzetti further ingratiated himself by composing the soundtrack for the film *Scipione l'Africano*, a paean to Italic neo-imperialism, and he conducted an excerpt from it – the 'Hymn to Rome' – for the Duce at the inauguration of the Cinecittà studios near Rome (1937).[85] The film won the Mussolini Cup at Venice's Fifth International Exhibition of Cinematographic Art.[86] The composer appears to have felt duty bound to defend fascism by exposing the selfishness of his fellow artists. In an article ('Our Musical Theatre – Observations and Notes') in the *Nuova antologia* (1 July 1938), he devoted two pages to the subject of 'artists and party hierarchy'. Artists, said, Pizzetti, have always blamed administrators, the public and even the state for 'all the ills that afflict the theatre', but they themselves deserve some of the blame. He went on to say that at a recent congress of musicians, promoted by the Confederation of Artists and Professionals for discussing proposals to be presented to the MinCulPop, at least ninety per cent of the subjects examined concerned 'purely material interests' rather than art. Musicians had given 'too simplistic and too convenient an interpretation' to the directives handed down by the regime's unions and corporations, as a result of the 'most deplorable nonchalance or incomprehension of the hierarchic principle, which is one of the fundamental postulates of the fascist ethic'. Graduated authority, said Pizzetti, must be respected in all fields, and 'the patently ridiculous concept of equality' was responsible for the mistaken belief held by many artists that membership in the Fascist Union of Musicians entitled them to have their works performed. They ought to have realized that the 'hierarchic concept [. . .] is based on worth, talent, character and merit-oriousness'. But who was to determine each musician's worth, talent, character and meritoriousness? Pizzetti did not say.

There are those who arm themselves with one of Mussolini's profoundly meaningful precepts or words of encouragement and shout that music must reach out to the people; and it is a most ignoble example of speculation on the part of some that such a precept is said to refer to what seems spontaneous and inspired according to the musical sense and aesthetic mentality of a mandolin-player. No less unworthy of respect or even tolerance are the statements made by all those who, in the name of their alleged aristocracy, refinement and modern way of feeling things, wish to have certain hieroglyphics, games and sound-combinations (which are nothing more than contemptible fictions and painful, vain creative efforts by the impotent) pass and be accepted as music.

What did Italian opera require? 'Love, above all. It already has an abundance of material provisions, for no Italian or foreign government has ever done for the musical theatre as much as the fascist Government has been doing for years and generously continues to do.'[87]

What more could the regime have desired of an Italian composer? In 1939 Pizzetti got the reward he had long been seeking. Upon learning of his nomination he wrote to thank Mussolini for 'raising me up to the Roman honour of the Academy'.[88] That year, he was also nominated president of the new Italian Institute of Music History; shortly thereafter he wrote an article about *The Rite of Spring* that demonstrated his anti-historical hostility towards certain non-Italian musical developments.

> [...] If the art of [Italian] primitives can be universally grasped, the reason lies in its spiritual content. But Stravinsky's primitivism [...] is that of an artist who does not have a real, authentic civilization behind him, but merely the elemental life of a people dominated by material things and by the senses – more by superstition than by religion, more by entirely material greed than by moral aspirations. If Stravinsky's music [...] makes us think of religious forebodings and rites, they are [...] the barbaric rites performed by savages before intentionally terrifying, grotesque masks: if they are not Negroid rites, they are Asiatic, Mongol, perhaps Russian, but certainly no longer those of civilized Europe. [...][89]

In June 1939, when he was beginning to enjoy his privileges as an academician, Pizzetti received a farewell letter from his former pupil Mario Castelnuovo-Tedesco, whose music was at that time nearly as well known outside Italy as Pizzetti's. Under the regime's new racial laws, Castelnuovo, who was Jewish, could no longer have his works performed in his native country, nor could his children continue to attend the schools at which they had formerly studied. He had decided to emigrate to the United States, and was scheduled to depart a few days later. 'I cannot tell you how painful it is [...] to leave this Country, my Parents and so many dear friends!' wrote the younger man. '[...] I shall carry with me [...] the unforgettable memory of you, of your artistic integrity, and of your precious teachings.'[90] There is no record of how this note affected Pizzetti; he was not, however, a man to stand up and protest against the new laws, any more than he had reacted against fascism's other acts of violence.

Pizzetti was astonishingly talented at having his cake and eating it. In February 1940, while finishing his *Epithalamium*, commissioned by Elizabeth Sprague Coolidge for performance at the Library of Congress in Washington, he began a symphony commissioned by the Japanese government for the 2,600th anniversary of the founding of the Empire.[91] That summer he accepted a gold medal for artistic merit from King Victor Emmanuel.[92]

Pizzetti's last substantial public statement as a fascist was a presidential speech made in 1942 at a plenary meeting of the Commission for the Study of Texts for the Autarchy of the Italian School System in Music Teaching Methods. Addressing himself to Bottai, then Minister of National Education, Pizzetti recalled the sense of honour and responsibility he and his colleagues had felt when, six months earlier, the ministry – by will of the Duce – had given them the task of devising a programme of musical self-sufficiency. In Pizzetti's opinion the results of the work carried out in the intervening time were superior to the highest hopes any of them had had at the first meeting. The commission, Pizzetti explained, had created twelve sub-committees (all financed by the government and all headed by Pizzetti), whose members had 'not only immediately applied their most active mental fervour', but had also shown their 'deep and vital love for their art and for the schools'. After praising his own and his colleagues' selflessness and dedication, he stated his belief that autarchy could quickly be achieved in this area, 'as the Duce and yourself [Bottai] so justly desire [. . .], precisely because Italian musicians have for years been working towards such an achievement, for love of their country and their art'. [93] If Pizzetti is to be believed, the demands of big egos and the requirements for economic survival never found a place among the considerations of Italian musicians – a state of affairs that would have distinguished them from their colleagues elsewhere, and indeed from most other human beings.

His analysis of the pre-autarchic situation was the one so beloved of the more provincial-minded Italian musicians: Italy was mother and teacher to all the other nations in matters musical; how ridiculous, therefore, that Italians were now accepting musical instruction from other countries. Unfortunately, several sub-committees, including those on choral music and music history, discovered that in their areas current Italian anthologies and texts were either inadequate or non-existent. The missing tools would have to be constructed as quickly as possible; meanwhile, time-honoured sources from abroad would continue to be used. Pizzetti generously adds that there was no more reason to remove Bach's *Well-Tempered Clavier* or the studies of Chopin, Kreutzer and Cramer from Italian students' courses of study than to eliminate the works of Paganini and Clementi from the syllabi of foreign conservatories. Passages from the works of Verdi, Puccini, Respighi 'and the best living

composers' should nevertheless be inserted into Italian examination programmes, and there should be less reliance on 'the most modern foreign
compositions'.

Although a manual of Italian musical nomenclature and an Italian treatise
on instrumentation were being planned, Pizzetti's address gives the impression that very little concrete action had been taken in most areas. 'We ask
you, Excellency, for two years' time' for the completion of the two books.[94]
Nine months later the fascist government fell, and with it fell all its unions,
corporations, commissions and sub-committees. Pizzetti, however, proved to
be a remarkably fine acrobat for a man in his mid-sixties: he landed on his
feet.

All of Pizzetti's declarations on fascism add up to very little. He was an
Italian musician trying to live and work and provide for his family, and he did
not inconvenience himself by letting his thoughts dwell upon the regime's
negative aspects. He may truly have believed that Mussolini was interested in
music – and indeed Mussolini was interested in music, in the same way in
which he was interested in every other facet of Italian life: as something that
might in some way augment the reputation of his country, his party, his
government, himself. The Staraces, the Farinaccis, the Bottais, the De Vecchis
– the high-level administrators – were not the people who kept the regime in
power for two decades. They, like Mussolini, were merely the beneficiaries of
the tacit or declared support provided by many thousands of second-, third-
and fourth-ranking bureaucrats, professionals, artists and intellectuals. These
thousands offered a largely opportunistic form of consensus that cemented
the regime's life-and-death control over the rest of the country's inhabitants.
Had the behaviour of Pizzetti and his colleagues really resulted from a true,
heartfelt conviction that fascism was the miraculous system its leaders
claimed it to be, it would be easier to accept. Then it could be said they were
blind, deluded, mad – perhaps even evil. But Pizzetti and most of his
colleagues were guilty of nothing so grand. Their self-seeking was small, grey,
banal and workaday: a mildly evil semi-delusion.

Ottorino Respighi is the only Italian composer of his generation whose name
still regularly appears on concert programmes beyond his country's borders –
if only for three colourful symphonic poems that he did not rate among his
most important works: The Fountains of Rome, The Pines of Rome and Roman
Festivals. Little information has come to light about his dealings with the
regime, and prevailing opinion on the subject has been well summarized in a
recent biographical sketch by Daniele Spini.

> Respighi [. . .] was certainly not in disgrace with the regime, much less
> suspected of heresy or even of rebellion. The honours he received – among
> them, election to the Accademia d'Italia in 1932 – and the frequent, major

productions of his operas in the most important Italian theatres, demonstrate that he was an officially recognized and consecrated artist during the early 1930s [. . .]. If, however, the historian is asked [. . .] to compare [Respighi's] attitude towards fascism with those of the other protagonists of Italian music during that period, it must be said that he comes off much better than many others. Elsa [the composer's widow] maintains that Respighi never became a member of the National Fascist Party, and she is supported by the testimony of Claudio Guastalla [Respighi's librettist and close friend . . .]. This in itself does not say much, but it certainly does not show a special mania for approving [the regime]. In addition, [. . .] one cannot attribute to him the beggarliness of a Mascagni or an Alfano, the ardent protestations of devotion (with accompanying requests for help) of a Pizzetti, or the activism of a Casella or a Malipiero [. . .].[95]

It may be, however, that Respighi did not attempt to ingratiate himself with the regime because he was the one composer of his generation whom the regime backed without being asked. Although Mussolini happily accepted the others' tributes, Pizzetti's musical asceticism, Malipiero's eccentricity and Casella's cosmopolitanism did not harmonize with fascism's belligerent, conformist, nationalistic principles. Respighi's palatable modernism, his brilliantly attractive orchestral spectrum and the ethnocentricity of his popular tone-poems were just what the regime needed to demonstrate that progressivism and fascism were natural allies. Mussolini would also have been drawn to Respighi for his relative circumspection and – Toni's manifesto notwithstanding – for his lack of interest in politico-aesthetic disputes that might have invoked government intervention on behalf of one faction or another. Consequently, the fascists opened doors for Respighi before he knocked.

Gian Francesco Malipiero's activism – referred to by Spini – was inconsistent. Relations between the regime and the man whom many musicologists consider the most original Italian composer of his generation were more revealing of his moodiness and persecution mania than of a rational political attitude. A clinical psychologist might have a better chance than a music historian at explaining Malipiero's dealings with the fascists. Nicolodi says that 'neither his pessimistic orientation nor his tedium vitae, neither his difficult relations with reality nor his poetics of the negative were sufficient antidotes against [. . .] the allurements of power';[96] but given Malipiero's personality, it is not surprising that the allurements were more often glimpsed and desired from afar than approached and possessed.

Malipiero wrote on numerous occasions to Mussolini and other fascist leaders to put forward his plans for rescuing Italian musical culture, to ask for a chance to talk with or play for the Duce, or to send the great man a score with dedication. But unlike the stuffy, moralistic tone of Pizzetti's letters or the business-like yet slightly awed quality of Casella's, Malipiero's are filled with morose self-pity and tiny thrusts at his enemies, real and imagined. On 25 March 1936 he addressed a letter to Mussolini, defending himself against a secret police report that had criticized his music history course at the University of Padua and had referred to him as a 'lunatic'.[97] Malipiero had heard of the attack, but apparently did not know exactly what had been said about him. The letter is so crabbed and crabby that the reader almost sympathizes with the anonymous attacker.

Excellency,

I think that my 'enemies' have once again tried to put me in a bad light by *denouncing me* to Your Excellency. More I do not know. I think it has to do with the Royal University of Padua, where I am giving a music history course in a very pleasant atmosphere.

I want Your Excellency to know that the moment for making a decision has come, and I should be happy if Your Excellency were the one to decide whether Italy will have one more musician or one less.

I could take pride in their campaign against me if it were fair and if I did not *now* have to think seriously about my *material* existence.

My moral, artistic [life] is absolutely in order, but I do not want to have to count on posterity. *My adversaries are trying to block every one of my activities within the fascist cultural institutions.* Why? If, with a few hisses, they manage to bury my works – even those that have been alive for twenty years on the world's stages – would it not be easier [still] to liquidate me forever? I could carry out the activities that I have been trying for ten years to put at the disposal of our culture (teaching of choral singing, rational simplifications of instrumental studies, creation of an Italian 'song book', synthetic, modern method for studying music history, etc.), but which no one dares either to reject or to accept.

Excellency, the memory of your words is still alive in me – words which, after each of the three audiences granted me, [raised] so many hopes in my soul; and my soul has the right to seek a bit of peace. I have had enough proofs to convince me that the Italian public, and the people, too, *if left in peace*, are perfectly capable of understanding all music, including my music.

The middlemen are the ones who stir up the public and profit by my *isolation* in order to lay traps for me. But it is late in the day.

To talk to the Duce of my *personal* situation at this moment [i.e. during the Ethiopian war] is perhaps a mistake, but since Your Excellency has read what my adversaries have written, I hope you will [also] read these lines, which represent:

(1) once again, the offer of all my efforts to participate in *real* fascist musical culture;

(2) a warning that my situation is very difficult. An urgent decision must be made, as I said above, as to whether Italy will have one more musician or one less.

My post at the Venice Conservatory is still that of a temporary employee; my teaching at the Royal University of Padua is an experiment.

It is late for starting a career [n.b.: Malipiero was fifty-four years old]. What I have done thus far either counts or doesn't count.

I know: I must not mix with mediocrities; everything or nothing; but unfortunately, too many people know this.

I would like to live in Rome. Could I not be transferred from my post in Venice (advanced courses for composers) to Rome, to Santa Cecilia? A word would be sufficient. I wouldn't look bad next to my friend Ottorino Respighi.

In Rome I would be in my own environment.

Should Your Excellency like to do something for me, it would suffice to arrange for me to meet with His Excellency Count De Vecchi di Valcismon [Minister of Education].

I would be extremely sad to have to emigrate. I love my Country too much. [. . .][98]

Malipiero did not get his transfer, but he did, in time, become the Fascist Union of Musicians' interprovincial secretary for Venice, a member of the union's national board, and director of the Venice Conservatory. But complaints continued. 'How many of my operas are played throughout the world?' he raged to Cornelio Di Marzio, president of the National Fascist Confederation of Artists and Professionals, in 1941. 'And what kind of success do they have? [. . .] Why do people want to eliminate a composer who is considered Number One abroad, and who brings much honour to his country? [. . .] My disgust has taken on alarming proportions.'[99] Malipiero's character rendered him useless to the regime except as a prestigious name to be added to its very long list of enthusiasts. His plans to reform musical education in Italy were never put into practice and his compositions were probably performed no more and no less often under fascism than they would have been under other political conditions.

The real, effective musical activist among the composers who in any way supported the regime was Alfredo Casella. Born in Turin, Casella received most of his musical education in Paris and remained there until he was thirty-two. He was polyglot, cosmopolitan and ardently interested in European musical developments, although fundamentally uninterested in opera. For all these reasons, Casella was the natural enemy of the Mascagnis, Pizzettis and Lualdis of Italian music. By the mid-1920s – a decade after returning to his native country – he had become leader and protector of the younger generation of composers and the bête-noire of the conservatives. A remark attributed to the outspoken conductor Antonio Guarnieri typifies the conservatives' attitude towards him: Casella mentioned that he had been born in the year of Wagner's death; Guarnieri replied, 'Misfortunes never come one at a time.'

Gavazzeni, like many other promising musicians born between 1900 and 1925, passed much of his adolescence and youth under Casella's influence. He said that 'Casella's image was the very image of a "teacher". He alone [. . .] was able to carry out that precise function in Italian musical life – a function that was at once stylistic and moral [. . .]. The strength of Casella's influence on one segment of public opinion was the sensitive reflection of an individual artistic existence that had nothing vague about it and that [. . . pursued] its goals with extreme lucidity.'[100] But the composer's devastating criticisms of the state of Italian musical life leave no doubt as to why many older musicians did not share Gavazzeni's admiration. The royal conservatories, Casella wrote in 1923, were useless; they should be reconstituted under private administration. There was only one permanent symphony orchestra (Molinari's) in the country, and the opera companies, apart from La Scala, were not worth discussing. Contemporary foreign composers such as Stravinsky, Scriabin, Schoenberg, Bartók, Szymanowski, Falla, Prokofiev and Honegger were virtually unknown to the Italian public, he said, while works by such major native composers as Malipiero were better known abroad than at home.[101] Within two years, however, Casella had begun to stir some strangely nationalistic and even naïvely fascistic ingredients into his cosmopolitan broth. In one of his occasional contributions to the American *Christian Science Monitor* (these continued throughout the late 1920s), he remarked with slightly uncomfortable pride that the European 'harmonic crisis' had been less severe in Italy than elsewhere. 'No Italian musician has indulged in the excesses of atonality', said the man who the previous year had brought Schoenberg to Italy for a concert tour of *Pierrot Lunaire*.

> Doubtless the common sense of the race has acted as a brake in this adventure. [. . .] Modern Italian musicians find themselves in possession of a musical language singularly traditional and at the same time new. While other schools are apparently still fighting against certain subversive dogmas, the Italian school makes use of an intelligent and salutary reactionism [sic]. [. . .] It is a big mistake to believe that 'reaction' always means a return to the past. In numerous instances, a 'reactionary' effort which sought to re-establish an equilibrium endangered by another and preceding movement has meant the salvation of an ideal. That is why I firmly believe that the apparently 'reactionary' musical thought of young Italy is singularly fortunate, not only for the musical renaissance of its own country, but also for the destinies of music in general.[102]

Casella's term 'salvation of an ideal' referred to the embryonic neo-classical movement; but there is a striking similarity between his pseudo-revolutionary terminology and that of the fascists. Pleased with 'the present national development and constantly growing national well-being', and with Italy's 'privileged situation' as a country without a viable parliament, Casella had openly declared his fascist sympathies by 1926 – 'although in retrospect', says Nicolodi, 'he tended to refer to himself as an enthusiast of the movement from the time of the march on Rome'.[103]

Casella's negative remarks on atonality and his interest in the neo-classical alternative must not be taken out of context. But that context is extremely complicated, and indeed comprises much of the history of European music in the second quarter of the century. The scope of this study is limited to the cultural–political arena – into which Casella ran, brandishing a sword. There was, he declared, a strong relationship between neo-classicism and fascism; both stood for order and reactionary revolution. Non-fascist practitioners of neo-classical techniques disagreed: they were convinced that their style was too refined, too aristocratic, to have anything in common with so roughshod and demagogic a movement as fascism. And Schoenberg, the Number One anti-neo-classicist, trotted out his most ponderously, aggressively ironic prose style to attack Casella's muddled thinking and to accuse him of 'picking my pockets', musically.[104] One of Schoenberg's supporters, the music sociologist Theodor W. Adorno, described Casella and all who thought like him as 'obtuse street musicians' of bourgeois–fascistic tendencies[105] – the pairing of those two adjectives having been particularly well calculated to enrage fascists, who claimed that their movement was anti-bourgeois and revolutionary. The argument was empty. As artists always do, Schoenberg, Casella and all the other major and minor musicians of the day were following their instincts and declaring others 'wrong'; and, as critics always do, Adorno was producing post-facto theories to support his own inclinations and to denounce others' post-facto theories.

Casella's real problem was the irreconcilability, which he refused to see, of his political and artistic ideas. He tried to belong to the fascist artistic hierarchy while representing the musical avant-garde – rather like trying to be simultaneously an orthodox follower of two religions. For although he delighted in the silliest forms of political support for the regime – even declaring proudly in print that he was born only four days before Mussolini[106] – he also mercilessly and at times exaggeratedly attacked the enemies of modernism. In 1926, for instance, he criticized the regime-approved Mascagni in an article for the *Christian Science Monitor*: 'Although he is the composer of *Cavalleria rusticana* (or rather for that very reason), [he] represents an anachronism and an art that has happily been past and buried for a quarter of a century. As a conductor he may have been very gifted, but the gaps in his musical culture betray him at every turn, the moment he conducts serious music.'[107] Mascagni was an embarrassment to the Italian avant-garde; but to decry him gratuitously abroad when he was the only living Italian composer whose music had a broad-based international public must certainly have been viewed by orthodox fascists as negative propaganda. For them, all

Italian glory was glory for the regime. Conservative Italian critics did not hesitate to retaliate. Raffaello De Rensis, for example, called Casella 'perhaps the most representative example of the opportunistic musician. He plays the part of the foreigner when in Italy and of the Italian when abroad.'[108] And Casella, along with Malipiero, was the principal target of Toni's reactionary manifesto.

Casella was convinced, however, that the regime smiled upon bold undertakings – including his own attempts to bring Italy into the mainstream of European music – and he paid musical as well as verbal tribute to fascist enterprises. Within weeks of the conclusion of the Ethiopian campaign, for instance, he had begun work on Il deserto tentato, a 'mystery' for the musical theatre.

> [It was] a mystery of predominantly religious and warlike character, evoking the abstract voices of virgin nature, which was anxious to be fertilized by human civilization; the intervention of a group of aviators, descending from the sky into that horrible desert, almost like modern Argonauts; their struggle against the dark forces of barbarism and the perils of nature; and finally peace, and the transformation of colossal ambe* into human constructions.[109]

But the glorification of western civilization in general and fascist progress in particular was not enough for Casella: he also wished to make the work a tool for revivifying melodrama by 'bringing it back to its point of departure – that is, to the holy representations and the ancient mysteries – renewing it, however, through a more up-to-date breath of modernity'.[110] No wonder, then – considering the grandiosity of Casella's intentions, and perhaps pretensions, and given the work's ostentatious dedication to Mussolini – that Casella felt hurt and betrayed when he and his fascist 'mystery' were attacked by many critics whose devotion to the regime was unquestionable and unquestioning. Their ad hominem assault may well have provoked him to write, some months later:

> I now believe that the problem of the so-called 'preliminary issue' of national character in works of art must be considered a thing of the past. [. . .] None of us, today, bothers to be 'national' when he writes music. [. . .] The current atmosphere in Italy is not that of times gone by [. . .]. One must not forget that it is much more important to be an historical artist (that is to say, one of the few who make history) than a national one. [. . .][111]

From a late twentieth-century point of view, the conscious quest for historical importance seems as outmoded an artistic intention as the need to give a work a distinctively national character. But perhaps Casella's virtual admission that he was seeking a place in the cultural firmament provides a

* An amba is an isolated, steep, flat-topped mountain, typical of certain regions of Ethiopia.

clue not only to his personality as a composer but also to the motives behind his enthusiasm for fascism. *Zukunftsmusik* and *Zukunftspolitik*: by adhering to what he saw as the most advanced musical and political movements of the day, he may have believed he was securing for himself a slice of historical authenticity, a right to artistic survival.

This explanation, if correct, does not detract from Casella's personal and professional generosity, nor is it meant as a condemnation of the fundamental egocentricity without which no artist can accomplish anything. It is simply an attempt to find a link between the openness, the kindness, to which virtually everyone who knew Casella has attested, and his support for an intrinsically and self-declaredly xenophobic, repressive regime. 'Today, the whole drama of our musical life (not to mention of all Italian art) lies in the divergence between "Europeans" and "provincials"', he said in 1938.[112] Taken by itself, this statement looks anti-nationalistic and therefore anti-fascistic; but Casella went on to describe 'Europeanism' as

> a spiritual movement which Italians are today called to participate in, not only for a thousand historical and cultural reasons, but also because of the fundamental nature of their political revolution. Unless one wishes to reduce it to [the dimensions of] a 'palace revolution', it must be accompanied by [. . .] an art that is no less 'modern' than the said political revolution, and that will put Italy decisively in first place within the European avant-garde.[113]

Thus Casella attempted to reconcile nationalism with internationalism. But as another European war began to seem unavoidable, his resolve wavered. The bend in his opinions was towards the right, in accordance with the regime's policies. He declared in 1939 that although twentieth-century Italian music had been influenced by Strauss, Debussy, Stravinsky and, to a lesser extent, Hindemith and the Viennese school,

> in the last fifteen years, the powerful, renewing breeze that Fascism has imprinted [sic] upon the whole life of the nation has even penetrated art, freeing it of all foreign subjection and giving new currency to our past, which had been forgotten for so many decades. The new sense of national dignity, faith in our own strength, boldness and, finally, love of danger have transformed artistic life, too, and have made real what for more than thirty years had been purely an aspiration and an attempt.[114]

The best Italian music of the day, said Casella, was

> profoundly independent [. . .] in its melody, which has remained free from Central European deformations [. . .]; in its harmony, which is so healthy and well-balanced, as is its rhythm [. . .]; in its instrumentation, which is the enemy of brilliant, virtuosic Russo-French sonorities; and in its forms, too, [. . .] which are high, severe references to great disciplines of the past [. . .]; and in its profoundly religious nature, which [. . .] hearkens back to the

ancient Roman and Catholic world. [...][115]

Casella was pleased that Italian composers had rejected atonality and other 'anti-historic' tendencies – a 'position that closely adheres to the political efforts of the Fascist Regime, which is at once tradition and revolution'.[116]

By 1941, Casella was excusing 'our generation' for having taken part in the 'European revolutionary movement', claiming that it had been 'momentarily' necessarily to rebel against nineteenth-century melodrama.[117]

> The end of that task of assimilation coincided with the advent of Fascism. Our emancipation from [...] foreign influences [...] dates in fact from that moment, as does the creation of an Italian style that is at once traditional and modern, and that therefore precisely reflects the characteristics of the nation's doctrine and of its political movement.[118]

Efforts on behalf of musical renewal were backed by the government, according to Casella, 'through various ministerial portfolios, union enterprises, and subsidies and prizes of every type; through assistance conceded to the operatic and symphonic arts; and through the rigorous control [exercised] over musical "exports" '. No other European government, he noted, had undertaken so vast an action – based, moreover, 'on the Regime's absolute respect for artistic freedom'. Thanks to the country's 'enviable' musical environment, Italy would again become 'a great musical power [...] There can be no doubt that the main credit for the Regime and for the Man who presides over it consists in having understood how to make each of us feel the worker's sense of proud, noble awareness that each of us [is] adding his stone to the majestic edifice of the new fascist order.'[119]

Casella's political thinking was either childishly naïve or incredibly confused – quite possibly both. In an autobiographical book completed after Mussolini's racial campaign had begun and published during the Second World War, he stated how proud he was that a follower of Hitler by the name of Casella, killed in the unsuccessful *Putsch* of 1923, had 'brought our obviously Italian name into the sacrarium of Germanic martyrs',[120] but spoke, within the following few pages, of his warm friendship for Ernest Bloch, George Gershwin and a multitude of Soviet composers.[121] What did he think Hitler represented to these people? How did he manage – not in 1923 or 1933, but in 1938 – to reconcile respect for Nazism with his belief in internationalism? Only when the horrors of war came extremely close would Casella begin to come to terms with the enormity of the situation.

*   *   *

Goffredo Petrassi was born at Zagarolo, near Rome, on 16 July 1904. He was musically self-educated until the age of twenty-one. By the time he received diplomas in composition (1932) and organ (1933) from the Santa Cecilia Conservatory, his international career as a composer had already begun.

Petrassi taught harmony, counterpoint and choral composition at the Santa Cecilia Academy from 1934 to 1936. Mario Labroca engaged him in 1935 to work in the music section of the MinCulPop's Ispettorato/Direzione generale del Teatro, and the following year he became Secretary of the Union of Music Societies, which was a division of the Centro Lirico Italiano. He was General Director of Venice's Teatro la Fenice from 1937 to 1940. His distinguished teaching career centred on the Santa Cecilia Conservatory, where he held the chair of composition from 1939 to 1959 and then instructed the advanced composition course until 1974, but he has also taught at Salzburg, Tanglewood, Siena and elsewhere. He has served as artistic director of the Accademia Filarmonica Romana (1947–50) and as president of the International Society for Contemporary Music (1954–6). Petrassi's compositions include operas, ballets and film scores, as well as orchestral, chamber, choral, and solo vocal and instrumental works. Among his best-known pieces are the Partita for orchestra (1932); Ninth Psalm (1934–6), *Coro di morti* (1940–1) and *Noche oscura* (1950–1), all for chorus and instrumental ensembles; the eight Concerti for orchestra (1933–72); and *Propos d'Alain*(1960) and *Beatitudines: testimonianza per Martin Luther King* (1968), both for baritone and instrumental ensemble. In this interview, he discusses his views on the composer's status under the fascist regime.

HARVEY SACHS: Maestro Petrassi, you were eighteen years old when Mussolini came to power, and you therefore spent all the early part of your adulthood under the regime. Will you tell me something of your musical experiences under fascism?

GOFFREDO PETRASSI: As far as the arts under fascism are concerned, we must distinguish between two periods. The arts were really free until 1932 or '33; then, in 1933, came the special laws with which the fascists made some regulations that curtailed many liberties. But before that, we in Rome, at least, heard music of all kinds, including many novelties, played in the normal course of events. I can speak as a spectator, because from the time of my boyhood, from 1919 on, I listened assiduously from the gallery of the Augusteum, a great, historic, 3,000-seat concert hall. All the important musicians of the day – conductors, instrumentalists and composers – passed through there. The new works that were performed in France, Germany and elsewhere were given almost immediately thereafter in Rome. I remember a very young Darius Milhaud who came to play his pieces for piano and orchestra [Five Etudes, Op. 63]; naturally, they were a colossal fiasco. Among other events, there was the tour of *Pierrot Lunaire* in 1924 with Schoenberg conducting.

HS: Stravinsky, too, came many times.

GP: Yes, very often. Foreign musicians circulated rather freely.

HS: Did Italian musicians at that time have a broad European cultural outlook?

GP: International culture was not very widespread among us – not because of a lack of information or of the means for getting it, but simply because the Italian cultural environment was backward, a victim of the nineteenth-century operatic tradition. There were, however, important exceptions, such as the *Rassegna musicale* which, under the editorship of Guido M. Gatti, gathered together the most advanced scholars of Europe-wide outlook. But none of this had anything to do with fascism: ideas, books and music itself circulated freely till the early 1930s.

HS: What was the nature of the limitations that came afterwards? We're not yet talking about restrictions made on racial grounds.

GP: No, those came only at the time of the Pact of Steel with Germany,* and we know what the tragic consequences were. The first restrictions were aesthetic and grew out of the confrontation between a group of conservative, even reactionary, musicians and a group of musical innovators.

HS: I imagine that the familiar figures of Mulè, Lualdi and Toni were to be found among the former.

GP: Mulè, Lualdi and Toni were the three fascist bosses reponsible for music. I can't say to what extent; but they were the paladins – and openly so. Behind them, however, stood some more qualified musicians, such as Respighi and, up to a point, Pizzetti. This group's political leader was Farinacci, who represented the darkest, most reactionary, provincial and narrow-minded side of the regime. They even had a degree of power – the power of political clout – for insuring that their ideas were respected. They tried to keep a national musical heritage alive; but although that heritage derived from a very rich past, it could no longer stimulate young composers looking towards their future.

HS: Did none of the young composers share the ideas of the conservative faction?

GP: Some did, but they have remained minor, forgotten figures.

HS: The spiritual leaders of the more forward-looking group were Casella and Malipiero.

GP: Yes. They were also more active and better known internationally. Within the regime they were connected with Bottai, who represented the more progressive and open-minded political faction.

HS: How did things change after 1932 or 1933?

GP: The restrictions didn't so much concern information – because Casella, for instance, travelled throughout the world and brought us news from every-where . . .

HS: . . . at least to those of you young people who were in Rome.

* The racial laws (September 1938) predated and paved the way for the Pact of Steel (May 1939).

GP: Yes, to us in Rome ... Perhaps it was the circulation of performers that became less lively than before. Even apart from the historic Toscanini case, certain foreign artists no longer appeared in Italy after the special laws and the wars in Ethiopia and Spain. I recall that Ansermet, for instance, did not return after 1933 – the year in which I heard him conduct, in Rome, the first performance of the Three Pieces from *Wozzeck*. For several years thereafter, however, one could play Schoenberg and Berg, and I remember the Italian première of *Der Wein* at the Venice Festival in 1934. Then, with the racial laws and the pact with Germany, many limitations were put into effect. Schoenberg was a Jew ...

HS: ... and Berg, being closely connected with him, was not in the odour of sanctity. One reads instead, in the music journals of the period, the names of minor German and Austrian composers who were clearly being pushed for purely political reasons. The name Werner Egk comes automatically to mind.

GP: Yes, Egk was an official musician in Germany, at least for a while. We had an influx of German musicians, composers and performers, and the level of importance of much of the German music that was played isn't worth discussing. These composers were not necessarily of secondary rank at the time, but they didn't interest us much: our interests were focused on other artistic cultures and types of expression.

HS: Were there Italian musicians, apart from those of Jewish origin, whose music was banned in Germany?

GP: Oh yes: Malipiero, Dallapiccola and I! From a racial point of view, all three of us were unexceptionable, although Dallapiccola had a Jewish wife. Our works were banned for aesthetic reasons. I was dumbfounded by the prohibition of my music, but my publisher wrote me that I was indeed on the list in Germany. Here, however, is an example of how confused the situation was. The Germans founded an international society for modern music, under the presidency of Richard Strauss, in opposition to the [non-Axis] International Society of Contemporary Music. Naturally, it was very temporary, set up as wartime propaganda. It was never spoken of again afterwards. But in Berlin in 1942 there was a big meeting of this new society and, as was logical, the Germans invited an Italian delegation. Who was in it? Pizzetti, Malipiero and myself – all chosen by Nicola De Pirro. Many friends advised me not to go, but I asked, 'How can I not accept?' And so I went with the others. Walking one day by the shop of Bote & Bock, Malipiero's German publisher, we went in and I bought a score of Malipiero's *Torneo notturno*; and he wrote a dedication in it – right there in Berlin, despite his being a forbidden composer in Germany. I've saved the document.

HS: Did you know De Pirro well?

GP: Yes. He directed the theatre and music division of the Ministry of Popular Culture, and he was part of Bottai's faction. De Pirro was a great friend of

Casella, Malipiero, Labroca and myself. In 1935 he hired Labroca for the music division of the Ministry, and Labroca then hired me and a friend of mine. So for ten months I was an employee of the Ministry of Popular Culture. We were rather curious employees, because we spent most of the day discussing music or singing, and only after some months went by did we learn to fill out an official form. We didn't know the bureaucratic jargon.

HS: What sort of work did you have to do?

GP: We had to reply to requests for railroad passes for singers, for instance, or for permits of other sorts – even passports. All these bureaucratic jobs were inconceivable to me, but I needed the salary.

HS: You weren't at it for long, in any case.

GP: Afterwards, I directed a [government-sponsored] concert agency. There, too, I did what I had to do, but I often had fun in the process. I looked at these things differently than a career bureaucrat would have done. I decided, for instance, that work would not begin if we hadn't all had a big *cappuccino* with chocolate sprinkled on top! I'm telling you these little bits of nonsense to describe my state of mind and that of my colleagues as well. Then, in 1937, Venice's Teatro la Fenice reopened after a few years of inactivity, and De Pirro asked me whether I wanted to direct it. I was afraid: I was thirty-three years old, and it was something unheard of for me, as if I had been asked to go to Africa for a conversation with Mustapha. Of course I had always attended opera performances at the Teatro Costanzi – which afterwards became the Royal Opera Theatre, where some extremely brilliant and culturally very important seasons had taken place. I pondered awhile, told myself that it would be an important experience, and then took heart and accepted – partly because the situation was attractive: I would be earning much more money, and I had to support my parents. I began to frequent various opera houses very attentively, and after a two- or three-month apprenticeship I was completely ready. I knew the singers, I knew what was needed to put on Verdi's *Don Carlo*, and so on. In short, I had learned my trade.

HS: Gui wrote, after the war, that under fascism there had been an astonishing number of useless employees at Florence's Teatro Comunale, each of them supported by one politician or another.

GP: Ah, but the Comunale was a politicized institution. The Fenice wasn't at all. The general manager – myself – was young; I engaged a very young conductor, Nino Sanzogno, who was twenty-six; the head of the press office was twenty-eight or twenty-nine. We were all very young, and therefore there was no bite to any attempted politicization.

HS: Or perhaps the Fenice didn't much interest the people in power . . .

GP: Right, they had little interest in it. I can say truly and in good conscience that no impositions were made upon me. As general manager, I would have had to execute any orders that arrived from the Ministry, but none ever came.

There was a reason for this: being a general manager was not my real profession. I already had a name as a musician, I enjoyed a certain respect, and people knew that I was ready to leave at any time if I couldn't realize the projects close to my heart. Not that I did anything that was forbidden by the regime ... I certainly could not have put on Schoenberg's or Berg's operas; but apart from the fact that the political situation would not have allowed it, the very nature of the Fenice, the material means at its disposal, would not have permitted it either. I did, however, do some things that could have aroused some suspicion.

HS: For instance?

GP: I did Busoni's *Arlecchino*, which had never before been performed in Italy, Ravel's L'*Heure espagnole*, Stravinsky's *Pulcinella* and, in 1938 – my first season – I did Strauss's *Elektra*, whose libretto had been written by Hofmannsthal, a Jew. I invited Strauss himself, and he came. He was very affable, very polished in manner, and I have a most beautiful memory of him. My veneration of Strauss the musician was total. I invited Béla Bartók for a concert dedicated to him. Then I did a *Carmen* – and although there was nothing courageous in that, we felt a quiver when Carmen sang her hymn to '*la liberté*'. That, too, was in '38, when the tightening-up had already taken place. I invited Gui to conduct, although he was known to be an anti-fascist, and he came for two years in a row. In short, I was never obliged to do or not to do anything specific.

HS: Did no one ever try to force you to accept this or that singer, for instance?

GP: Of course people tried, as they do in every theatre in the world, and I was perfectly free to say no.

HS: Were you able, at the Fenice, to observe the workings of the musicians' and performers' corporations and unions?

GP: Right, there was that business. Like everyone else, I was a member of those corporations – it was obligatory – but I didn't really take part in their activities. Mulè and Lualdi represented the Fascist Union of Musicians in the Chamber of Corporations. The union and the corporations certainly wielded their share of influence, but they were politicized mainly to protect the interests of Italian musicians. After England and France instituted sanctions [against Italy] at the time of the Ethiopian war, the autarchy plan was formed. This had its ridiculous aspects. One couldn't, for instance, print foreign words like *ouverture* or *suite* on a programme.

HS: When you refer to the protection of Italian interests, do you mean the minimum quotas for Italian music in the repertoire?

GP: Yes, the quotas – nationalistic protectionism. And it wasn't all negative. Looking back on it now, under a democratic regime with total freedom of information, it may appear restrictive – and so it was. But thanks to Italian slyness, if you will, or common sense, or even sense of humour, it wasn't entirely respected. In Rome, for instance, during the first years of the war, the

Corporation of Artists and Professionals organized two seasons of concerts and chamber theatre at the Teatro delle Arti, and we did some rather extraordinary things there without taking the autarchy programme into account. The directors of that corporation were rather more on Bottai's side than on the other, which made some very advanced proposals possible. We were even protected to an extent – very discreetly – by the Princess of Piedmont, whose anti-fascist role is well known.

HS: So you had returned to Rome from Venice.

GP: In 1939 I was named instructor of composition at the Santa Cecilia Conservatory in Rome, and I left Venice the following year to take up my new post. Like Dallapiccola, who went to the Florence Conservatory at the same time, I was appointed 'for eminence'.

HS: Were directives concerning teaching imposed upon you by the authorities?

GP: I taught the last three years of the higher composition course, and I felt absolutely free. There was no attempt to make me teach one way as opposed to another. I didn't concern myself at all with the Conservatory's regulations, either before or after fascism, because one of the first orders I gave myself on taking up teaching was never to become the director of a conservatory. And I've succeeded. I've never had anything to do with the bureaucratic side of the Conservatory. The director could, of course, inform us [of orders from above]. But I don't even know what such directives might have been. Perhaps they were silly things regarding uniforms and the like. There was an attempt to use only textbooks by Italian authors, in deference to the autarchy plan, but it was never followed up.

HS: What was the attitude of the musicians of the 'Generation of 1880' towards fascism?

GP: Virtually all of them went along with it. In what spirit? Each according to his own personality. Pizzetti was a member of the Royal Italian Academy; he was officially invested and even had a political function. Malipiero was the most petulant. He wrote letters to everyone, complained about not being played and about being misunderstood, and was always asking for help. I know this because, during my ten months at the Ministry, Malipiero was constantly applying to De Pirro. Perhaps he did this in a slightly ironic vein, but also with a great deal of hysteria. Casella behaved differently. He was the regime's unofficial composer, and he felt a certain responsibility for his conduct. He certainly made obeisances to fascism, but his autobiographical book, I segreti della giara, was dedicated to Bottai, and thus to one of the less obsequious political personalities. Unlike Malipiero, who dedicated his Giulio Cesare to Mussolini, Casella never went so far as to practise the cult of personality through flattery, despite the fact that he was highly placed in official circles. In the euphoria created by the Ethiopian war, he wrote Il deserto tentato,* an opera, which was the least interesting of his theatrical endeavours.

* Dedicated to Mussolini.

HS: We now come to the younger musicians.

GP: Yes, we come to my attitude and to that of Dallapiccola. Dallapiccola was at first a fervent fascist – so fervent that he sometimes annoyed us, his friends. At the time of the sanctions he took a firm stand in favour of the Italian Empire and against the British. There was the famous motto on his Tre laudi: 'Paradise in the shadow of the sword.' Then, with the coming of the special laws and above all the racial laws, things changed for him and he became a passionate anti-fascist. As for me, I never gave real, outright support to the regime except in one sole case – and a rather ambiguous one at that. I wrote a Ninth Psalm for chorus and orchestra, whose text invokes a legislator, in order that men recognize their responsibility as men. Mussolini was symbolized by this legislator. But it must be remembered that I had this idea in 1934 and that Dallapiccola's hymns were written in 1935 – in other words, at a time when popular consensus towards fascism was at its maximum in Italy and when international infatuation with and attention for Mussolini was also at its height. Still, to avoid having people think that I was trying to flatter or glorify a specific individual, I dedicated the Psalm to my parents. It was easy, obviously, to identify Mussolini in the law-maker; but there was also the idea of personal human responsibility – an idea I always continued to pursue in successive works, during and after the war.

HS: Wasn't there also, among composers – especially those who were not well known – a bit of cynicism in manipulating the regime's rhetoric for their own selfish ends?

GP: One cannot exclude that possibility, and it was even understandable in a certain sense. This is a human attitude, especially among young people, and I don't see it as a grave fault. The serious fault was to have used the political situation to obtain very substantial personal advantages. Perhaps what I am saying could also be interpreted as cynical; I believe, however, that the fault is more or less serious depending upon one's age and the scope of the advantages that one has gained. If a young composer wanted to have one of his orchestra or chamber pieces performed and asked a politician to use his influence to that end, I would call the fact in itself human rather than immoral. And what could this young composer have gained? Certainly no economic advantage. It may well have been a stepping-stone in the process of getting somewhere, little by little, in one's career, but I don't think it could be called anything more than that.

HS: But were there not composers or performers who were pushed forward by this method to the exclusion of others who may have been more capable?

GP: There could certainly have been such abuses. I still remember that one conductor – I didn't know him, but he must have been frightful – used to go to rehearsals in his black shirt. Before starting to conduct, he would pull out a revolver and set it on the music stand! But this is a story from the backwoods –

and of course this individual was the butt of everyone's jokes. There are always such people everywhere: they are the servants of those in power. It's a sort of meanness that certainly existed in Italy but that never reached the upper echelons.

HS: Did the anti-fascist movement make itself felt among musicians during the war?

GP: There was the episode of the general strike in Rome when the city was occupied by the Nazis. It was carried out very courageously, and some of my students at the Conservatory informed me of it in advance. The Nazis and fascists were very surprised by it. Before the war, Massimo Mila was imprisoned for his anti-fascist ideas. Gui kept a foot in each camp, and others demonstrated a certain rebelliousness. The *Wozzeck* episode at the Rome Opera in 1942 is indicative of the spirit of cultural independence and resistance to the fascists and the Germans.

HS: Was there a precise moment when the fraudulence of fascism became clear to you?

GP: We knew from the start that there was opposition to the regime, that there were anti-fascists in Paris, and that many people had protested against the Spanish civil war. But of course the news we received described all anti-fascists as criminals. With the beginning of the Second World War, however, anti-fascism began to grow stronger and more lively. I felt very torn, because I was friendly with many young anti-fascist painters with whom I argued about these things. I continued to have faith – very ingenuous and wavering – because I had taken seriously the oath that we had had to swear. But I lost my illusions when I realized that despite Mussolini's having said, once, that Italy had eight million bayonets, there were only 7,999,000.* It was then that I began to doubt – symbolically at first. I was lacerated for a long time, torn between the nationalistic idea of continuing to believe in certain values that were being swept away, and the gradual emergence of an ever more burning reality – a return to square one.

* 'Mussolini in October 1936 coined his famous phrase about having "eight million bayonets", but in 1939, after three further years of rearmament, Italy still did not have enough bayonets for the 1.3 million rifles which was all that the army could muster. These rifles, moreover, were of a design introduced as long ago as 1891, yet they were not to be replaced during the entire war.' Denis Mack Smith, *Mussolini's Roman Empire*, p. 172.

CHAPTER IV

Performers

The sad tale of Italian musicians' opportunistic reactions to fascism does not end with the country's composers. Performing musicians, too, did their best to ingratiate themselves with the regime. The story of their consensus is less important and therefore more quickly told than that of the composers, but their dossiers in Mussolini's office files are bursting, all the same, with letters of adulation, invitations to performances, pleas for help in obtaining jobs and requests for private audiences and autographed photographs. Launching a successful career as a performer is often extremely difficult, no matter what merits an individual may have, and among musicians the struggle to succeed sometimes emphasizes or even creates personality defects similar to those that mark many politicians: egomania, paranoia, ruthlessness and a need to occupy the limelight. Many performing artists and politicians need to be approved of and loved by masses of people, the value of whose collective reaction is never questioned.

Many celebrated opera singers were particularly susceptible to the Duce's posturing and self-aggrandisement; perhaps they saw him as an incarnation of the tenor-hero, *sans peur et sans reproche* – Siegfried and Radamès, Tamino and Manrico, in one individual. The act at Palazzo Venezia was indeed that of a masterly if overtly exhibitionistic performer who had an extraordinary capacity for convincing any audience that the role of the moment was a true expression of the player's own feelings.

No Italian opera star was more enthusiastic towards Mussolini than Beniamino Gigli, one of the greatest tenors of the century. Gigli's memoirs, published shortly before his death (1957), begin with the disarming admission that he was born with no special talents except his voice, and this statement is amply substantiated by his political behaviour. His attitude towards fascism and Nazism is treated gingerly in the book. About a meeting with Mussolini in 1925, for instance, Gigli says: 'He bombarded me with questions about the Metropolitan, the popularity of Italian opera in America, and the Italian hospital in New York. I found it easy to talk about such subjects; but if he had referred to politics, I would have been reduced to silence.'[1] He seems to have been quite proud of his encounters with Hitler and other high German officials. Following a concert Gigli gave in Berlin in 1933, 'Hitler shook hands with me and said that he loved Italian music'.[2] Two years later, 'Hitler came to my benefit concert for the winter assistance fund [. . .] and made me a gift of an autographed photo of himself'.[3] Although he was sufficiently politically aware to refuse to perform in Britain at the time of the anti-Italian sanctions imposed during the Ethiopian war, he later claimed political ignorance as an excuse for his numerous appearances in Nazi Germany. He sang for Göring and Ribbentrop at an Italian embassy function and continued to perform for Hitler, of whom he says: 'Our encounters [. . .] were extremely brief and formal to the point of stiffness. I knew nothing of his political activities' – this at a time when even the most apolitical musicians in Europe knew that every one of their German Jewish colleagues had either been chased out of Germany or had met with some other form of persecution – 'and I never had occasion to exchange anything but polite phrases with him.'[4] Gigli was delighted to have participated in a performance of *Aida* in Berlin with the Scala ensemble in 1937, which 'Hitler applauded tirelessly',[5] and to have sung for the Führer when he visited Rome the following year. The tenor admitted that despite his great professional admiration for Toscanini, he avoided working with him during the 1930s because the conductor's anti-fascist political sympathies 'were foreign to me, and I have never been able to understand how he let them control his life. For me', says Gigli, 'Italy was Italy, under any regime whatsoever.'[6]

But Gigli's attitude towards fascism was not so strictly a matter of formality as his post-war memoirs suggest. In his *Confidenze*, a book published at the height of the war, at least one paragraph could have been written by one of Mussolini's most trusted propagandists:

> [. . .] For some years now, thank God and thanks to the new Italian government, Italy has regained a splendid and powerful standing for all her children [. . .]. The same Italians who not more than thirty years ago were considered – in North America, for example – inferior even to the Chinese, have now leapt to the highest level of esteem throughout the world.[7]

The same year, Gigli sent a wire 'To His Excellency Benito Mussolini, Head of Government, Duce of Fascism', thanking him for 'the nomination as commissioner of the Confederation of Lyric Artists [, which] fills me with pride because it puts me more directly at the service of the Great Chief[.] I shall set aside every duty in order to carry out this appreciated job with ardently fascist faith and supremely Italian artistic spirit.'[8] And on 14 July 1943, ten days before the Grand Council of Fascism removed Mussolini from power, the beleaguered dictator received a heart-warming letter from the ever-enthusiastic Gigli:

DUCE!

With real joy and great satisfaction I have learned of the decision by which lyric artists will become part of the [Union of] Artists and Professionals.

I am sure that my joy and satisfaction will be shared by those who fall within this classification, [and] who are not the least important among those who hold our adored country's name high in Italy and abroad.

To you, Duce, we owe this intense satisfaction – to you who never overlook the encouragement and protection of everything that is beautiful and right.

On my own behalf and on behalf of the entire profession, thanks and boundless devotion.[9]

Giacomo Lauri Volpi, another celebrated tenor, matched Gigli in his dedication to Mussolini. In 1927 his friend Amilcare Roni, president of the National Veterans' Association, wrote to the Duce's secretary to request an autographed photo of Mussolini for the singer. According to Roni, Lauri Volpi was 'a former Infantry Captain who fought valorously throughout the [First World] War [. . .] and [who] has always been a militant member, pure of heart, of the Fascist rank-and-file'. He quotes Lauri Volpi's request: 'I have photographs of the King, Diaz, Badoglio and Caviglia, and am only lacking that of the Man I most admire – because he is Italy's Caesar and Napoleon, of whom we dreamt in 1915 when we raced to the front, and who today is awakening the miracles [sic], the admiration and the envy of the whole world.'[10]

This flattery did not spare Lauri Volpi the criticism of the fascist press for his egomaniacal professional demands, which were listed in a 1931 report: net fee of 20,000 lire per performance; exemption from all taxes; only famous colleagues as co-performers, with his name featured above theirs on large posters and in press advertisements; freedom to 'interpret in his own way'; permission to do dress rehearsals in his street clothes; right to five days' sick-leave; publication of his photo in all local newspapers; 1,000 lire-worth of tickets for each performance, including a prime seat for his wife; and an option to choose the operas in which he would make his first and last appearances of the season.[11] These requirements were extraordinary even by the standards of a profession in which high-handed behaviour is common.

Mussolini received Lauri Volpi in 1930 and 1939 and probably on other occasions, and the tenor regularly sent him obsequious notes and copies of embarrassing works of fiction that he had authored. He and his wealthy Spanish wife lived in Valencia and were extremely grateful to the Duce for his support of General Franco's faction in the Spanish civil war. Through Mussolini they donated 30,000 lire in support of fascist cells abroad. In their favour, they also gave a considerable amount of money to Italian charities – but always by sending cheques to Mussolini, ostensibly to let him decide which charities were most meritorious, but more likely to make sure he knew how generous they were.[12]

Two other great tenors of the time also have dossiers in Mussolini's files. Tito Schipa was friendly enough with party secretary Starace to use the familiar *tu* form with him, and he repeatedly and often successfully requested audiences with the Duce. But he ruined his record during the Second World War: in applying for permission to give concerts in Spain and Portugal, he forged the signature of an Italian friend in Valencia (not Lauri Volpi) on a guarantee that Italy would receive its fair share of revenue on Schipa's foreign earnings. When questioned by the Minister of Exchange and Currency, Schipa admitted the fraud and was not prosecuted.[13] The other tenor, Aureliano Pertile, was one of the select core of artists who worked regularly with Toscanini at La Scala. He waited until 1932, when it was clear that the Maestro would not be returning to the theatre, to ask Starace to

> intercede with the Duce so that he will allow me the great honour of a conversation with him. I have been singing in all the world's theatres for twenty years, carrying out an impassioned labour of Italian-ness. [...] As a fervent fascist, I would consider it a prize for my long efforts to be able to pay my devout respects to the Chief, so beloved of all Italians. [...] Fascist greetings.[14]

The case of Riccardo Stracciari is more pathetic. He was one of the most successful Italian baritones of the first three decades of the century – still in his prime when he joined the Fascist Party early in 1921, a year and a half before the march on Rome. Like so many singers, Stracciari failed in his salad days to provide for his years of vocal decline, which came upon him sooner than he had anticipated. Beginning in 1932, he, his wife and various friends bombarded Mussolini with complaints about the cold treatment he was 'inexplicably' receiving at theatres where he had formerly been a welcome guest. Inquiries were made by the Duce's office, but both La Scala and the Rome Opera stated that their forthcoming seasons were 'already planned' – which, in theatre language, means that the person in question is not wanted. Undaunted, Maria Stracciari continued to hound Mussolini's chief secretary, who finally ordered the prefect of Imperia, where the singer lived, to tell the angry lady that the Duce's office could not intervene in her husband's case.[15]

Each year the onslaught was renewed, with similar results. In December 1934, for instance, Mussolini's office chief replied to a plea from Azalea Mazzoni, a friend of the Stracciaris':

> His Excellency the Head of Government, and His Office acting for Him, abstains, for understandable reasons, from making recommendations on behalf of artists or works of art. Out of special regard, [this office] has nevertheless not failed to take an interest, repeatedly, in Grand Officer Riccardo Stracciari, by making his desires known to the proper organizations. As things stand, however, I do not envisage a possibility of repeating such treatment [...].[16]

In 1936, Signora Stracciari again appealed to Mussolini: her husband was gravely ill and they had no money to cover his medical expenses. The Duce granted the necessary funds; Stracciari recovered, sang occasionally until 1942, and died in 1955.

The soprano Toti Dal Monte, a leading star at La Scala, the Metropolitan and Covent Garden during the 1920s and 1930s, seems to have had a more frivolous attitude towards fascism than the enthusiastic Gigli, Lauri Volpi and Stracciari. She dealt with Mussolini as she would have treated a theatre impresario in whose good graces she wished to remain. Her dossier in the Duce's files consists largely of memoranda regarding flowers she sent to the dictator's wife and wedding gifts for his children. A note from Mussolini's office chief to his boss two days after the Duce had received the singer in a private audience (January 1937) shows that her efforts did not always pay: 'Signora Toti Dal Monte has asked whether news of the welcome given her by the DUCE – from which she is still in an emotionally-charged state – will be given to the press.' Mussolini's reply: 'Too late – it doesn't seem appropriate.'[17] Five years later, while Mussolini was presumably worrying about Allied advances in North Africa, 'la Toti' asked him to intervene with the Scala administration in getting her the role of Norina in a forthcoming production of *Don Pasquale*, since the soprano originally chosen for the part was pregnant. The Duce referred the matter to De Pirro. In her memoirs (1960), Dal Monte mentions with unconcealed pride that Mussolini and Hitler occasionally attended her performances during the 1930s, and that the two leaders greatly appreciated her work.

Titta Ruffo, the great Pisan baritone, wrote his autobiography in 1937, at the age of sixty. *La mia parabola* is an uncommonly interesting book in its genre, but it ends, with no explanation, in June 1924, when Ruffo was at the height of his career; the reason for the abrupt stop was political. In June 1924 the Socialist Party secretary, Giacomo Matteotti, who had been speaking in the Chamber of Deputies against fascism's totalitarian objectives, was kidnapped and murdered. The episode shook millions of Italians, and personally affected Ruffo, whose sister, Velia, was Matteotti's wife. The singer, whose anti-fascist beliefs were already common knowledge, virtually stopped performing in Italy. In 1926 he was accused – incorrectly, in his son's view – of financing anti-fascist, anti-monarchical publications abroad.[18] Politically inspired vandals destroyed a plaque honouring Ruffo in Pisa's opera house, and the Milanese branch of the Corporation of Entertainment violently condemned his alleged anti-fascist activities. Foreign Minister Dino Grandi, acting on a suggestion from the Corporation's secretary-general, had the singer's passport confiscated.[19] The document was soon given back; once abroad, however, Ruffo found that his performances were frequently interrupted by fascist sympathizers.

Ruffo's son, who summarized the baritone's declining years in a 1977 addendum to *La mia parabola*, has described a particularly nasty incident in Marseilles, where Ruffo was to sing in *The Barber of Seville* in February 1931.

> Papà was not intimidated [...] by the anonymous epistolary and telephoned threats [...], by the punches and slaps he received at the door to the theatre as he was entering to make ready for the performance, or by the traitorous behaviour of the impresario, who was in on the plot. Once he had put on his make-up and combed his hair in such a way as to hide his painful head contusions, he went before the public all the same. He was greeted by the shouts and insults of *agents provocateurs*, which were answered in kind by the numerous [anti-fascist Italian] exiles present in the house; but notwithstanding the easily imaginable uproar that had been unleashed to still his voice, he honoured his contract and finished the performance [...].[20]

Intimidation continued even after Ruffo's retirement from the stage:

> On the morning of 16 October 1937, two policemen came to get him at his home in Rome, where he had gone to visit his family. [Ruffo was then living in France.] They took away his passport and [...] delivered him over to Regina Coeli prison. There he was photographed and fingerprinted for the police records; his money, cufflinks, collar-button, suspenders and shoelaces were confiscated, and he was placed in a cell.[21]

The arrest had been ordered by Mussolini, mainly on information volunteered by the impresario Walter Mocchi, whose testimony was transcribed by the political police.

> I have known the baritone Titta Ruffo for many years, as he was under contract with me [...] at Buenos Aires's Teatro Colón and at other theatres belonging to me. On the afternoon of [October] 7th, I was going to Rome on the express train from Livorno [...].
>
> [...] I saw Titta Ruffo in the corridor. [...] I mentioned to him that a cinematographic society was being created under the presidency of Vittorio Mussolini [the Duce's son], who intended to produce films of operas. I further specified that these productions would begin with Rigoletto, and I therefore told him that it was the right moment for him to step forward again. [n.b.: Rigoletto had been one of Ruffo's most celebrated roles.]
>
> He told me that he had already received an invitation in this regard from people in Florence who are involved in the Society, to which he had responded with a definite refusal – first, because he no longer wanted to sing, and secondly and principally because he did not want to have any contact at all with people with whom he was irreconcilable. This circumstance made it easy for Titta Ruffo to show his political feelings of unadulterated aversion towards the Regime – [feelings] already known to me as a result of having had an argument of a political nature with him years ago [...].
>
> I thought I ought to point out to Titta Ruffo all the innumerable works carried

out by the Regime, the pre-eminent position that the Fascist Government has given Italy in the world, and [. . .] the moral and physical education now being imparted to fascist youth. At that point, Titta flew into a temper, stigmatizing [. . .] the education of young people; and I can cite the words he spoke: that these young people are being educated as cannon fodder, to be servile, with no sense of dignity, etc., etc. When I mentioned that young people brought up in this way had in seven months avenged the shame of Adowa [Italy's Ethiopian defeat in 1896], he abruptly interrupted the conversation and we left each other with barely a goodbye.[22]

Word of Ruffo's arrest caused a minor stir in the international press, as a result of which he was released after three days' imprisonment. His passport, however, was not returned to him, and he was forced to remain in Italy, where he spent the war years in failing health. Among major Italian singers of the period, he was the only one to refuse to have any truck with fascism.

Conductors reacted to Mussolini less exuberantly than singers, for the most part, but they were not great protesters. Victor De Sabata, the best-known Italian conductor of the day, Toscanini excepted, was by all accounts a man of no political sophistication whatsoever. As La Scala's principal conductor following Toscanini's departure, De Sabata often conducted for visiting fascist and Nazi dignitaries. He toured Nazi Germany, appearing with Italian and native ensembles, and conducted at the 1939 Bayreuth Festival. Mussolini's office kept a dossier on him, but the only item of even minor significance in it is an effusive letter (November 1932) in which De Sabata thanked the Duce for having sent him an autographed photo ('allow me to express the great emotion that your gesture arouses in me, Excellency') and offered his 'profound devotion'.[23]

Bernardino Molinari, who conducted Rome's Augusteum Orchestra with great competence and success from 1912 to 1943, was a more enthusiastic fascist than De Sabata. Mussolini must have enjoyed Molinari's company, because he always granted him an audience when the latter requested one. As principal conductor of the capital's most important orchestra, Molinari must also have met Mussolini often at official receptions. His letters to the Duce and his staff demonstrate that he was mainly interested in recounting his accomplishments – with the excuse, naturally, that they brought glory upon Italy. On 18 April 1930, for example, Molinari invited Mussolini to attend his forthcoming performance of the Verdi *Requiem* at the Augusteum and asked him to 'grant me a brief audience, as I wish to inform you of my artistic activities and of plans for the future in regard to Italian propaganda'.[24] Six weeks later, on returning from an American tour, Molinari wrote to complain that the Italian ambassador had not attended his Washington concert, whereas the German ambassador always attended German artists' concerts.

Molinari also asked for and received an autographed photo of the Duce which, as he wrote (1937?), 'fills my soul with profound emotion. [. . .] Your image will accompany me everywhere as my dearest memento and most precious talisman, and I shall be proud to show it, even in the most distant countries, to all the admirers of the new Italy created by Your Excellency's faith and work.'[25]

Gino Marinuzzi conducted the opening performance of Boito's *Nerone* at the newly nationalized Rome Opera in 1928, and was active at that house, elsewhere in Italy and abroad – including Nazi Germany – throughout the fascist period. Like Molinari, he often asked to speak with Mussolini, to give him autographed copies of his compositions, and to tell him of his activities. In May 1936, for instance, as the Ethiopian war was drawing to a close, Marinuzzi wrote: 'Excellency, the immense desire to hear again in person that voice which, from last October [declaration of war] to today has made us tremble with holy pride, filling us with reawakened energy and giving us the certainty of triumphal and totalitarian [sic] Victory, prods me to ask you to receive me for a few seconds.' The request was granted.[26] Marinuzzi had qualms about the establishment and operational methods of the various theatre corporations, consortia and inspectorates, but he does not seem to have mentioned them to Mussolini or to anyone else in power.

Although the Duce's motives are not clear, he was in some way involved in the process of taking the principal conductorship of the Rome Opera from Marinuzzi and giving it to Tullio Serafin in 1934. Serafin, who had thirty years' professional experience behind him, was a hard-working, thoroughly knowledgeable, reliable artisan; he had previously been principal conductor at La Scala, the Colón of Buenos Aires and the Metropolitan Opera in New York. Mussolini had first invited Serafin to take the Rome position in 1926, when the Teatro Reale dell'Opera was just in the planning stages, but Serafin, happy with his position at the Metropolitan, had turned the offer down.[27] Four years later, Mussolini summoned him to a private meeting in Rome to repeat the offer.[28] In a letter from New York nine months later, Serafin reminded the Duce that at their meeting 'I undertook to write to Your Excellency before signing a new contract at the Metropolitan. The administration of this theatre, with which I am under contract until May 1932, is asking me to commit myself further, allowing me the option of determining the length of my new contract.' He said that 'the problem of the reconstruction of the Lyric Theatre [. . .] about which Your Excellency wished to question me' was too complicated to discuss by letter, and suggested a further meeting. 'I'll await him in Rome', noted Mussolini on the letter.[29]

Serafin was still hesitant about leaving the Met and must have asked the company's general manager, Giulio Gatti Casazza, to make representations on his behalf. On 30 April 1931 Gatti wrote to the Italian ambassador in

Washington, Giacomo De Martino, stating his fear that the Italian government and the City of Rome 'intend to induce Maestro Tullio Serafin to leave the Metropolitan, in order to dedicate his activity to the Royal Theatre in Rome, beginning with the 1932–33 season'. Gatti suggested that De Martino tell the Duce that this would be a great loss to the cause of Italian opera at the Met. He pointed out that Serafin's position was equal to that of Artur Bodanzky, who was in charge of German repertoire, and that it would be difficult to find another Italian conductor of equal prestige to balance that of Bodanzky.[30] The Met's principal patron, Otto Kahn, presented the case in the same light directly to Mussolini, whom he greatly admired, and the Duce once again backed down. But, as Serafin later reported, '[. . .] at his third "assault" I had to give in; and so it was announced at a press conference on 28 July 1934 that Tullio Serafin had been named artistic director and principal conductor of the Royal Opera Theatre. Gatti Casazza telephoned in alarm from New York, but I had to confirm that I could no longer leave my country.'[31]

In 1936, Serafin became national conductors' representative to the musicians' union; but his contacts with Mussolini and other leading fascists appear to have remained limited to ceremonial occasions. There are no obsequious or self-seeking letters from him in the dossier Mussolini kept. He never joined the party – an omission that did not pass unnoticed by job-hunters who had become party members in order to further their careers. The cabinet chief of the MinCulPop silenced criticism by saying: 'That Maestro Serafin is not furnished with a party card [. . .] is superfluous. Serafin is at the Royal [Opera Theatre] by the explicit desire of the Duce, who gave peremptory instructions [. . .] to resolve every difficulty in order to encourage the Maestro to stay on [. . .].'[32] According to people who knew him, Serafin privately expressed anti-fascist and anti-monarchic opinions, and he was commonly thought to have been a Freemason, which was officially condemned by fascism. But he made no public statements and was left in peace.

Although Vittorio Gui had the distinction of being the only musician to have signed Croce's manifesto of anti-fascist intellectuals, he had been allowed to found and conduct the Florentine orchestra and to play an important part in the Maggio Musicale. According to Leonardo Pinzauti's history of the festival, Gui was persecuted by Florentine fascists who were aware of his opinions. He continued to work freely, however, and eventually met Mussolini, who could not take his eyes off all the conductor's First World War medals.[33] Gui conducted in Hitler's Germany and did not hesitate to replace Toscanini at the Salzburg festival when the older conductor withdrew in protest over the Nazi takeover of Austria in 1938. Gui's peccadillo of thirteen years earlier had obviously been forgiven.

Among major Italian instrumentalists, Enrico Mainardi seems to have been the most eager to ingratiate himself with the regime. He was one of the best-known cellists of his generation; he often appeared in duos with such pianists as Wilhelm Backhaus, Ernö Dohnányi, Edwin Fischer and Carlo Zecchi, and he recorded Strauss's *Don Quixote* under the composer's baton. When, in 1932, he was told that he would have to give up his Italian citizenship in order to maintain his important teaching position in Germany, Mussolini intervened to establish a master class in cello for him at the Santa Cecilia Academy in Rome.

As Nicolodi has pointed out, the Duce's gesture was not a private favour to Mainardi. Mussolini was simply making one of his periodic and not very well-concerted attempts to 'reinforce national culture by bringing together the best [native] artistic energies.'[34] Mainardi, however, chose to interpret Mussolini's interest as a personal compliment, and he occasionally thereafter sent the Duce some rather choice words of self-praise. 'I take the liberty of allowing myself to give you this news about myself', he said towards the end of one such letter (3 July 1934), 'in order that you, Excellency, take it – as I fervently hope – as proof of my iron will to keep the promise I made you as an Italian, a fascist and an artist, in the surge of emotional recognition for your great goodness towards me.'[35] On the eve of the Second World War Mainardi took the trouble to wire Mussolini from Berlin: 'I have the honour of informing you that the German Minister of Education has given me a cello master class at the Berlin State Academy[.] With ever grateful and devout spirit[,] Enrico Mainardi.'[36]

Like their counterparts among the composers, most Italian performers of the period played Mussolini's game. He used their reputations to glorify fascist Italy; they used or tried to use the regime to increase their stocks of laurel wreaths and material benefits. The True Believers among them were politically ignorant, the know-nothings frivolous, and the cynics, if there were any, appear contemptible. Hannah Arendt's phrase about the banality of evil is too good for any of them: theirs was the banality of opportunism – the terrain on which evil grows.

*   *   *

The conductor Gianandrea Gavazzeni was born in Bergamo on 27 July 1909, and studied at the Santa Cecilia and Milan conservatories. He began his career as a pianist, opera répétiteur and composer. Several of his compositions achieved considerable success in Italy, but he stopped writing music at the age of forty and forbade further performances of his works. His conducting career got underway in the mid-1930s, since which time Gavazzeni has worked with virtually every major Italian operatic and instrumental ensemble and many foreign ones, including the Vienna State Opera, the Metropolitan Opera, the San Francisco Opera, and the Bolshoi. He was artistic director of La Scala from 1965 to 1968. He has published books on Donizetti, Pizzetti (who was his principal teacher) and Mussorgsky, a series of diary excerpts and other autobiographical works, a great deal of musical and literary criticism, and a vast number of articles on a wide variety of subjects.

HARVEY SACHS: How many of the musicians you knew during the fascist period were really anti-fascists?

GIANANDREA GAVAZZENI: Massimo Mila was actively anti-fascist. He was condemned by the Special Tribunal, went to prison, and later participated in the partisan war. There were others, but I knew only Riccardo Malipiero, whom I often saw during his time as a partisan. Vittorio Gui was of notoriously anti-fascist opinions.

HS: But this certainly doesn't mean that all the others supported the regime.

GG: Decidedly not. The situation is very difficult not only to judge but even to analyse, and not only regarding music but for culture in general. Arnoldo Mondadori, the publisher, said that at the time of the big European success of Erich Maria Remarque's *All Quiet on the Western Front*, he immediately had an Italian translation printed. When the edition was ready, however, in an excess of zeal he went to Mussolini to ask whether he could put it on the market. Mussolini replied, 'If you hadn't asked me, the book could have gone into circulation. Since you've come and asked me, my answer is No.' This episode may tell us something about cultural life at that time.

HS: At least until the Italo-German alliance began to force the fascists' hands.

GG: Even then, however, we find certain anomalies, as in the case of the famous Italian première of *Wozzeck*, which took place in Rome in 1942, at the height of the war, at the height of the 'Axis', and at a time when the music of Berg and of the other composers of the 'Viennese School' was banned in the Reich. But right from the beginning, when Giovanni Gentile, Minister of Education under Mussolini and philosopher of the regime, initiated the *Enciclopedia Treccani*, he put many anti-fascist men of culture to work on it – men who could not teach because they had not sworn fidelity to the regime, as was obligatory in their profession. Even when Gentile received orders to put only fascist party members to work, he refused to obey. The music critic Gastone Rossi-Doria, a well-known anti-fascist, always worked for Gentile as a music editor of the encyclopaedia, which was his sole means of survival.

HS: But Rossi-Doria also contributed to the *Rassegna musicale* and was later a member of the Italian Institute of Music History. I don't understand how such things were possible while musicians who truly supported the regime held so much power. I'm thinking of the usual names – Toni, Lualdi, Mulè – that keep reappearing in all the documents of the period.

GG: There was certainly favouritism: this group of musicians, decidedly well placed in the regime, had advantages that they would perhaps not have had if a liberal–democratic government had continued in power. But this doesn't mean that they were able to reduce others to silence. Differences were debated freely.

HS: How were these three able to become so solidly entrenched?

GG: It came about partly as a result of their already existing musical and cultural tendencies, of their narrowness in regard to what was happening in the rest of Europe, and of their provincialism. The most open among them was Lualdi. He was undoubtedly intelligent, cultured – he was also a writer – and he could have succeeded as a musician even without fascism had he maintained a dialogue with other tendencies and cultures. With the regime, however, he saw a possibility of assuming a different kind of importance.

HS: Because the regime encouraged provincialism?

GG: Yes; but there were also psychological factors transcending the political ones. It is typical of composers to feel that they are not valued highly enough, that they are misunderstood; and Lualdi, Toni and Mulè sensed a lack of esteem on the part of the whole other side of their musical world . . .

HS: You mean Casella, Malipiero, and so on . . .

GG: Yes, the up-to-date people who were open to what was happening in Europe and the rest of the world. And so they developed these attitudes, which also derived from their temperaments. They hardened their positions and took advantage of the general political climate of the regime.

HS: Toni was critic of Il *popolo d'Italia* as well as a composer.

GG: His temperament was highly inflammable – typical of people from the Romagna. He was basically a good man but rather provincial, and he certainly was a fascist in the truest sense of the word.

HS: And Mulè?

GG: As a composer, Mulè was part of the post-*verismo* current – the residue that followed *verismo*'s lucky period – with that smidgen of impressionism translated catch-as-catch-can into Italian or into dialect (for Mulè was Sicilian, and his music had a strong Sicilian ethnophonic and even folkloristic component). But he was always an upright, good, and competent person who never assumed factional attitudes. And he certainly wasn't lacking in either talent or likeableness.

HS: I have the impression that Lualdi, on the other hand, was more overbearing.

GG: Yes, somewhat, as I myself once discovered. In Bergamo, we used to publish a little literary–artistic journal in which I had attacked the programme of the 1932 Venice festival, saying it contained the names of too many reactionary musicians. I was twenty-three at the time and, like all young people, quite an avant-gardist. Lualdi sent a controversial letter to the journal in which he denied the accusation and attacked me. When the festival opened, Corrado Pavolini and Gian Battista Angioletti* gave me the job of writing articles about it for *Italia letteraria*. On arriving in Venice, I went to the festival office to pick up my pass. Lualdi's secretary said, 'Oh, but you're no longer the correspondent for *Italia letteraria.*'

'What do you mean I'm not? The editor has given me the job.'

'Oh no,' she said, 'Maestro Lualdi, who is president of the board of the magazine, has sent a telegram to the editor saying that he doesn't want you to be the correspondent.'

'All right,' I said, 'I'll buy my own tickets and send the articles anyway, because I've been asked by the editor to do the report.' In fact, Pavolini had wired the office in the meantime saying, 'I am unaware that Lualdi has editorial responsibilities.' And so I wrote my articles.

HS: Various tendencies, however, coexisted within the Venice festival, just as they did at Florence's Maggio Musicale and elsewhere.

GG: Certainly. Lualdi, Casella and Labroca all worked to organize the Venice festival, although the last two followed the opposite line to Lualdi's in regard to musicians and works to be programmed. Casella was not an anti-fascist, but he supported musicians of pan-European tendencies and was himself a follower of a pan-European culture that was the complete opposite of the provincial or governmental culture followed by the Lualdis, Tonis and Mulès.

HS: You knew Casella well . . .

GG: He was on the judging commission for piano when I took my confirming examination at the Musical High School of Santa Cecilia in Rome. We later became very good friends. He was a man of exceptional generosity and culture – a true teacher.

HS: For many years, however, he supported many of the lines proposed by the regime. He was very much involved in many of the music education committees that the regime invented, and in that sense he was close to the fascists.

GG: Yes, in that sense he was; but his whole culture and all his work were absolutely European. And in fact he was attacked by Lualdi and Toni, though not by Mulè.† Do you want to know in what way Casella was a fascist? Simply that he wasn't an active anti-fascist. Above all, he was fundamentally uninterested in politics. I don't believe that anyone ever had interesting political conversations with him: he existed outside that dimension and apart from historical or political culture.

HS: One could also say that about many performing musicians of that period.

GG: Look at De Sabata, for instance: he never had anything to do with political

* Corrado Pavolini was a Florentine writer, playwright and stage director; Gian Battista Angioletti was a Milanese novelist and essayist.
† But in 1932 Mulè was one of the signatories of Toni's manifesto, which was an indirect attack on Casella and Malipiero (see Chapter One).

ideas. I knew him very well – I was devoted to him. He was so possessed by his musical demon that nothing else existed. He lived in his circumscribed, stupendous world, born of his exceptional musical nature. Talking about politics with De Sabata would have been impossible.

HS: He even conducted in Germany during the war, and for several Fascist and Nazi party officials in Italy.

GG: Yes, he once conducted for some German cabinet minister or other who had come to La Scala with Mussolini – because he was the most important conductor in Italy at the time. To refuse would not only have been an open act of hostility: it never would have entered his mind. It would have been futile to ask him who Mussolini, Göring and Göbbels really were or what they did. He was completely out of this world, in that sense. Even Toscanini, whose opposition to the regime was fully justified, was not basically a person with whom one could have a concrete political discussion. He had his moral standards – sometimes very just but other times not so just. I remember him getting very angry, in private, with Adolf Busch for having remarried after the death of his first wife. He used to say that a man could have many mistresses but only one wife. He had had great affection for the first Mrs Busch and had felt very close to her – and he couldn't tolerate the idea of a second one. These are things that in a certain sense constitute part of a person's greatness – these negative limitations, this blindness towards the continuously changing reality of individual lives, of a society, of a culture. That may be why they were so great – De Sabata with his characteristics, Toscanini with his: they didn't understand life or reality. We who are infinitely smaller can, on the other hand, keep one eye on reality, on what goes on around us.

HS: Another conductor who was somewhat compromised by fascism was Bernardino Molinari.

GG: Molinari was a man of very great merit. Italian symphonic life was given its greatest forward impulse by the Augusteum, which he governed and guided dictatorially. He was a musician and conductor of many virtues, an orchestra builder; and he introduced a great deal of modern music to Rome, from Stravinsky onwards. Even the music that he himself didn't feel able to conduct he had other conductors perform. I remember a performance of Schoenberg's *Verklärte Nacht* – I don't remember who was conducting – that was greeted with a public uproar – some people applauding, others hissing, still others shouting.

HS: Did Molinari believe in fascism?

GG: Oh yes, he was a believer. In fact, I remember an evening in Milan, when he had come to conduct a concert at La Scala in memory of Respighi. My father and I had known him for years, since the period when we had lived in Rome, and he and his wife came to dinner at our home. Molinari and my father had a brief political set-to that my father then let drop, because he understood that it was useless to argue – that this was a man who understood music but nothing at all of other realities.

HS: Maestro, your father was a well-known anti-fascist.

GG: Yes, he was actually a militant anti-fascist, and he had had great problems in the 1920s. But I remember that in 1932, when we weren't yet thinking about [the imminence of] a future war or about what was going to happen to the world, he told me, 'Look, who knows when fascism will end. You have to live and work in this environment. Become a party member, because if you don't, you may see the last jackass overtake you.' And in fact, I became a party member in 1932. But I never, not even once, set foot in my local party headquarters or took part in a public demonstration. In any case, we young musicians couldn't have cared less, for the most part. We reacted with indifference to the regime. There were a few conservatory students who took part in the so-called GUF – Fascist University Group – but all the rest of us were indifferent. The Milanese fascist group to which I belonged had the words 'permanently unavailable' written on my file: I was never available to do anything.

HS: Did you ever have political difficulties, apart from the Lualdi incident?

GG: Look, I never took a heroic stand, but I did take a rather free one. When, for example, the Germans made provisions against Jewish musicians and against the German avant-garde, I wrote a very tough article that *Italia letteraria* published on its front page – and no one criticized me for it. When a group of reactionary, fascist musicians mounted a campaign against what they called the international Bolshevist tendencies of Malipiero, Casella and others, I wrote a series of articles for the *Meridiano di Roma*, whose editor-in-chief was Massimo Bontempelli. There were other dissenting voices, and the debate took place freely. Then, at an international music congress held in Florence, I gave a lecture on the musician's status in those years. My speech displeased Ugo Ojetti, the president of the congress – a man of noteworthy culture and intelligence who, however, had given his full support to fascism. I had defended the isolation and aristocracy of the modern composer in the face of the directives about art for the masses, art for the people – in the rhetorical sense of 'people' – that the regime had indicated as the goal of all artists. Ojetti was irritated and told his colleagues that my lecture should have been read in advance, because, he said, it was an anti-fascist lecture. But, as I said, I never took a 'heroic' stand. It wasn't my nature.

HS: Do you know anything about the money given by the MinCulPop to various artists, musicians, men of letters and others? It was clearly a way of endearing the regime to many people . . .

GG: It was a pay-off fund, a sort of welfare payment, and also a small corrupting influence, by means of which the regime created a certain attitude of benevolence towards itself. Among the people who received these pay-offs was Vincenzo Cardarelli, one of Italy's twentieth-century poets – a writer who was important in certain movements such as the *Ronda*, which produced one of the first neoclassical literary journals.* He had gone hungry all his life, so the regime handed him a few little pay-offs. Not that Cardarelli interested the regime as . . .

HS: . . . as someone who could have given fascism some positive publicity?

GG: Exactly: it wasn't for that, but in order to create, as I said, a feeling of benevolence, perhaps even of a passive nature, towards the government, and a base of consensus in the literary and cultural field.

HS: But there were also famous people: among musicians, Mascagni was the one who was given the most; and then there was Barilli, too . . .

GG: Barilli was never a fascist, but he, too, had starved all his life. He never had a home – he always lived in furnished rooms or miserable boarding houses.

HS: But Mascagni? How could he have allowed himself to accept public funds?

GG: Because he, too, despite all that he had earned, had a family and a rather disorderly way of life. He always needed money. But above all, he took the money as a subsidy for the performance of his operas, which he then conducted. In this case, the money was given for specific work.

HS: This, to me, is an important aspect of Mussolini's neo-imperialism. It's a little reminiscent of ancient Rome's important personages, including the Senate: under the first emperors, they could have rebelled and tried to replace despotism with some other system; but it was too easy for them to stand in the imperial sunshine and not do anything, not have to make decisions.

GG: This is typical of all absolute regimes, don't you think? There are always those who are neither for nor against but who stand around, just trying to live.

HS: In the newspapers and journals of the time, there are many government provisions regarding music, especially proposals for musical education. Almost all of them are reasonable and interesting, but nothing much seems ever to have come of them.

GG: Just as in the post-war period! How many study sessions have been held, how many plans have been drawn up in these last forty years! There have been musicians concerned with pedagogy who have examined the problem thoroughly, and the Ministry of Public Education has promoted committees and commissions. And nothing has yet been done – or, at best, only absolutely insufficient measures have been undertaken.

HS: So you're saying that if we look at today's schools, we can see more or less how . . .

GG: . . . how they functioned in those days. Absolutely. There was, for instance, a certain Maestro [Achille] Schinelli who tried to do a lot for choral singing in

* La *Ronda* was a Roman literary monthly published from 1919 to 1923; its contributors were for the most part opposed to both D'Annunzian ultra-romanticism and contemporary experimentalism.

the schools. He had children singing, as in Germany and the Anglo-Saxon countries, not just ditties, but the classics of polyphony. He ought to have been able to go far, because he was a man of high official standing, very much aware of the workings of the Ministry. Yet he hardly got anywhere, despite having dedicated much of his life to the problem.

HS: Every month, new directives about conservatory curricula were published, and very often a new one would cancel one from the previous month. It sometimes seems schizophrenic.

GG: We can still say, however, that the conservatories functioned better then than now – partly, of course, because the number of students was much lower. In those days, few conservatories existed, and only in regional or provincial capitals; but even the civic music schools, which didn't have equal standing with the conservatories, were productive! In recent years, new conservatories have sprung up everywhere, but look at the training of orchestra musicians. There is a crisis situation in Italy regarding string players, for example, and you can hear that in the quality of our orchestras. Today, as a result of the utopian idea of generalized culture, many obligatory complementary subjects have been introduced into the curriculum, and these impede young people – especially those who play string instruments – from having sufficient practice time. Real violinists, violists and cellists are formed between the ages of ten and fifteen; those who aren't formed at that age are never formed at all. Fifty years ago, musicians who had the ability and desire to develop their general culture did so on their own. The important thing, however, was to produce capable instrumentalists.*

HS: Did the regime allow much freedom of action to conservatory directors, or did they have to take seriously the constant succession of directives issuing from Rome?

GG: There was a great deal of autonomy on the directors' part. Those who had the personality to express their autonomy also had freedom of action. Pizzetti, for instance, was a great director of the Milan Conservatory. He didn't spend a lot of time there, but those three hours a day that he did spend really counted. The same for Mulè in Rome, Cilea in Naples, and Lodovico Rocca, whose career as a composer was completely sacrificed to the Turin Conservatory.

HS: You were saying that Italian orchestras were better at that time . . .

GG: Just think of the Augusteum Orchestra in Molinari's day: it was at top European level; it could go on tour anywhere, as could the Scala Orchestra – the one that Toscanini took on the great North American tour [of 1920–1] and that then became the orchestra of the Ente Autonomo. Bologna! The Bologna strings were famous!

HS: And the musical 'corporations'?

* But see Forino's complaint (1930), very similar to Gavazzeni's, in Chapter Two.

GG: That was entirely a castle in the air. It led to nothing concrete. Despite having lived through that period, I never understood what 'incorporation' consisted of for musicians. It was of use to Lualdi and Mulè for becoming representatives in the Chamber of Corporations. The musicians' union, which existed before the corporations, carried out few practical acts: it set up an embryonic mutual welfare fund – the beginning of social insurance – which was then developed after the war. But apart from this, the organization of concerts by contemporary composers was also useful. You have only to think of the early activities of young musicians like Petrassi, Dallapiccola and Salviucci.*

HS: Maestro, you were thirteen years old when Mussolini came to power and thirty-six at the end of the war. What is your overall judgment, today, of that period in Italian musical life?

GG: It may be a weakness owing to age or an experience drawn not only from music but also from what happens in me, in my family life and in the outside world: I refuse more and more to pass judgment on men and on things. I shall never come to the point of saying that everything happens because it must happen, for clearly certain things could have gone differently – but always *if* this had happened and *if* something else had not. But reality consists in the things that do happen. As to the musicians who wrote favour-seeking letters: do you think there aren't artists and men of culture today who haven't written to [President Sandro] Pertini or [Prime Minister Bettino] Craxi?

---

* Giovanni Salviucci, one of the most promising composers of his generation, died in 1937 at the age of thirty.

CHAPTER V

Foreigners, Alliances, Racism and War

Marguerite Yourcenar has written of 'the hollow reality hidden behind fascism's bloated façade' – a façade that fooled those foreign writers who allowed themselves 'to be enchanted once again by the traditional, picturesque Italian, or who rejoiced at seeing the trains run on time (at least in theory), without dreaming of asking themselves towards which station the trains were running'.[1]

Many foreign artists who visited fascist Italy came away with a superficially rosy view of the country's political orientation, and their impression was strengthened by the regime's apparent benevolence towards foreign artistic currents. For although the fascist movement was ultra-nationalistic, and although the xenophobic and racist elements at its outer extremes were always tolerated and sometimes encouraged, the official attitude of Mussolini's government towards art from beyond its borders was initially highly tolerant. The most progressive Italian musicians of the day complained about the small amount of major new foreign music presented to the public, but that problem was by no means limited to Italy, nor was it politically induced. Works by virtually every foreign composer of repute, performed by virtually every well-known foreign artist, were heard in Italian cities throughout the first decade of fascist rule and well into the second. A list of foreign musicians who performed at the Teatro di Torino (Turin) between 1925 and 1930 – many of whom offered contemporary music from their countries – includes the conductors Richard Strauss, Rhené-Baton, Hermann Scherchen and Ernest Ansermet; the pianists Egon Petri, Alfred Cortot, Artur Rubinstein, Rudolf Serkin, Wilhelm Backhaus, Harold Bauer and Sergei Prokofiev; the violinists Jacques Thibaud, Georges Enesco, Adolf Busch, Bronisław Huberman, Jascha Heifetz and Fritz Kreisler; the Fisk Jubilee Singers (a black American choral group) and the Russian State Chorus; the Lener Quartet from Hungary and the Pro Arte Quartet from Belgium; cellist Pablo Casals, harpsichordist Wanda Landowska, guitarist Andrés Segovia, and bass Paul Robeson. Eleven nations are represented on the list – including the Soviet

Union, the fascists' *bête-noire* – as are numerous Jews, who were later to be excluded from Italian musical life, blacks, and one future opponent of fascism, Casals.[2] In Rome, the Augusteum's concerts between 1923 and 1933 included many of the musicians just mentioned, as well as the conductors Leopold Stokowski, Igor Stravinsky, Désiré Défauw, Pierre Monteux, Otto Klemperer, Fritz Busch, Sir Thomas Beecham, Dimitri Mitropoulos and Ernest Bloch; the pianists Ignace Paderewski, Leopold Godowsky, Vladimir Horowitz, Artur Schnabel, Rudolf Firkušný, Walter Gieseking, Alexander Brailowsky, Annie Fischer and Sergei Rachmaninoff; the violinists Nathan Milstein, Váša Příhoda, Yehudi Menuhin and Ferenc Vecsey; the violist Paul Hindemith; and the cellist Gregor Piatigorsky.

Contemporary foreign composers were also well represented. During the seasons 1935–40, immediately preceding Italy's entry into the war, operas and/or ballets by Bartók (an outspoken anti-fascist), Bloch (a Jew), Falla, Honegger, Kodály, Ravel, Roussel, Richard Strauss, Stravinsky and lesser figures were presented in major Italian theatres; and the repertoire of instrumental works by foreigners extended to such 'extremists' as Schoenberg and Berg and to the Soviets Prokofiev and Shostakovich. The circumstantial evidence of the musical repertoire helped persuade many native and foreign musicians that Mussolini was a good man and fascism a fundamentally wholesome system.

The most celebrated figure among the bamboozled was Igor Stravinsky. By 1922, when the fascists came to power, even the most modestly perspicacious observer of international musical developments could have predicted that Stravinsky was destined to remain at the forefront of twentieth-century composers. Although he had just turned forty, his curriculum already included such influential creations as *The Firebird*, *Petrushka*, *The Rite of Spring*, *The Nightingale*, *Les Noces*, *Histoire du soldat*, *Mavra*, *Pulcinella* and the Symphonies of Wind Instruments. Stravinsky had been living in western Europe at the outbreak of the First World War and had stayed away from his native Russia following the Revolution, to which he was categorically opposed. His views on politics were agnostic ('I am opposed to the right, abhor the left, and am out of sympathy with the center', he would say of the French political situation in 1937);[3] but, according to Robert Craft, as 'a man with an obsessive, almost pathological need for order', Stravinsky tended to 'feel comfortable with oligarchies and autocracies'.[4] Thus, like many another intelligent person whose familiarity with Italy during the 1920s and 1930s was limited to brief visits, Stravinsky was taken in by the appearance of efficiency that characterized the fascist era.

His love of Italy pre-dated the advent of fascism, and he had at first intended to move to Rome rather than Paris when he left Switzerland in 1920. 'I consider myself to be partly Italian by sympathy and affection', he once told a reporter.[5] His enthusiasm for Mussolini was encouraged, possibly initiated, through contact with colleagues and acquaintances among the Futurists, including Giacomo Balla, Carlo Carrà, Fortunato Depero, Umberto Boccioni, Marinetti, Pratella and Russolo, and through his friendship with D'Annunzio. Craft reports:

> In September 1925, Stravinsky played his [Piano] Sonata in a series of contemporary-music concerts in Venice – 'Sotto il Patronato di S[ua] E[ccellenza] Benito Mussolini,' this in large letters on the program, as if the dictator were seeking the support of the avant-garde. A Stravinsky festival, free of political auspices, had already taken place in Rome, in April, with two concerts conducted by him, a third in which he played his Concerto, and a production of Histoire du Soldat by Pirandello. From then until the Second World War, Stravinsky regularly fulfilled engagements with Italian orchestras, and conducted his stage works at La Scala and the Rome Opera. In 1930, Mussolini invited him to the Palazzo Venezia.[6]

Before his first meeting with the Duce, Stravinsky revealed some of his political opinions to Alberto Gasco, music critic of Rome's La tribuna.

> I don't believe that anyone venerates Mussolini more than I. To me, he is the one man who counts nowadays in the whole world. I have travelled a great deal: I know many exalted personages, and my artist's mind does not shrink from political and social issues. Well, after having seen so many events and so many more or less representative men, I have an overpowering urge to render homage to your Duce. He is the saviour of Italy and – let us hope – of Europe.[7]

Afterwards, Stravinsky told Gasco that 'the mental image I had formed of this formidable man was exactly right. The conversation I had with him has made an indelible impression on me. This pilgrimage to Rome will remain one of the happiest events of my life.'[8]

Three years later, Mussolini sent Stravinsky his thanks for birthday greetings, and in 1934 he gratefully acknowledged receipt of the score of the composer's Duo concertante.[9] By now, Craft says, 'Stravinsky preferred Mussolini's Fascism to British and French democracy, and when the Manchester Guardian described his music as "democratic" (22 February 1934), he underscored the word and drew a large question mark next to it in the margin'.[10] Stravinsky visited Ciano once and Mussolini twice during a visit to Rome in the spring of 1935,[11] and told reporters: 'Unless my ears deceive me, the voice of Rome is the voice of Il Duce. I told him that I felt like a fascist myself. Today, fascists are everywhere in Europe.... In spite of being extremely busy, Mussolini did me the great honour of conversing with me for three-quarters of an hour. We talked about music, art, and politics.'[12] By the end of the year, says Craft,

> [Stravinsky] was defending [Italy] against the 'misunderstanding democ-

racies'. For example, in a letter to Yakov Lvovich Lvov, in Trieste, December 5, 1935, Stravinsky says: 'It is a great pity that I cannot accept the kind invitation of the Ministry of Propaganda for the performance of *Oedipus* set for March 15', and he goes on to express sympathy for 'the difficult position that Italy, glorious and unique, now rejuvenated and thirsting for life, has been put in by worldwide obscurantism. . .'.[13]

This was written when Italy was fighting in Ethiopia; and so was a letter (14 July 1936) to Yury Schleiffer, a Russian refugee resident in Rome.

On leaving Rome in March I delivered . . . the second volume of my *Chronicles* [memoirs] with a dedication to Il Duce, as well as a small gold medal (representing Napoleon and Marie Louise), with the request that Depirro [*sic*] present them to Il Duce together with the expression of my profound admiration for him and for his work. In presenting this small gold token to the Treasury of the Italian State, I feel the satisfaction of participating in the fine deeds with which Italian patriots have shown allegiance to their party. I had also asked Signor Depirro that there be no publicity. . . . In the past, Il Duce has always acknowledged the receipt of music, books, or messages from me. . . .[14]

Craft points out that 'by this time, the "fine deeds of Italian patriots" included the bombing of defenseless Ethiopian villages. On October 13, Stravinsky accepted *"avec joie"* a request to begin a concert in Naples the following month with the Fascist Hymn.'[15]

Despite his close friendships with many Jewish musicians and his declared hatred of racism, Stravinsky continued to perform in Italy after the anti-semitic campaign had been officialized in 1938 and right up to the outbreak of war – after which, as a French citizen, he would have been considered an enemy alien. He worked in and received honours from Franco's Spain; and although he detested the Nazis, he did everything possible to insure the continued flow of his royalties from Hitler's Germany, and even performed there before the war. Although his desire to maintain good relations with the other fascist countries seems to have been fundamentally opportunistic, his feelings towards fascist Italy were clearly of a different, more profoundly positive nature.

Béla Bartók was probably the most decidedly anti-fascist of the major non-Italian composers. Although he performed in Italy during the pre-war years, he clearly disliked what he saw there. Writing to his friend, Mrs Oscar Müller-Widmann, in May 1937, he explained why he and his wife had decided to take their summer holiday in Austria:

Originally we wanted to go to Italy (to the Dolomites), but my hatred of Italy has grown to such unnatural proportions that I simply cannot make up my mind to set foot in that country. This may seem a very strained and unnatural point of view; but I have no wish, at least during my few weeks' holiday, to be continuously bothered by Italian aggressiveness. Actually, they say that Austria has also been infected with the Nazi poison, but it is not so obvious there.[16]

At the time of the *Anschluss*, ten months later, Bartók – many of whose works had been published in Vienna – was requested to fill out a questionnaire that asked whether he was 'of German blood, related race, or non-Aryan' and what his First World War record had been.

'Naturally neither I nor Kodály filled it out', he wrote to Mrs Müller-Widmann – although both he and his colleague were racially 'pure' by Nazi standards. 'Our point of view is that such inquisitions are contrary to right and law. (In a way that is too bad, because one could make some good jokes in answering [. . .]: "Where and when were you wounded?" "Answer: March 11, 12, and 13, 1938, in Vienna!" ' – the days on which the Nazis assumed control of Austria.[17]

Of his native Hungary, Bartók wrote that 'the "civilized" Christian people are almost entirely devoted to the Nazi system; I am really ashamed that I come from this class'.[18] In 1940, he accepted a teaching position in the United States, where he died in near penury five years later. Before leaving Budapest, however, he had made out a will that contained a strange and touching clause:

> If after my death they want to name a street after me, or to erect a memorial tablet to me in a public place, then my desire is this: as long as what were formerly Oktogon-ter and Korond in Budapest are named after those men for whom they are at present named [i.e. Hitler and Mussolini], and further, as long as there is in Hungary any square or street [. . .] named for these two men, then neither square nor street nor public building in Hungary is to be named for me, and no memorial tablet is to be erected in a public place.[19]

Although Arnold Schoenberg was one of the most celebrated musicians in Europe, his first-hand professional contacts with Italy seem to have begun and ended with the performances of *Pierrot Lunaire* that he conducted in various Italian cities in March and April 1924. He later expressed his conviction that the self-proclaimed 'expert judges' had shown more hostility towards his work during that tour than had the true 'art-lovers'.

> I was indeed honoured that Puccini, not an expert judge but a practical expert, made a six-hour journey, despite his illness, to hear my work, and afterwards said some very friendly things to me. That was good, strange though my music may have remained to him. But on the other hand it was characteristic that the loudest disturber of the concert was identified as the director of a conservatoire. [. . .] I have to conclude that the Italian public may not have known what to make of my music. [. . .][20]

Schoenberg's music continued to be heard in Italy, although infrequently, until 1937; from 1938 onwards, it was banned as a result of the racial laws. Anton Webern was not well enough known before the Second World War to have played an important role in international musical activities; Alban Berg was thus the only member of the Schoenberg–Berg–Webern school to have established anything that resembled a steady relationship with Italy during the fascist period.

Berg travelled to Italy for professional reasons in 1933 and 1934 and would almost certainly have continued to do so had he not died in 1935. Hitler's rise to power in Germany had put Berg in an impossible position: although he was an 'Aryan', his music was associated with that of Schoenberg who, in addition to being the leading Jewish composer of the day, was also the father of a compositional technique regarded by the Nazis as decadent and un-German. 'Since the Berlin Reichstag fire [spring 1933]', Berg wrote to Malipiero in 1934, 'not a single note of mine has been heard in Germany [. . .]. And in my own country [Austria] things are not much different. For with the present tendency [. . .] to glorify the Jews as martyrs, I *am hardly ever performed*.'[21] Not only was Berg's pride hurt: if his works were not performed, he received no royalties. The enthusiasm with which he was received in Italy in 1933 and 1934 was, therefore, important to him both morally and materially. Willi Reich, a disciple of all three masters of the Second Viennese School, has described Berg's delight with the music congress held in Florence in conjunction with the first *Maggio Musicale* (1933). Berg – with Strauss, Milhaud, Malipiero, Bartók, Roussel and Ernest Křenek – was a guest of honour.

> [. . .] He was celebrated both by his hosts and by the international public. I was constantly at his side as his travel-manager and interpreter and there were days of cloudless gaiety. With the utmost conscientiousness he visited all the meetings of the congress, and even the most boring of them was a source of purest pleasure when one could watch how he sketched on the back of the resumé of the congressional speeches [. . .].[22]

Berg noted in his letters to his wife that he enjoyed Italian cuisine, but he was condescending about Italian musical tastes:

> In Italy they are just discovering Richard Strauss. Not so surprising: a people whose primal instinct is for noise can't be as far advanced musically as a people with a primal instinct for melody or for rhythm. [. . .] You only have to hear a folk melody here. First condition, as loud as possible; second, rhythm; melody non-essential. Three or four notes are enough, taken up and down the scale.[23]

Berg met Italian notables, including a fascist minister of state and the Duke of Aosta, and was pleased with 'a tea given to us by the Fascist musicians'. He took 'fresh courage' from 'the appreciation I'm shown in this truly international circle'.[24] All the more reason why, in the summer of 1934, he was distressed to find that his 'Lyric Suite' had been stricken from the programme of the Venice Biennale, scheduled for September. He incorrectly attributed the action to pressure from the German government, and wrote in that sense to Malipiero, who was on the festival's executive committee. The real problem, however, was that both the 'Suite' and the *Wozzeck* excerpts, which Berg had proposed as an alternate choice, had already been heard in Italy: the Biennale's regulations specified that only works new to the country could qualify for performance. Once this misunderstanding was cleared up, Berg proposed his *Der Wein*, which was given its Italian première under the direction of Hermann Scherchen at the Teatro la Fenice on 11 September. The composer and his wife attended and were gratified by the warm reception given his work.[25]

The Venice trip was Berg's last journey abroad: he died in his native Vienna fifteen months later. In an obituary in the *Rassegna musicale* (January 1936), Guido Maria Gatti called Berg a 'rare example of a completely unbending artistic conscience, in good times and bad' – an obvious reference to the composer's problems with the Nazis. For the time being, Italians could still feel a certain national moral superiority to the Germans.

No performing musician was more celebrated during the first half of the twentieth century than Ignace Jan Paderewski, who had served as the first prime minister of independent Poland, after the First World War. His position on the political spectrum is pinpointed by his opinion of the Mexican dictator Porfirio Díaz, who had made 'a great impression' on him at the turn of the century: 'He was indeed a remarkable man. As long as he was there the country was orderly and prosperous. He was just the man for those people, an iron-handed man. At that time there were no bandits – there was perfect peace and order in the whole country.'[26]

And of course, a quarter-century later Paderewski openly admired Mussolini. After a benefit concert given by the pianist for the Santa Cecilia Academy in the mid-1920s, the association's president, Count Enrico di San Martino, asked what he could do to show appreciation. Paderewski replied that he wanted very much to meet Mussolini.

> The request was immediately granted, and the meeting turned out to be very interesting since Paderewski – so in love with Italy and so sensitive to national questions – was indeed an enthusiastic admirer of Mussolini, who at that time was *à la page* for the world public. And Mussolini, for his part, could not have been indifferent to Paderewski's conversation, in which one felt so much energy, so much strength, so much genius [...].[27]

Paderewski visited Mussolini again – apparently at the latter's request –

following a concert he gave in Rome in November 1932. Their conversation lasted two and a half hours, and the dictator gave his guest a large autographed photo of himself.[28] A few months later Paderewski's biographer, Rom Landau, saw the photo with its 'impressive dedication' on display in the pianist's home in Switzerland and asked his opinion of Mussolini. 'I think he is a very great statesman', said Paderewski. 'I am a great admirer both of Mussolini and of Italian Fascism. I must admit, though, that last time I visited the Duce I was rather less impressed than on my earlier visits.'[29]

The pianist's admiration for the Duce took a real plunge when Mussolini came out in favour of the German–Soviet 'Non-Aggression Pact' of 1939. Aniela Strakacz, wife of Paderewski's secretary, described the pianist's reactions in detail in a book published after the war.

> [...] Mussolini's declaration that the partition and enslavement of Poland by Hitler and Stalin constituted a 'settlement of the Polish question' was, as Paderewski expressed himself at the time, 'a nail driven into Poland's coffin.' What I didn't know, though, was that the President [Paderewski] had written a letter to Mussolini.
>
> Sylwin [Strakacz] tells me that in his letter Paderewski categorically protested against Mussolini's statement [...]. Paderewski was aware that because of the political situation this was probably the last letter he'd be able to write directly to Mussolini. So, in the second part of the letter, mindful of the persistent rumours that Italy would enter the war on Germany's side, the President formulated the following warning.
>
> It is rumoured that Mussolini is being subjected to strong pressure from Hitler to have Italy enter the war. Paderewski warns Mussolini that Germany will lose the war. He is positive the United States will not permit Great Britain to be routed and, if the need arises, will actively come to England's defense. Ruin awaits Italy, should she suffer defeat along with Hitler. But even if Hitler were to win the war [...] a victory-drunk Hitler would [...] reach out for the Italian regions in the north which Italy recovered from Austria after the last war. [...] And he would doubtless strive to reduce what would be left of Italy to a vassal state.
>
> [...] Her history, tradition, and culture link Italy with the West and not with Germanic barbarism, to which ancient Rome succumbed. [...]
>
> [...] Now, six months later [April 1940], Mussolini has replied to Paderewski's letter. But he apparently feared to put his answer down in writing because the reply was verbal and limited to a few sentences which the Italian consul general [in Lausanne] read to Paderewski from a slip of paper [during a secret visit]:
>
> [...] Il Duce requests Mr. Paderewski to take into consideration the difficult political situation in which Italy finds herself as a result of a war that is being waged at her doorstep. Il Duce's sentiments toward Poland and the Polish nation have not changed. Il Duce believes the war will end soon in a German victory. Italy must make sure she will have a voice when the

terms of the future peace, affecting the fate of many countries, are discussed. Il Duce believes he will then be in a position to render many a service to the Polish nation, and assures the Polish people they can always count on his friendship and help. Il Duce asks Mr. Paderewski not to judge him by his words, which are often dictated by circumstances beyond his control, but by his acts, which will ever remain friendly to Poland.

The conversation terminated with the consul's request that Paderewski treat Mussolini's statement as strictly confidential. I have jotted it down just as Sylwin, who was present at the meeting, told it to me. Sylwin also says that the President now considers Mussolini's entry into the war a certainty. Paderewski remarked sadly that Mussolini will destroy by his own hand everything he has done for the development of Italy and which in part might have atoned for the suffering that Fascism had imposed upon the Italian people. Italy will again be faced with chaos and bolshevism, she will revert to the state in which Mussolini found her at the time of his march on Rome. [. . .].[30]

Paderewski obviously still believed that Mussolini had been good for Italy, despite the brutality of his methods. Two months later, however, when the Duce declared war against France, the pianist's view changed: 'I'm sorry for Italy. The Italian people will pay dearly for Mussolini's mistake. Apparently the cup of Fascist sins has run over and God will now mete out his punishment.'[31] The eighty-year-old pianist died the following year, at the most depressing moment in the war, and was duly eulogized in the Italian press.[32]

Fritz Kreisler played often in Italy during the fascist period and visited informally with Mussolini on several occasions. The violinist reported in a 1931 interview that at their first meeting, the Duce nicknamed Mrs Kreisler 'Sherlock Holmes':

When Mussolini greeted us Mrs. Kreisler said, 'You are a violinist, too.' 'No,' he said, 'that is ridiculous. I can't play the violin.' [. . .] 'Then what are those marks on your neck?' she asked. 'I thought I had invited artists,' he said. 'I find I am harbouring detectives. But you are wrong. Those marks are from my playing with, not as an artist upon, the violin.'[33]

The same interviewer asked whether Mussolini was a better violinist than Kreisler's old friend, Albert Einstein. Kreisler laughed and said: 'I would [. . .] have to hear them together, and what an occasion that would be! A violin contest between Einstein and Mussolini! Superb! And this you would see: [. . .] those two men, each so serene, so supreme in his own field – you would see them trembling, with the sweat rolling down their brows.'[34]

The idea that the Duce was 'supreme in his own field' was commonly held by musicians throughout those years. During a working visit to Rome only two months after the fascists had come to power, Otto Klemperer heard Mussolini make a speech and – according to the conductor's biographer, Peter Heyworth

– 'was much impressed by his programme of work and discipline. "It's a face one doesn't forget" ', Klemperer wrote to his wife;[35] and he agreed to conduct 'Giovinezza' before his first performance in the capital.[36] Like Kreisler, Bruno Walter, and many another foreign musician of Jewish origin, Klemperer continued to make music in fascist Italy until he ceased to be invited.

The entire Vienna State Opera ensemble performed at Venice's Teatro la Fenice in September 1934, under the baton of its artistic director, Clemens Krauss, who was soon to abandon the company for a greener pasture: Hitler's Berlin State Opera. Otto Strasser, the orchestra's principal second violin, reported that

> The most famous and most interesting listener sitting in the auditorium [...] was Benito Mussolini. Through him, our visit was given an apparently intentional political accent, for the next day he invited the entire ensemble to a farewell dinner at the Hotel Excelsior on the Lido [...]. Austria's Federal Chancellor, Dr Dollfuss, had been murdered two months earlier, and Dr Schuschnigg had taken office as his successor. Dr Pernter, the [Austrian] Minister of Education, spoke on behalf of the [...] guests, after which Mussolini read a speech in halting German. He declared that just as he had stood behind Dollfuss, so he would stand behind Schuschnigg. History has shown to what extent he kept his word. I, however, did something I hardly ever do: I got him to give me his autograph, which I still have today [1974].[37]

It is not surprising that Strasser wanted Mussolini's autograph – as, no doubt, did most of the other members of the ensemble. For Jews and others who opposed Hitler, Mussolini was the self-proclaimed protector of Austrian neutrality and the opponent of nonsensical racial theories; for those who were pro-Nazi, Mussolini was Hitler's admired mentor, the man who had imposed 'order' on a 'decadent democracy'; and until he unwisely transformed his country into a German satellite, he was able to continue to pose as a Man of Reason and Strength. Once the transformation process had begun, however, the pose became ever less convincing. Between 1935 and 1939, Mussolini invaded and conquered nearly defenceless Ethiopia, aided the Spanish Falangists, declared the Italians to be 'Aryans' and the Jews – who accounted for little more than one-tenth of one per cent of the country's population – to be dangerous racial enemies. He trounced tiny Albania and stood silently by as Hitler annexed one country after another, including Austria. All these acts began to make even the most credulous, well-disposed foreigners – and a good many Italians – wonder who the real Mussolini was and what he really believed.

There had been early racial warning signals, in the field of music as elsewhere, but they had come from cranks. In 1933 Guido Visconti di Modrone, nobleman and amateur musician, had stated publicly that 'our music should go back to being [...] the pure expression of our soul and of our race'. But the Jews were not his target.

> One fine day, [. . .] the Italian nation threw its doors open to the Negroes: they were supposed to come here, to this land where art was born and where it has flourished for centuries, to teach us the new rules. And the Negroes came among us as conquerers and dominators. Their music, if thus it may be called, has taken hold, with its deafening noises and asthmatic rhythms.

The civilized music of the white race, said Visconti, had been pushed into the background; music no longer helped to 'raise the spirit, to bring it repose, comfort and joy [. . .]'. Since 1929 he had been saying that it was necessary to react against jazz bands 'as against cocaine and such alcoholic beverages (all imported from abroad) as gin, whiskey and cocktails; and that a crusade of this sort [. . .] ought to interest the Church, the press, Educational Institutions and, not least, the Government'. This idea had been 'approved even at *the highest level*, precisely where *"one can do as one pleases"*,' but to no avail. Too many black-skinned musicians were becoming popular in Italy, said Visconti. And he concluded: '[Let's have] nationalism in music, nationalism in all the arts [. . .]'.[38]

Two years later, the critic Alberto Ghislanzoni published a more generally and therefore more ominously xenophobic article ('New Italian Music Must Be Anti-European') in a government-funded magazine. In every civilized country, he said, in every field, new ideals, horizons, visions and constructive forms were developing. But Italian musicians hardly seemed to be aware of what was happening.

> The best known and oldest Italian composers (those born between 1875 and 1895, approximately), did not take part in the [First World] War – with some very praiseworthy exceptions; [. . .] they did not feel it, either internally or externally, as a great destructive and renewing force. [. . .]
> Nor did they experience the *squadrismo* period of the fascist struggle – they did not, even at a distance, feel its fascination, its intimate beauty and its colossal propelling power [. . .]. They peacefully kept up their daily grind [. . .] as if the philosophical and social directions that were ripening [sic] in their own country did not concern them in the least.
> [. . .] They realized only very late that there existed a Regime that was somewhat different from previous ones – and then they all lined up, Indian file, in the ranks. [. . .]
> Unfortunately, however, the cultural system and the spiritual orientation have remained as they were [. . .]. [It is] bad and unacceptable that these people still insist upon directing young [musicians] towards artistic concepts and forms that are very foreign to us Italians [. . .].
> Thus the self-negating spirit of little, democratic, Umbertine and Masonic Italy still dominates these mild but often vain and argumentative artistic consciences. We still hear [. . .] 'Art is universal', 'Art has no borders'. [. . .]

The Italian characteristics of [...] some of their works are limited to the authors' surnames. [...]

They are dominated by the greyness of a composite, internationalistic way of thinking and sensibility. Yet some of them who today find themselves more welcome in certain foreign Masonic-musical environments wish to represent 'fascist art' before the world. [...]

I hardly need to add that these people use texts by Riemann, d'Indy or Schoenberg for teaching composition; those of Rimsky-Korsakov and Strauss for orchestration; and those of Riemann, Combarieu or Adler for music history.

Ghislanzoni believed that the Nazis had gone too far in eliminating such gifted people as Hindemith from Germany's musical life; but it was equally wrong of Italians, he said, to maintain 'in eminent administrative positions artists who are congenitally bound to that stale internationalistic concept [of music]'.[39] But the notions of Ghislanzoni and others like him had no influence on official artistic policy as expressed through the various corporations, consortia and inspectorates – nor could they affect Mussolini's racial thinking: the motivation for the adoption of racial laws in Italy was purely political.

Jewish communities had existed in Italy since before the birth of Christ, and the years between the annexation of Rome into the Kingdom of Italy in 1870 and the first stirrings of fascist anti-semitism in the early 1930s were the least troubled period in their existence. According to Meir Michaelis's excellent study, *Mussolini and the Jews,*

All students of Italian Jewry, whether Jewish or Gentile, Fascist or anti-Fascist, are agreed that there was virtually no Jewish problem in modern Italy. The late Cecil Roth, among the foremost authorities on the subject, affirmed [...] that after 1870 there was no country in either hemisphere where Jewish conditions 'were or could be better' [...].[40]

In its short history, pre-fascist united Italy had had one Jewish and one half-Jewish prime minister, and Jews had held many other high-ranking political and military positions. In the arts, they were strikingly prominent: the novelist Italo Svevo, the poet Umberto Saba and the painter Amedeo Modigliani – to give only the best known names – were all of Jewish origin. These facts do not demonstrate a complete absence of popular anti-semitism, but they do clarify the official position. At a practical level, anti-semitism could not arouse widespread interest in a country in which Jews accounted for only one one-thousandth of the population.

Most Italian Jews accepted Mussolini, who left them unmolested for the first fifteen years of his regime. Michaelis points out that

[...] under Fascism the number of Jewish university teachers continued to be disproportionately high, and so did the number of Jewish generals and admirals. Nor was the Fascist Party by any means *judenrein*. Guido Jung, on being appointed Minister of Finance [1932], became an *ex officio* member of the Fascist Grand Council. Alberto Liuzzi, a baptized Jew with an Aryan wife, attained the rank of consul-general in the Fascist militia. Margherita Sarfatti was the Duce's first official biographer as well as co-editor of his monthly review, *Gerarchia*, for which only trusted Fascists were permitted to write. Gino Arias was the chief theorist of the *Stato corporativo* and a regular contributor to both *Gerarchia* and *Il popolo d'Italia*; another regular contributor was Carlo Foà, an eminent Jewish physiologist. Giorgio Del Vecchio was the first Fascist Rector of the University of Rome.[41]

Numerous foreign Jews, too, declared their solidarity with Italian fascism. Among those connected in some way with music, the most enthusiastic was Otto H. Kahn, the American financier responsible more than any other individual for the Metropolitan Opera's well-being in the early decades of the century. The May 1926 issue of *Musica e scena* contained a full-column article about this 'strong and convinced sympathizer with Italy and with fascism' who had been created a 'high officer of the Italian Crown and a knight officer of Sts. Maurice and Lazarus, decorations he well deserves for all he has done and will continue to do for Italy and Italians'.[42] Elsewhere, Kahn was quoted as referring to fascism as Italy's 'saviour from Bolshevism'.[43]

Mussolini's personal feelings towards the Jews were mixed, and he did, for instance, limit their accession to the highest echelons of power and unofficially exclude them from the Accademia Reale d'Italia. But he was probably sincere when he stated, late in the 1920s, that he believed there were no 'pure' races and that there was no Jewish question in Italy. His privately expressed contempt for Hitler ('a horrible sexual degenerate, [...] a dangerous madman') and for National Socialism ('savage barbarism [...] murder and killing, loot and pillage and blackmail are all it can produce')[44] – echoed in gentler terms by the Italian press in the early days of the Nazi regime – reassured not only Italian Jews, but the majority of the Italian population, for whom the Germanic peoples were the 'historic' enemy.

Most Italian musical publications were virtually free of anti-semitism before 1938. The lead article of the July 1928 issue of *Musica d'oggi* was a lengthy piece by H. R. Fleischmann entitled 'Jewish Music', which refers very positively to Jewish musicians of the immediate past and the present and to recent books on Jewish music. Similar in tone was an article ('Jewishness in Music') by Paul Nettl, published four years later in the *Rassegna musicale* (September-December 1932). And most Italian newspapers and journals gave a great deal of attention to the 1934 première of *Il Dibuk*, an opera by the non-Jewish Lodovico Rocca on a wholly Jewish subject. In the May-June issue of the *Rassegna musicale*, Gavazzeni called it 'the most important artistic event of the season'.

From 1933 on, as famous musicians of Jewish origin began to lose their positions in Germany, Italian music magazines reported their appointments to positions in other countries – albeit without entering into the moral issue. The editors of Musica d'oggi nevertheless printed Alfred Brueggemann's highly tendentious 'Letter from Germany' (July 1933) regarding the Nazis' treatment of Jewish musicians: the critic admitted that 'a certain amount of wheat has been thrown away with the chaff', but went on to say that the Aryan musicians who were replacing Jews would have to prove that they themselves had not been poisoned by Semitic and Bolshevik ideas. He reported the departure of the 'brilliant but eccentric' Klemperer – 'admirable despite his often nearly intolerable extravagances' – and that of Bruno Walter, 'for personal reasons.'[45] But six months later, the same magazine published a 'Letter from Vienna' in which Fleischmann called the events in Germany a boon for Austrian musical life, what with the arrival of Walter, Klemperer, Zemlinsky and Schnabel, and 'above all', on account of Toscanini's first Vienna Philharmonic concerts.[46] Klemperer, during his visits to Italy in the mid-1930s, was so delighted to find anti-semitism virtually absent from Italian life that he considered moving there with his family, although he quickly discarded the idea for professional reasons.[47]

As if in protest over what was happening in Germany, the directors of the Santa Cecilia Academy scheduled a concert of Kurt Weill's music (excerpts from his operas Mahagonny and Der Jasager) early in 1934. Giorgio Nataletti, in a lengthy article in Musica d'oggi, called Weill 'one of the composers most representative of today's Germany' – although he ought to have said 'yesterday's Germany';[48] and Luigi Colacicchi, in the Rassegna musicale, heaped praise not only on the Jewish composer and his Jewish interpreters (the conductors Maurice Abravanel and Robert Blum), but, amazingly, on Weill's decidedly – not to say stridently – anti-fascist librettist, who was also a Jew:

> Der Jasager in particular found a willing audience; and this was natural, [. . .] given its highly accessible human value, which is partly a result of the very beautiful poetic text [. . .] by Bertold [sic] Brecht. [. . .] Kurt Weill's thematic idiom is [. . .] popular in inspiration, but not popular in the folkloric [. . .] and mannered sense. It is, rather, genuinely popular and spontaneous, reflecting the musical attitude of the day. [. . .][49]

The music of Ernest Bloch, much of whose work was meant to be specifically Jewish in character, was also well received in Italy: Pannain had written admiringly and at length about it as early as 1929;[50] the world première of the composer's Sacred Service – a setting of the Hebrew liturgy – was given by the Turin Radio Orchestra in 1934; and a major production of his opera, Macbeth, was presented at Naples' Teatro San Carlo in March 1938, when the anti-semitic campaign was unofficially underway.

When Wilhelm Furtwängler resigned from the Berlin State Opera in 1934 in protest over the Nazis' ban on Hindemith's *Mathis der Maler*, the *Rassegna musicale* stated that Germany had lost (temporarily, as it turned out) 'one of the few real musicians left | . . . | since the advent of the Nazi regime' – an indirectly 'pro-semitic' declaration.[51] A year later the same journal carried H. H. Stuckenschmidt's warning that Germany's musical repertoire 'shows signs of bogging down in the most narrow-minded conventionality.' As an example, he cited Paul Graener's *Der Prinz von Homburg*, which had been touted as 'the representative opera of the Third Reich', but which 'has had a rather modest degree of success'.[52]

Whatever Mussolini's private opinion of Hitler may have been, by 1936 he was beginning to pay him the compliment of imitation – in the field of racism, among others. One of the pioneers of 'Aryan' philosophy in Italy was Giulio Cogni, a young Tuscan composer, critic and writer who had lived in Germany. In the fall of that year, with Mussolini's encouragement, Cogni published *Il razzismo*, a book in which he described fascism as an outstanding example of the Nordic race's virtues – thus giving impetus to the process through which Italians were to be transformed into Aryans. According to Michaelis, however, 'Cogni took care to dissociate himself from German anti-Semitism, stressing the superiority of the Italian Sephardi Jew over the German Ashkenazi Jew and denying the existence of a Jewish problem in Italy | . . . |.' Although this opinion earned him a rebuke from Göbbels, he repeated it the following year in another book, *Il valore della stirpe italiana* (*The Merit of the Italian Race*). Commented Neville Laski, president of the Board of Deputies of British Jews: ' "The Italian Press, significantly enough, had fairly favourable reviews and appreciations of |Cogni's| book, and I am told that papers, known for their anti-racial views, did not have the courage to criticise the pseudo-scientific theories of this new Italian racial authority." ' Cogni's Germanophile ideas disgusted most fascists and non-fascists alike, and the Holy Office put *Il razzismo* on the Index. Mussolini quietly withdrew his support for Cogni without, however, abjuring racism.[53] When he made up his mind that an alliance with Nazi Germany was Italy's best option, he simultaneously decided upon an actively anti-semitic policy. Some musicians may have been forewarned in August 1937, when *Il musicista*, monthly bulletin of the National Fascist Union of Musicians, devoted its first five pages to Ghislanzoni's report on 'Chancellor Hitler's Speech on Modern Art' – an address that had taken place the previous month at the opening of the House of German Art in Munich. The author cites the Führer's assertion that after the First World War, Judaism 'took control of public opinion' in the field of art and culture by 'taking advantage of its |Judaism's| position with the press, abetted by so-called art criticism | . . . |'. The Jews did this 'not only to confound, little by little, natural ideas about the essence and duties of art, and about its goals, but above all to destroy general healthy feeling in this area'. This, said Hitler, was where the responsibility lay for certain lies, such as that 'art is international'. Ghislanzoni allowed that the situation had not reached so dangerous a point in Italy, but declared that Hitler was fundamentally right all the same.[54]

More directly distressing to Jewish musicians was 'The Jewish Musical Blood-Sucker', an article published four months later in Il Tevere, a widely read fascist daily. Francesco Santoliquido, the author of this savage outburst, was a not wholly unknown composer in his mid-fifties who had never entered the mainstream of contemporary Italian music. His article opened with an attack on Casella who, he said, had been sent to Italy twenty years earlier as a prophet of French musical fads and 'with the precise task of conquering this great musical market for the Jewish cause'.

> I can almost visualize the last, moving embrace, at the Paris station, between Alfredo Casella and Henry Prunières, who at that time was the High Pontiff of the brand-new international Jewish musical church. He undoubtedly told Casella to be inexorable, to stab the execrated Giuseppe Verdi pitilessly, to destroy *romanticism, lyricism, feeling* (all horrible prerogatives of the Italian Catholic soul), and to inoculate us instead with *cerebralism, materialism* and *cynicism* – talents that make up the power and superiority of the Jewish soul (?).

Santoliquido proceeded to insult Emil Hertzka, former director of the avant-garde Viennese Universal-Edition – apparently unaware that the object of his attack had died five years earlier. He also lashed out at the American patroness of contemporary music, Elizabeth Sprague Coolidge: Casella had managed to make her his 'great protectress', said the writer, because she was deaf. The author then denounced Jewish solidarity, giving as a rather far-fetched example the Jews of Tunis who, he said, had been mobilized by their Chief Rabbi to attend the concert of an unnamed visiting European Jewish pianist, thereby bringing 25,000 francs to the local theatre's box office; whereas when Alfred Cortot appeared under the same roof a few weeks later, half the seats were empty and the take barely reached 10,000 francs. And the Jews of Rome had somehow been similarly mobilized to fill the Augusteum for a concert by Ernest Bloch. 'This, then,' Santiliquido quickly concludes, 'is how the Jews have carved a place for themselves in the European musical world. This is how they have managed to make their musical sensibility, or rather *insensibility, all the rage.*' He said, without giving examples, since there were none to give, that the Jews had tried to destroy Debussy in France, Richard Strauss in Germany, and Verdi in Italy – fortunately without success.

> [...] It is worthwhile to establish unequivocally the fact that Alfredo Casella and his friends *are not innovators at all*, as they so generously define themselves; they are, rather, simple and modest *imitators* of such Jewish

musicians as Stravinsky [sic!], Honnegger [sic!], Milhaud etc.

The music of Italy's so-called modernists and innovators derives [...] from these [foreign, Jewish] musicians. It is music without a country!

It is music that cannot find a place for itself in the ardent, jealously autarchic national atmosphere created in Italy by Fascism.

It is music that must now find a place for itself only in countries where internationalism triumphs.

But the writer added that he was no reactionary – lest such a thought might have entered anyone's head:

I admire the Stravinsky of The Firebird and Petrushka, just as I admire the Honegger of King David and the Bloch of Schelomo and even the Schoenberg of the Gurrelieder. But I am firmly determined to fight the Italian imitators of this exotic art, which is not the thing for our people. [...]

We do not want to be inoculated with the Jewish intellectual seed, and we do not want to become bastards, even if only in a spiritual sense.[55]

Santoliquido's shabby article was not primarily anti-semitic. In trying to make the Jews seem a powerful group that was subtly seeking to debilitate Christian culture, the writer was simply using anti-semitism as a tool for carrying out *ad hominem* attacks on Casella, Prunières, Hertzka and Mrs Coolidge – none of them Jewish except Prunières – who represented progressive musical tendencies he could not abide. His attitude was even more deplorable than 'sincere' anti-semitism, for he was making a particularly small, defenceless Italian ethnic group responsible for problems with which it had virtually no connection. Certainly the Jews had not been responsible for Casella's music receiving more attention than Santoliquido's. Selfishly motivated, incorrect and illogical though it was, Santoliquido's article was nevertheless given prominent place in an official fascist newspaper. The warning signals had been sounded.

In 1938 Mussolini drew up and published a ten-point 'Manifesto of the Race' that declared that Italians were Aryans, that Jews were not, and that intermarriage of Aryans with non-Aryans was not to be allowed. Michaelis says:

The ordinary people in Italy, according to an acute Western observer, received [the Manifesto] with 'resentful shame', chiefly owing to the fact that their leader had 'stooped to copy the example of German neo-barbarism'. Pope Pius XI publicly branded it as a 'disgraceful imitation' of Hitler's Nordic mythology, adding that it ran directly counter to the noblest traditions of that Roman Empire which the Fascists had hitherto professed themselves so anxious to restore. The King of Italy voiced similar views in private, expressing astonishment at the fact that his Prime Minister should have seen fit 'to import these racial fashions from Berlin into Italy'.[56]

But Mussolini held real power: the king, the pope, and hundreds of thousands of other Italians who knew he was wrong on this and many other matters had already swallowed his excesses in various areas in order to maintain their personal status quo, and were unlikely to exert themselves now on behalf of a tiny group of people who, in any case, were not being deprived of their homes or herded into concentration camps, but 'merely' losing their civil rights and, often, their jobs and extensive properties.*

The best-known Italian Jewish musician of the time was the composer Mario Castelnuovo-Tedesco, a Florentine who had studied under Pizzetti and had received encouragement from the ever-generous Casella. Toscanini, too, had taken an interest in his works, several of which he had performed with the New York Philharmonic, and with such soloists as Jascha Heifetz and Gregor Piatigorsky. During the 1930s Castelnuovo's music was being performed within and outside Italy at least as frequently as that of any other Italian composer of his generation.

Castelnuovo appears not to have had any interest in politics, although his criticism of neo-classicism, published in the magazine *Pegaso* (1929), contains a phrase rendered ambiguous by the double meaning, in Italian, of the word *regime* – the political sense, and the more general sense of any sort of system. 'The true work of art', he said, 'is born in regimes of freedom, not of coercion.'[57] Mussolini selected Castelnuovo-Tedesco to write incidental music to the drama *Savonarola* by the journalist Rino Alessi, which was presented as a massive outdoor spectacle in Florence's Piazza della Signoria in the spring of 1935. Years later, the composer wrote:

> I never knew the why or the wherefore: [...] I had never dedicated a piece to [Mussolini] (as many Italian artists used to do, to ingratiate themselves); nor had I ever approached him. On the contrary, an instinctive antipathy had always led me carefully to avoid finding myself in his path. I think, in fact, that I am one of the very few Italians who never saw Mussolini in the flesh! [...] I believe his choice was determined by two reasons: the fact that I was then considered 'the Florentine musician' *par excellence*, and therefore may have seemed the right man for that [...] task; and probably also because, knowing that I was Jewish, he thought I would have fewer scruples in the event that the

---

* The resolutions adopted by the cabinet on 2–3 September 1938 eliminated Jewish teachers and students at every educational level, from elementary school through university, allowing Jewish communities to set up separate schools; and they withdrew Italian citizenship obtained after 1 January 1919 from foreign-born Jews. The Grand Council of Fascism's resolutions of 6–7 October 1938 banned 'marriage of Italians to members of the Hamite, Semite and other non-Aryan races'; expelled foreign Jews who had not been resident in Italy at least since 1 January 1919, who were under sixty-five years of age, and who were not married to Italians as of 1 October 1938; and declared that Jews could not '(a) be members of the National Fascist Party; (b) own or manage businesses of any sort that employ 100 or more people; (c) own more than fifty hectares of land; (d) do military service in peacetime or wartime'.

Ecclesiastical authorities created the problems that were foreseen at the time, but avoided by submitting the text for the Cardinal Archbishop's approval.[58]

But if, in 1935, being Jewish could be an advantage in Mussolini's eyes, the situation soon changed. In his unpublished autobiography, *Una vita di musica*, Castelnuovo discloses that 'one of the first ominous hints' of the coming anti-semitic campaign reached him in January 1938 when Giulio Bignami, a young Florentine violinist who had learned the composer's Second Violin Concerto ('The Prophets') for a forthcoming performance with the Turin radio orchestra, came to see him.

> [. . .] With a crestfallen, confused expression on his face, he told me that he had been called to the Florence radio station for a telephone conversation with the General Administration in Rome 'regarding the requested replacement of Castelnuovo-Tedesco's concerto'. Bignami thought that I was not happy with his performance and that I had been the one to request the 'replacement'. I assured him that I was very satisfied [. . .]. I asked him who the conductor of the concert [. . .] was to be, and he replied that it was a German, a Nazi [. . .]. I then thought it must have been the conductor himself who [. . .] had refused to conduct a Jewish composer's work [. . .]. I therefore advised Bignami to accept the replacement; and although I [. . .] was slightly disturbed, I did not make much of the matter at the time. Then, two weeks later, I had a letter from my colleague Renzo Massarani (also a Jew, employed by the Society of Authors [and Publishers]). He was greatly worried, and let me know of another prohibition that had arrived by telephone: this time, it was the Mendelssohn [Violin] Concerto! [. . .] I then began to be seriously worried, and I tried to find out whether it was a matter of the individual initiative of some over-zealous functionary. I asked Alessandro Pavolini [Fascist Federal Secretary for Florence] who, however, answered evasively (naturally). I then turned to D'Annunzio [. . .], and through him I learned that there were no written orders, but that these 'instructions' were handed down, one at a time, by telephone, from the Ministry of the Interior or of Propaganda. [. . .][59]

Nothing startling happened to Castelnuovo-Tedesco during the next few months; but on returning to Italy (2 September 1938) from a brief trip to Switzerland with his elder son,

> [. . .] we read in the papers the first of the so-called 'racial laws'. [. . .] It was the one that forbade Jewish children to attend public schools; and it made them pariahs and outlaws from infancy on! [. . .] It was a terrible blow. I could have tolerated anything – the end of my professional activity, the expropriation of my private goods – but not this! I can still see the desperate expression on Pietro's face as he read the 'sentence' [. . .]. On returning to Florence, I talked briefly with [my wife] Clara: '[. . .] If this is how they're beginning, *anything is possible!* The only thing left is to leave!'[60]

To circumvent Italian censorship, Castelnuovo-Tedesco returned to Switzerland to write to three friends in the United States – Toscanini, Heifetz and the American violinist Albert Spalding – requesting their help in obtaining visas allowing them to emigrate to the United States. 'Toscanini immediately sent me [. . .] a telegram to assure me that Heifetz and Spalding [who, unlike Toscanini, were American citizens] would provide an affidavit, and that they would all try to find some kind of work for me.' Obtaining Italian exit visas proved more difficult, but after overcoming many difficulties the Castelnuovo family set sail for New York in the summer of 1939.

> What I felt at that moment [. . .] cannot be called sorrow, regret or spiritual suffering: it was an almost physical torment, a tearing asunder, a mutilation. It seemed to be a dress rehearsal for Death; and indeed, since that time something in me has been absolutely dead: not Hope, but Illusion. What has kept me alive has been love for those dear to me and for music. However much affection I have come to feel over the years for my adopted country, I have no longer been able to become attached to people and things; I have lived as if suspended in mid-air, in a cloud, waiting [. . .].[61]

The composers Renzo Massarani and Vittorio Rieti were also Jews who, like Castelnuovo-Tedesco, had acheved a fair degree of recognition during the inter-war period. Casella, in 1925, had called Rieti, Massarani and Labroca the three most important Italian composers under the age of thirty.[62] Rieti spent much of that period in Paris, and presumably his uprooting from Italy was not as dramatic as Castelnuovo's.* He eventually emigrated to the United States, where he held various important teaching positions, and where his works were championed by such artists as Toscanini, Mitropoulos and Balanchine.[64]

Massarani's situation was more complicated. As an ardent 'fascist of the first hour' who had participated in the march on Rome, he held artistic–bureaucratic positions under the regime and contributed to the newspaper, L'impero. But the musicologist J. C. G. Waterhouse says that when the racial laws were adopted,

> [Massarani's] works were banned, and much material was destroyed during World War II. He emigrated to Brazil, where he took citizenship in 1945 and

---

* A secret report from the Italian embassy's press attaché in Paris to the MinCulPop in Rome in November 1939 mentions that Margherita Sarfatti, who was then living in exile, 'had received [. . .] the musician Rietti [sic] – same race – who has even given some concerts at the Royal Embassy, under the artistic management of Signora Cerruti' – the Jewish wife of the Italian ambassador. Far more surprising than the existence of the secret report is the fact that a country that had officially forbidden marriages between Gentiles and Jews had posted a mixed couple to head one of its most important diplomatic missions abroad, at a particularly tense moment in Franco-Italian relations, and that the Paris embassy openly encouraged the participation in officially sponsored activities of people who had been deprived of many of their civil rights at home.[63]

wrote music criticism [. . .]. But after his traumatic experiences, far worse than any suffered by Rieti and Castelnuovo-Tedesco, he preferred to forget about his own music. He forbade its republication and performance, and refused access to the manuscripts even of his best compositions.[65]

Italian Jews who played in orchestras, sang in choruses, or were in other ways employed by musical organizations also lost their jobs after the promulgation of the racial laws. Vittore Veneziani, a former Martucci pupil who had directed La Scala's excellent chorus since 1921, was one of the better-known performing musicians who found themselves unemployed from one day to the next. Cesare Ferraresi, a violin student at the Milan Conservatory, was expelled in 1938 because his mother was Jewish. He was later readmitted on a technicality, and he graduated in 1940; but at the time of the German occupation he was deported to a concentration camp. Ferraresi survived and, after the war, served as concertmaster of various major Italian orchestras and as a member of the outstanding Trio di Milano. Less fortunate was Renato Levi, a music-lover who ran a music shop near La Scala and who had been befriended by many well-known musicians: he died in a German concentration camp in 1944.

By the autumn of 1938 Jewish composers and performers had effectively been eliminated from Italian musical life, and the fascist press did not refrain from gloating. Il telegrafo, the Ciano family's newspaper, crowed happily over the change in the Florentine musical scene:

> This year – thank God – soloists, conductors, interpreters, composers and directors of Jewish race have been excluded from both the symphonic season and the 'Maggio Musicale'. There no longer figure on the programme those names which had been raised to seventh heaven by snobbery and Jewish racial solidarity, and which had brought the high-class Florentine public (or the part of it that gives itself musicological airs) to our most important theatre. More than ever before, this public has a duty to attend these artistic events, now that in this field, too, we have been freed of Hebrew idols and idol-worship. It will be a non-Platonic, non-theoretical, non-superficial way of showing one's personal support of Fascism, the reviver of all noble initiatives, animator of a reborn, totalitarian awareness of Italian-ness.[66]

However clear the racial laws may have been, their application was confused. The main article of the August–September 1938 issue of Musica d'oggi was dedicated to Mozart's librettist Lorenzo Da Ponte – a Jew who had converted to Catholicism – on the centenary of his death. The lead article in the October issue of the same magazine was a well-balanced, positive piece on the Jewish composer Max Bruch, on the centenary of his birth. The March 1939 issue of the Rassegna musicale mentions some recent work of the Jewish musicologist and critic Alfred Einstein. The same magazine's issue of May

1942 contains an obituary on the Jewish cellist Emanuel Feuermann, who had died in exile in the United States. And an article on Strauss's *Elektra* in the April 1941 issue of *Musica d'oggi* speaks very well, and by name, of Hugo von Hofmannsthal, the work's Jewish librettist. Naturally, the fact that these men were Jewish is never mentioned; but in Germany praise of them would have been impossible.

An incident typical of the situation has been recounted by a violinist who was a student at the Milan Conservatory in the late 1930s. He was about to play a famous caprice by Wieniawski on a concert in the Conservatory's Great Hall, shortly after the racial laws had taken effect, when an administrator came to him and asked: 'Wasn't Wieniawski a Jew?'

'I have no idea', said the student. After several minutes of dithering, a solution was found: when the violinist went on stage, he announced to the audience that instead of playing the caprice by Wieniawski, he would play a caprice by an anonymous composer. He then played the Wieniawski piece he had prepared, and no one said a word.

Despite such minor infringements, and although overt anti-semitism never took root among Italians – official physical persecution of Italian Jews having occurred only during the German occupation, from September 1943 to April 1945 – protest against Mussolini's racial policy was extremely limited and muted and largely ineffectual, among musicians as among other professional groups. The same *Musica d'oggi*, for instance, that sometimes allowed neutral or even pro-Jewish remarks to slip into print also published items such as the 'letter from Germany' (October 1940) that reported a Berlin performance of Handel's *Judas Maccabaeus*, whose title had been changed to *The General* and whose text had been rewritten. 'A way has thus been found', said the correspondent, 'for playing an undeniable musical masterpiece without having to celebrate the deeds of a people which, having become the parasite of other peoples, has brought upon itself a degree of ostracism that is incompatible with any sort of enthusiasm.'[67] To their credit, major personalities in the Italian musical world at least refrained from jumping on the anti-semitic bandwagon, although some of them occasionally allowed ambiguous remarks to surface. Among these, the most surprising came from the broad-minded Casella, who was married to a Jewish woman. (Yvonne Muller was his second wife; the first, Hélène Kahn, was also Jewish.) In an article published in February 1939, Casella accused many important Italian composers – without naming names – of 'internationalism', and called their music 'the product of international Judaism'. Verdi, he said, had often been accused of anti-modernism because his music was un-Wagnerian. (Casella had made just such a statement many years earlier.)

> And today, in fact, our contemporary music is likewise being defined 'anti-
> modern' in certain foreign circles – predominantly Jewish and snobbish

|circles| of an extremist nature. Our position, however, corresponds to the history and traditions of our country and our race, and is in perfect agreement with the political atmosphere of the Regime, which has raised the nation's existence to a European | . . . | and imperial level.[68]

How sad that Casella had lowered himself, in this respect, to the level of Walter Mocchi, the opportunistic former banana merchant and opera impresario, who had been put to work writing articles in which he thanked the regime for such accomplishments as its 'guardianship of the Race and struggle against Judaism'.[69] Besides, Casella was in effect accommodating the theories adopted by people like Santoliquido in their attacks on him, or by the ever-watchful Lualdi, who took advantage of the changed situation to launch a new offensive against progressivism. In the preface to his book, L'arte di dirigere l'orchestra (the art of conducting), which was written in 1939, Lualdi first admonished young musicians to pay attention to the 'great Chief' who 'daily incites us to boldness, courage, pride in our existence, dangerous living and conquest', and then proceeded to demolish the most bold and courageous musical ideas then in circulation, which he lumped together as

the Italian and international musical cabbala [.] From 1918 to 1938 |i.e. until the racial laws went into effect| | . . . it| laid its aggressive plans in three strongholds: Vienna (Universal-Hertzka), Berlin (Rudolf Steiner and his musical repercussions – Schoenberg, first and foremost), and Paris. |The cabbala's| Italian publicity agency and branch office were located in Turin, under the insignia of Il pianoforte |later re-named Rassegna musicale|, the self-indulgent little journal around which all the fans of ugly music took their stand – as did our home-grown members of and sympathizers with the atheistic, bolshevik musical International; the 'nerve centre' from which, for twenty years, a futile attempt was made to derail and poison our musical taste, our national artistic conscience, and our younger generations of artists | . . . |; the authorized interpreter and false prophet of a mob of foreign and native Messiahs, of whom nothing more is heard today, or who have been cut down to their proper size | . . . |; the standard-bearer of all the worst, most decadent drawing-room snobberies. All this has now begun to totter because – with the loss of Vienna and Berlin – it finds itself having to gravitate around a single, sadly reduced survivor: Henry Prunières and his Revue musicale | . . . |.[70]

Lualdi chose to rant on this subject in a book on conducting because precisely at that moment he was so delighted at seeing his star in the ascendant – at seeing the conservative, ethnocentric faction of the Italian musical hierarchy apparently on the verge of a decisive victory over the radical, cosmopolitan element – that he could not refrain from jumping for joy. Once he began to talk about conducting, he dropped the political polemics, except for a swipe at Toscanini, whom he accused of having been led astray (read: out of the fascist fold) as a result of his 'unfortunate character and dangerous friendships'.[71]

Italian audiences, like their counterparts in the Reich, were no longer allowed to listen to music by such native-German-speaking but non-Aryan degenerates as Mendelssohn, Offenbach, Mahler, Weill and Schoenberg; instead, they could feast upon – indeed could hardly avoid – the works of such racially pure foreigners as Werner Egk, Ottmar Gerster, Wilhelm Kempff, Carl Orff and Norbert Schultze. German performing artists also took advantage of the newly Jew-free Italian musical scene by appearing ever more frequently in their Axis ally's theatres and concert halls. The list of conductors, instrumentalists and singers who worked in Italy between 1938 and 1943 includes nearly every important German musician of the day. In addition to such established artists as Furtwängler, Walter Gieseking, Wilhelm Backhaus, Carl Schuricht and Edwin Fischer, many youngsters were given a hearing in Italy. Thirty-three-year-old Herbert von Karajan, for instance, conducted concerts at La Scala in 1941 and then led *Don Giovanni* and Beethoven's Ninth Symphony at the following year's *Maggio Musicale*.

Italian musicians, too, profited from the growing Rome–Berlin friendship, as this very incomplete list indicates:

De Sabata conducted the Berlin Philharmonic during the 1935–6 season.[72]

Lualdi conducted the Berlin Radio Orchestra in 1936.[73]

Marinuzzi conducted the Munich State Opera in 1936.[74]

The entire Scala ensemble under De Sabata toured Germany in 1937.[75]

The Santa Cecilia Orchestra under Molinari toured Germany (seventeen concerts in Berlin, Munich and other important cities) in 1937.[76]

The tenor Giacomo Lauri Volpi and the conductor Antonino Votto were among the artists who participated in a special Italian opera season in Germany in 1938.[77]

Enrico Mainardi became principal professor of cello at the Berlin State Music Academy in 1939.[78]

Molinari conducted the Berlin Philharmonic during the 1940–1 season, and many other Italian artists (e.g. Toti Dal Monte and violinists Arrigo Pelliccia and Gioconda De Vito) were also performing in Germany.[79]

The Rome Opera, with well-known singers and conductors, performed seven operas in Berlin in 1941. Göbbels was among those in attendance.[80]

The Scala Orchestra under Marinuzzi toured Germany in 1941, with a repertoire consisting entirely of works by German, Austrian and Italian composers.[81]

In the autumn of 1941, Gui conducted *Aida* in Vienna, Franco Ferrara conducted a concert in Königsberg and Mariano Stabile sang in Graz.[82]

In the spring of 1942, Casella conducted his Symphony, Op. 61, in Vienna, and Gui and Mario Rossi conducted in Berlin.[83]

One by-product of the Axis alliance was a book by the German musicologist Hans Engel on the history of musical relations between Germany and Italy. According to *The New Grove*, Engel 'wielded a sharp sword in the cause of the pursuit of knowledge'.[84] But in the case of *Deutschland und Italien in ihren musikgeschichtlichen Beziehungen*, his weapon seems rather blunt. 'Our choice of subject requires no explanation', he said. 'The current political situation is not at all its only justification.' If not the only justification, however, it was an important one; for besides stringing together trite generalizations about 'the Germanic peoples' longing for southern lands' and 'Italians' longing for northern profundity',[85] Engel provided his theses with 'historical and racial bases. [. . .] The racial question, he said, 'has emerged so strongly into the foreground that the problem of racial relations between Germany and Italy must be set at the forefront of our considerations.'[86] Dismissing as 'amateurish' the hypothesis propounded by 'race researcher' H. F. K. Guenther – to the effect that the Germanic *Volk* was made up of 'six basic races' – Engel favoured Friedrich Keiter's no less silly theory of three basic European facial types, one of which was allegedly common both to large numbers of northern Italians and to Germans. This helped to explain why there had been so constant a cross-pollination between Germanic and Italic music, said Engel. While warning students of the subject not to seek 'the racial provenance' of composers in specific details of their works, he asserted that those works' 'racial style may be recognized in a general way'.[87]

Engel avoided direct attacks on Jews and other groups, and there was nothing especially racial in his exposition of the historical links between German and Italian music. He did, however, provide a racial chart – remarkable for its grotesque over-simplifications and general unintelligibility – which deserves to be reproduced as the last word on 'inter-Aryan' musical relations. (See table pp. 192–3)

Amid all the nonsense and all the shabby acquiescence of the period, one musical protest stands out: Luigi Dallapiccola's *Canti di prigionia* for chorus and instrumental ensemble.

> I was working on my first opera, *Volo di notte*, [. . .] when curious rumors began to circulate at first very discreetly, later in more obvious fashion. Could Fascism have unleashed a race campaign after the model of that of the dastardly Adolf Hitler?
>
> In an issue of the *Corrispondenza Politico-Diplomatica* in the middle of February 1938, such rumors were hastily denied. However, knowing from experience what interpretation to give to official denials, we all had the impression that the Fascist government was lying once more.
>
> Five months later, on July 15th to be exact, there appeared in the papers the

grotesque 'race manifesto'; this was even more shocking because it was tainted by pseudo-science. On the afternoon of September 1st, the race campaign was officially inaugurated.

[. . .] How should I describe my state of mind when I learned from the radio of the decision of the Fascist government on that fateful September afternoon? I should have liked to protest; but, at the same time, I was aware that any gesture of mine would have been futile. Only through music could I express my indignation. [. . .] [n.b.: Dallapiccola did make a non-musical statement against the racial laws by marrying his Jewish companion, Laura Coen Luzzatto.]

I had just finished reading *Mary Stuart* by Stefan Zweig. Through this book, I became acquainted with a short prayer written by the Queen of Scots during the last years of her imprisonment:

> O Domine Deus! speravi in Te.
> O care mi Jesu! nunc libera me.

My intention was to transform the prayer of the queen as an individual into a song for all mankind. I wanted to dwell at length upon the word 'libera' in music, to have this divine word shouted by everyone. [. . .]

In sketching the *Preghiera di Maria Stuarda*, I had no preconceived idea of the general construction of the *Canti di Prigionia*. However, one number alone seemed to me too little to express my protest completely. I had to find other texts, of other illustrious prisoners, of other individuals who had fought for liberty and for the triumph of justice. [. . .]

Boethius, the sixth-century philosopher, provided me with the text for the second number, written in the summer of 1940. This was to be a sort of scherzo in which the 'apocalyptic' character should be very much in evidence [. . .]. Among the various aspects of terror is the terror that freezes; there is not only that which finds its natural outlet in a shriek. I chose the first of these aspects [. . .].[88]

Dallapiccola had difficulty in finding a third and final text.

On August 19, 1940, my wife and I happened to be at Covigliaio, a small mountain retreat [north of Florence]. That evening, the radio brought Hitler's fearful speech to the Reichstag. The imminence of air attacks on England was announced. [British Foreign Secretary] Sir Samuel Hoare, answering Hitler, urged the people to pray.

At last I hit upon it! [. . .][89]

The composer chose a passage from Gerolamo Savonarola's *Meditatio* on the psalm, *In Te Domine speravi*, and was then able to complete the work.

The first performance of the *Preghiera di Maria Stuarda* took place on the Flemish radio at Brussels on April 10, 1940. It was the last time in Italy that I was able to hear a Belgian broadcast. Four weeks later came the Nazi invasion.

The first performance of the entire work took place at Rome, amongst all

	Southern Italy	Northern Italy (S. Alpine)	Southern Germany (N. Alpine)	Northern Germany	North-east
Physique					
Colour*	mainly brown-eyed	→—————		mainly blue-eyed	
Facial shape	pointy		average		flat
Build	small	large			very large
Psyche	integrated	(unint)	(int)		unintegrated
	open	closed	open	closed	
	changeable				dull
involuntary nerves	excitable	cheerful		cool	apathetic
Musical talent	34%	66% (area of greatest mus. talent)	74%	26% (of musicians)	
music	melody	mixed / polyphonists	homophonists	linear polyphony	
Characteristics	temperament			quiet passion	
	pathos			feeling	
	gesture			pensiveness	
	bel canto		lied	choir	
	coloratura		lied		
	ornamentations in folk-music				
Excess	brilliance			pendantry	
	pretty sound			structure overloading	
	simplistic-infantile			erudite-dry	
				heavy	
Humour	comic	satyric	merry		sharp

Traits		Italian	German
16th cent.	Lasso	Italian charm	German awkwardness
17th cent.	Hirsch	tempered style	hardwork
			morose seriousness
18th cent.	Quantz	more artistic	great voices
		moving expression	no singers
		charlatans	
19th cent.	Mozart	richly melodic songs	national sound
	Schubart	melody	affected harmony
	Paisiello	ear-tickling singing	eye-itching (notes)
	Wagner	flowery form	formal chaos
		ornamental fury	unholy erudition
	Nicolai	too little philosophy	too much philosophy
	Verdi	vocal music	instrumental music
		vocal polyphony	symphonic
		opera	concert
		mainly sung	highly expressive

L. Torchi 1884

* The colouring of Northern Italians, according to Keiter, is connected as a direct transition to the Alpine Germans. In Styria 30% have blue eyes, in Northern Italy 20%. Those with brown eyes are altogether dominant; in the South 80% have dark brown eyes. The head shape is said to be elongated in the South, with a clear-cut tendency towards pointiness.[90]

kinds of difficulties, on the afternoon of December 11, 1941. The city presented a sinister aspect: police cordons everywhere and radios bellowing all over. On that day, Mussolini declared war on the United States.

After the Rome performance, personalities and circumstances barred the way for the *Canti di Prigionia*. This state of affairs lasted till the end of the war. [...][91]

Throughout the spring of 1940, as Hitler's troops wolfed down more and more of western Europe, Mussolini's resolve to partake of the territorial spoils grew until he had whipped himself into a frenzy.[92] The Duce's rashest act and fatal error was to bring Italy into the Second World War alongside Germany. His military advisers knew that the country was unprepared for such a venture, but they either assumed that he had information they did not have about the Germans' capabilities or were simply afraid to oppose him. He had assumed the role of commander-in-chief and now held virtually complete control over the nation. Since there was no appeal from his decisions, no bureaucrats, military or civilian, were willing to risk their careers on any issue that might conceivably have interested him. 'He alone', says Mack Smith, 'could decide when the traffic police should change into their white summer uniforms, or when the military band on the Lido should begin its series of Sunday concerts.'

> From 1939 onwards this psychological quirk became more noticeable and more dangerous. Thus on 21 April 1940, when the whole fate of Italy was in the balance, Mussolini found time to discuss and authorise the felling of a tree stump on the Via dell'Impero. On 16 May, since he had to approve details of the Rome opera season, he demanded the inclusion of *Tannhäuser* rather than *Parsifal*, and no doubt this was because of some intricate theory about its effect on public morale.[93]

Or because, as he often said, he liked *Tannhäuser* but did not like *Parsifal*. On 10 June, without seeking the advice of his cabinet or military leaders, Mussolini declared war on Britain and France and attacked the latter, which was already on the verge of surrendering to the Germans. Italy's territorial gains in France were practically nil, and within a year Mussolini lost Ethiopia, was stymied in the Balkans and found himself having to depend increasingly on the Germans to keep his regime from collapsing. He nevertheless declared war on the Soviet Union shortly after the Germans had opened the eastern front, and on the United States four days after the Japanese attack on Pearl Harbour. By 1942 Italy's situation was becoming desperate, and it worsened through the first half of the following year.

Mussolini had ranted a great deal in public, during the months leading up to the attack on France, about the need for increased military productivity – even at the cost of 'bringing all civilized life to a halt'.[94] Now the nation was doubly hoodwinked: the government's schemes for increasing military capacity were too disorganized, too small-scale and too late to bring Italy even the most fleeting material victories; but the war effort did indeed cause a great reduction in and eventually the virtual elimination of those aspects of life that are usually referred to as civilized.

Most Italian musicians were presumably not delighted with the prospect of war, but few publicly expressed their feelings on the subject. Those who did make statements spoke in favour of the war and were either ignorantly or dishonestly optimistic about it. Lualdi – who, as usual, led the way among the fascist music-bureaucrats – proclaimed in August 1940 that after only two months of war, it was still hard to realize that this was the most important event in Italian history since the fall of Rome 1,400 years earlier. A mere fifteen years of fascism had sufficed to bring down the French and British empires, he crowed; and he went on to describe this turn of events as 'a great miracle, never before witnessed in History. And the determining factor will have been the irresistible, fateful march of a new, revolutionary civilization and a new concept of the State and the World, rather than a series of brutal, barbarian invasions.'[95] After heaping praise on Mussolini and Hitler, Lualdi predicted that the arts would flourish after the war and that the important figures in Italian culture would receive economic assistance from the government. Enthusiasm, passion and native intelligence were, he said, the qualities that gave Italy its spiritual primacy over other countries. Having got that rather generic declaration off his chest, Lualdi produced a series of more pointed articles for the *Giornale d'Italia*.

> For us Italians, one of the gravest and brightest duties | ... | will be to represent, alone, in the Europe of tomorrow, the bastion and the torch, the centre of expansion and the line of defence of Roman-ness, of Latin-ness – of Latin and Roman art, thought, spirit and classical culture. The *Ville lumière* (because all the rest was | ... | 'the provinces') had lost much of its enlightening energy in recent years; but many continued to | ... | consider it | ... | not merely a beacon of European and world civilization, but also a beacon and first line of defence of Latin, Roman and classical civilization – which is as good as saying civilization itself, |for Latin civilization| is the mother of all civilizations. | ... |
>
> In France, one cannot speak of music without keeping literature in mind. In this, too, Italy was teacher to other Nations; she then let herself be led by the hand. This is another position to be reconquered, another bright tradition to be rejuvenated. | ... |
>
> | ... One has only to think| about the spiritual phenomenon that will have to operate through fascist and imperial Italian impulses and influence within whole nations, peoples and continents, in order to realize and convince oneself that the torch of eternal Latin culture and art – neglected and abandoned by France – must now glow, thanks to the miraculous spiritual virtue of a Man to whom a great people has worthily responded upon the

Capitoline hill. Let them learn to look no longer towards Paris but towards Rome for their proper beacon.

Raffaello De Rensis was also ready to plunge his tiny dagger into French culture which, bound and gagged, could not defend itself. His pro-war articles on 'The Centuries-Old Struggle between Italian and French Music' demonstrates the born propagandist's ability to mix largely irrelevant facts with highly debatable opinions and jingoistic nonsense.

> | ... | The French language stimulates insufficient melody and supports it but weakly, |because the language is| but lightly accented, full of feeble sounds and silent *e*'s, and rather unpleasantly nasal; and its poetry is uniform and arhythmical. | ... |
> | ... | The political factor | ... | has always blinded French objectivity in judging Italian art. | ... | This illogical situation, tolerated for centuries, could last no longer. On 10 June 1940 Italy was forced to declare war on France in order to obliterate forever an unjust subjection and a false sisterhood.

De Rensis ended his statement with the hope that Italian form and spirit would once again govern French music.[96]

Musicologist Remo Giazotto, rewriting history in order to associate music with the need to defend fascist Italy, declared in an article published in August 1940 that Giuseppe Verdi, forty years in his grave, had prefigured the spirit of fascism in works written before the Duce's birth. His argumentation is remarkable even by fascist standards.

> Giuseppe Verdi's musical art should be enjoyed in a working atmosphere; his ethical values are sacrosanctly reserved for the people who sweat to earn their daily bread | ... |. Verdi worked as an Italian *citizen*, when the martyrs of our Risorgimento were working to create the Italian *citizen*. | ... | Every note of his songs is a palpitation of faith in his country, a breath of freedom.
> Working atmosphere, atmosphere of toil, atmosphere of faith. Work, toil and faith know no respite; this is true of the nation that believes and wills; this is true of our nation, which lives, acts and makes history in Mussolini's name. | ... |
> To create is an activity necessary to human well-being. But of what use would the products of that creativity be if their value were not justly recognized? | ... |
> No sooner had the new era, the fascist era, commenced than Italy began to feel a need to collect, popularize and review its spiritual values, in keeping with the new awareness, with the new concept of the country's historic and artistic traditions. | ... | The spiritual atmosphere created by Fascism is particularly conducive to meditation, to concentration and to encyclo-paedism |*sic*|. | ... | In the fascist atmosphere, this meditative, organizational process is doubly significant: it is, above all, the conquest and exaltation of our past; and it should also be the solid basis | ... | for creative work. | ... |
> Take Verdi, for example. In the nineteenth century that name was

venerated and exalted because it represented [sic] a propitious symbol of the political aspirations of the day. | ... | They loved him selfishly and fanatically, just as a child loves his closest relatives | ... |. But we today love Verdi as a man loves and respects his father. Verdi is an absolute reality in our fascist times, a reality that soars in sunlight and free air. | ... |

Mussolini's century is that of the defence of spiritual and earthly values. Italians live today in the atmosphere of this battle, this hand-to-hand combat. For the fascist people, defending their music is almost like defending a wheat or grape harvest. We go to the theatre today with this fascist awareness. | ... |

This is why there is a strong, virile love for Verdi. An Italian fascist hears in Verdi's music the taste [sic] of its land. We have won the battle for wheat; we can eat bread made entirely from our wheat. Verdi's music is entirely our music. | ... | Verdi's music is bread: pure bread that inexhaustibly refills the larder with its purely Italian generosity.

The sun that illuminates and enlivens the musical world of Giuseppe Verdi is the same one that blesses our land.[97]

As the war dragged on, and as prospects for Italian world domination shrank, statements of mystical or perhaps hallucinatory fascist faith such as Giazotto's, and Lualdi- and De Rensis-like outbursts of premature glee, became fewer. Not that there were any published protests: even if someone had decided to make one, it would not have escaped the press censors' scissors. Such 'slips' as were made in past days were no longer possible. Mila came closer than anyone else to talking out of turn when, at the end of a long review, in the *Rassegna musicale*, of a book on Petrassi by D'Amico, he remarked – not without irony: 'Although he is not drowning in a shapeless vacuum of internationalism', Petrassi must maintain 'his European consciousness – that way of being Italianly, perhaps Romanly, European – in which all of us – Petrassi, D'Amico and I – believe.'[98]

For most non-Jewish musicians, life went on as usual, war or no war. The king awarded First Category diplomas for artistic merit to Mascagni, Cilea, Pizzetti and Giordano;[99] musicologist Fausto Torrefranca persuaded Mussolini's sister, Edvige Mancini, to tell her brother that Torrefranca was underpaid in comparison with his colleagues – especially in view of his 'thirty-five years of tenacious work and hard struggle against foreign schools';[100] the Duce continued to receive musicians who wished to be congratulated on their achievements or to have their complaints looked after; and the elder statesmen of Italian music continued to jostle each other on the issue of who was to be included in the Accademia d'Italia.[101]

As the war continued, money became increasingly hard to find for Italian musical institutions. Appearances, however, were kept up for a while. In the spring of 1941, for instance, Marino Lazzari, Director-General of the Education Ministry's Fine Arts section, confirmed the government's intention to 'broaden the areas of culture in the conservatories' and to see to 'the development of the Unions' and Recreation Associations' Exhibitions and to the granting of scholarships and subsidies. Fresh air will enter our opera houses and concert halls [. . .].'[102] Fresh air did indeed enter many such buildings during 1943, 1944 and 1945, but in a way not intended by Lazzari. Pizzetti's commission for autarchy in musical instruction provided useless work for a number of music administrators. And the MinCulPop put eight 'student managers' on its payroll, for on-the-job training in running the state-supported *enti autonomi* – as if the hardy race of arts bureaucrats had been on the verge of extinction rather than badly in need of thinning out.[103] Despite drops in attendance – down, even at La Scala, by eight per cent during the 1940–1 season[104] – a few commissions for new works still trickled down to composers from time to time. Antonio Veretti, for example, was paid by Venice's Teatro la Fenice to write an opera, *La scuola del villaggio*, set – surely not by coincidence – in Japan.[105] Under the circumstances, he couldn't very well have set it in the Midlands, the Pale of Settlement or Paris in the 1920s.

Or could he? A few hardly less astonishing facts spring forth from the pages of the music journals of the day. The Autumn 1942 series of contemporary operas, ballets and choral works, held at La Scala and the Rome Opera, included not only compositions by Italians (Ghedini's *Re Hassan*, Casella's *La donna serpente*, Felice Lattuada's *La tempesta*, Respighi's *Belfagor*, Dallapiccola's *Volo di notte*, Busoni's *Arlecchino*, Petrassi's *Coro di morti* and the world première of Malipiero's *I capricci di Callot*, but also the Italian premières of four foreign works: *Carmina Burana* by the German, Nazi-sanctioned Carl Orff; *Amphion* by the Swiss Honegger; *The Miraculous Mandarin* by the decidedly anti-fascist Bartók, then living in exile in the United States; and, most astonishing, *Wozzeck* by Berg – who, although 'Ayran' (and dead) had nevertheless been a subversive adherent of the 'Jewish–cosmopolitan–bolshevik' Schoenberg and his teachings.[106] The inclusion of *Wozzeck*, with the twenty-seven-year-old Tito Gobbi in the title role, seems to have been De Pirro's idea;[107] but Serafin, the sixty-four-year-old conductor, 'threw himself into the study of [the work] with the enthusiasm of a twenty-year-old', according to Fedele D'Amico. 'It is a landmark for Italian musical culture – the real point of departure for venturing into one of the vastest of modern musical experiences.'[108]

Such an event could not have taken place in Germany or the territories it occupied, and the same was true of many other performances and articles – some of them worth listing – that the Italian authorities allowed to pass.

Late 1940: Stravinsky's *Histoire du soldat* was given at Rome's Teatro delle Arti.[109]

February 1941: 'Igor Stravinsky and His Most Recent Works', a lengthy and highly laudatory lead article by Alberto Mantelli, was published in the *Rassegna musicale*.[110]

Autumn 1941: The publication of *Mikrokosmos* by Bartók ('an artist and pedagogue of highest quality') was announced in *Musica d'oggi*.[111]

Early 1942: Stravinsky's *Renard* and *Mavra* were performed in Rome, his *Fireworks* in Milan, and his *Pribaoutki* in Turin; Prokofiev's *The Prodigal Son* was given in Rome.[112]

Rassegna musicale, May 1942: Massimo Mila, in a column on recent recordings, discussed works by Stravinsky, Prokofiev and Bartók.[113]

Musica d'oggi, May 1942: 'During the siege of Leningrad, the Russian composer Dmitri Shostakovich composed his Seventh Symphony, which was inspired by Russia's tragic experiences. The first performance (followed by a radio broadcast) took place in Kuibychev [provisional seat of government].'[114]

Spring 1942: The 'Pro Musica' society of Bologna sponsored a concert series that included music by Berg, Stravinsky and Hindemith.[115]

Musica d'oggi, August–September 1942: An article on contemporary Hungarian music praised Bartók and Kodály.[116]

Rassegna musicale, September–October 1942: Nicola Costarelli, in a substantial article on twelve-tone music, explained the system and, without mentioning Schoenberg or any other exponents, advised open-mindedness. 'Art must be judged through [individual] works', he said.[117]

April–May 1943: The Teatro delle Arti's *Manifestazioni musicali* included works by Stravinsky and Hindemith.[118]

Shostakovich's symphony, inspired by the Russian war effort, raised an obvious question: why had major Italian composers not been similarly inspired? The issue was set forth by 'Tito Silvio Mursino' – anagram and pseudonym of Vittorio Mussolini, the Duce's eldest son – in *Il messaggero*, a Rome daily.

> [. . .] So far as I have heard, composers in the other countries [i.e. belligerent countries other than the USSR] have hitherto continued to go their separate ways, as if detached from the immense events that are taking place before their eyes [. . .]. In Italy there has been no such attempt: we have had a few nice songs, some listenable anthems and marches, but nothing more. [. . .]
> Thus we come back to the *vexata quaestio*: the lack of involvement in the war on the part of our intellectuals. The old proverb – 'When the cannon speaks the Muses are silent' – would, in that case, be proved right. But I am not of that opinion. The great Italian Muse has been silent for quite a while, and perhaps only the war will encourage her to sing. [. . .] Never has Italian Art made such

progress, aroused such arguments and had so much success as in these three years of war. [!] [. . .]

[. . .] But, I maintain, one must at least try [. . .] to come up with something related to the drama we are living through, which will decide our fate for centuries. Why can't |Giorgio| De Chirico give us a fine modern battle canvas? Why can't |Arturo| Martini sculpt, in eternal marble, the heroism of a conquerer of enemy fortifications? Why can't |Riccardo| Bacchelli set his mind to a fourth volume of *Il mulino sul Po* [*The Mill on the Po*]? Why can't Dalla Piccola [*sic*] see the way towards composing a symphony on the theme of war? [. . .] You are Italians and fascists, and as such you cannot continue to paint flowers and bottles, to sculpt the heads of countesses and important personages, to write the same old plays about cuckolds in evening dress, or to compose barcarolles forever. [. . .] In the silence of your studies, [. . .] think seriously about doing something yourselves for this tremendous struggle, which must be won not only by gunfire but also and above all by the spirit. [. . .][119]

Mussolini Junior's summary of what he apparently believed some of the country's leading contemporary masters were doing – churning out Feydeau-like comedies and tossing off tuneful songs for gondoliers to warble – gives an idea of his level of cultural awareness. He noted that he had used those four names only because they were well known, not because he considered their bearers more guilty than their colleagues. But if some of the music Dallapiccola was writing or thinking about writing during that period was indeed connected with 'the theme of war' and related issues, its tone was not the optimistic, heroic one 'Mursino' had in mind.

Shostakovich, whose patriotism had allegedly inspired the work that provoked Vittorio Mussolini's article, was later reported to have said: 'Actually, I have nothing against calling the Seventh the Leningrad Symphony, but it's not about Leningrad under siege, it's about the Leningrad that Stalin destroyed and that Hitler merely finished off.'[120] If this quotation is correct, the symphony was intended more as a protest against dictatorship than as a description of national wartime heroism: its message was *sic semper tyrannis*. Neither the Duce nor his son would have approved.

But the Duce's approval or disapproval of anything soon became irrelevant. The Allied invasion of Italy began in Sicily on 10 July 1943, and the impossibility of the country's situation brought the Grand Council of Fascism to pass a motion of no confidence in the government. After two decades of opportunistic dithering, the king had Mussolini arrested. Marshal Pietro Badoglio became prime minister and announced that the war would continue. Secret peace negotiations were initiated with Britain and the United States but proceeded so slowly that Italy's German allies had time to occupy much of the peninsula, while the other side rained destruction from the air on Italian cities. An armistice between Italy and the Allied forces, signed on 8 September, proved to be the starter's gun for a year and a half of murder and destruction that far surpassed anything in the country's turbulent history. While the king's government was regrouping at Brindisi in the south, preparing to declare war against Germany, the Nazis freed Mussolini from prison and installed him as puppet dictator of a fascist republic head-quartered at Salò on Lake Garda; its control extended over much of the north. All the major parties that had been suppressed under fascism – the Christian Democrats (led by Alcide De Gasperi), the Communists (Palmiro Togliatti), the Liberals (Croce) and the Socialists (Pietro Nenni) and their splintered-off Reformists (Giuseppe Saragat) – formed a coalition government, still at Brindisi, in 1944, first under Badoglio and then under Ivanoe Bonomi, who had been one of the last pre-fascist prime ministers. The Allied front, massively assisted by Italian partisans, moved northwards, encountering terrible resistance from the Germans and from what remained of the fascist Italian forces.

To speak of the effect of these conditions on the country's musical activities sounds almost silly: Allied air attacks on the cities left many historic theatres unusable. Among the most important of them, Genoa's Teatro Carlo Felice (1828) was destroyed, Florence's Teatro Comunale (1862) was partially devastated and La Scala's auditorium (1778) was largely demolished. Some of the ensembles these and other theatres had housed attempted to carry on under reduced circumstances and makeshift conditions: the sheer economic survival of their employees made this imperative, and providing some sort of entertainment for the populace was considered good for morale.

Individual musicians and others professionally connected with music had to fend for themselves. Even the very, very few of them who had previously had a better than adequate income soon found their resources badly eroded by uncontrollable inflation. Those who lived in Rome, which underwent little physical destruction but was occupied by the Germans from September 1943 to June 1944, faced the nightmare in a variety of ways. Mascagni, now eighty and fading, gratefully accepted lunches sent him by Pope Pius XII.[121] Casella, twenty years younger but ill with cancer, lived in constant fear of being torn from his Franco-Jewish wife and their daughter, who were subject to arrest and deportation. One evening, having been tipped off about a raid on their apartment, the family split up and hid in the homes of friends, not to reassemble until the 'Jew hunt' had ended.[122] Shortly after the German retreat, Casella began work on his *Missa solemnis pro pace*, with which he was to end his career as a composer.

After Mussolini's fall, Pizzetti was nominated by the first Badoglio government to preside over a study commission whose job was to make provisions for the reorganization of the conservatory system; this gave him a modest source of income. But 'how can one work', he asked his diary in March

1944, 'when one's heart is strangled with anguish?'. On 3 June he complained that 'we have no water, no electricity, and the telephone no longer works'. Then, two days later: 'Last evening, after sundown, the Anglo-Americans entered Rome and the Germans abandoned it. Great event! And God save and protect Italy! And save and protect all my family, and me for them!'[123]

Beniamino Gigli, who had performed for the German troops throughout their occupation of the capital, and indeed until the very eve of their retreat, could not understand why he was treated as a *persona non grata* when they departed.

> I now discovered, to my surprise, that because I had 'sung for the Germans', I had become a traitor. The accusation was made not by the Allies but by my own compatriots. Threatening crowds besieged my residence in Rome; for months I dared not go out.
>
> One day an English officer came to investigate. 'Of course I sang for the Germans,' I told him. 'I've sung for everyone. I've sung for the English and the Americans. I sang under the fascist government, just as I would have sung under the bolsheviks or under any other government that had found itself governing Italy. I can't see why this makes me a traitor. And you?' The officer laughed and went away.
>
> This unpleasant situation lasted about nine months. In the spring of 1945 things seemed to calm down. I began to appear in public again. On 12 March I sang in a concert at [Rome's] Teatro Adriano [to raise money] for refugees. Many asked me afterwards: 'When will you start singing opera again?' I thought to myself: 'I'll wait until they ask me.' I did not have to wait long.[124]

Gigli resumed his operatic career two months later. His disingenuous answers to the accusations of collaborationism satisfied many people; for others his reputation remained tainted.

One of Rome's most venerable theatres – the Argentina (1732), where the first production of Rossini's *Barber of Seville* had taken place – was chosen as the venue for a popular opera series given for Anglo-American troops in 1944–5. 'They were accompanied by young local ladies,' wrote one of the theatre's historians, 'and together they watched the productions while chewing gum and putting their feet up on the seats in front of them and on the boxes' rails. More than a few of them made love in the recesses of the upper levels, and it is not unlikely that numerous war babies were conceived to Puccini's melodies [. . .]'.[125]

Further to the north, conditions were more difficult for musicians. Alfano, who had recently retired as director of the Turin Conservatory, saw most of his possessions destroyed during a bombing raid in November 1942; an imploring letter to the Duce, who was then still in the saddle, brought him a cheque for the considerable sum of 50,000 lire.[126] In the same city a year and a half later, the aged Jewish composer Leone Sinigaglia died of cardiac arrest when the Germans came to his door to deport him. In Florence, no sooner had Mussolini's fall been announced in July 1943 than Titta Ruffo rushed to his window and began to sing the 'Marseillaise'; an exultant crowd gathered outside and gradually joined in the singing. It was the very last time the sixty-six-year-old baritone sang in public – and it was too soon. When the Germans occupied the city six weeks later, Ruffo had to go into hiding: friends looked after him, and he changed residence frequently to avoid discovery. In August 1944, as the British Eighth Army fought its way into the city, he barely managed to escape from the building he was living in before the retreating Germans blew it up.[127] Less fortunate was his friend Lina Cavalieri, the seventy-year-old former diva, who had been as celebrated for her beauty as for her voice, and who was also living in Florence: she died under the Allies' bombs early in 1944.

At least two young composers – Riccardo Malipiero (nephew of Gian Francesco) and Bruno Maderna – joined the partisans, as, no doubt, did many uncelebrated musicians throughout the country. Maderna's activities landed him in a concentration camp, but he survived to become one of the most influential Italian musicians of his generation. Pariso Votto, who had long headed Florence's Teatro Comunale and *Maggio Musicale* under the fascist aegis, joined the partisans as the Allied front approached, and resurfaced in his old position a few months later under Allied protection.

Dallapiccola, whose *Canti di prigionia* were inspired by the racial campaign and the events leading up to the war, now conceived a new large-scale work closely related to the horrors of the war itself. *Il Prigioniero* – an opera based on Philippe Auguste Villiers de l'Isle-Adam's *La Torture par l'espérance* and Charles de Coster's *La Légende d'Ulenspiegel et de Lamme Goedzak* – began to gestate while its composer lived in constant fear for his Jewish wife's survival. As in the *Canti*, Dallapiccola clothed his protest under the mantle of historical allusion.

> Between 1942 and 1943 | ... | it became increasingly clear to me that I must write an opera which, in spite of its background and historical setting, could be both moving and timely; a work that would portray the tragedy of our times and the tragedy of persecution felt and suffered by millions of individuals. I would turn to free men; why should I concern myself with the | ... | incongruities of the Fascists in any |specific| country? | ... |[128]

Dallapiccola had felt a 'glorious burst of joy' when Mussolini's fall was announced ('the happiest day of my life'),[129] but soon found himself living under Nazi occupation in Florence. Shortly after the Germans arrived in the city, he and his wife moved to a friend's country villa at Borgunto, near Fiesole.

> On November 6th Igor Markevitch arrived on his bicycle to tell me that the rounding up of Jews had begun. Six days later, we left for Como, where we

would be prepared for a possible escape into Switzerland. But if we should have gone, I would have had to remain without news of my mother for months or even years. [...] We returned to Borgunto. [...]

[...] On December 9th of that terrible 1943, my wife decided, for the sake of us all, that she ought to take shelter for some time in the city, in a house placed at her disposal by a generous friend. Every night at dusk I went to see her, carefully choosing a different route every time. [...] Reassuring news brought my wife back to Borgunto.

Between Christmas Eve and New Year's Eve [...] I prepared a final draft of the libretto [of Il Prigioniero] which, on January 4, 1944, I read in San Domenico [Fiesole] at the home of my friends, the Bonsantis. [...]

At the last words of the Prisoner, who unconsciously mutters 'Freedom?' though giving the word a definitely questioning tone, there was a minute of silence. Alessandro Bonsanti [writer, literary critic and – many years later – mayor of Florence] spoke first: 'For me', he said, 'I dare to hope it will be the Fascists who will end at the stake.'

[...] At the beginning of February the villa in Borgunto was requisitioned by the Nazi command. No way lay open but to return to the city, and then to change our residence from time to time. This we did until friends cordially took us in so that we might await with them through interminable days and nights the moment of liberation.

The air-raid sirens blew their warnings seven or eight times a day. [...] What robbed me of all peace of mind, in the most humiliating manner, was the treacherous persecution, the anonymous denunciation, the arrogant prose of the newspapers, the petty Fascist officials who would stare meaningfully after anyone they met on the street. [....]

The summer of 1944 was quite long, but, with God's help, August 11 arrived, and with it, the liberation of the entire city of Florence took place. [...][130]

In April 1945 Allied and partisan forces captured the rest of northern Italy; by the end of the month the liberation was complete. Party leaders who had voted Mussolini out of power in 1943 and who had later fallen into his clutches at Salò – among them his son-in-law, Ciano – had long since been shot at his orders. Now Mussolini, Starace, Farinacci and other fascist leaders were shot by partisans; their bodies and that of the Duce's mistress, Clara Petacci, were brought to Milan and exposed to public vilification in Piazzale Loreto.

Gentile was shot by Tuscan partisans in 1944; Bottai (one of those who had voted against Mussolini at the Grand Council meeting) escaped from the country, joined the French Foreign Legion under a false name and eventually returned to Italy, where he died in 1959. Lualdi was removed from the directorship of the Naples Conservatory in 1944 but became head of the Florence Conservatory three years later, remaining there until his retirement in 1956. Mulè, who was Lualdi's exact contemporary, lost his position at the Santa Cecilia Conservatory in 1943 and opted for retirement thereafter. Toni, who had remained dedicated to Mussolini to the end (he had asked to visit the Duce as late as October 1944, when most of the rats had long since abandoned the ship), became music critic for Milan's right-wing *La notte*; in collaboration with Serafin he published *Stile, tradizioni e convenzioni del melodramma italiano* (1958–64). Labroca's post-war career was entirely honourable. He continued to carry out administrative jobs fairly and intelligently and served as president of UNESCO's International Musical Council from 1958 to 1960.

The *verismo* composers who had been honoured by the regime all survived its defeat: Mascagni died in misery three months after the war's end; Giordano survived him by three years, Cilea by a further two. Of the leading members of the *Generazione dell'80*, Respighi had died in 1936. Casella, despite his illness, continued to be a source of inspiration and stimulation to young musicians until his death in 1947. Malipiero, when the war ended, continued to complain. Instead of whispering *mea culpa* as quietly as possible and trying to draw a heavy curtain over his relations with the regime – as nearly all his colleagues were doing – he noisily criticized those European composers who had emigrated to America just before the war and who were now accusing their 'Axis' brethren of collaborationism. No, no, said Malipiero: those who had stayed behind were the ones who had had to undergo wartime physical privations.

> [Spring 1945] An informative article by Darius Milhaud has arrived from America; it speaks of refugee musicians in the United States. These *martyrs* [...] lived in safety, in Dollar Paradise [...]. Conflicting ideologies and racism endangered many very famous musicians, but we'd better settle right now which side the martyrs are to be found on. Homesickness for one's country is certainly a serious form of suffering for those in exile, but bombings, revolutions, hunger, etc., etc., don't make life very pleasant.[131]

How convenient not to understand that most of those who had abandoned their native countries would have been deported and killed had they not done so, and that if the war had gone well for Mussolini and Hitler – whose efforts Malipiero and most of his colleagues had tacitly or enthusiastically supported – the musicians who had taken refuge abroad would eventually have suffered worse than mere privations. 'America [is] no longer the country that willingly welcomed me, through my operas, between the two wars', said Malipiero, shaking his crown of thorns. 'What has happened to hospitality these days?'[132] And to Pizzetti he wrote:

> I am increasingly perplexed about 'our' future. The *de profundis* would no longer be sufficient [for us], and perhaps not even a 'Requiem Mass'. [...] After all I've gone through for so many years, they [Casella's alleged supporters] want to make me out to have been a favourite of the fascists! I've had the short end

of *two* sticks! [. . .] We're living with death, with the dead. What are all these twitchings? The process of decomposition of a cadaver, the swarming of worms. A miserable, nauseating spectacle.[133]

Malipiero felt that life was proceeding normally only when he was sure that everyone was against him (and therefore did everything within his power to incite everyone to act against him), but Pizzetti had a talent for getting what he wanted out of life. By mid-May 1945 he had been named representative for the National Federation of Entertainment Workers on the Royal Opera House's advisory committee.[134] He continued to teach composition at Santa Cecilia until 1958 and to compose prolifically. His new works were always given major productions, and he was said to be well connected within the ruling Christian Democratic party. His last opera, *Clitennestra*, had its première at La Scala in 1965; Pizzetti died three years later at eighty-eight – survived only by Malipiero, among his contemporaries, who died in 1973 at the age of ninety-one. In this respect Malipiero even beat Stravinsky, the only great foreign composer of that generation to maintain a continuing relationship with Italy after the war. The Russian master reserved the premières of *The Rake's Progress* (1951), *Canticum sacrum* (1956) and *Threni* (1958) for his beloved Venice, and was buried in that city's cemetery-island, San Michele, in 1971.

Dallapiccola and Petrassi became the best-known Italian composers of their generation. Castelnuovo-Tedesco – a decade older – postponed his first post-war visit to Italy until 1948. His name had been mentioned for the directorship of the Naples Conservatory, but he determined to maintain his working base in the United States. From his old summer home in Tuscany, he wrote to Pizzetti:

Usigliano is as beautiful as ever! Here, for the first time, I've felt 'at home' again [. . .]. But in the cities I felt ill at ease – even in Florence, which I found beautiful, still, but where too many things have changed (at least for me . . .). And being there in a hotel, as a guest, seemed to me unnatural! Suffice it to say that the only place where I felt comfortable was at the Cemetery, before my Parents' tombs [. . .]. You are right: Italy is the most beautiful country in the world! [. . .] But for me, perhaps, it is a 'Paradise Lost'.[135]

CHAPTER VI

The Toscanini Case

And Toscanini? Toscanini returned to Italy in triumph a year after the war's end, fully vindicated for the stand he had taken during the previous two decades. The maturation of his opposition to Mussolini and Hitler is the most singular episode in the story of music under fascism – all the more so when set beside the sad spectacle offered by nearly all the other *dramatis personae*. Yet Toscanini's anti-fascism continues to be regarded by many people, especially within Italy, as insincere or even self-seeking. Such a misrepresentation of his beliefs and actions comes from a lack of knowledge of the man and the situation – a situation that has been much illuminated by recently rediscovered archival material.

The political views Toscanini acquired in his youth were straightforward and unsophisticated. His father, an irresponsible tailor with a strong sense of adventure, had left home in his youth to join Garibaldi's irregular army and to help in Italy's struggle for reunification and independence. Claudio Toscanini had participated in the successful northern Italian and Sicilian campaigns of 1859–60, and in the disastrous battles of Aspromonte (1862), Condino and Bezzecca (1866). The remaining forty years of his life were given over to insignificant anti-royalist and anti-clerical political activities, unsteady application of his trade, scatter-brained business ventures, drink, vaga-bonding and – above all – the recounting of his youthful exploits.[1] Arturo, born in 1867, did not inherit his father's interest in alcohol or money-making schemes, and he was quite the opposite of Claudio in ability to concentrate on his work. What he did absorb from his father was an intense dislike of the Church and the monarchy, strong nationalistic sentiments, and the un-shakeable belief that the Trent and Trieste regions, which were still in Austrian hands, rightfully belonged to Italy.

At the outset of the First World War this belief led Toscanini to favour Italian intervention against the German-speaking powers. Criticism of his enthusiasm is legitimate, but he at least had the courage of his convictions: although he was forty-eight when Italy entered the war and had been active as a conductor for twenty-nine years – including periods as director of La Scala and the Metropolitan Opera – he immediately gave up all his regular engagements, conducted only benefit performances for the duration of the conflict and contributed to funds for musicians who had been reduced to penury by wartime unemployment. It was eventually necessary for him to sell his home to provide for his family. In 1917 Toscanini formed a military band and took it to the front, performing during the victorious assault on Monte Santo and at the disastrous rout at Caporetto. He was decorated for bravery under fire.[2]

The government's inability to deal with post-war turmoil persuaded Toscanini that drastic changes were needed in the country's political structure. Early in 1919 he attended a political meeting held in Milan by Mussolini, who was then advocating a bolshevik-like platform. Never a man for compromise solutions, Toscanini was positively impressed by this apparently forceful programme – an impression that was strengthened by the admiration for Mussolini expressed by many of the conductor's intellectual acquaintances, including Marinetti. When, at the last moment, Mussolini decided to put forward a list of candidates in Milan for the parliamentary elections of November 1919, Toscanini's name appeared on the slate. Marinetti had persuaded him that although there was no chance of victory, the fledgling movement needed a name as famous as his to gain credibility. The new *fasci di combattimento* received fewer than 5,000 votes, in contrast to 170,000 for the Milanese socialists. Not even Mussolini was elected; his political career was considered finished, but he had merely lost his taste for elections. Toscanini's unwanted political career was indeed over – at least officially. He did, however, pay the then considerable sum of 30,000 lire that he, like the other candidates, had pledged in order to cover the party's expenses.[3]

Toscanini made his next political gesture a year later, when he took his newly formed Milanese orchestra (soon to become the orchestra of the reorganized La Scala) to perform in Fiume (Rijeka), contested between Italy and Yugoslavia. The city had been occupied by D'Annunzio's troops. Even the horrors of the world war had left Toscanini's nationalism intact, and he appears to have been pleased by the display of military exercises, including battle cries, that the poet's men put on for the orchestra. D'Annunzio decorated Toscanini and his musicians and made a revoltingly fulsome speech in honour of the 'Symphoniac' and his 'Orphic Legion'.[4]

By this time, Mussolini and his adherents had veered sharply to the right and had adopted violence as a means of obtaining power. On the eve of the march on Rome, Toscanini, who had by then reorganized La Scala as the first *ente autonomo*, told a friend of his disgust: 'If I were capable of killing a man', he said, 'I would kill Mussolini.'[5]

The new prime minister, however, wished to be considered a cultivated man, and La Scala, for economic reasons, needed to remain in the government's good graces. When Mussolini visited Milan a few weeks after taking office, he had himself photographed with the entire company, including Toscanini. But shortly thereafter, in December 1922, during a performance of *Falstaff*, the conductor had his first skirmish with supporters of the new regime. As he entered the pit to start the last act, a group of fascists began shouting at him to conduct the party hymn, 'Giovinezza'. Toscanini signalled the orchestra to go on with the opera, but the disrupters would not be silent. He broke his baton and left the pit, shouting and cursing. After a long wait, a member of the administrative staff announced that the anthem would be played at the end of the performance, and Toscanini then returned to the pit. Maria Labia, who was singing the role of Alice Ford recalled:

> When the opera ended the manager told us: 'Stay where you are, everybody, and sing the hymn to piano accompaniment.' Toscanini intervened: 'They're not going to sing a damned thing; the Scala artists aren't vaudeville singers. Go to your dressing rooms, all of you.' And we went. The hymn was played by the piano [alone] because the orchestra, according to Toscanini, did not know it.[6]

Still more upsetting to Toscanini, however, was Giuseppe Gallignani's suicide in December 1923, after having been abruptly fired from the Milan Conservatory directorship, perhaps for lack of enthusiasm for the regime.[7] A few months later the conductor declared he would leave La Scala if the fascists carried out their threat to take control of the theatre's board of directors. Senator Mangiagalli, the mayor of Milan, warned Mussolini of this possibility and its potential consequences in a letter of 6 June 1924:*

> [. . .] La Scala now has world-wide prestige and fame, thanks to Toscanini. [. . .] He may have his defects, but he also has great moral virtues. His disinterestedness is total, as a result of which he has hurt himself by remaining at La Scala to insure its primacy. He has turned down fabulous offers [from abroad], and he would not accept the cheque for 100,000 lire that we offered him as a bonus payment. La Scala is his passion; it is the temple of art, and he does not want it profaned by selfish interests or party passions. [. . .] The fascist party wishes to have three fascist municipal representatives [on the Scala board]; but besides disrupting the harmony among the various political groups, this would give Toscanini the impression of a political act. He won't hear of it. Can we allow Toscanini to leave and La Scala to lose its prestige? [. . .][8]

Toscanini had his way. He might have been temporarily reconciled with the fascists; but that very month the murder of Giacomo Matteotti enraged him.

* See also pp. 76–7.

Late in 1924, when rumours that he was to be offered a senatorship were circulating, his wife confidentially asked Ugo Ojetti to help forestall such an offer. At one time, she said, her husband would have been proud of such an honour, but now he would certainly reject it, 'and who knows what words he would use?'. Ojetti made sure that the offer was never made.[9]

Toscanini's friendship with the Liberal Senator Luigi Albertini, whom the fascists had ousted from the editorship of the *Corriere della sera*, helped greatly to develop his awareness of the dangers of fascism. In April 1925, however, he turned down the senator's request that he sign Benedetto Croce's anti-fascist manifesto. He may have felt he did not have the right to endanger La Scala's economic survival by making his political beliefs public. The same year, however, when the government ordered that pictures of Mussolini and the king appear in every public building, including theatres, Toscanini countermanded the order at La Scala, Italy's most important theatre. As long as he remained there the pictures were not displayed. Mussolini also decreed in 1925 that on the 21st of April – a national holiday honouring the Birth of Rome – all places of public entertainment were to play 'Giovinezza' before beginning their performances. Toscanini circumvented the command by scheduling a rehearsal rather than a performance for that evening. He received word from government authorities that he was not to reuse the trick the following year. A few months later, Toscanini met Mussolini – for the last time, it seems, and at the latter's command – at the Milan prefecture. It was probably this meeting that Toscanini later described as a long harangue on the Duce's part. The conductor, who was kept standing, stared at a spot on the wall over Mussolini's head, restraining his notorious temper but refusing to reply to the accusations of bad behaviour and the threats of dire consequences for La Scala. The official press release stated blandly: 'HIS EXCELLENCY MUSSOLINI, the Prime Minister, had a conversation with Maestro ARTURO TOSCANINI and took a lively interest in La Scala's activities and in the important concert tour the Maestro will soon begin in New York.'[10]

Ignoring government orders and Mussolini's threats, Toscanini kept the theatre dark on 21 April 1926. Mussolini, who arrived in Milan a day or two later for an official visit, sent for La Scala's administrators and declared that if they could not control Toscanini, they ought to replace him – otherwise, they would never again see the Head of Government in their theatre. He wished, he said, to attend the world premiere of Puccini's *Turandot*, which was scheduled for the 25th; 'Giovinezza', he insisted, must be played when he entered the house.

But Toscanini *was* La Scala in the 1920s. For the administrative staff, who existed above all to carry out his orders, it was an unprecedented and unenviable task to convey an order to Toscanini, who was at least as irascible and, in his own, field, as important as Mussolini. In the end, they simply told him what the Prime Minister had said. Toscanini retorted that he didn't mind having 'Giovinezza' played if they would get someone else to conduct it – and *Turandot*. In 1926, Toscanini was more essential than Mussolini to La Scala's well-being: *Turandot* was performed with the Maestro and without the Duce. The next day's *Corriere della sera* – which had been pruned of its openly antifascist writers – reported:

> During the interval the audience awaited Mussolini's previously announced arrival. But the prime minister did not wish to attend, and explained the reason behind his sensitive gesture: he did not want his presence in any way to distract the public, whose attention had to be entirely devoted to Puccini and his last work. Mussolini will attend a later performance of *Turandot*.

Some days later Toscanini, who was close to nervous exhaustion at the end of a particularly demanding season, had to cancel his remaining performances and go to the seaside for a rest. The fascist press used the occasion to circulate rumours that he had left La Scala forever because he objected to the new law instituting a national corporation of opera-house managers. In effect, the fascists were giving La Scala a chance to dump Toscanini and Toscanini a chance to withdraw without hurting his pride.[11]

Toscanini stayed at La Scala, but the rift between the conductor and the Italian government was real and growing, and word of it became international news. The managers of the New York Philharmonic, with which Toscanini had made a phenomenally successful debut as guest conductor a few months earlier, were delighted. They hoped to wrest him away from La Scala and make him their principal conductor. Although their wish was eventually fulfilled, the process proved slower than they had hoped. Not until the summer of 1928 did he decide to leave La Scala, effective the following spring.

His last Milan season was in many respects the most memorable of all – especially the triumphal tour to Vienna and Berlin with which it ended. Public and critics in Austria and Germany reacted with stupefied admiration. Mussolini, who closely followed reports on all things Italian in the foreign press, must have been thoroughly pleased to read such national-pride-inducing statements as the following:

> [...] Let us hope that the German artists who attended this performance [*Falstaff* in Berlin] have learned something; in any case, the Italian opera company has given us a delightful but dangerous measuring-stick for judging German art. [...] [Alfred Einstein, *Berliner Tagblatt*]
> [...] La Scala's performances moved and shook the public [...] [It was] a success without precedent in the modern history of opera in Germany. [...] [Karl Holl, *Frankfurter Zeitung*]
> [...] In Berlin, the excitement rose to such a fever pitch that it actually made us fear for German art, for the prestige of German musical culture. [...] [H. R. Gail, *Bayerischer Courier*][12]

Consummate propagandist that he was, Mussolini knew how to turn such material to account. On returning to Milan, Toscanini received a pompous telegram from the Duce: 'La Scala's performances made known not only the great historic virtues of an artistic organization, but also the new spirit of Contemporary Italy, which unites to its will to power the necessary harmonious discipline required in every field of human activity.' Toscanini understood Mussolini's implication: like it or not, by contributing to the glory of La Scala he was also contributing to the glory of the new fascist society. He replied that 'today, as yesterday and as always, I am serving and shall serve my Art with humility but with intense love, certain that in so doing I am serving and honouring my Country'.[13] He must have thought, as he wrote that sentence, that he performed such a service wherever he was working, whether within or outside of Italy. But he could not have imagined that seventeen years were to pass before he would next perform with an Italian organization.

Toscanini's departure from the Italian musical scene was not entirely voluntary, nor was it wholly politically induced. He was sixty-two years old in 1929 and had decided to concentrate on the concert repertoire, which was less taxing, physically, than the multi-faceted business of rehearsing and performing opera. The growing strength of the Italian musicians' and theatre workers' unions disturbed him, too – not because of their economic demands, which he considered just, but because of their desire to have more say in the running of the organization, which he believed would lead to chaos. In addition, the New York Philharmonic was at the time one of the greatest orchestras in the world, and Toscanini was being offered an unprecedented salary (over $100,000, net, for fifteen weeks' work) to make it into *the* greatest. He still intended, however, to conduct in Italy when the artistic circumstances were right and when he would not have to put up with fascist interference.

When he took the Philharmonic on its first European tour in the spring of 1930, the itinerary included four Italian cities: Milan, Turin, Rome and Florence. The presence of Crown Prince Umberto at the Turin concert made the playing of the Royal March obligatory; Toscanini might have been willing to conduct it if regulations had not required that it be followed by 'Giovinezza'. Under the circumstances, he refused. A compromise was eventually reached: after the orchestra was seated and tuned, a military band came out to play the hymns. In Rome, the queen and other members of the royal family wished to attend a performance, and a possibly more serious incident was averted only when they wisely announced that their presence would be unofficial. No anthems were played.

This episode no doubt encouraged Toscanini to believe that he could continue to use the weight of his fame in order to go about his business as if the fascists did not exist. The regime, however, was increasingly displeased with his behaviour, and the chief of Mussolini's Political Police began to build up a dossier of reports from paid informers throughout Europe. The first important notice referred to his 1930 visit to Berlin with the New York Philharmonic.

> [...] having been asked repeatedly to attend a reception that was being organized in his honour at the headquarters of the local [Italian] fascist party organization, the Maestro always replied that he could not participate because he was tired. When pressed, and when asked whether he would authorize the sending of a telegram in his name to the Duce, in which he would state that he did not agree to the function only *because he was tired, he replied sharply that he was not attending because he was an anti-fascist, because he held Mussolini to be a tyrant and oppressor of Italy, and that rather than breaking with these convictions, he was prepared never to return again to Italy.*[14]

A copy of this report was handed to Mussolini, who underlined the phrases here reproduced in italics and brought the information to the attention of Foreign Minister Dino Grandi. Toscanini had become someone to be watched; but he did not fully recognize the danger implicit in his position until the following year, when he found himself at the centre of an incident that caused greater international embarrassment to Mussolini's government than any event since the Matteotti affair.

Toscanini had accepted an invitation to conduct two concerts (14 and 16 May 1931) at Bologna's Teatro Comunale, with the house orchestra, to mark the seventy-fifth birthday of the composer and conductor Giuseppe Martucci (1856–1909), whom he had greatly admired. The programmes were to consist entirely of Martucci's music, and Toscanini refused payment for the engagement. By chance, a Fascist Party festival was also taking place in Bologna that week. On the day of the first performance, Toscanini was told by the Deputy Mayor, Giuseppe Lipparini, that the Minister of Communications, Costanzo Ciano, and the Under-secretary of the Interior, Leandro Arpinati, would be in the theatre, and that he would therefore have to begin the concert with the Royal March and 'Giovinezza'.[15] As Toscanini later described the episode:

> This happened a few minutes after the last rehearsal, at which I had warmly exhorted the members of the orchestra to take their places only two minutes before the performance, with a maximum of concentration, conscious of the reverent and loving demonstration that they had been called to participate in – in order that no sounds other than Martucci's music should make contact with the public. I concluded: 'Gentlemen, be democrats in life but aristocrats in art.' I could not, therefore, accommodate Professor Lipparini's request – as unexpected as it was out of place – and allow the concert suddenly to take on a gala or political character, since no preliminary sign or newspaper advertisement had announced this. Instead, I very gladly accepted the conciliatory proposal later formulated by the Prefect of Bologna together with

the Deputy Mayor, which they communicated to me at five in the afternoon. The proposal was set forth in these terms: when the ministers entered the theatre, a band would play the national anthems in the lobby of the Comunale. But at eight o'clock the situation changed. The conciliatory formula did not satisfy the Ministers, and we were back at the earlier order; and I remained more steadfast than ever in my conviction about maintaining the commemorative character of the evening. At nine-thirty [the concert's scheduled starting time] Mr Brianzi of the Municipal administration telephoned me [to say] that I could go to the theatre, advising me that Their Excellencies would refrain from attending the concert. And I fell right into the ambush.[16]

With Toscanini as he arrived late at the Comunale were his wife, Carla, their younger daughter, Wanda, and a family friend – a lawyer named Muggiani. (The conductor's son, Walter, had been assigned to accompany Martucci's widow to the concert. He had arrived in a different car and had entered by the main door.) On getting out of his car, Toscanini found himself surrounded by fascist youths. One of them – Leo Longanesi, a young journalist who later invented the mindless and widely-used phrase, 'Mussolini is always right', and who, still later, achieved celebrity as author, editor, caricaturist and publisher – asked him whether he would play 'Giovinezza'.

'No.'

Longanesi hit Toscanini in the face and neck and shouted insults that were echoed by others in the crowd.* Toscanini's wife, chauffeur, and friend managed to rescue him from the onslaught and to get him back into the car. When the harm had already been done, some *carabinieri* (national police) who had been standing by in their plumed ceremonial hats, came over and told the chauffeur to get going. The Toscaninis were sped back to their hotel.[18]

Rumours of the attack quickly circulated in the packed theatre, where the public was already impatient as a result of the long delay. A functionary finally announced that the concert was being postponed because the Maestro was indisposed. Many members of the public began to shout, 'It's not true! It's not true!'. Armed black-shirted guards, apparently panic-stricken, shut the exits but were then ordered to reopen them. The public surged into the streets, and one orchestra musician said there was so much commotion in the centre of

---

* Public revelation that Longanesi was the perpetrator of what in Italy became famous as the 'Bologna slaps' came only in 1984, with the publication of his biography by Indro Montanelli and Marcello Staglieno. Longanesi was not well enough known in 1931 to have been recognized by Toscanini or by many others present, and the secret was kept in the Longanesi family for half a century. (It was, however, suspected by several journalists, and this suspicion was known to Mussolini's police informers.) The authors report that the Toscaninis were being put up at one of Bologna's best hotels at the city's expense but fail to mention that the conductor had refused a fee or that his participation had drawn sell-out crowds to concerts whose ticket prices had been raised for the occasion, for the Comunale's benefit.[17]

Bologna that a revolution seemed to have broken out.[19]

Respighi and his wife were in the audience that evening; they had heard of the 'Giovinezza' dispute in the afternoon and realized that something untoward must have happened. 'Respighi was beside himself', wrote his wife in a letter to Walter Toscanini many years later, '[. . .] and said it was a disgusting and shameful thing for Italy. I took Respighi and Mary Molinari [Bernardino Molinari's wife] with me and we left by the stage [door] . . . '[20] They drove to Toscanini's hotel, where the conductor was nursing cuts on his face and neck. He had no serious injuries, but Elsa Respighi later described his mood as that of a caged beast.[21] Two hundred fascists were soon parading from party headquarters to the hotel, where they gathered beneath Toscanini's windows and shouted insults and obscenities; there was some fear that they might begin hurling objects as well. Mario Ghinelli, the local party secretary, asked to speak with a member of the Toscanini party. The conductor and his son were ruled out as negotiators because of their quick tempers; Carla Toscanini went instead, but the fascists refused to deal with a woman. Respighi then volunteered to represent the family. He was told that the Toscaninis were to leave the city before sunrise: their safety could not otherwise be guaranteed. Elsa Respighi and Mary Molinari helped them to pack their bags as quickly as possible, and the Toscaninis departed at 1.20 a.m., arriving in Milan by sunrise.[22]

Arpinati phoned Mussolini immediately after the attack, and Gaetano Cesari, who was in town to report on the concerts for the *Corriere della sera*, bribed a telephone operator to report what had been said. The operator told him that Mussolini had responded to the news with these words: 'I am really happy. It will teach a good lesson to these boorish musicians.' He ordered the Milan prefecture to take away the Toscaninis' passports and to place their house under surveillance.[23]

The following day, Toscanini sent a telegram to Rome:

To His Excellency Benito Mussolini,
Last evening, while going with my family to Bologna's Teatro Comunale to carry out a kind act of friendship and love in memory of Giuseppe Martucci (having been invited there by the Mayor of the city for a religious and artistic commemoration, not for a gala evening), I was attacked, injured and repeatedly struck in the face by a contemptible gang. The Under-secretary of the Interior was present in Bologna. – Not fully satisfied with this, the gang, its ranks swollen, stood threateningly under the windows of the Hotel Brun, where I was staying, uttering every sort of insult and threat against me. Not only that: one of its leaders enjoined me, through Maestro Respighi, to leave the city by six a.m., not being able to guarantee my safety otherwise. I am communicating this to Your Excellency so that, despite the silence of the press or false information, Your Excellency will be able to have precise news

of the deed, and so that the deed be remembered.

Salutations

Arturo Toscanini[24]

Although Mussolini never replied to Toscanini's message, he did, according to the composer Vincenzo Tommasini, tell a mutual acquaintance: 'He conducts an orchestra of one hundred people; I have to conduct one of forty million, and they are not all *virtuosi*.'[25]

The Italian press, which was completely under fascist control, either refrained from mentioning the incident or threw the blame for it entirely upon Toscanini. Longanesi – without, of course, mentioning his part in the affair – wrote an article for the official newspaper (appropriately named *Assalto* – assault) of the Bologna Fascist Federation; it was reprinted in several papers throughout the country.

> Thursday evening, we were the protagonists of a confirmation of Bolognese Fascism that was not only political but also aesthetic.
>
> In all the theatres of Italy, Maestro Toscanini had for some time been playing the part of the pure aesthete who soars above politics and is contemptuous of the miserable laws of governments, or rather of his Government. In the name of musical purity, of a decadent aestheticism conceived by people who had picked up the crumbs of Wagnerism, our concert performer had decided not to play the Royal March at the beginning of performances attended by a member of the Government or the Royal Family. |n.b.: Longanesi was equivocating: he well knew that Toscanini had not refused to perform the Royal March, but rather to follow it with 'Giovinezza', as the regime required.|
>
> 'I don't want to infect the air, the atmosphere of the hall, with profane music, with political anthems', he said; 'I don't want to disrupt the religiousness attendant upon the elevation of a piece of music.' |n.b.: This was, of course, a completely inaccurate 'quotation'.|
>
> Defending himself with such a foolish aesthetic rule, fit for Anglo-Saxon old maids, our holy man proclaimed his sublimity before every performance, as well as his abstention, if thus we may call it, from the simple duties that no citizen refuses to carry out.
>
> Bellini, Verdi and Rossini, artists of much greater imagination than our concert performer, would have laughed at such pained and sublime religiousness. | ... |
>
> But our Maestro | ... | had already instinctively discovered – sly and astute man that he is – that the canons of musical religiousness proved to be of assistance in building up his fame: the more his bizarre ideas took shape and were re-echoed, the more the public's admiration and awe grew. It is an old trick of *fin-de-siècle* Nietzscheans, an old type of rhetoric that defines genius by its anomalies, a pose in use fifty years ago, at the time of the development of medical theories about the characteristics of genius, when it was commonly believed that artists were high-strung, that they vibrated like telegraph wires,

and that they had one sole God: Art; one sole law: Art; one sole discipline: Art.
[. . .]

True to this aesthetic, our Toscanini got himself up in an ascetic face for the
ladies in the first tier of boxes, invented half-light, interrupted performances
because somebody had dropped a penny, and swore before Art not to play
the Royal March. Musical Italy didn't say a word; it remained open-mouthed
and gawking before the new orchestra chieftain. Toscanini adopted Wilde's
motto, 'A king may bow before an artist's brush', raised his baton as if it were
Wotan's sword, and proclaimed his musical republic. With the business about
'I won't pollute the religious atmosphere with the Royal March', he even
managed to create a political stand for himself; from holy mystic he turned
into holy warrior, a Saint Expeditus of symphony concerts, in frock-coat and
patent-leather shoes.

But in Wagnerian and Rossinian Bologna [n.b.: Rossini was connected with
the Bologna Conservatory from 1837 to '48; Wagner's *Tannhäuser*, *Lohengrin*,
Tristan and *Parsifal* all received their first Italian performances in the city], the
illustrious lay-apostle found an audience that believed in a stronger religion
than his: that of the State. The Bolognese fascists asked Maestro Toscanini –
mystic or not, but thus far an Italian citizen, thanks to his birth and civil status –
to respect what every other citizen of the Realm respects. The public would
not have been prevented from applauding the illustrious Maestro had he
conducted the Royal March or allowed someone else to conduct it.

As the news reports have stated, our little musician replied to the
authorities' and fascists' invitations with a repeated, insolent No. This was
followed by a few slaps, some heckling and the end of an aesthetic.[26]

Less sarcastic but equally misleading was the report that appeared in the
fascists' national daily, *Il popolo d'Italia*:

Maestro Toscanini's inexplicable behaviour met with just retaliation from
the Bolognese Fascists. For some time the Maestro, like a god angry with
everyone, had been showing off his attitude. Not even for the sake of
propriety and courtesy could he conquer his contempt for logic and common
sense. The belief that playing the national anthems would have been an
offence against art is an outrage to the sensibilities of fascists and of the Italian
people. The reaction was therefore legitimate.

It only remains to be asked whether Maestro Toscanini was the best person
to carry out the Martucci commemoration, when we recall that he recently
travelled through Italy with exotic groups and programmes [n.b.: the New York
Philharmonic playing standard symphonic repertoire], flaunting the indignation of a misunderstood genius in his own country's face. We must conclude
that it would have been much better to ignore the Maestro who, in political
matters, was anti-Bolshevik in order to win a little medal [n.b.: presumably a
reference to his First World War decoration which, however, had nothing to do
with Bolshevism], and in artistic ones was angry simply over rivalries at La
Scala [n.b.: where he had had no rivals].

In any case, however, let no one who has the sensitivity and the spirit of the race and of the country forget the signs of our faith and of our unity. Not to understand this would mean setting oneself outside art and life and exposing oneself to severe lessons from those who have a clear-cut sense of duty, pride and Italian and fascist logic.[27]

Finally, in *La tribuna*, the following conclusion was drawn: '[. . .] A slap at the right time and place can sometimes have a salutary effect – above all, that of reconfirming, and sonorously, that the old formula of art for art's sake is not very suitable *today*.'[28]

But the fascists did not know their man. Toscanini was interested in art for humanity's sake. 'The lesson they wanted to teach me', he wrote, '[. . .] was to no avail, nor will it be to any avail in the future, for I would repeat tomorrow what I did yesterday if the same conditions prevailed in Italy or in any other part of the world.'

> I know perfectly well how great the moral, political and patriotic value of a national anthem played at the right time is – and I have never refused to play that of the Nation to which I belong in any situation, so long as its moral and patriotic meaning was unmistakable.
>
> Did I not cross Italy and North America shortly after the war, at the head of the Scala orchestra, in a long series of concerts of national propaganda, playing my Country's anthem everywhere? And have I not conducted it innumerable times, in my forty-five-year career, for patriotic events [. . .], for gala evenings and at Exposition openings, in the presence of the monarchs? And did I not conduct it on Monte Santo under enemy fire? [. . .]
>
> *To conclude:* Am I, then, to take newspapers like the Resto del Carlino [Bologna] or the Corriere della sera [Milan] seriously when, overnight, they replace the Hosannas to Toscanini with the Crucifixus? When they, like the Popolo d'Italia, even find my person unsuitable for commemorating Giuseppe Martucci? And all the others that have actually called me unpatriotic? How tiny are these people, and of what little value is all this business, barely deserving of my compassion!
>
> 'The spine bends when the soul is bent.' It is true. But the conduct of my life has been, is, and will always be the echo and reflection of my conscience, which does not know dissimulation or deviations of any type – reinforced, I admit, by a proud and scornful character, but clear as crystal and just as cutting – always and everywhere ready to shout the truth loudly – that truth which, as Emerson so rightly says, always comes into the world in a manger, but is rewarded by having to live until it is completely enslaved by mankind.[29]

Mussolini's delight over what had happened to this 'boorish musician' cannot have lasted long. Artists and intellectuals throughout the country soon began to learn something of the incident, and the foreign press carried detailed if not always accurate accounts of it. Letters and telegrams bearing messages of solidarity reached Toscanini from all over the world: one informer for the political police estimated that the conductor received 15,000 such messages, and stated that an extra postman had been taken on to deal with the overload.[30] Leading Italian musicians came to visit Toscanini, although they knew that their movements were being reported by the police. Serge Koussevitzky cancelled his scheduled concerts at La Scala in protest over the affair, declaring that 'Maestro Toscanini does not belong only to Italy but to the whole world'.[31] Béla Bartók presented a protest resolution at a meeting of the UMZE (New Hungarian Music Society): 'The UMZE is deeply shocked and roused to indignation by the news of the grave assault that has been made on Arturo Toscanini. The Society wishes to assure him of its most wholehearted sympathy and solidarity and salutes him with the utmost admiration.'[32] Ossip Gabrilowitsch, pianist and conductor, and his wife Clara Clemens, daughter of Mark Twain, took a train from Zurich to Milan as soon as they heard of the Bologna incident. According to Gabrilowitsch:

[Toscanini] greeted us most cordially and seemed spontaneously inclined to describe the entire Bologna experience. He did so with undisguised indignation against the Fascist factions who had set the trap for him. In the expression of his feelings the great artist before us also divulged the great man. [. . .] His declaration of dislike for the present state of affairs in Italy was expressed in bold, round phrases. And this declaration he has repeatedly given outside the privacy of his home, so that no one can mistake his attitude. 'Truth,' he said, 'truth we must have at any price, and freedom of speech, even if that price should be death. I have said to our Fascists time and again: You can kill me if you wish, but as long as I am living I shall say what I think.'[33]

All this negative publicity caused Mussolini to order that Toscanini be closely observed – that his mail be opened, his telephone line tapped and the comings and goings at his home reported – and that all potentially useful information be passed on to the Duce's office. Five days after the Bologna incident, a telegram typical of the dossier's contents was sent from Milan to Rome.

Ministry of the Interior
CIPHER OFFICE   *Telegram*/24583 (6) EAS
FROM MILAN 19.5.31 8:20 O'CLOCK RECEIVED 10:30 O'CLOCK
MINISTRY INTERIOR GEN. ADMIN. [illegible code letters and numbers follow]

No 019228 Yesterday Maestro *Toscanini* did not leave own home stop During day telegrams and letters brought to him among which one sender Esposito and a visiting card from Lawyer Cuciniello stop Following people went to visit Maestro Toscanini Dr Ravagio family doctor, Maestro [Vittorio] Vanzo [conductor], Maestro Mario Castelnuovo Tedesco, Signor Calzini, Maestro Giordano, Maestro Polli, Signor Gonnelle and Signora Vercelli stop Inform that [the following] have been identified and have confessed having taken part in group that shouted 'viva Toscanini' the other evening in front of the same's residence Giovanni Bodrone, Ernesto; Missiroli, Roberto; Gilli, Carlo;

Ferticucci, Carlo; Giovanardi, Eugenio; Arienti, Lodovico; and Valcarenghi, Aldo, all students |at the| Liceo Berchet except Gilli |who is| first year student jurisprudence stop Aforementioned Valcarenghi confessed himself instigator yesterday evening's demonstration and distributor of the famous libels of 'Giustizia e Libertà' among schoolmates stop* All students except Gilli confess having received said libels stop Yesterday evening during symphony concert Teatro alla Scala at end of the first part several youths in top Gallery shouted 'viva Toscanini' greeted by long applause noteworthy part of public filling theatre stop Through prearranged |police| forces nine individuals were quickly stopped |and| identified as those responsible stop These for the most part confessed |and| are being held pending further checks stop Meanwhile several hundred fascists gathered before said theatre |and| with singing of 'Giovinezza' headed towards |Toscanini's house in| Via Durini where they put on demonstration hostile towards Maestro Toscanini stop Pre-arranged forces |of| public order were able to avert attempted invasion building stop Fascist column then went Galleria Vittorio Emanuele |n.b.: centre of Milanese popular social life| where broke up orderly fashion after having sung Fascist anthems stop Public order normal stop

Prefect FORNACIARI[35]

The contents of Mussolini's file on Toscanini have long been known. A recently rediscovered classified dossier, however, held by the Chief of the Political Police (*Ministero dell'Interno, Direzione Generale di Pubblica Sicurezza, Divisione Polizia Politica, fascicoli personali*), demonstrates the extent of the government's worry over the Bologna incident's domestic and foreign repercussions. The file preserves over a hundred reports, all unsigned, from informers in ten Italian cities and in France, Germany and Switzerland, as well as requests from the Ministry to local prefects for information on individuals known to have been politically sympathetic towards Toscanini. A sampling of the material shows the level of concern and confusion.

Rome, 15 May: 'This morning a rumour has been spread | ... |, especially in foreign press circles, that Maestro Toscanini has been manhandled by the Fascists. The wildest conjectures have been made | ... |.'[36]
Milan, 16 May: '|Toscanini| has always had everything from his country: awards, honours, celebrations, offerings, praise from the press. If Toscanini acts this way, what should those people do who have suffered injustice, sorrow,

---

* Valcarenghi was the son of the co-director of the Ricordi Company. Marinuzzi, his wife and daughter happened to be visiting the Valcarenghis when agents arrived to arrest the young man. 'My father rushed to the prefect, Fornaciari,' wrote Lia Pierotti Cei Marinuzzi many years later, 'to try to convince him to minimize the incident. But Fornaciari was furious. "I'll send him into internal exile!" he thundered. "I'll show him, and others like him!" We feared for the fate of our dear friend. He was given a three-year prison sentence, but fortunately he was released a few months later because he was so young.'[34]

slander, never an act of recognition? [. . .] Those responsible will do what is necessary so that the Maestro will talk about us [fascists] as little as possible.'[37]

Milan, 16 May: 'Nothing is spoken of in Milan except the Toscanini episode in Bologna. [. . .] I made the rounds of all the main newsstands [. . .] to find a copy of "Resto del Carlino", but was unable to find a copy. Sold out! [. . .] His Excellency Gen. Sen. Carlo Porro [. . .] said that the Maestro has so boundlessly high an opinion of himself that he thinks he is on a level with the Sovereigns. [. . . Toscanini's] deed in Bologna, according to Porro, is more the cowardly deed of a thoroughly cowardly person than a political action. But that's not how it is seen in the city's cafés. [. . .] At the Campari, [one man] told me that we need 100 Toscaninis in Italy, or rather in Milan, and that there are thousands and thousands who see things Toscanini's way but don't have the courage to say so. [. . .] [Another man] told me that for many people, Toscanini's action in Bologna was an occasion for great jubilation, because it is interpreted as a big-gun intellectual's show of contempt towards the Regime. In reality, [he said,] the intellectuals are all against the Regime [. . .] but they are fearful, like the bourgeoisie. The fact that Toscanini actually said NO to Ciano and Arpinati emboldens vast numbers of people who hope that others will repeat the gesture.'[38]

Rome, 17 May: 'In the Transatlantico [press room of the Chamber of Depu ties], the most interesting subject was the slap given Toscanini. [Fascist leaders] Balbo, Manaresi, Riccardi, Bacci, Ferretti Lando, Diaz, Rossoni, Pierazzi and other lesser people gathered around Arpinati, who was join- ed by Ciano. Arpinati recounted the story. He wanted to have Toscanini arrested, but he said that the Duce, reached by telephone, replied that the matter should be dropped. [. . .] Meanwhile, the Rome correspondents of foreign newspapers have received urgent telegrams requesting details [. . .].'[39]

Rome, 17 May: Telegram from the Ministry of the Interior to the Prefect of Milan: 'Pol[itical] Pol[ice] – Confidential personal stop – Please wire information moral political behaviour social economic conditions certain Cav[aliere] Andreoletti who when speaking with Signorina Colombo of the Teatro Scala administration about well-known Toscanini incident expressed himself in terms disloyal [to] Regime. CHIEF OF POLICE Bocchini'[40] [n.b.: Several similar messages regarding other people were sent the same day. The replies have not been preserved.]

Naples, 17 May: 'The Toscanini incident [. . .] has aroused unanimous disdain and disapproval in all circles, even in the most markedly fascist circles. The slap given the great, elderly conductor by an anonymous, third-rate hero is considered a mad, reprehensible gesture, and the solidarity of "Popolo d'Italia" with so vulgar an act of hooliganism is spoken of with unanimous harshness.'[41]

Florence, 17 May: 'Many [. . .] think that [the incident] can severely damage our country, since Maestro Toscanini is well known for his obstinacy and since he spends much of his life abroad. He will therefore not fail to carry out anti-Italian propaganda.'[42]

Milan, 17 May: '[. . .] for years [. . .] every editor at "Popolo d'Italia" has known of Toscanini's anti-fascist beliefs.'[43]

Milan, 20 May: '[. . .] People are saying that if some poor devil had done less, much less, than Toscanini, he would have been sent into internal exile. [. . .] Everyone is now opening newspapers in the hope of seeing that a strong action has been taken against Toscanini. It is feared that if he is given the option of leaving the country, he could be used as an emblem [. . .] against us [. . .].'[44]

Naples, 19 May: '[. . .] people are saying that Toscanini is a genius, and that one can't ask him to do what one would ask of a village bandmaster; that it should be recalled that Toscanini conducted the national anthems under fire at the front; that artistic events should not be mixed with politics; that this fact will alienate much good will towards us abroad; that through this method they have forced an artist into exile [. . .].'[45]

Zurich, 20 May: 'The anti-fascist press is of course taking advantage of the incident; but what is making an enormous impression everywhere, even on the friends of Fascism, is the fact that the celebrated Maestro Toscanini was attacked in Bologna by fascists. [. . .]'[46]

Milan, 20 May: '[. . .] I believe that the incident is not of such minor importance as I had first thought; I am, rather, beginning to realize, from the great amount of talk about it everywhere, that it has given ammunition to a certain nasty movement. [. . .]'[47]

Milan, 20 May: '[. . .] If anyone is disliked, hated, in Milan, it is Toscanini, because he is a coward and a bully [. . .]. Everyone knows it. Well, now people are speaking well of him: they're saying he is a man of character, of strength, of courage.'[48]

Milan, 20 May: 'Monday evening 18 May, at the Teatro alla Scala, which was filled with an elegant audience for a great symphony concert, at a certain moment – as if obeying a silent order – cries of *viva* were addressed to Maestro Toscanini from the orchestra seats, the galleries and the boxes. The demonstration was nearly unanimous and lasted several minutes. Alone among the public applauding the Maestro (who was not even present), old man [Tito] Ricordi, a good patriot (of the well-known Music Publishing House), stood up austerely and shouted, *Viva l'Italia,* for God's sake! And from the galleries, jammed with students from the Polytechnic and the University, there came an even more heated reply: "Yes, *viva l'Italia!* But *viva, viva* Toscanini, Italy's glory!" There was no violence. It was noted that the Milanese aristocracy filling the boxes joined the demonstration for Toscanini with obvious enthusiasm. [. . .]'[49]

Rome, 21 May: '[. . .] a rumour is circulating, namely, that the "campaign" against Maestro Toscanini was fuelled by His Excellency Ciano and H. E. Arpinati, who were offended because the National Anthems were not played in their presence.'[50] [n.b.: This sentence has been crossed out, either by a functionary in the Ministry of the Interior who wished to ingratiate himself with Under-secretary Arpinati, or by Arpinati himself, who had access to it.]

Milan, 21 May: '[. . .] From now on, the cries of *viva* Toscanini will have to be understood as down with Fascism. This is absolutely not the moment for either slaps or beatings. It is urgent that many leaders in Milan be changed in order to attempt a fascist reconstruction; otherwise (in Milan) there may be some nasty surprises [. . .].'[51]

Paris, 23 May: '[. . .] Newspapers of every political leaning have given [. . .] importance to the act of the Bolognese fascists. There have been many comments in Parisian artistic circles, which of course side with the musician. [. . .]'[52]

Milan, 27 May: '[. . .] a demonstration [at La Scala] of solidarity with Maestro Toscanini [. . .] provoked a certain reaction in the souls of many fascists, especially the students who belong to the GUF [Fascist University Groups]. Thus, on the evening of Friday, 22 May, 70 of them trickled in [to La Scala]. Their admission was paid by the [Fascist] Federation and the GUF. The students occupied the [Scala] Gallery. That evening the concert was conducted by the German [*sic*] Fritz Reiner. There was a nice patriotic demonstration to the tune of the national anthems [. . .]. The students, however, were watchful, and noticed people who made unkind comments regarding the demonstration and Fascism. These incautious people got what they deserved. One with a short beard, later identified as a professor at the Liceo di Milano – although he denied it – was slapped by a few students and then led to Police Headquarters [. . .]; three other youths, [. . .] who said the Maestro might as well have been asked to play the anthems of every country, including Russia and Spain, [. . .] were followed by a group of five students from the GUF. [. . .] following explanations and arguments, [the five] handed out a good dose of punches [. . .]. A taxi driver expressed his poor opinion of the fascist students and made insulting statements against the regime [. . .]; one athletic student [. . .] grabbed the driver and gave him a good, hard lesson. [. . .] I have just learned that the GUF's Directorate has met to discuss initiating a series of punitive expeditions, because the spread of anti-fascist propaganda, which is carried out especially in the bosom of certain intellectual circles, can no longer be tolerated.'[53]

Milan, 27 May: 'There is a great deal of electricity in the air, and in so stating, I am not overdramatizing. [. . .] Anti-fascists are indignant towards the perpetrators who manhandled Toscanini and friends in Bologna, and towards Prof. Bruno [of the Milanese police headquarters] for having caused terror and despair in many Milanese families as a result of the arrests he ordered for students from the Liceo Berchet [who demonstrated in Toscanini's favour . . .]; and most of the old Fascists, devoted to the Duce, are indignant because [. . .] Bruno is creating an atmosphere of victimization that will work entirely negatively for [. . .] Fascism. Those of our young people who committed the grave crime of applauding Arturo Toscanini on his return from Bologna, in a moment of fanatical enthusiasm for him, ought at most to have been given a spanking [. . . ;] but to have [. . .] turned our houses upside down, searching for documents attesting to a criminal organization against the Fascist State and the Duce, and then to have taken these young people away from us, and even to have sent some of them to prison – believe me, this is the best system for creating real anti-fascism and for creating martyrs cheaply. [. . . Regarding the counter-demonstration against Toscanini:] When the demonstration had moved into Piazza della Scala, the most hot-headed participants shouted: "What does Toscanini do? – He makes us sick! – What is Toscanini? – A pederast! – What is Toscanini's wife? – A whore! – What is Toscanini's daughter? – A whore!" This dialogue caused real indignation among those present. Many asked themselves whether this is the Fascist style of the new generations. [. . .]'[54]

Lugano, 2 June: 'There is a lasting, painful impression everywhere regarding the mistreatment suffered by the highly celebrated Maestro Toscanini, and the anti-fascist newspapers continue to maintain that the slap was given him by His Excellency Arpinati.'[55]

Trieste, 3 June: 'The Toscanini affair still continues to arouse comment. In general, it is said that for the simple reason that Toscanini is an Italian luminary in the musical field, nothing should have caused [fascists] to lower themselves to such deeds.'[56]

Berlin, 4 June: 'My attention has been drawn to the following telegraphic dispatch, sent [. . .] from Milan today to Berlin's democratic "Vossische Zeitung", published in this evening's edition under the headline, "Will Toscanini be able to conduct at Bayereuth [sic]?": "The Bayereuth festival's director, Mrs Winnifried [sic] Wagner, has asked Toscanini when at the earliest he will be able to be in Bayereuth for the new production of 'Parsifal', for which his speedy arrival is desired. Toscanini has passed the question on to Italian government authorities, with a request to have his passport returned so that he may leave with his family by the end of this week, if possible [. . .]. The Italian government's reply is still being awaited. Meanwhile, the Deputy, Hon. Scorza, president of the Fascist Students' Association, in a speech to Milanese Fascist students, branded as anti-fascists all those who have shown their adoration for Toscanini, and emphasized that for the Italian people it is superfluous to be judged abroad by its conductors and singers. Foreign crowds have always gone into ecstasy over them, while the talents and work of [other] Italians abroad have been repaid by contempt and whippings. Today, Italy's good name depends exclusively upon Mussolini's genius." [. . .]'[57]

St Moritz, 21 June: '[. . .] since the evening of the 10th of this month, Maestro Toscanini, together with his wife and daughter, has been staying in the Villa "Chantarella" in St Moritz-Dorf. Almost every day, he receives the hotel manager, Emil Thoma-Badrutt, a well-known anti-fascist, and the piano teacher Robert Gruner. Yesterday, a commission made up of various leaders of anti-fascist parties came to congratulate him on having escaped from danger and for his decisive stand against Fascism. [. . .]'[58]

How strange, in the midst of all this, and how typical of Mussolini's ability to turn everything to account, was his comment to Emil Ludwig – probably made very shortly after the Bologna incident:

'Music seems to me the profoundest means of expression for any race of men. This applies to executants as well as to composers. If we Italians play Verdi better than do Frenchmen or Germans, it is because we have Verdi in our blood. You should hear how Toscanini, the greatest conductor in the world, interprets him.'

'The very mention of the man is an argument against what you have just been saying', [Ludwig] replied [...]. 'You could not find any German to conduct Beethoven so well as this remarkable Italian; and yet I have heard Verdi better produced in Germany than anywhere in Italy. [...]'

'You are only right in respect of exceptions', said Mussolini. [...][59]

And when, a dozen years later, the deposed and ailing dictator – now ruling the infamous Salò Republic as a German puppet – was queried by Nino D'Aroma about his musical preferences, he remarked: 'Among conductors, Toscanini. The man is contemptible for his behaviour; as an artist, however, he is immense. I, for my part, shall never deny the extraordinary emotion he gave me with his Beethoven concerts, nor the friendship he offered at his peril to our *fasci [di combattimento]* in 1919.'[60]

Mussolini had certainly demonstrated his gratitude in odd ways; for although the fascists never again dared to assault Toscanini physically, they kept close tabs on him throughout the 1930s and occasionally attacked him in the press. And the conductor did have a way of provoking the Duce. Late in 1931, for instance, spies informed the chief of the Political Police that Toscanini had been welcomed as a conquering hero by anti-fascist Italians in New York[61] and that he had given a large sum to the 'Giustizia e Libertà' organization in Paris.[62] Another report revealed that the French Prime Minister, Edouard Herriot, had made Toscanini a Commander of the Legion of Honour in 1932, and that when the two men happened to meet during an Atlantic crossing some months later, Herriot told Toscanini 'that His Excellency Manzoni, who was then the [Italian] ambassador to Paris, had let it be known that the granting of such an honour to Maestro Toscanini would not be much appreciated by the Duce. [...] Herriot is said to have been greatly astonished by Manzoni's out of place and politically ill-advised observation.'[63] Several documents indicate that Mussolini attempted to bring Toscanini back into the fold in the summer of 1934. For instance:

> The Duce is said to have personally offered Toscanini the direction of the Royal Opera Theatre [Rome] and, at the same time, the general directorship of all Italian theatres; but Toscanini is said to have contemptuously refused. When friends pressed the Maestro [...] to consider the offer, pointing out that it had come from the Duce himself, Toscanini is said to have answered in these words: 'I don't give a damn.'[64]

In October 1935, shortly after the government had banned the sale of foreign newspapers within Italy, agents intercepted a subversive telephone conversation between Toscanini and a woman identified only as Signora Ada.

(This was almost certainly Ada Mainardi Colleoni, wife of the cellist Enrico Mainardi; she is reputed to have been one of Toscanini's lovers during that period.)

> TOSCANINI: It's a really dirty piece of work to put a country in this situation! It's unheard of that a person can't read the paper he wants and has to believe everything that they print! It's unbelievable stuff! And it isn't even clever, because it will generate still more doubts. To force a people this way . . . with a slip-knot at its throat! [. . .] You have to read and know only what they want. . . . There must be only one mind! This is no longer living!
> ADA: It's frightful! Worse than Russia! For the previous few days the newsvendors had already had orders not to display foreign papers. [. . .] You can see that they're plotting something.
> T: No, it's only this: the people must be kept in complete ignorance . . .
> A: It gives you a feeling of suffocation.
> T: I can't wait to leave, because I can't stand it any longer! These things shock me . . . To see people enslaved this way! [. . .] They grab you by the throat here, they choke you! You have to believe what that mind [i.e. Mussolini's] believes . . . And I'll never believe what he believes . . . I never have believed it! I was weak only for a moment [n.b.: clearly referring to his support for Mussolini in 1919] and now I'm ashamed of myself! [. . .] We've reached the bottom of the barrel . . . Yet there are people who feel nothing, who live like this . . . But for me it's a kind of suffering that annihilates me.[65]

A notation on the transcript reads: 'Which proves what we already knew, that Toscanini is indomitable.'

For Toscanini, Italy had been reduced to a holiday site – a place where he could spend periods of rest between engagements elsewhere. He continued to receive many invitations to conduct major ensembles throughout his country, and he gave serious consideration to some of them. In the end, however, he realized that some degree of personal compromise would always have been required, had he accepted, and he resisted all temptations. Mario Labroca, for example, reported sounding Toscanini out in 1936 about the possibility of his conducting at the *Maggio Musicale*.

> [. . .] I asked him point-blank: 'Would you like to return to Italy to conduct?' I expected one of his violent reactions, but instead he replied very naturally: 'Certainly I would like it!' 'Then why don't you come back?' I persisted. I was moved. He remained silent, and he, too, was moved. He said: 'Thank you, Labroca', and that was all. I tried to persist, to assure him of the welcome he would receive, of the certainty that no untoward incident would take place. He listened as if the invitation interested him, but said no more. I had the impression of having touched a sensitive spot.[66]

When in Italy, Toscanini occasionally attended other people's perform-ances – police informers duly noted the names of people who greeted him –

and was as outspoken both in public and in private as Gabrilowitsch's statement has indicated. His rented summer villa on the Isolino San Giovanni, a tiny island in Lago Maggiore, became a meeting place for anti-fascist artists and intellectuals. Family movies from the mid-1930s show assemblages of writers and musicians (Erich Maria Remarque, Rudolf Serkin, and Adolf, Fritz and Hermann Busch) who had fled Hitler's Germany, as well as such improvised entertainments as a burlesque of the Fascist Youth Corps' marches – choreographed by Cia Fornaroli, Toscanini's daughter-in-law, who had been prima ballerina and head of the ballet school at La Scala until her family connections had cost her her job.

Toscanini had long since begun to extend his anti-fascist protest to other countries. In 1930 and 1931 he had been the first non-native-German-speaking conductor to appear at the Bayreuth Festival – where he had performed, *gratis*, *Tristan*, *Tannhäuser* and *Parsifal* – but he broke his promise to return in 1933 because of Hitler's accession to power. Toscanini had been a devout Wagnerite since his youth, and his letter of renunciation (28 May), addressed to Winifred Wagner, the composer's daughter-in-law, was painful to write:

> The sorrowful events that have wounded my feelings as a man and as an artist have not yet undergone any change, contrary to my every hope. It is therefore my duty today to break the silence I had imposed upon myself for two months and to notify you that for my peace of mind, for yours and for everyone's, it is better not to think any longer about my coming to Bayreuth.
> With unchangeable friendship for the House of Wagner
>
> Arturo Toscanini

That decision – which he later referred to as 'the deepest sorrow of my life' – led him to accept a long-standing invitation to conduct the Vienna Philharmonic, first in Vienna itself (1933) and then also in Salzburg (1934–7), where he gave his last performances of complete, staged operas. He was to have returned in 1938, but when Austrian Chancellor Kurt von Schuschnigg made concessions to Hitler in February of that year, Toscanini immediately cabled the festival's directors, saying that he would not return. His renunciation brought him many letters and telegrams of solidarity and gratitude, not only from opponents of Nazism, but also from key figures in the Italian anti-fascist movement-in-exile. Chief among these were Luigi Sturzo, founder of the Popular (Catholic) Party, who sent Toscanini copies of an article he had written about him and that had been published in French, Belgian and Swiss newspapers; and Gaetano Salvemini, who was at that time professor of history at Harvard. Salvemini's letter of 18 February 1938 is worth quoting in its entirety.

Dear Maestro,

I have been repeating to myself for two days that it would be absurd on my part to inflict one more letter on you, amidst who knows how many other letters and telegrams that you will be receiving these days. But so be it. Whether it is absurd or not absurd, I have to write to you, to tell you of my emotion, admiration, recognition and enthusiasm for the new proof of generosity and character that you have given by refusing to go to Salzburg.

In these Borgia-like years, you are the only person whose moral light remains immovable amid the universal baseness. Among those who speak to the future, you are the only one who has always remained faithful to the pure and beautiful tradition of the Italian soul. You are the only one who, at those important moments when we were lost in the darkness of despair, shouted words of faith, duty and hope at us.

In her three thousand year history, Italy has produced the most unheard-of contrasts: Marcus Aurelius and Romulus Augustulus, St Francis and Alexander VI, Dante and Stenterello, Leonardo da Vinci and Bertoldino.* Fate has not been so adverse today as may seem, at first glance, to be the case, to those of us who have been scattered through the world by the tempest. To those cowards who bow down before the Great Beast, taking it to be Italy, we can teach that Italy is today represented not by Mussolini but by Toscanini.

Thank you, dear Maestro, for the good you do us, for the strength you give us – not to speak of the pure happiness for which we are indebted to your art.

May our Italy live forever – the Italy of Mazzini, which still continues, through you, dear Maestro, to speak to the world in terms worthy of her history and her nobility.

G. Salvemini[67]

When Toscanini's friend and colleague Bruno Walter begged him not to abandon Salzburg, Toscanini cabled back: 'My decision[,] however painful[,] is final. I have only one way of thinking and acting. I hate compromise. I walk and I shall always walk on the straight path that I have traced for myself in life. Cordial greetings.'[68] And to the Festival's administrators, who gave him a deadline (10 March) by which to inform them whether he had changed his mind, he replied: 'I am surprised by your insulting telegram and I am surprised that the finality of my decision was not already understood from my first cable.'[69] Within a few days Hitler had entered Austria, and a month later an overwhelming majority of the Austrian people voted in favour of unification with the German Reich. That summer, Wilhelm Furtwängler, Hans Knappertsbusch and the avowedly anti-fascist Vittorio Gui conducted what had been Toscanini's Salzburg productions.

---

* As Salvemini well knew, Italy was the victim rather than the progenitor of the Spanish Pope Alexander VI Borgia. Stenterello was a good-natured simpleton in late eighteenth-century Florentine popular theatre. Bertoldino was a similar figure in early seventeenth-century comedy.

Toscanini had further involved himself in the struggle against fascism by travelling to Palestine at his own expense in December 1936, to conduct without fee the first concerts of a new orchestra – now known as the Israel Philharmonic – made up of Jewish refugees from Nazi persecution in Central Europe. His action had elicited the gratitude of Albert Einstein, himself in exile at Princeton University:

Honoured Master!

I feel the necessity of telling you for once how much I admire and honour you. You are not only the unmatchable interpreter of the world's musical literature, whose creations deserve the highest admiration. In the fight against the fascist criminals, too, you have shown yourself to be a man of greatest dignity. I also feel most deeply thankful because you have given the soon-to-be-founded Palestine Orchestra a push forward of inestimable significance.

The fact that such a contemporary exists balances many of the delusions one must continually experience from the *species minorum gentium*!

With love and greatest respect, cordial greetings from your

A. Einstein.[70]

Toscanini returned to Palestine, again at his own expense, in 1938. En route, he stopped in Rome, where he was followed by a spy for the political police.

12 April 1938. Last Friday I heard the following exchange in the lobby of the Quirinale Hotel. A gentleman approached Maestro Toscanini and said to him: 'Welcome back among us, Maestro. When will we have the great good fortune to hear you conduct again in Italy?' Toscanini replied: 'I would rather die than conduct again in Italy', and, after a brief, brusque salutation, he moved away from his interlocutor. [...] Someone said that Toscanini had been called to Rome to be asked to conduct on the occasion of Hitler's visit to Italy, and that he contemptuously refused. It is also said that he warmly defends German Jews whenever an occasion presents itself.[71]

Toscanini had also begun to accept invitations to conduct in countries in which he had not previously appeared (except, in some cases, on tour with American or Italian ensembles): France, Holland, Sweden, Switzerland, and especially England, where he gave extraordinarily successful concerts with the BBC Symphony Orchestra from 1935 to 1939. In a sense, he was dancing a circle around the fascist-controlled countries. His withdrawal from Salzburg caused the mayor of Lucerne to ask him to conduct there in the summer of 1938; Toscanini's acceptance was the cornerstone upon which the Swiss city built itself an enduring European music festival of major proportions. Fascist party bosses in Italy were not pleased with Toscanini's openly contemptuous behaviour. What truly incensed them, however, was the frenetic rush of Italian music lovers and of the cream of Italian society to attend his concerts across the border. The Political Police went into paroxysms of activity not seen since the weeks following the Bologna incident, and informers' reports began once again to flow.

> *Rome, 4 August* 1938: '[...] The "key" to these [musical events] is a Wagner concert to be conducted by Toscanini on the 25th of this month at 4 p.m. in the park opposite the villa at Tribschen [...] where Wagner lived from 1866 to 1872 [...]. The thousand seats are already completely sold out, 350 of them to Italians from Milan, Genoa, Turin and Rome. I don't believe that the purchase of these tickets on the part of some of them has been made only out of great love of art. It is surprising that among those who have reserved a place we find Signora Alfieri, wife of the Minister of Popular Culture. [...] Our Ambassador in Berne, His Excellency Attilio Tamaro, [...] has assured me that he has given instructions that no official Italian representative in Switzerland attend the concert. [...]'[72]

When Toscanini applied to Milan police headquarters to have his passport renewed so that he could leave for Switzerland, the local chief telephoned the Interior Ministry in Rome for permission to grant the request; the matter was referred to Mussolini, who gave his authorization.[73] At the same time, however, he ordered that Italians returning from the concert in cars be stopped, but he later decided merely to have their license plates noted.[74]

One of the informers dispatched to Lucerne reported that in addition to Mrs Alfieri, the concert was attended by such notables as Countess Volpi di Misurata, wife of a leading fascist financier and government minister; Remigio Paone, Director of Italian theatres; Marchioness Marconi, widow of the physicist and inventor; the composers Italo Montemezzi and Vincenzo Tommasini; Senator Giacomo De Martino; the wife of Senator Borletti; members of the Puccini family; the well-known Milanese lawyer Luigi Ansbacher; possibly the former Prime Minister Ivanoe Bonomi; Count Giovanni Ascanio Cicogna; the publisher Leo Olschki; and dozens of other artists, intellectuals and aristocrats. What most irritated Mussolini, however, was the presence of Maria José, consort of Crown Prince Umberto. By attending the concert, the princess was making a small but significant protest gesture – by the standards of the day. Toscanini undoubtedly knew this; but he also knew that however admirable she may have been as an individual, Maria José represented the royal family, which was in thrall to Mussolini. When she went back stage to greet the conductor after the performance, hoping that he would autograph her vocal score of the Verdi *Requiem*, he refused to see her. Carla Toscanini, greatly embarrassed, ran back and forth between her husband in his dressing room and the princess just outside the door, trying to persuade one or the other to back down. Both were adamant. But Toscanini, as usual, had his way: his room was on the ground floor, and passers-by soon saw the white-haired conductor climbing out the window.[75]

The Lucerne episode led to dozens of telegrams and telephone calls and hundreds of pages of reports to and from the Political Police regarding all Italians whose license plates had been noted by informers. The government seems to have gained no useful information from these efforts; but Farinacci's newspaper, Il *regime fascista* of Cremona, published a libellous article against the conductor and those who admired him.

THE HONORARY JEW

Toscanini has conducted a concert in Wagner's honour at the Tribschen museum. Even the Swiss press reproved this gentleman who, merely because he knows how to conduct an orchestra, thinks he has the right to act basely.

Indeed, when two non-Jewish young ladies presented him with a bouquet of flowers at the end of the first part, he threw down his baton and abandoned the podium. But the most interesting fact is that the 'great democrat' declared himself willing to give a concert for the people without earning a penny – except that ticket prices were stupefying: 22.55 Swiss francs. Thus no plebeian could attend. It is true that he was not paid, but he asked for 100 seats in the theatre, hotel rooms for himself and his family, and the same for the numerous Jews who accompanied him.

Toscanini's disinterestedness cost the concert organizers 6000 Swiss francs; if one adds to that the gifts presented to him, the figure rises to 40,000 Italian lire. [...]

Since Toscanini is doing all this in a purely anti-fascist spirit, we would like to know who those Italians were who went there [...]. This should not be difficult, because we know the numbers of the Italian cars' license plates.

Well, then – so that people won't say that we take shots in the dark – we invite our comrades in Milan to look up the owners of the automobiles bearing the following plates: MI 1–4505, MI 4215; comrades in Florence, the car FI 1–4395; and comrades in Rome, the cars 6288 and 4–1857.[76]

The Milanese and Florentine papers hastily found and printed the names of the car owners,[77] but there is no record of reprisals. Some of the calumnies in the article are gratuitous; some accusations contain a small portion of truth. The concert organizers probably did put Toscanini and his immediate family up at hotels and provide tickets – but certainly not a hundred of them – to the event. These are customary practices. The prices were raised – quadrupled – for Toscanini's concert, a sure sell-out, in order to subsidize the rest of the new-born festival. The article conveniently does not mention that as the demand for tickets had been so overwhelming, Toscanini agreed to conduct a second one two days later, again without drawing a fee, and with the tickets at normal prices. He probably did run away from the floral presentation, as he had been known to do on other occasions: Toscanini superstitiously associated such doings with mortuary rites.

On returning to Italy for a holiday later that summer, Toscanini and his wife had their passports taken away by the fascist authorities. Galeazzo Ciano, who was then Foreign Minister, wrote in his diary: 'The Duce is annoyed because many Italians, and above all the Princess of Piedmont [Maria José], went to Lucerne for [Toscanini's] Wagner concert. But the withdrawal of the passport is related to a wiretap, from which it seems that Toscanini attacked the Duce for his anti-Semitic policy, terming it "medieval stuff".'* Ciano also warned Fulvio De Suvich, Italy's Ambassador to the United States, not to become involved in the affair: 'The Duce flies into a rage if you talk to him about Toscanini.'[78] De Suvich, however, was worried about what the American reaction to the incident would be if Toscanini did not reach New York in time for his October engagement. He broached the matter with Mussolini, who agreed to give back the passport if the conductor would request it of him. Toscanini would not bend even to that degree – although his wife wrote (16 September) to the Chief of the Political Police to warn that there could be 'unpleasant interpretations and comments on the part of the foreign press' if the passport were not forthcoming.[79] Toscanini considered escaping in a hydroplane that would take him from the Italian to the Swiss part of Lake Maggiore: this appealed to his sense of adventure, but he feared there might be reprisals against family and friends. A Swiss journalist, friendly with Walter Toscanini, threatened to make an uproar in the world press, and Mussolini realized that he had created unnecessary problems for himself.[80] In a brief note (6 August 1938), the Duce's office chief informed him that Toscanini 'insists on having his passport renewed as soon as possible. Bocchini [Chief of the Political Police] asks whether he may grant it.' At the top of the page, the exasperated Duce scrawled 'Sì';[81] and in a note to the Chief of Police he ordered: 'return the passport'.[82]

Toscanini spent the war years in New York. He joined the Mazzini Society – a group of liberal and socialist Italian expatriates who favoured the

---

* The transcript of this conversation – again between Toscanini and 'Signora Ada' – reads, in part:
    T: Who knows where it will all end. Anything is possible!
    A: What makes you see red is the lying, the bad faith . . .
    T: [. . .] They don't even have the sense to say: 'Let's disguise things.' They want people to be stupid.
    A: In fact, they're reducing them to that, little by little!
    T: [. . .] I'm going to the Isolino within the next few days, and I'm going to do everything to have things moved out . . . because I don't know what could happen next.
    A: Yes, it's for the best. But I don't think they can push things too far . . .
    T: There's no limit now. Tomorrow they'll say: 'Give me your money, do this . . .' They're capable of anything. Promises no longer exist; they don't remember today what they said yesterday. It's shameful! When it was a matter of [the laws regulating] foreigners, okay; but now, there are people who have worked for years, who have done so much! [Jewish] children can't go to school . . . this is medieval stuff!
    A: Yes, exactly.
  The bottom of the transcript bears the words: 'by order of the Duce take away Toscanini's passport'.[83]

establishment of an Italian republic following the downfall of fascism, for which they all fervently hoped. Their leaders included Salvemini, the art critic Lionello Venturi, church historian Giorgio La Piana, author and literary historian Giuseppe Antonio Borgese, Colonel Randolfo Pacciardi, Alberto Tarchiani (later Italy's ambassador to the United States) and Count Carlo Sforza, who was a cabinet minister both before and after the fascist period. Toscanini was asked to accept the presidency of the society; he refused the office but offered his continuing support.[84] Salvemini later wrote that 'our most effective argument in our criticism of fascism was Arturo Toscanini. [. . .] He did not write or give lectures, but his very existence was a formidable accusation against a political regime that could have chased such a man out of his country.'[85] Early in 1943 Salvemini and La Piana published their booklet, What to do with Italy, and dedicated it 'To Maestro Arturo Toscanini who, in the darkest days of fascist crimes, of Italy's dishonour, of the world's madness, remained intransigently faithful to the ideals of Mazzini and Garibaldi and, with tenacious faith, anticipated the dawn of the second Italian Risorgimento'.[86]

The Toscanini family assisted large numbers of refugees from Europe in securing American entry visas, jobs and homes. Once the United States had entered the war, Toscanini added numerous benefit concerts to his regular performance schedule. The proceeds from most of these went to the Red Cross, but some performances raised money for United States Government war bonds. The fascists made the most of this: they claimed that Toscanini was paying for bombs that were destroying his country. And when Toscanini conducted the American première (19 July 1942) of Shostakovich's Seventh ('Leningrad') Symphony, which was said to symbolize Russian resistance to the German invasion, the Roman daily, Il messaggero, apostrophized:

> O you good Bolognese fascist who, in days that have now been forgotten by too many people, gave him those sonorous slaps when he refused to play the national anthems, stirring up an enormous international clamour – why didn't you increase the dose which he so deserved, so as to render him permanently unable to work? You would have made it impossible for this Italian to debase Italy before the enemy today.[87]

The article was signed by 'Tito Silvio Mursino' – alias Vittorio Mussolini.

On 25 July 1943 Toscanini conducted a live radio programme of Verdi excerpts with his NBC Symphony Orchestra in New York. He had just left the stage with soprano Gertrude Ribla after a performance of the aria 'Pace, pace mio Dio' from La forza del destino when an announcement was broadcast into the hall and over the air: Mussolini had been deposed. Toscanini rushed back on stage, clasped his hands and gazed heavenwards, in a sign of thanksgiving, while the audience, equally beside itself, applauded, cheered, screamed and all but tore the studio to pieces. That same day, printed posters were pasted all over La Scala's sign-boards: '*Evviva Toscanini, Ritorni Toscanini*'.[88] The lawyer who had paid to have those placards printed and had then put them up with his own hands was arrested and beaten when the fascists resumed control of the city a few weeks later. His enthusiasm for Toscanini cost him seven teeth.

The Mazzini Society broke up soon after 8 September 1943, when the Allies concluded the armistice with the king and Badoglio. Sforza, Tarchiani and their faction accepted the compromise, but Salvemini and the others insisted that any dealings with anyone who had been tainted through collaboration with the fascists – above all the king and Badoglio – were immoral and politically unwise. Toscanini decidedly favoured the latter opinion, and when Salvemini asked him to make a public statement, in print, to represent their point of view to the Allies, he accepted. This was the only significant, individual public statement Toscanini ever made on any subject, and the editors of *Life* magazine gave him the editorial page of their issue of 13 September 1943. He wrote directly in English and with great care; but a member of his family claims that a critical reference the conductor made to the Church's position on fascism was removed by the editors before publication.[89]

In his declaration ('To the People of America'), Toscanini said he felt that he could act as interpreter of the wishes of the Italian people, who had been 'choked for more than twenty years'. He asserted – and this was his main point – that the king and Badoglio 'cannot be dissociated in any way from the fascist and military clique. They cannot be the representatives of the Italian people: they cannot in any way conclude peace with the Allies in the name of Italy, so betrayed by them.' He predicted that there would be a revolution in Italy, and that for this to 'result in orderly democratic government, as we hope, it will be necessary for the Allies to support all democratic elements currently arrayed against the King and Badoglio'. These 'elements', however, included the long-suppressed socialists and communists, and the idea of dealing with them instead of supporting the king and Badoglio was unlikely to be greeted with enthusiasm by Roosevelt and Churchill.

Toscanini also suggested that Italy's frontiers be left as established before Mussolini's accession, that economic assistance be given the new government, and that 'the Allies permit our volunteers to fight against the hated Nazis under the Italian flag with conditions substantially similar to those of the Free French', in order to facilitate an unconditional surrender of the Italian armed forces. Citing Shakespeare's *Henry* VI he said:

> Do not forget that we Italians have been the first to endure the oppression of a tyrannical gang of criminals, supported by that 'fainthearted and degenerate King' of Italy – but that we have never willingly submitted to them. Countless thousands of men and women in Italy shed blood, met imprisonment and

death, striving fiercely against that horde of criminals, enduring also the apathy and indifference of the world then full of admiration for Mussolini.[90]

When Sforza wrote Toscanini to explain why, in his opinion, the Allies were right to continue to accept the king as titular head of Italy, Toscanini replied in typically unequivocal fashion:

From this moment on you may consider me a *traitor to my Country*! Not even to save Italy could I come to terms with those who have shamefully betrayed her for more than twenty years! I would not even be able to speak to or look at those two wretches. I feel sorry for you.... Our tastes are very different.... Your politics may be intelligent and shrewd, but I condemn them and despise them – and I declare myself against you and the Allied government that has fully demonstrated its complete ignorance and ineptitude in understanding the honest and simple Italian soul. Their policy towards Italy has been a shameful fiasco – and, as Dorothy Thompson says, a complete disaster. Their *'unconditional surrender'* is ridiculous.... And now they want to put the anti-fascist forces in the hands of those who have betrayed them for long and, alas! sorrowful years![91]

An Italo-American, Gian Luca Cicogna, protested to Toscanini: 'Your article [...] thoroughly disgusted me. Why don't you continue to busy yourself only with music and leave politics alone, since you understand nothing of it[?] Who authorized you to express the feelings of Italians towards His Majesty the King[?] I respond to your ignorant statements with a: Long live the King, Long live the House of Savoy!'[92]

Toscanini's reply:

No – I have never had the bad taste to express to the American people the feelings of those shameless Italians who, like you, admire and respect that degenerate, cowardly King of Italy who has betrayed *everything* and *everyone*.

A constitutional monarch betrayed the Constitution and invalidated the Statute, making a free people the slaves of a gang of criminals!

For more than twenty years he sanctioned by his signature all the iniquities that his *worthy* cousin Mussolini, the mad criminal, set before him. In the end, to save himself, he even betrayed Mussolini and the ignominious alliance with Germany. Where can you find a more vile being??? Where??

No – Noble Gian Luca Cicogna – my letter to the American people interpreted the feelings of the other Italians ... the good ones – the pure ones – those who sincerely love Italy and freedom.... You have nothing to do with it – nor do those fascists who de-fascisticized themselves at the last moment out of convenience and cowardice! ... You misunderstood my letter.[93]

On 12 June 1944 *Life* magazine carried a lengthy article entitled 'An Italian Manifesto', co-signed by Salvemini, Toscanini, Borgese, La Piana, Pacciardi and Venturi. Once again, they urged the British and Americans to stop supporting the king's government, but this time they went further in their

condemnation of Allied policy. The plea – desperate, heartfelt and im-
passioned – was largely disregarded.[94]

Some months earlier Toscanini, who had previously turned down several
lucrative offers to appear in commercial films, had contributed his services to
the making of a propaganda short for the United States Office of War
Information. He conducted the NBC Symphony in the overture to La forza del
destino and another Verdi work, the Hymn of the Nations – a cantata written for
London's International Exposition of 1862. The piece makes use of the
themes of 'God Save the Queen', the 'Marseillaise' and Italy's 'Mameli Hymn',
whose first line Toscanini changed from 'O Italia, patria mia' (O Italy, my
country) to 'O Italia, patria mia tradita' (my betrayed country); and he wrote a
bridge passage at the end and added the Socialist 'International' and 'The
Star-Spangled Banner' in tribute to the other two major allies. The film was
distributed in the liberated portions of Europe.[95]

As the war dragged on and Italy's situation became increasingly desperate,
Toscanini grew more and more restive. 'I think of my poor, dear Italy,' he wrote
to his daughter, Wally, in November 1944, 'mishandled and torn asunder by
enemies and friends alike, and I don't know why I'm not there to do more than
what I can do here.'[96] He found some consolation in the visits of other Italian
exiles whose anti-fascist convictions he shared, and one of these, Armando
Borghi – a well-known anarchist whom Toscanini and Salvemini had helped
to free from detention by American immigration authorities – wrote of
their acquaintanceship in Il mondo a few months after the conductor's death.
Borghi pointed out that until the United States entered the war, the anti-
fascists were a small minority among influential Italo-Americans.

> | ... | As far as the roughnecks of the colony were concerned, Toscanini had
> betrayed Italy and the Duce, and, as Don Basilio says, calumny always leaves its
> mark. | ... | Let's reflect upon the fact that Toscanini was the only world celebrity
> |of Catholic origin| who never went to visit the Pope, never surrounded himself
> with priests and friars and nuns, never conducted music in church |n.b.: he did so
> on three or four occasions, but never for religious functions|, never gave benefit
> concerts for religious organizations, either in Italy or in America.
>
> Toscanini had shouted his No to fascism right in its historic capital: Bologna,
> in the heart of the Po Valley | ... | whose agrarian Don Rodrigos |n.b.:
> reference to the villain in Manzoni's I promessi sposi| had provided fascism with
> its first scoundrels and financiers. Toscanini's No in Arpinati's home territory
> was a bomb blast. Mussolini understood this | ... |.
>
> | ... Toscanini| was a thousand times stronger than the rest of us, who acted
> with 'political' preparation and premeditation. He was defenceless at the time of
> fascism's rise; he was not furnished with the armour of suspicion that we had
> and that came of our political convictions. Toscanini was | ... | absorbed by
> the majesty of his art. But his interior world predestined him to be what he
> was. | ... |

[. . .] Had it not been for the 'now you see me, now you don't' attitude towards the rescue, not of poor devils, but of big guns like Farinacci and Starace [. . .], the dissensions among the anti-fascist leaders [in New York] would have remained in the background. This necessity *not to soften*, in what was then the conclusive hour of the war, showed everyone and everything in its true light. In that hour Toscanini openly ranked himself against compromise and against the compromise-brokers. As a result, he broke with the Mazzini Society, at the moment in which it was about to become a Noah's Ark for saving the black-shirt big guns of the entire colony. [. . .]

We were often in touch at that time. We discussed politics and post-fascist society. We also discussed anarchy, which he found a 'reasonable' ideal. He laughed at those who called him a future Paderewski. In fact, he had never accepted, nor did he later accept, honours or decorations that he could have had for the asking in Italy, in America, in the whole world. [. . .][97]

At war's end, Toscanini contributed one million lire towards the reconstruction of La Scala, which had been semi-destroyed by Allied bombs in 1943, and gave a special concert in New York that raised $30,000 for Italian welfare societies, especially the War Orphans Committee. At the end of that performance, New York Mayor Fiorello La Guardia and the new Italian Ambassador, Tarchiani, went to greet him in his dressing room. They found themselves turned away: Tarchiani was one of those who had compromised with the so-called demo-fascists; Toscanini would not see him.[98]

In February 1946, when the Italian government announced that a referendum on the abolition of the monarchy would be held in June, Toscanini made up his mind to go home, to conduct a concert for the reinauguration of La Scala. Seventy-five per cent of Milan's historic centre had been destroyed or seriously damaged during the last twenty months of the war, but – typical of the Milanese mentality – the first important building to be put back in shape was La Scala. Antonio Greppi, the city's first post-war mayor, stood staunchly behind the popular slogan 'bread and theatre'. With permission from the Allied occupation forces, financial support from a variety of Italian sources and painstaking work on the part of La Scala's chief engineer, Luigi Lorenzo Secchi, and his staff, the 168-year-old house was nearly ready for use on 25 April, the first anniversary of the liberation.

Toscanini had arrived in Italy two days earlier and had begun to lay down the law. Jewish musicians who had lost their positions at La Scala in 1938 and who had also managed to survive the German occupation were to be re-engaged – first among them, Vittore Veneziani, the chorus director. Others who had fallen into political disfavour under fascism were also given back their jobs. Many people wrote to Toscanini – some to welcome him back, others to excuse or ingratiate themselves, still others to describe their wartime sufferings. The most interesting of these letters came from Oreste

Noto, a music journalist, who, after the war, was secretary of the National Order of Lyric Artists.

Milan, 24 April 1946
Dear, Great Maestro,

[...] Allow me to relate a bit of my story. In the 15 June 1940 issue of my Giornale degli Artisti, which I managed to publish a couple of times a month, despite its being a target of the so-called fascist Unions, I printed a news item that had been given me by poor Enrico Bonacchi, who died in an extermination camp at Mauthausen. [The item] was about the great celebrations then being prepared in Rio de Janeiro for your return to that city after so many years. [...] The item appeared on the front page in bold-face type, and was followed by some remarks of mine that concluded thus: 'While Rio de Janeiro is preparing triumphal honours for Arturo Toscanini, the greatest ambassador of Italian Beauty, we are left with nothing but regret at having lost him'. That did it! The world came tumbling down.

Grand Officer Filippo Criscuolo – cocaine addict, trickster and downright thief – head of the Prefecture's Press Office during the proconsulate of Prefect Marziali, had the issue confiscated immediately, and sent two ruffians in his service to take me away from my home [...]. As soon as I was brought before him, he upbraided me with the most vulgar, Neapolitan phrases that ever issued from the mouth of a filthy street urchin. A few days later, the fascist king's public prosecutor notified me of a decree that put an end to my periodical.

I was literally knocked to the ground, with no resources: [...] all theatre people turned their backs on me, except a Polish Artist, the tenor Franco Beval – anti-fascist as only a truly free man can be – who took me on as his secretary and thus gave me at least a piece of bread (albeit with nothing to go with it) for myself and my womenfolk.

But the story was not to end there; [...] I was arrested on 28 October. Accusation: I had said, in a bar near the Teatro Lirico, that the fall of France had settled nothing, that the war would be long and terrible all the same, and that the Axis would be completely destroyed by it. Quick trial and sentence; and after 68 days of preliminary incarceration at San Vittore [Milanese prison] (where, in November, December and the first days of January, they threw buckets of cold water over me, *naked*, after having beaten me – almost all my teeth and my right clavicle were broken), I was condemned to three years of internal exile and sent to Lacedonia, a little village in Irpinia [province of Avellino ...].

There I remained until 25 July 1943, when I fled with my companions in misadventure on the day of the so-called coup d'état. I arrived in Milan with the hope of resuming my activities, and I found my house destroyed by the bombardments of February 1942, and my family evacuated [...].

[...] On the 8th of September I had to go into hiding, in order not to be arrested again, but my wandering life did not last long. Poor Bonacchi, who had had permission from the [Allied] Intelligence Corps to accept the administration of the [German] 'Soldatensender' Orchestra, was arrested at the instigation of that lurid figure, Walter Mocchi, author of the '16 Points' of Verona [policy statement of Mussolini's 'Salò Republic'], right-hand-man of Mezzasoma and Bombacci [important personages in the Salò government], chief and superintendent of the so-called Para-union Cooperative of opera companies, and perpetrator of the 'republic's' most repulsive propaganda. I was commanded by the Intelligence Corps to replace [Bonacchi], and I remained in that position until it was discovered that I had given 28 orchestra members' cards to 28 members of the Intelligence Corps, three of whom [. . .] were arrested in Mantua after having tried to blow up the local military headquarters of the SS, and were found to be in possession of the cards. Arrested again in Milan, and accused of a crime for which I would have been shot, I was moved to Verona and interned in the basement of the National Insurance Institute, where the General Command of the SS was located. After eight days of indescribable tortures to make me confess the names of those to whom I had given cards, I managed to escape, together with other prisoners [. . .].

Finally, on 25 April [1945], I fought alongside the railroad workers of Palazzo Litta, where we had hidden large- and small-calibre arms.

With peace restored, Mariano Stabile, who had organized within the National Order of Lyric Artists all the singers worthy of the name, asked me last October to become Secretary of the Order.

[. . .] The war has ended, the fascist tyranny has ended, and the Mocchis and those who protect them will also come to an end. And our Country will belong to Italians – the pure ones, who are in love with art and with their Country.

Today, dear Maestro, in recompense for all my sufferings, I ask only one thing of you: to allow me the joy of seeing you again and of kissing your hand again, and I am certain that you will not deny me this joy.[99]

On 11 May La Scala, still smelling of fresh paint, was filled to nearly twice its normal capacity, and the audience included government officials and the leaders of the major political parties. Even Ferruccio Parri, legendary resistance leader and head of the post-war government of national unity, was present. Greppi, whose son had died as a partisan fighter, had wanted to make a brief speech before the concert, but Toscanini had vetoed the idea: there had already been plenty of talk; concerts were for music. Although the concerts Toscanini conducted later in that brief season included a good deal of American, Soviet and other 'Allied' music that had not been performed in Italy during the war years (accompanied, naturally, by a substantial dose of German classics), for the first programme he chose music by Italian composers only – Rossini, Verdi, Boito and Puccini. Outside the theatre, tens of thousands gathered in Piazza della Scala and in Piazza del Duomo – both closed to traffic – and in the arcaded Galleria that connects them, to listen to the performance on loudspeakers. The concert was broadcast throughout

Italy and via short wave to much of the rest of the world. At precisely nine p.m., as the nearly octogenarian Toscanini walked onto 'his' stage for the first time in sixteen years, the people in the theatre leapt to their feet, applauding frantically, shouting 'Toscanini! Toscanini!' and weeping. The dictatorship, the war and the prolonged mass sufferings were a thing of the past. At the end of the last piece, the applause and cheering went on for thirty-seven minutes. Backstage, the orchestra gave Toscanini a commemorative gold medallion bearing the inscription: 'To the Maestro who was never absent – his Orchestra'.[100]

The press coverage given to Toscanini's return would be inconceivable in other countries and under other conditions. As usual, he granted no interviews and made no comments to journalists, but his views on contemporary Italian events were known. Several political commentators affirmed that Toscanini's baton did more for the anti-monarchic cause than all the orations of De Gasperi, Togliatti and Nenni combined.[101] Toscanini's influence cannot be evaluated, but certainly the conductor was pleased with the results of the referendum, held three weeks after the Scala inaugural, which led to the establishment of an Italian Republic. Although he could have resumed the direction of La Scala, by then Toscanini's activities were largely confined to New York, where working conditions satisfied him. He conducted occasionally at La Scala until 1952 and spent long holiday periods in Italy until 1955, a year after his retirement. Toscanini died in New York a few weeks before his ninetieth birthday. What he himself had referred to as his 'proud and scornful character, but clear as crystal and just as cutting', had saved him from the shame that touched most other musicians in fascist Italy.

> You are too poisoned by the atmosphere that surrounds you to be able to value people like me, who have remained and will remain above the mud (not to give it a worse name) that is drowning the Italians!!! You are all living, now, in the midst of shame and dishonour, without giving any sign of rebellion. [. . .] I can only believe that you've never understood me, never valued me at my *real* and *true* worth! I was too far above you, and your vantage point deceived you . . . You've mixed me up with the Molinaris, the Pizzettis and other, similar *animals*. [. . .] I am disgusted at belonging to the family of artists . . . who, with a few exceptions, are not men, but poor beings, full of vanity . . . Life no longer holds any interest for me, and I would pray God to take it away from me immediately if it weren't for my firm, *never diminished hope* to see the *criminals* swept off the face of the earth before I go. [. . .] Live happily and healthily if you can . . .
>
> Arturo Toscanini,
> letter to a lady in Rome,
> New York, 16 May 1941.[102]

Epilogue

Aldous Huxley asked himself in 1925 why Italy was no longer the 'musician's paradise' described by Charles Burney in the eighteenth century. 'What has happened to Italian genius nowadays?' Huxley wondered.

> It still exists, I think; but it has been deflected out of music, as it was deflected out of the visual arts, into politics and, later, into business and engineering. The first two-thirds of the nineteenth century were sufficiently occupied in the achievement of freedom and unity. The sixty years since then have been devoted to the exploitation of the country's resources; and such energy as has been left over from that task has gone into politics. One day, when they have finished putting modern comfort into the old house, have turned out the obstreperous servants and installed a quiet, honest housekeeper – one day, perhaps, the Italians will allow their energy and their talent to flow back into the old channels. Let us hope they will.[1]

Well, the obstreperous servants were indeed turned out, though the degree of circumspection and honesty of post-war leaders is as melancholy a subject in Italy as in any other country. The modern comforts have been installed, too, though often not in the wisest manner. And the country's musical life? It goes on much as before. A few important Italian composers, conductors, singers and instrumentalists maintain the nation's international standing. Some Italian musicologists and critics – over-reacting, perhaps, to the xenophobia of the fascist period – have become self-hating, blind xenophiles, oddly nostalgic about the Vienna and Berlin of the 1920s and early 1930s, and persuaded that even today, whatever goes on north of the Alps is necessarily more serious and therefore better than what happens at home. The inevitable transformation of the popular, nineteenth-century operatic repertoire into High Culture – a process already well advanced before the Second World War – is complete: the same casts that appear at the Metropolitan, Covent Garden, and the Vienna State Opera also sing at La Scala; the less wealthy houses, and sometimes even La Scala, often use controversial stagings to divert people's attention from the third-rate singing; and the public for new operas is minuscule. Occasional uprisings – usually insignificant and wrong-headed – among the 'guardians of bel canto' in the galleries are the only remnant of traditional operatic life.

It is not possible to believe that the state-run Italian conservatories were any more depressing, fossilized and anti-musical under the fascist regime than they are today. Unfortunately, those adjectives describe conservatories under every governmental system in every country: important musicians who have written memoirs have all born witness to this for generations. The right individual instructor can make a school worthwhile for a lucky student, but few young people are so fortunate. Indeed, only the luckiest or toughest students survive the experience. The unique feature of Italian conservatories is their paralysing bureaucratic superstructure which, by its very nature, discourages original initiative on the part of the faculty and administration.

If the conservatories are pre-fascistic in their timeless non-functioning, there is one sector of Italian musical life that can truly be described as the inheritor of the fascist tradition. The state-subsidized opera houses have remained in thrall to the major political parties, which use them as prestigious showcases of their power. Thus, in addition to the backroom and bedroom politics that are an inevitable facet of theatre life everywhere, Italian operatic culture is today beset by the day-to-day problems of hard-core party politics. There is a tacit agreement among Christian Democrats, Communists and Socialists to maintain a decorous balance in the administration of each theatre – and the smaller parties accept this situation in the hope of an occasional handout from their big brothers. Anyone – even a major composer or performer – who wishes to be a *sovrintendente*, *direttore artistico*, or *segretario generale* of one of these institutions must enlist the support of one or another party, either by joining outright or, at the very least, by demonstrating that his or her heart is in the right place. Sometimes, the best people for these jobs in a certain theatre at a certain time also form the right political combination; more often the desirable party mix creates an undesirable artistic compromise. And since the administrators are nearly always strange bedfellows who tend to feud a great deal among themselves, the divorce rate is phenomenally high. A chronic instability is thus created in the day-to-day functioning of Italian opera houses. Remarkably, under such conditions, some of them manage to maintain a decent level of production and occasionally to rise above the humdrum. Most, however, are a shambles. The politicization of the performing arts, so crudely initiated by the fascists, has been brought to a high level of refinement by their successors; and the *enti autonomi*, as they exist today, are a travesty of the system worked out at La Scala in the 1920s. One of history's tiny, consoling ironies, however, is that Mussolini's true spiritual heirs have to limit their activities to hiring and firing the 'eternal Italian tenors and mandolin-players' of whom he was so contemptuous.

What interests me is the psychological, emotional manner in which people were fascists. It was a sort of mental block [. . .] at the adolescent phase. [. . .] Fascism and adolescence continue to be permanent, historic phases in our lives – adolescence in our lives as individuals, fascism in our lives as a nation. It's a sort of eternal childhood, a dumping of responsibility on others, living with the comfortable feeling that someone is thinking for you. One time it's your Mama, another it's Daddy, and then there's the mayor or the Duce, and the bishop and the Madonna and television. [. . .] I think I recognize fascism's eternal premise in the provincial mentality, in a lack of awareness of real, concrete problems, in a refusal to deepen one's individual relationship to life – out of laziness, prejudice, unwillingness to inconvenience oneself, and presumptuousness. [Fascist attitudes include] being proud of one's ignorance and trying to assert oneself or the group to which one belongs, not through the strength that grows out of capability or experience, or by measuring oneself against culture, but through bragging, making meaningless statements and displaying imitative rather than true qualities. [. . .] Fascism cannot be combatted unless we identify it with the stupid, shabby, empty-wishful part of ourselves – a part that belongs to no political party, a part of which we ought to be ashamed. In order to get rid of it one cannot simply say: 'I am active in an anti-fascist party'. Because we all have that quality within ourselves; 'fascism' once gave it a voice, authority and credibility.

Federico Fellini[2]

Notes

Legend of Italian music journals: MO = *Musica d'oggi*, Milan, Ricordi; MS = *Musica e scena*, Milan, Sonzogno; NIM = *La nuova Italia musicale*, Milan; RM = *La rassegna musicale*, Turin
Legend for Archivio Centrale dello Stato, Rome (indicated: ACS): SPD = Segreteria particolare del Duce (Mussolini's private office); CO = corrispondenza ordinaria; CPC = Casellario politico centrale (central political files); MI = Ministero dell'Interno; DGPS = Direzione generale di Pubblica sicurezza (general administration of public safety); DPP = Divisione Polizia Politica (political police division); FP = Fascicoli Personali (confidential files)
NA = National Archive, Washington
SAC = St Anthony's College, Oxford

INTRODUCTION (pp. 1–3)
1 H. Sachs, *Toscanini*, London, Weidenfeld & Nicolson, 1978
2 F. Nicolodi, *Musica e musicisti nel ventennio fascista*, Fiesole, Discanto, 1984

CHAPTER I: THE TERRAIN (pp. 5–32)
1 D. Mack Smith, *Italy: A Modern History*, Ann Arbor, University of Michigan Press, 1969, p. 313
2 Ibid., p. 327
3 Ibid., p. 325
4 Ibid., p. 340
5 Ibid., pp. 348–9
6 Ibid., pp. 368–70
7 G. Salvemini, *Le origini del fascismo in Italia*, Milan, Feltrinelli 1966, pp. 388–90

8 R. De Rensis, *Mussolini musicista*, Mantua, Paladino, 1927, pp. 13–14
9 Ibid., p. 14
10 Ibid., p. 17
11 Ibid., p. 18
12 Y. de Begnac, *Palazzo Venezia: Storia di un regime*, Rome, La Rocca, 1950, pp. 650–1
13 De Rensis, op. cit., p. 18
14 Begnac, op. cit., p.650
15 De Rensis, op. cit., p. 21
16 V. E. De Fiori, *Mussolini: The Man of Destiny*, New York, Dutton, 1928, p. 52
17 De Rensis, op. cit., p. 21
18 M. Sarfatti, *Dux*, Milan, Mondadori, 1926, pp. 251–2
19 De Rensis, op. cit., pp. 21–2
20 E. Ludwig, *Talks with Mussolini*, London, George Allen & Unwin, 1932, p. 210

21 Begnac, op. cit., p. 650
22 De Rensis, op. cit., p. 22
23 Ibid., p. 23
24 Ibid., p. 23
25 Ludwig, op. cit., p. 211
26 F. Sapori, L'arte e il Duce, Milan, Mondadori, 1932, p. 61
27 N. D'Aroma, Mussolini segreto, Bologna, Cappelli, 1958, pp. 304–5
28 De Rensis, op. cit., p. 33
29 MO, X–1, Jan. 1928
30 B. Mussolini, Opera omnia (ed. E. and D. Susmel), Rome, G. Volpe, 1979, Vol. XLI, p. 424
31 D. Mack Smith, Mussolini, London, Weidenfeld & Nicolson, 1981, p. 175
32 A. Petacco, Riservato per il Duce, Milan, Mondadori, 1979, p. 75
33 Ibid., p. 76
34 MO, VII–7, July 1925
35 Petacco, op. cit., p. 13
36 MO, IX–10, Oct. 1927
37 Salvemini, op. cit., p. 406
38 E. R. Tannenbaum, L'esperienza fascista, Milan, Mursia, 1972, pp. 180–1
39 Mack Smith, Mussolini, p. 128
40 Tannenbaum, op. cit., p. 182
41 Mack Smith, Mussolini, p. 123
42 G. Bottai, Politica fascista delle arti, Rome, Signorelli, 1940, pp. 165–6
43 MO, XVI–3, March 1934
44 MO, XVIII–2, Feb. 1936
45 Nicolodi, Musica e musicisti nel ventennio fascista, p. 342
46 Ibid., p. 343
47 Ibid., p. 347
48 Ibid., p. 428
49 Ibid., p. 465
50 La Stampa, Turin, LXVI–300, 17 Dec. 1932, p. 3
51 Ibid., p. 3
52 B. Pizzetti (ed.), Ildebrando Pizzetti: cronologia e bibliografia, Parma, La Pilotta, 1979, pp. 235–9; and Nicolodi, op. cit., pp. 143–5
53 A. Casella, I segreti della giara, Florence, Sansoni, 1941, p. 259
54 B. Pizzetti, op. cit., pp. 242–3
55 Casella, op. cit., p. 202
56 MS, I–3, March 1924
57 MS, III–8–9, Aug.-Sept. 1926
58 MS, III–12, Dec. 1926
59 MO, IX–8–9, Aug.-Sept. 1927
60 MO, X–4, April 1928
61 MO, XI–1, Jan. 1929
62 Ibid.
63 MO, XII–11, Nov. 1930
64 MO, XIV–1, Jan. 1932
65 MO, XIV–10, Oct. 1932
66 RM, XIV–1, Jan. 1941
67 This and successive quotations in this chapter come from the Annuario musicale italiano, Rome, Fratelli Palombo, 1940

CHAPTER II: INSTITUTIONS (pp. 33–100)

1 MO, VI–1, Jan. 1924
2 Facsimile in L'illustrazione italiana, Milan, 13 June 1948
3 H. Sachs, conversation with Elena Cesari Silva, October 1983
4 A. Casella, 'The Teaching of Music in Italy', in Christian Science Monitor, 12 September 1925
5 RM, II–8, Sept. 1929
6 L. Forino, Come si studia nei conservatori di musica. Considerazioni e proposte, Rome, Edizioni dell'Annuario musicale, 1930
7 MO, XV–4, April 1933
8 MO, VII–3, March 1925
9 MS, III–8–9, Aug.-Sept. 1926
10 MO, XVII–11, Nov. 1935
11 MO, VI–1, Jan. 1924
12 MO, VIII–6, June 1926
13 MO, IX–4, April 1927
14 MO, X–1, Jan. 1928
15 RM, I–2, Feb. 1928
16 MO, X–2, Feb. 1928
17 Quoted in MO, XVI–5, May 1934
18 RM, VII–5, Sept.-Oct. 1934

19 MO, XVIII–1, Jan. 1936

20 RM, X–2, Feb. 1937

21 MO, XIX–6, Jan. 1937

22 MO, XX–10, Oct. 1938; and RM, XI–10, Oct. 1938

23 Sachs, Toscanini, pp. 60–1

24 MS, III–5, May 1926

25 MS, III–8–9, Aug.-Sept. 1926

26 MS, III–11, Nov. 1926

27 MO, X–3, March 1928

28 MO, IX–6, June 1927

29 MO, XII–5, May 1930

30 Ibid.

31 NIM, IV–3, March 1931

32 NIM, IV–10, Oct. 1931

33 NIM, V–1, Jan. 1932

34 Sachs, op. cit., p. 197

35 NIM, V–1, Jan. 1932

36 NIM, IV–5, May 1931

37 MO, XIII–7, July 1931

38 MO, IX–3, March 1927

39 NIM, IV–8, Aug. 1931

40 MO, XIV–3, March 1932

41 L. Pierotti Cei, Il signore del golfo mistico, Florence, Sansoni, 1982, p. 380

42 MO, XX–3, March 1938

43 MO, XIV–6, June 1932

44 Annuario musicale italiano, 1940

45 MO, XIV–8–9, Aug.-Sept. 1932

46 Annuario musicale italiano, 1940

47 Pierotti Cei, op. cit., pp. 304–5

48 Ibid., pp. 359–60

49 G. Scanni (ed.), Musica e società, Bari, Dedalo, 1975

50 V. Gui, 'Per la vita musicale italiana di domani', in Il ponte, I–4, Florence, July 1945, pp. 308–14

51 Ibid.

52 Nicolodi, op. cit., pp. 17–18

53 MO, XVIII–2, Feb. 1936

54 Nicolodi, op. cit., p. 18

55 MS, III–6–7, June-July 1926

56 NIM, V–1, Jan. 1932

57 MO, XVI–3, March 1934

58 MO, XVII–4, April 1935

59 RM, VII–5, Sept.-Dec. 1935

60 Nicolodi, op. cit., p. 19

61 MO, XVIII–5, May 1936

62 MO, XX–5, May 1938

63 RM, XI–7–8, July-Aug. 1938

64 Nicolodi, op. cit., p. 20

65 Ibid., pp. 23–4

66 MO, XXI–5, May 1939

67 MO, XXII–4, April 1940

68 Nicolodi, op. cit., p. 25

69 ACS CPC 3321.29776

70 MS, III–8–9, Aug.-Sept. 1926

71 A. Casella, 'The Costanzi as a State Theater', in Christian Science Monitor, 31 July 1926

72 MO, IX–10, Oct. 1927

73 De Rensis, Raffaello, Musica vista, Milan, Ricordi, 1961, p. 80

74 Pierotti Cei, op. cit., pp. 253–4

75 Ibid., p. 255

76 MO, X–3, March 1928

77 ACS SPD CO, 555.902, No. 7658

78 Ibid., No. 7659, 15 Jan. 1923

79 Ibid., No. 7639, 10 Jan. 1923

80 Ibid., No. 7641, 17 Jan. 1923

81 Ibid., No. 7646, 8 May 1923

82 Ibid., No. 7650, 19 May 1923

83 Ibid., No. 7649, 19 May 1923

84 Ibid., No. 7647, undated

85 Ibid., unnumbered, undated, but clearly from late 1923 or early 1924

86 Ibid., same document

87 Ibid., No. 7661, 6 June 1924

88 Ibid., same document

89 Ibid., No. 15758, 12 July 1929

90 Il popolo d'Italia, 21 Nov. 1929

91 ACS SPD CO, 555.902, No. 1947922, 1 July 1930

92 Ibid., No. 1947923, 2 July 1930

93 Ibid., No. 1947928, 7 July 1930

94 U. Tegani, La Scala nella sua storia e nella sua grandezza, Milan, Valsecchi, 1946, p. 272

95 ACS SPD CO, 555.902, unnumbered, 6 April 1932

96 Ibid., unnumbered, 28 June 1932

97 Tegani, op. cit., pp. 272–3

98 ACS SPD CO, 555.902, unnumbered, undated

99 Ibid., unnumbered, 21 Oct. 1932

100 Ibid., unnumbered, undated

101 Ibid., unnumbered, 29 Oct. 1932

102 Ibid., unnumbered, 29 April 1933

103 Ibid., No. 1539260, 1 May 1933

104 Ibid., No. 1538412, 30 Oct. 1933

105 Ibid., unnumbered, 15 March 1934

106 Ibid., unnumbered, 30 March 1935

107 Ibid., unnumbered, 31 March 1935

108 Ibid., unnumbered, 1 April 1935

109 Ibid., unnumbered, 21 Feb. 1939

110 Ibid., unnumbered, undated, unsigned

111 Ibid., unnumbered, 26 June 1941

112 Ibid., unnumbered, 5 June 1943

113 D. Rubboli, 'Quelle serate di quarant'anni fa', in *Sipario*, XI–456–7, May-June 1986, p. 30

114 MO, XX–3, March 1938

115 RM, X–1, Jan. 1937

116 MO, XIX–1, Jan. 1937

117 G. M. Ciampelli, *Ente concerti orchestrali* (E.C.O.): *Sei anni di vita*, 1924–1929, Milan, 1929, p. 20

118 F. Nicolodi, 'Su alcuni aspetti dei festivals tra le due guerre', in *Musica italiana del primo novecento – 'La generazione dell'ottanta' – Atti del convegno – Firenze 9–10–11 maggio* 1980 (ed. F. Nicolodi), Florence, Olschki, 1981, p. 142

119 Ibid., p. 162

120 Ibid., p. 162

121 Ibid., pp. 163–4

122 Ibid., p. 168; letter of 3 April 1932

123 Ibid., pp. 167–8

124 MO, XVI–8–9, Aug.-Sept. 1934

125 RM, VII–5, Sept.-Oct. 1934

126 L. Pinzauti, *Il Maggio Musicale fiorentino dalla prima alla trentesima edizione*, Florence, Vallecchi, 1967, p. 12

127 Ibid., p. 12

128 Ibid., p. 17

129 Ibid., p. 22

130 Ibid., p. 12

131 MO, XV–4, April 1933

132 RM, VI–3, May-June 1933

133 MO, XVI–4, April 1934

134 Ibid.; Pinzauti, op. cit., p. 35

135 MO, XVI–11, Nov. 1934

136 19 May 1935; quoted in Pinzauti, op. cit., p. 42

137 Ibid., p. 48

138 Ibid., p. 48

139 Ibid., p. 49

140 RM, X–V, May 1937

141 Pinzauti, op. cit., pp. 57–8

142 MO, XX–5, May 1938

143 Pinzauti, op. cit., p. 61

144 *Atti del terzo congresso internazionale di musica, Firenze, 30 aprile – 4 maggio 1938–XVI*, Florence, Le Monnier, 1940

145 RM, XII–5, May 1939

146 MS, III–11, Nov. 1926

147 MO, IX–3, March 1927; MO, IX–4, April 1927

148 MO, XII–6, June 1930

149 MO, X–1, Jan. 1928

150 MO, X–2, Feb. 1928

151 MO, X–12, Dec. 1928

152 MO, XII–3, March 1930

153 MO, XII–4, April 1931

154 MO, XVI–1, Jan. 1934

155 MO, XVIII–7, July 1936

156 Ibid.

157 MO, XIX–4, April 1937

158 RM, IX–12, Dec. 1936

159 MO, XIX–1, Jan. 1937

160 RM, X–3, March 1937

161 RM, XII–1, Jan. 1939

162 MS, III–8–9, Aug.-Sept. 1926

163 RM, VII–3, May-June 1934

164 MO, XVIII–2, Feb. 1936

165 MO, XVIII–5, May 1936

166 MO, XIX–5, May 1937

167 MO, XX–3, March 1938

CHAPTER III: COMPOSERS
(pp. 101–47)

1 J. Parrott, *Ashkenazy: Beyond*

Frontiers, London, Collins, 1984, pp. 60–1

2 G. Marotti, *Giacomo Puccini intimo*, Florence, Vallecchi, 1942, p. 171

3 Sachs, *Toscanini*, p. 125

4 A. Marchetti, 'Tutta la verità sull'*Inno a Roma* di Puccini', in *Nuova rivista musicale italiana*, IX, 1975, pp. 396–409

5 G. Puccini (S. Puccini, ed.), *Lettere a Riccardo Schnabl*, Milan, Emme edizioni, 1981, p. 84

6 Ibid., pp. 92–3

7 Ibid., p. 105

8 Ibid., pp. 136–7

9 Ibid., p. 139

10 Ibid., p. 190

11 Ibid., p. 192

12 Ibid., p. 201

13 Marotti, op. cit., pp.168–70

14 Ibid., p. 169

15 MO, VII–3, March 1925

16 G. Tintori, *Palco di proscenio*, Milan, Feltrinelli, 1980, p. 196

17 M. Morini (ed.), *Pietro Mascagni*, Milan, Sonzogno, 1964, Vol. I, pp. 402–5

18 Ibid., pp. 404–5

19 Ibid., p. 409

20 Nicolodi, *Musica e musicisti nel ventennio fascista*, p. 42

21 G. Orsini, *Vangelo d'un mascagnano*, Milan, Vecchi, 1926, p. 190

22 Nicolodi, op. cit., pp. 40–1

23 De Rensis, *Musica vista*, pp. 79–80

24 MS, III–6–7, June-July 1926

25 Nicolodi, op. cit., pp. 373–5

26 Ibid.

27 MO, IX–10, Oct. 1927

28 MO, IX–11, Nov. 1927

29 L. Salvatorelli and G. Mira, *Storia d'Italia nel periodo fascista*, Turin, Einaudi, 1956

30 Nicolodi, op. cit., p. 59

31 L. Mascagni, letter to Vittorio Gianfranceschi, 23 Oct. 1929, in Museo Teatrale alla Scala

32 Nicolodi, op. cit., p. 59

33 G. Cogo, *Il nostro Mascagni*, Vicenza, Cristofari, 1931, p. 167

34 Ibid., p. 10

35 Ibid., p. 11

36 Nicolodi, op. cit., p. 383

37 Ibid., pp. 3834

38 NA, Personal Papers of B. Mussolini, also some official records of the Italian Foreign Office and the Ministry of Culture, 1922–44, T586; 029901/A – 029907/A

39 NA, 029908/A

40 NA, 029910/A

41 NA, 029911/A – 029912/A

42 NA, 029912/A – 029913/A

43 NA, 029937/A – 029938/A

44 NA, 029938/A – 029939/A

45 NA, 029917/A – 029936/A

46 Nicolodi, op. cit., p. 398

47 Ibid., pp. 398–9

48 Ibid., p. 401

49 Morini, op. cit., I, pp. 423–6

50 Nicolodi, op. cit., p. 401

51 Ibid., p. 400

52 Ibid., p. 400

53 F. Nicolodi, 'Mascagni e il potere', in *Mascagni*, Milan, Electa, 1984, p. 224

54 Nicolodi, *Musica e musicisti nel ventennio fascista*, p. 58

55 A. Jeri, *Mascagni: Quindici opere mille episodi*, Milan, Garzanti, 1940, p. 168

56 NA, 029942/A – 029945/A

57 NA, 029947/A

58 Nicolodi, op. cit., p. 405

59 NA, 029947/A

60 NA, Special Report No. 42; and R. Cantore, 'Sul borderò del duce', in *Panorama*, Rome, 22 Feb. 1987, pp. 106–121

61 NA, 029948/A – 029949/A

62 Nicolodi, in *Mascagni*, p. 225

63 Nicolodi, *Musica e musicisti nel ventennio fascista*, p. 332

64 Ibid., pp. 331–2

65 Morini, op. cit., p. 256

66 Nicolodi, op. cit., pp. 328–9

67 M. Mila, 'La Messa di Pizzetti', in *Cronache musicali*, 1955–1959, Turin, Einaudi, 1959, pp. 160–2

68 Mack Smith, *Italy*, pp. 381–2

69 Salvemini, *Le origini del fascismo in Italia*, p. 58

70 Reprinted in E. R. Papa, *Storia di due manifesti*, Milan, Feltrinelli, 1958, pp. 59–69

71 Reprinted in ibid., pp. 92–102

72 B. Pizzetti (ed.), *Ildebrando Pizzetti*, p. 217

73 Nicolodi, op. cit., pp. 434–5

74 B. Pizzetti, op. cit., p. 233

75 Nicolodi, op. cit., pp. 432–3

76 Ibid., p. 435

77 Ibid., pp. 436–7

78 Ibid., p. 437

79 Ibid., p. 437

80 B. Pizzetti, op. cit., p. 243

81 RM, IX–1, Jan. 1936

82 Nicolodi, op. cit., p. 365

83 B. Pizzetti, op. cit., p. 262

84 Ibid., p. 264

85 Ibid., p. 267

86 Ibid., p. 268

87 I. Pizzetti, 'Il nostro teatro di musica – Osservazioni e appunti', in *Nuova antologia*, LXXIII–1591, Rome, 1 July 1938, pp. 3–19

88 Nicolodi, op. cit., p. 440

89 *La Tribuna*, 20 March 1939; quoted in B. Pizzetti, op. cit., pp. 277–8

90 B. Pizzetti, op. cit., pp. 278–9

91 Ibid., pp. 282–3

92 Ibid., p. 284

93 I. Pizzetti, 'Autarchia musicale italiana', in *Le arti*, Florence, V–1, Oct.-Nov. 1942, pp. 27–33

94 Ibid.

95 D. Spini, 'Ottorino Respighi (1879–1936), Profilo biografico', in *Ottorino Respighi*, ed. G. Rostirolla, Turin, ERI, 1985, pp. 74–5

96 Nicolodi, op. cit., p. 200

97 Ibid., p. 364

98 Ibid., pp. 364–5

99 Ibid., p. 368

100 G. Gavazzeni, *Il suono è stanco*, Bergamo, Conti, 1950, p. 290

101 MO, V–2, Feb. 1923

102 A. Casella, 'Young Italy and Its Role', in *Christian Science Monitor*, 14 March 1925

103 Nicolodi, op. cit., p. 245

104 A. Schoenberg, 'Il fascismo non è un articolo d'esportazione', in A. Schoenberg, *Analisi e pratica musicale*, ed. I. Vojtech, Turin, Einaudi, 1974, pp. 79–87

105 Nicolodi, op. cit., p. 250

106 MO, XII–12, Dec. 1930

107 A. Casella, 'The Musical Season in Rome', in *Christian Science Monitor*, 15 May 1926

108 A. Casella, *I segreti della giara*, Florence, Sansoni, 1941, p. 209

109 Ibid., p. 284

110 Ibid., p. 284

111 Ibid., p. 308

112 Ibid., pp. 310–11

113 Ibid.

114 A. Casella, 'Problemi e posizione attuale della musica italiana', in *Le arti*, Florence, I–3, Feb. 1939, pp. 256–64

115 Ibid.

116 Ibid.

117 A. Casella, 'Tendenze e situazione della musica contemporanea in Italia', in *Il libro italiano nel mondo*, II–5–6, Rome, 1941, pp. 99–105

118 Ibid.

119 Ibid.

120 Casella, *I segreti della giara*, p. 211

121 Ibid., pp. 229, 245, 274

CHAPTER IV: PERFORMERS (pp. 148–65)

1 B. Gigli, *Memorie*, Milan, Mondadori, 1957, p. 234

2 Ibid., p. 286

3 Ibid., p. 294
4 Ibid., p. 298
5 Ibid., p. 303
6 Ibid., p. 153
7 B. Gigli, *Confidenze*, Rome, Istituto per l'Enciclopedia De Carlo, 1942, pp. 143–4
8 ACS SPD CO 545.962
9 Ibid.
10 ACS SPD CO 510.381
11 NIM, IV–8, Aug. 1931
12 ACS SPD CO 510.381
13 ACS SPD CO 527.895
14 ACS SPD CO 14.532
15 ACS SPD CO 124.343
16 Ibid.
17 ACS SPD CO 126.563
18 T. Ruffo, *La mia parabola*, Rome, Staderini, 1977, p. 301
19 Ibid.
20 Ibid., p. 302
21 Ibid., pp. 302–3
22 Ibid., pp. 303–4
23 ACS SPD CO 196.025
24 ACS SPD CO 546.775
25 Ibid.
26 ACS SPD CO 107.493
27 MS, III–8–9, Aug.-Sept. 1926
28 ACS SPD CO 532.655
29 Ibid.
30 Ibid.
31 T. Celli and G. Pugliese, *Tullio Serafin, Il patriarca del melodramma*, Venezia, Corbo e Fiore, 1985, p. 104
32 ACS SPD CO 500.007
33 L. Pinzauti, *La musica e le cose*, Florence, Vallecchi, 1977, p. 148
34 Nicolodi, *Musica e musicisti nel ventennio fascista*, p. 299
35 ACS SPD CO 133.995
36 Ibid.

CHAPTER V: FOREIGNERS, ALLIANCES, RACISM AND WAR (pp. 166–206)

1 M. Yourcenar, *Denier du rêve*, preface, Paris, Gallimard, 1971
2 M. Bernardi, *Riccardo Gualino e la cultura torinese*, Turin, Centro studi piemontesi, 1970
3 V. Stravinsky and R. Craft, *Stravinsky in Pictures and Documents*, New York, Simon & Schuster, 1978, p. 662
4 Ibid., p. 551
5 Ibid.
6 Ibid.
7 A. Gasco, *Da Cimarosa a Stravinsky*, Rome, De Santis, 1939, p. 452
8 Ibid.
9 V. Stravinsky and R. Craft, op. cit., p. 662
10 R. Craft (ed.), *Stravinsky, Selected Correspondence*, Vol. III, New York, Knopf, 1985, p. 219n.
11 V. Stravinsky and R. Craft, op. cit., p. 324
12 Ibid., p. 552, from *Il Piccolo*, 27 May 1935
13 Ibid., p. 552
14 Ibid.
15 Ibid.
16 J. Demeny (ed.), *Béla Bartók Letters*, London, Faber & Faber, 1971, p. 251
17 H. Stevens, *The Life and Music of Béla Bartók*, New York, Oxford University Press, 1967, p. 85
18 Ibid.
19 Ibid., pp. 90–1
20 W. Reich, *Schoenberg*, New York, Praeger, 1971, p. 170
21 M. Carner, *Alban Berg*, London, Duckworth, 1975, pp. 68–9
22 W. Reich, *Alban Berg*, London, Thames & Hudson, 1965, pp. 90–1
23 A. Berg, *Letters to His Wife* (ed. B. Grun), London, Faber & Faber, 1971, pp. 407–8
24 Ibid., p. 409
25 M. Carner, op. cit., pp. 68–70
26 I. J. Paderewski and M. Lawton, *The Paderewski Memoirs*, London,

Collins, 1939
27 E. di San Martino, *Ricordi*, Rome, Danesi, 1943
28 A. Strakacz, *Paderewski as I Knew Him*, Rutgers University Press, 1949, pp. 147–8
29 R. Landau, *Ignace Paderewski*, New York, Crowell, 1934, p. 267
30 Strakacz, op. cit., pp. 255–8
31 Ibid., 259
32 RM, XIV–7–8, July-Aug. 1941
33 Quoted in L. Lochner, *Fritz Kreisler*, London, Rockliff, 1951, p. 257
34 Ibid., pp. 257–8
35 P. Heyworth, *Otto Klemperer, His Life and Times*, Vol. I, Cambridge, Cambridge University Press, 1983, p. 168
36 Ibid., p. 167
37 O. Strasser, *Und dafür wird man noch bezahlt*, Munich, Deutscher Taschenbuch, 1978, p. 84
38 G. Visconti di Modrone, 'Nazionalismo nella musica', in *Realtà*, June 1933, pp. 613–20
39 A. Ghislanzoni, 'La nuova musica italiana dev'essere antieuropea', in *Antieuropa*, VII–9, Rome, Sept. 1935
40 M. Michaelis, *Mussolini and the Jews*, Oxford, Clarendon Press, 1978, pp. 3–4
41 Ibid., p. 52
42 MS, III–5, May 1926
43 NA, Personal Papers of B. Mussolini, also some official records of the Italian Foreign Office and the Ministry of Culture, 1922–44. T 586, RG 59, etc.
44 Michaelis, op. cit., p. 75
45 MO, XV–7, July 1933
46 MO, XVI–1, Jan. 1934
47 P. Heyworth, letter to H. Sachs, 16 April 1986
48 MO, XVI–1, Jan. 1934
49 RM, VII–1, Jan.-Feb. 1934
50 RM, II–2, Feb. 1929
51 RM, VII–6, Nov.-Dec. 1934

52 RM, VIII–5–6, Sept.-Dec. 1935
53 Michaelis, op. cit., pp. 116, 127, 187
54 *Il musicista*, IV–8, Rome, Aug. 1937
55 F. Santoliquido, 'La piovra musicale ebraica', in *Il Tevere*, XV–40, 14–15 Dec. 1937, pp. 1 and 3
56 Michaelis, op. cit., p. 153
57 Nicolodi, *Musica e musicisti nel ventennio fascista*, p. 246
58 M. Castelnuovo-Tedesco, *Una vita di musica*, unpublished, Vol. I, pp. 329–30
59 Ibid., pp. 354–6
60 Ibid., pp. 366–7
61 Ibid., pp. 373–4
62 *Christian Science Monitor*, 29 Aug. 1925
63 NA (see note 43)
64 J. C. G. Waterhouse, 'Rieti, Vittorio', in *The New Grove Dictionary of Music and Musicians*, London, Macmillan, 1980, Vol. XVI, p. 11
65 Ibid., Vol. XI, p. 798
66 *Il telegrafo*, 31 Dec. 1938, in Pinzauti, *Il Maggio Musicale fiorentino*, p. 64
67 MO, XXII–10, Oct. 1940
68 *Le arti*, I–3, Feb. 1939, pp. 256–64
69 W. Mocchi, 'Ventennale', in *La verità*, Rome, 31 Oct. 1942, p. 371
70 A. Lualdi, *L'arte di dirigere l'orchestra*, Milan, Hoepli, 1940, pp. 27–8
71 Ibid., p. 32
72 RM, VIII–4, July-Aug. 1935
73 MO, XVIII–2, Feb. 1936
74 MO, XVIII–11, Nov. 1936
75 RM, X–5, May 1937
76 MO, XIX–8–9, Aug.-Sep. 1937
77 MO, XX–4, April 1938
78 RM, XII–3, March 1939
79 MO, XXIII–1, Jan. 1941
80 MO, XXIII–5, May 1941
81 MO, XXIII–8–9, Aug.-Sep. 1941
82 MO, XXIII–10, Oct. 1941

83 MO, XXIV–4, April 1942
84 *The New Grove*, op. cit., Vol. VI, p. 167
85 H. Engel, *Deutschland und Italien in ihren musikgeschichtlichen Beziehungen*, Regensburg, Bosse, 1944, pp. 7–8
86 Ibid., p. 9
87 Ibid., pp. 10–11
88 L. Dallapiccola, 'The Genesis of the *Canti di prigionia* and *Il prigioniero*: an Autobiographical Fragment', in *The Musical Quarterly*, XXXIX–3, New York, G. Schirmer, July 1953, pp. 355–72
89 Ibid.
90 Engel, op. cit., pp. 28–9
91 Dallapiccola, op. cit.
92 D. Mack Smith, *Mussolini's Roman Empire*, London, Penguin, 1979, p. 215
93 Ibid., p. 229
94 Ibid., p. 146
95 A. Lualdi, *Per il primato spirituale di Roma*, Rome, Editoriale degli Agricoltori, 1942
96 R. De Rensis, 'La lotta secolare tra musica italiana e francese', in *Augustea*, Rome, XIV–12–13, 1 and 15 July 1941
97 MO, XXII–8–9, Aug.-Sep. 1940
98 RM, XV–9–10, Sep.-Oct. 1942
99 MO, XXII–11, Nov. 1940
100 ACS SPD CO 539.866
101 B. Pizzetti (ed.), *Ildebrando Pizzetti*, pp. 289–92
102 MO, XXIII–4, Apr. 1941
103 MO, XXII–8–9, Aug. Sep. 1940
104 MO, XXIII–4, April 1941
105 RM, XIV–3, March 1941
106 MO, XXIV–7, July 1942
107 RM, XV–12, Dec. 1942
108 Ibid.
109 RM, XIII–12, Dec. 1940
110 RM, XIV–2, Feb. 1941
111 MO, XXIII–10, Oct. 1941
112 RM, XV–1, 4 and 5; June, April and May 1942
113 RM, XV–5, May 1942
114 MO, XXIV–5, May 1942
115 RM, XV–6, June 1942
116 MO, XXIV–8–9, Aug.-Sept. 1942
117 RM, XV–9–10, Sep.-Oct. 1942
118 RM, XVI–3, March 1943
119 T. S. Mursino (alias V. Mussolini), 'La settima sinfonia', in *Il messaggero*, Rome, 17 April 1943
120 S. Volkov (ed.), *Testimony: The Memoirs of Dmitri Shostakovich*, New York, Harper & Row, 1979, p. 156
121 Morini, *Mascagni*, Vol. II, p. 123
122 E. Zanetti, 'Gli ultimi anni', in *Alfredo Casella*, ed. F. D'Amico and G. M. Gatti, Milan, Ricordi, 1958, p. 25
123 B. Pizzetti, op. cit., pp. 293–5
124 Gigli, *Memorie*, p. 333
125 G. Tirincanti, 'Il teatro Argentina', quoted in M. Rinaldi, *Due secoli di musica al teatro Argentina*, Florence, Olschki, 1978, p. 1417
126 Nicolodi, op. cit., p. 312
127 T. Ruffo, *La mia parabola*, p. 306
128 Dallapiccola, op. cit.
129 Ibid.
130 Ibid.
131 G. F. Malipiero, *Il filo d'Arianna*, Turin, Einaudi, 1966, p. 133
132 Ibid., p. 139
133 B. Pizzetti, op. cit., pp. 296–7
134 Ibid., p. 295
135 Ibid., pp. 301–2 (letter of 2 Sep. 1948)

CHAPTER VI: THE TOSCANINI CASE (pp. 207–40)
1 Sachs, *Toscanini*, pp. 5–8
2 Ibid., pp. 132–6
3 Ibid., pp. 139–40
4 Ibid., p. 144
5 Ibid., p. 154
6 M. Labia, *Guardare indietro: che fatica!*, Verona, Bettinelli 1950, p. 117
7 See Chap. II, p. 34
8 ACS SPD CO, No. 7661, 6 June 1924

9 U. Ojetti, I taccuini, Florence, Sansoni, 1954, pp. 156–7

10 Sachs, op. cit., p. 174; and ACS SPD CO, No. 7666, undated

11 Sachs, op. cit., p. 179

12 A. Fraccaroli, La Scala a Vienna e a Berlino, Milan, Corriere della Sera, 1929

13 E. A. Teatro alla Scala, 'Cronistoria della stagione 1928–29', p. 142

14 MI DGPS DPP FP 51/B. No. 446

15 Sachs, op. cit., p. 209

16 G. Barblan, Toscanini e la Scala, Milan, Edizioni della Scala, 1972, facing p. 360 et seq.

17 I. Montanelli and M. Staglieno, Longanesi, Milan, Rizzoli, 1984

18 Wanda Toscanini Horowitz, interviewed by Edward Downes, Metropolitan Opera broadcast, March 1967

19 M. Labroca and V. Boccardi, Arte di Toscanini, Turin, ERI, 1966, p. 137

20 Letter of 6 Nov. 1967; copy in Fondo Respighi, Fondazione G. Cini, Venice

21 E. Respighi, interviewed on RAI, Aug. 1977

22 Sachs, op. cit., pp. 209–10

23 Ibid., p. 210

24 Barblan, op. cit., facing p. 360 et seq.

25 Sachs, op. cit., p. 213

26 Reprinted under headline: 'L'incidente provocato da Toscanini in una nota de L'assalto', in La tribuna, 19 May 1931

27 Il popolo d'Italia, Milan, 16 May 1931

28 'In margine: Effetti salutari di uno schiaffo', in La tribuna, 20 May 1931

29 Barblan, op. cit., facing p. 360 et seq.

30 MI etc., No. 346

31 Sachs, op. cit., p. 214

32 J. Szigeti, With Strings Attached, New York, Knopf, 1967, pp. 347–8

33 C. Clemens, My Husband Gabrilowitsch, New York, Harper & Bros., 1938, p. 206

34 L. Pierotti Cei, Il signore del golfo mistico, p. 293

35 SPD SAC, Nos. 088760–1

36 MI etc., No. 435

37 Ibid., No. 434

38 Ibid., No. 413

39 Ibid., No. 433

40 Ibid., No. 427

41 Ibid., No. 419

42 Ibid., No. 418

43 Ibid., unnumbered

44 Ibid., No. 415

45 Ibid., No. 411

46 Ibid., No. 378

47 Ibid., No. 384

48 Ibid., No. 403

49 Ibid., No. 339

50 Ibid., Nos. 399–400

51 Ibid., No. 375

52 Ibid., No. 358

53 Ibid., Nos. 365–6

54 Ibid., Nos. 328–32

55 Ibid., No. 347

56 Ibid., No. 337

57 Ibid., No. 343

58 Ibid., No. 323

59 E. Ludwig, Talks with Mussolini, pp. 211–12

60 N. D'Aroma, Mussolini segreto, p. 304

61 MI etc., No. 308; Nos. 304–5

62 Ibid., No. 310

63 Ibid., No. 288

64 Ibid., No. 283

65 SPD SAC, Nos. 088788–9

66 Labroca and Boccardi, op. cit., pp. 142–3

67 H. Sachs, 'Toscanini, Hitler, and Salzburg', in Grand Street, New York, Autumn 1986

68 Ibid.

69 Ibid.

70 Photocopy of letter in Casa natale

di Toscanini, Parma

72 MI etc., No. 267

72 Ibid., No. 4

73 Ibid., No. 40

74 Ibid., No. 3

75 A. Della Corte, *Toscanini visto da un critico*, Turin, ILTE, 1958, pp. 319–20; and Friedelind Wagner, interviewed by H. Sachs, 1978

76 *Il regime fascista*, Cremona, 1 Sep. 1938, No. 207

77 Della Corte, op. cit., p. 321

78 G. Ciano, *Diario 1937–1938*, Bologna, Cappelli, 1948, entry for 7 Sep. 1938

79 MI etc., No. 29

80 Sachs, *Toscanini*, pp. 267–8

81 SPD SAC, No. 088801

82 MI etc., No. 26

83 Ibid., No. 39

84 Sachs, op. cit., p. 270

85 Salvemini, *Memorie di un fuoruscito*, Milano, Feltrinelli, 1960, p. 178

86 G. Salvemini, *L'Italia vista dall'America* (ed. E. Tagliacozzo), Milan, Feltrinelli, 1969, Vols. I and II, p. 165

87 T. S. Mursino (alias V. Mussolini), 'La settima sinfonia', in *Il messaggero*, Rome, 17 April 1943

88 Sachs, op. cit., pp. 280–1

89 Ibid., p. 281

90 A. Toscanini, 'To the People of America', in *Life*, 13 Sep. 1943

91 Salvemini archives, Rome

92 Ibid.

93 Ibid.

94 G. Salvemini *inter alia*, 'An Italian Manifesto', in *Life*, 12 June 1944

95 Sachs, op. cit., p. 283

96 Barblan, op. cit., p. 370

97 A. Borghi, 'Esilio americano', in *Il mondo*, 14 May 1957

98 Sachs, op. cit., p. 288

99 O. Noto, unpublished letter of 24 April 1946, from Milan, to A. Toscanini; anonymous source.

100 H. Sachs, op. cit., pp. 288–90

101 RAI–2 (TV), 'I giorni della Repubblica', 3 June 1986

102 A. Toscanini, unpublished letter of 16 May 1941, from Riverdale, New York; anonymous source.

EPILOGUE (pp. 241–3)

1 A. Huxley, *Along the Road*, London, Triad/Paladin, 1985, pp. 28–9

2 F. Fellini, *Fare un film*, Turin, Einaudi, 1980, pp. 155–6

Bibliography

Barblan, Guglielmo. *Toscanini e la Scala*. Milano, 1972
Barilli, Bruno. *Il sorcio nel violino*. Torino, 1982
Begnac, Yvon de. *Palazzo Venezia: Storia di un regime*. Roma, 1950
Berg, Alban (ed. B. Grun). *Letters to His Wife*. London, 1971
Bernardi, M. *Riccardo Gualino e la cultura torinese*. Torino, 1970
Biddiss, Michael D. *The Age of the Masses*. London, 1977
Bottai, Giuseppe. *Politica fascista delle arti*. Roma, 1940
Carner, Mosco. *Alban Berg*. London, 1975
Casella, Alfredo. *I segreti della giara*. Firenze, 1941
Castelnuovo-Tedesco, Mario. *Una vita di musica*. Unpublished
Cavaglion, Alberto. *Nella notte straniera*. Cuneo, 1981
Celli, Teodoro, and Pugliese, Giuseppe. *Tullio Serafin*. Venezia, 1985
Ciampelli, G. M. *Ente concerti orchestrali*. Milano, 1929
Ciano, Galeazzo. *Diario, 1937–1938*. Bologna, 1948
Clemens, Clara. *My Husband Gabrilowitsch*. New York, 1938
Cogo, G. *Il nostro Mascagni*. Vicenza, 1931
Craft, Robert (ed.). *Stravinsky, Selected Correspondence*. Vol. III, New York, 1985
D'Amico, Fedele, and Gatti, Guido M. (eds.). *Alfredo Casella*. Milano, 1958
D'Aroma, Nino. *Mussolini segreto*. Bologna, 1958
De Felice, Renzo. *Storia degli ebrei italiani sotto il fascismo*. Milano, 1972
De Fiori, V. E. *Mussolini: The Man of Destiny*. New York, 1928
Della Corte, Andrea. *Toscanini visto da un critico*. Torino, 1958
Demeny, J. (ed.). *Béla Bartók Letters*. London, 1971
De Rensis, Raffaello. *Musica vista*. Milan, 1961
De Rensis, Raffaello. *Mussolini musicista*. Mantova, 1927
Engel, Hans. *Deutschland und Italien in ihren musikgeschichtlichen Beziehungen*. Regensburg, 1944
Failoni, Sergio. *Senza sordina*. Roma, 1946
Fellini, Federico. *Fare un film*. Torino, 1980
Forino, Luigi. *Come si studia nei conservatori di musica*. Roma, 1930
Fraccaroli, Arnaldo. *La Scala a Vienna e a Berlino*. Milano, 1929

Gasco, Alberto. *Da Cimarosa a Stravinsky*. Roma, 1939
Gavazzeni, Gianandrea. *Il suono è stanco*. Bergamo, 1950
Gigli, Beniamino. *Confidenze*. Roma, 1942
Gigli, Beniamino. *Memorie*. Milano, 1957
Gregory, Tullio, *inter alia* (ed.). *Filosofi, università, regime*. Rome, 1985
Gui, Vittorio. *Battute d'aspetto*. Firenze, 1944
Heyworth, Peter. *Otto Klemperer*, Vol. I. Cambridge, 1983
Huxley, Aldous. *Along the Road*. London, 1985
Jeri, A. *Mascagni: Quindici opere mille episodi*. Milano, 1940
Kämpfer, Dietrich. *Luigi Dallapiccola*. Firenze, 1985
Labia, Maria. *Guardare indietro, che fatica!* Verona, 1950
Labroca, Mario, and Boccardi, Virgilio. *Arte di Toscanini*. Torino, 1966
Landau, Rom. *Ignace Paderewski*. New York, 1934
Laqueur, Walter (ed.). *Fascism: A Reader's Guide*. London, 1976
Lochner, Louis. *Fritz Kreisler*. London, 1951
Lualdi, Adriano. *L'arte di dirigere l'orchestra*. Milano, 1940
Lualdi, Adriano. *Per il primato spirituale di Roma*. Roma, 1942
Ludwig, Emil. *Talks with Mussolini*. London, 1932
Mack Smith, Denis. *Italy: A Modern History*. Ann Arbor, 1969
Mack Smith, Denis. *Mussolini*. London, 1981
Mack Smith, Denis. *Mussolini's Roman Empire*. London, 1979
Malipiero, Gian Francesco. *Il filo d'Arianna*. Torino, 1966
Marinetti, F. T. (ed. R. W. Flint). *Selected Writings*. New York, 1971
Marotti, G. *Giacomo Puccini intimo*, Firenze, 1942
Michaelis, Meir. *Mussolini and the Jews*. Oxford, 1978
Mila, Massimo. *Cronache musicali, 1955–1959*. Torino, 1959
Montanelli, Indro, and Staglieno, Marcello. *Longanesi*. Milano, 1964
Morini, Mario (ed.). *Pietro Mascagni*. Milano, 1964
Mussolini, Benito (ed. E. and D. Susmel). *Opera omnia*. Roma, 1979
Nicolodi, Fiamma. *Musica e musicisti nel ventennio fascista*. Fiesole, 1984
Nicolodi, Fiamma (ed.). *Musica italiana del primo novecento*. Firenze, 1981
Nolte, Ernst. *Three Faces of Fascism*. New York, 1969
Ojetti, Ugo. *I taccuini*. Firenze, 1954
Origo, Iris. *A Need to Testify*. New York, 1984
Orsini, G. *Vangelo d'un mascagnano*. Milano, 1926
Paderewski, Ignace J., and Lawton, Mary. *The Paderewski Memoirs*. London, 1939
Papa, Emilio R. *Fascismo e cultura*. Venezia, 1974
Papa, Emilio R. *Storia di due manifesti*. Milano, 1958
Parrott, Jasper. *Ashkenazy: Beyond Frontiers*. London, 1984
Petacco, Arrigo. *Riservato per il Duce*. Milano, 1979
Pierotti Cei, Lia. *Il signore del golfo mistico*. Firenze, 1982
Pinzauti, Leonardo. *Il Maggio Musicale fiorentino*. Firenze, 1967
Pinzauti, Leonardo. *La musica e le cose*. Firenze, 1977
Pizzetti, Bruno (ed.). *Ildebrando Pizzetti: cronologia e bibliografia*. Parma, 1979
Pound, Ezra (ed. R. M. Schafer). *Ezra Pound and Music*. London, 1978
Prieberg, Fred K. *Musik im NS-Staat*. Frankfurt a. M., 1982

Puccini, Giacomo (ed. S. Puccini). *Lettere a Riccardo Schnabl*. Milano, 1981
Reich, Willi. *Alban Berg*. London, 1965
Reich, Willi. *Schoenberg*. New York, 1971
Rinaldi, M. *Due secoli di musica al teatro Argentina*. Firenze, 1978
Rostirolla, G. (ed.). *Ottorino Respighi*. Torino, 1985
Ruffo, Titta (ed. R. Titta, Jr.). *La mia parabola*. Roma, 1977
Sachs, Harvey. *Toscanini*. London, 1978
Salvatorelli, L., and Mira, G. *Storia d'Italia nel periodo fascista*. Torino, 1956
Salvemini, Gaetano. *Le origini del fascismo in Italia*. Milano, 1966
Salvemini, Gaetano (ed. E. Tagliacozzo). *L'Italia vista dall'America*. Milano, 1969
Salvemini, Gaetano. *Memorie di un fuoruscito*. Milano, 1960
Salviucci, Paolo. *La musica e lo stato*. Milano, 1953
San Martino, Enrico di. *Ricordi*. Roma, 1943
Sapori, Francesco. *L'arte e il Duce*. Milan, 1932
Sarfatti, Margherita. *Dux*. Milano, 1926
Scanni, G. (ed.). *Musica e società*. Bari, 1975
Schoenberg, Arnold (ed. I. Vojtech). *Analisi e pratica musicale*. Torino, 1974
Stevens, Halsey. *The Life and Music of Béla Bartók*. New York, 1967
Strakacz, Aniela. *Paderewski as I Knew Him*. Rutgers, 1949
Strasser, Otto. *Und dafür wird man noch bezahlt*. Muninch, 1978
Stravinsky, Vera, and Craft, Robert. *Stravinsky in Pictures and Documents*. New York, 1978
Szigeti, Joseph. *With Strings Attached*. New York, 1967
Tannenbaum, Edward R. *L'esperienza fascista*. Milano, 1972
Tegani, Ulderico. *La Scala nella sua gloria e nella sua grandezza*. Milan, 1946
Tintori, Giampiero. *Palco di proscenio*. Milano, 1980
Volkov, Solomon (ed.). *Testimony: The Memoirs of Dmitri Shostakovich*. New York, 1979
Wiskemann, Elizabeth. *Europe of the Dictators, 1919–1945*. Glasgow, 1966
Wulf, Joseph. *Musik im Dritten Reich*. Frankfurt a. M., 1983
Yourcenar, Marguerite. *Denier du rêve*. Paris, 1971
Various authors. *Mascagni*. Milano, 1984

Index

Abravanel, Maurice, 179
Academy, Italian Royal, 110–11, 121, 126–9, 131, 145, 178, 197
Achron, Joseph, 90
Adami, Giuseppe, 104
Adami Corradetti, Iris, 42
Adler, Guido, 177
Adorno, Theodor W., 136
Adriatico nostro, 96
Alaleona, Domenico (composer and teacher, 1881–1928), 34, 43
Albanese, Licia, 42
Albertini, Cesare, 88
Albertini, Luigi (editor, *Corriere della sera*, 1871–1941), 57, 210
Alessi, Rino, 93, 119, 183
Alfano, Franco (composer, 1876–1954), 7, 24, 28, 30, 34, 44, 60, 70, 89, 93, 98, 132, 202
Alfieri, Dino (diplomat, 1886–), 94, 230
Amadori, Sante, 42
Amendola, Giovanni (journalist and politician, 1882–1926), 123
Ancona, 87
Angioletti, Gian Battista, 160
Annuario musicale italiano, 33
Ansbacher, Luigi, 88, 230
Ansermet, Ernest, 142, 166
anti-semitism, 42, 47, 94–5, 149, 162, 169, 177–88, 232, 237; *see also* racial laws
Apostel, Hans, 93

Aprea, Tito, 119
Arangi Lombardi, Giannina, 63
Arendt, Hannah, 157
Arias, Gino, 178
Arpinati, Leandro, 18, 213, 215, 221–2, 224, 236
Arte fascista, L', 96
Asciolla, Dino, 42
Ashkenazy, Vladimir, 101
Assalto, 216
Auber, Daniel-François-Esprit, 56
Avanguardisti, 43, 97
Aytano, Aldo, 60

Bacchelli, Riccardo, 200
Bach, Johann Sebastian, 14, 36–7, 95, 130
Backhaus, Wilhelm, 157, 166, 189
Badini, Ernesto, 65
Badoglio, Pietro (chief of staff and prime minister, 1871–1956), 150, 200–1, 234–5
Balanchine, George, 185
Balbo, Italo, 221
Baldovino, Amedeo, 42
Balilla (youth organization), 43, 97
Balla, Giacomo, 168
Ballo, Ferdinando, 97
Barbieri, Fedora, 42
Barblan, Guglielmo, 30, 42
Baretti, Il, 49
Bargello, Il, 93

Bari, 87
Barilli, Bruno, 119, 124, 163
Bartók, Béla, 89, 92–3, 135, 144, 167, 169–71, 198–9, 219
Barutidella, Adolfo, 43
Bauer, Harold, 166
Battistini, Mattia, 6
Bayreuth, 154, 224
Bechi, Gino, 42
Beck, Conrad, 94
Beecham, Sir Thomas, 167
Beethoven, Ludwig van, 14–15, 37, 47, 72, 95, 189
Beer, G., 111
Begnac, Yvon de, 12–14, 119
Bekker, Paul, 92
Bellincioni, Gemma, 6
Bellincioni Stagno, Bianca, 43, 119
Bellini, Vincenzo, 56, 70
Belluzzo, Giuseppe, 20
Beltramelli, Antonio, 13
Benedetti Michelangeli, Arturo, 42
Benvenuti, Giacomo, 93
Berg, Alban, 56, 91–3, 142, 147, 158, 167, 171–2, 198–9
Bergamo, 159; Teatro delle Novità, 69
Bergonzi, Carlo, 42
Berio, Ernesto, 30
Berio, Luciano, 30
Berlin, 142, 149, 157, 189, 211, 213; Berlin Philharmonic, 94–5, 189; radio orchestra, 189; State Opera, 179; State Music Academy, 189
Berlioz, Hector, 56
Beval, Franco, 238
Bianchi, Giovanni, 97
Bianchi, Michele, 66
Biggini, Carlo Alberto, 20
Bignami, Giulio, 184
Bizet, Georges, 6, 116, 144
Bizzelli, Annibale, 16
Blanc, Giuseppe, 30
Bloch, Ernest, 38, 89, 139, 167, 179, 181–2
Blum, Robert, 179
Boccabati, Giulia, 43

Boccherini, Luigi, 18
Bocchini (Chief, Political Police), 221
Boccioni, Umberto, 168
Bodanzky, Artur, 156
Böhm, Karl, 95
Boito, Arrigo, 239; Nerone, 73, 155
Bologna, 6, 34, 59, 87, 99, 124, 199; Teatro Comunale, 59; fascist intellectual convention, 75; Mostra del Novecento Italiano, 96; see also under Toscanini
Bonacchi, Enrico, 238–9
Bonaventura, Arnaldo (musicologist, 1862–1952), 34
Bonavia, Ferruccio, 92
Bonci, Alessandro, 6
Boni, Guido, 62
Bonomi, Ivanoe, 201, 230
Bonsanti, Alessandro, 119, 204
Bontempelli, Massimo, 26, 162
Bonucci, Arturo, 34, 43
Borgatti, Giuseppe, 6
Borciani, Paolo, 42
Borgese, Giuseppe Antonio, 233, 235
Borghi, Armando, 236
Borletti, Senator, 74, 79–81, 230
Borodin, Alexander, 82
Bossi, Marco Enrico, 6, 34
Bottai, Giuseppe (journalist, fascist minister, 1895–1959), 20–1, 28, 46–7, 54, 81, 94, 112–14, 120, 130, 141, 145, 204
Bottini (Fascist Federal Secretary, Milan), 80
Boulanger, Nadia, 93
Bovio, Libero, 110
Brahms, Johannes, 94
Brailowsky, Alexander, 167
Brengola, Riccardo, 42
Britten, Benjamin, 93
Bruch, Max, 186
Brueggemann, Alfred, 179
Brugnoli, Attilio, 34
Bruscantini, Sesto, 42
Buenos Aires, 56; Teatro Colón, 71, 108, 153, 155

Burney, Charles, 241
Busch, Adolf, 161, 166, 227
Busch, Fritz, 90, 95, 167, 227
Busch, Hermann, 227
Busoni, Ferruccio (composer, 1866–1924), 56, 70, 92; *Turandot*, 56, 95; *Arlecchino*, 56, 144, 198; *Doktor Faust*, 56, 95

Caldara, Emilio, 57
Campanini, Cleofonte, 6
Campogalliani, Ettore, 30
Caniglia, Maria, 42, 85, 94, 119
Cantelli, Guido, 42
Cardarelli, Vincenzo, 119, 163
Carelli, Emma, 71–2
Carisch (music publishers), 85
Carisch, Guido, 88
Carlo Lodovico di Borbone, 102
Carmirelli, Pina, 42; 'Casetta abissina', 97
Carosio, Margherita, 42
Carpi, Giannino, 42
Carrà, Carlo, 168
Carro di Tespi (mobile theatre), 63–4
Caruso, Enrico, 6, 17, 56
Casalini (fascist official), 61
Casals, Pablo, 166–7
Casati, Alessandro, 20, 35
Casavola, Franco (composer, 1891–1955), 30; *L'alba di Don Giovanni*, 90
Casella, Alfredo (composer, 1883–1947), 6–7, 25–7, 34–6, 39–40, 47, 53, 70–1, 89, 92–3, 94, 96, 116, 121, 132–9, 141, 143, 145, 159–60, 162, 181–3, 187, 190, 201, 205; *La favola di Orfeo*, 90; *Il deserto tentato*, 93, 137, 145; *La donna serpente*, 198; *Missa solemnis pro pace*, 201; subsidized, 119; and Mussolini, 136–7; and fascism, 136–9
Casella, Hélène (*née* Kahn), 187
Casella, Yvonne (*née* Muller), 187
Casimiri, Mons. Raffaele, 47
Castelnuovo-Tedesco, Clara, 184
Castelnuovo-Tedesco, Mario (composer, 1895–1968), 24, 89, 93, 129, 183–6, 206, 219; *Savonarola*, 93, 183; *Una vita di musica*, 184
Castelnuovo-Tedesco, Pietro, 184
Catania, 65–6
Christian Science Monitor, 71, 135–6
Church, Roman Catholic, 10, 111, 234; see also Holy Office
Cicogna, Giovanni Ascanio, 88, 230
Cinecittà, 128
Clausetti, Carlo, 88
Clemens, Clara, 219
Clementi, Muzio, 37, 50
Cogni, Giulio, 180
competitions, 10, 96–8
Colacicchi, Luigi, 179
Colasanti, Arduino, 34
Colombo, Anita, 80–1, 84, 116, 221
Colonna, Prospero, 102
Combarieu, Jules, 177
concert societies, 87–8
congresses, 10, 92, 94–5, 116
conservatories, 19, 33–43; see also under cities
Consolo, Ernesto, 34, 42
Coolidge, Elizabeth Sprague, 130, 181–2
Copertini, Spartaco, 96
Coppola, Piero, 94
Corelli, Arcangelo, 13, 15
Corelli, Franco, 42
Corporation for the Theatre, 75–6
Corriere della sera, Il, 23, 57, 85, 126, 210–11, 215, 218
Corrispondenza Politico-Diplomatica, 190
Corti, Mario, 42, 47
Cortopassi, Damiano, 97
Cortot, Alfred, 166, 181
Costa, Andrea, 107
Costarelli, Nicola, 199
Coster, Charles de, 203
Couperin, François, 48
Craft, Robert, 167–9
Cremona, 18, 116
Crepax, Gilberto, 34
Criscuolo, Filippo, 238
Crispi, Francesco, 7, 104
Cristoforeanu, Florica, 63

Critica fascista, 20
Croce, Benedetto (philosopher and senator, 1866–1954), 47, 49, 55, 93, 123, 125, 201; *see also* Manifestos

Dallapiccola, Luigi (composer, 1904–75), 16, 42, 70, 90, 93–4, 142, 145–6, 165, 200, 206; *Volo di notte*, 95, 190, 198; *Canti di prigionia*, 190–1, 194, 203; *Il prigioniero*, 203–4
Dal Monte, Toti (soprano, 1893–1975), 26, 152, 189
D'Amico, Fedele (music critic, 1912–), 26, 42, 198
D'Amico, Silvio, 47, 197
D'Annunzio, Gabriele (poet, 1863–1938), 8, 55, 111, 122–3, 168, 184, 208
Da Ponte, Lorenzo, 186
Debenedetti, Giacomo, 94
Debussy, Claude, 6, 36, 38, 48, 55, 82, 87, 106, 138, 181
De Capitani d'Arzago, Giuseppe, 79, 118
De Chirico, Giorgio, 200
Défauw, Désiré, 90, 167
De Filippo, Eduardo, 63
De Filippo, Peppino, 63
De Filippo, Titina, 63
De Fiori, V. E., 13
De Gasperi, Alcide, 201, 240
Delcroix, Carlo, 91–2
Della Ciaia, Azzolino, 37
Della Corte, Andrea (musicologist, 1883–1968), 25, 46–7, 53, 92, 94
Del Monaco, Mario, 42
De Luca, Giuseppe, 6
De Lucia, Fernando, 6, 34
Del Vecchio, Giorgio, 178
De Martino, Giacomo, 156, 230
Dent, Edward J., 92–3
Depero, Fortunato, 168
De Pirro, Nicola, 21, 54, 68–9, 142–3, 145, 152, 169, 198
Depretis, Agostino, 104
De Rensis, Raffaello, 11–16, 38, 60, 119, 137, 196
De Robertis, Giuseppe, 123

De Rosa, Dario, 42
De Sabata, Victor (conductor, 1892–1967), 82, 91, 96, 154, 160–1, 189
Desderi, Ettore, 30, 96
De Sica, Vittorio, 63
De Stefani, Alberto, 73–4
De Suvich, Fulvio, 232
De Vecchi di Val Cismon, Cesare Maria, 20, 40, 128, 134
De Vito, Gioconda, 189
Diaz, Armando, 221
Díaz, Porfirio, 150, 172
Di Marzio, Cornelio, 58–9, 134
Di Stefano, Giuseppe, 42
Dohnányi, Ernö, 157
Dollfuss, Engelbert, 175
Donizetti, Gaetano, 56, 70
Dopolavoro nazionale, 64
Dresden Staatsoper, 95
Dubois, Théodore, 37
Durante, Francesco, 37

early music, 37, 44, 56, 87, 93–5, 122; *see also under composers*
Ebert, Carl, 92
Egk, Werner, 142, 189
EIAR (national radio), 64, 91, 97, 121
Eichheim, Henry, 90
Einaudi (publishers), 52
Einaudi, Giulio, 50
Einaudi, Luigi, 49
Einstein, Albert, 174, 229
Einstein, Alfred, 92, 186, 211
Emmanuel, Maurice, 94
Enciclopedia italiana (Treccani), 19, 123–4, 158
Enesco, Georges, 166
Engel, Hans, 190
enti autonomi, 57–64, 69–70, 73–5, 77, 91, 198, 208, 242
Epoca, 107
Ercole, Francesco, 20, 118
Espresso, L', 47
Ethiopia, 7, 21, 42, 119, 137, 142, 144–5, 149, 155, 169, 175, 194

Fabbroni (Scala staff musician), 85
Facta, Luigi (prime minister, 1861–1934), 9
Falla, Manuel de, 89–91, 135, 167
Farinacci, Roberto (fascist leader, 1892–1945), 18, 116, 119–20, 141, 204, 231, 237
Farulli, Piero, 42
Fasano, Renato, 30
fasci di combattimento, 20, 208, 225
Fascist Party, 8–9, 19, 28, 124, 136, 146, 168–9, 178, 213; Grand Council of, 19–20, 75, 149, 178, 183, 200; membership in, 40–1, 64, 67, 71, 105, 116, 132, 150–1, 156, 162, 183, 185; mentality of, as seen by Toscanini, 240, and Fellini, 243
Fauré, Gabriel, 14
Favero, Mafalda, 63, 89
Fedele, Pietro, 20
Federzoni, Luigi, 53
Fellini, Federico, 243
Fermi, Enrico, 110
Ferone (Scala board member), 81
Ferrara, 87
Ferrara, Franco, 42, 119, 189
Ferraresi, Cesare, 42, 186
Ferrari Trecate, Luigi, 30, 34
Ferri, Enrico, 107
festivals, 10, 16, 21, 89–96
Feuermann, Emmanuel, 187
Finzi, Aldo, 90
Firkušný, Rudolf, 167
Fischer, Annie, 167
Fischer, Edwin, 95, 157, 189
Fisk Jubilee Singers, 166
Fiume, 8, 87, 208
Fleischmann, H. R., 178–9
Florence, 6, 87, 153, 183, 186, 203–4, 212; Conservatory, 24, 33–4, 98, 123, 204; Teatro Comunale, 27, 143, 201, 203; *Maggio Musicale*, 27, 70, 88–9, 91–5, 116, 127, 156, 171, 186, 189, 203, 226; University of, 48; Teatro della Pergola, 59; Politeama, 61, 72, 92; International Music Congresses, 92, 94, 116, 162, 171

Foà, Carlo, 178
Foa, Vittorio, 51, 54
Forges-Davanzati, Roberto, 113–14
Forino, Luigi (cellist, 1868–1936), 34, 38–40, 164
Forlì, 5, 12
Fornaroli, Cia, 227
Forzano, Giovacchino, 63, 107, 120
Françaix, Jean, 93
Francescatti, Zino, 85
Franci, Benvenuto, 63
Franco, Francisco, 169
Frassinelli (publishers), 52
Frescobaldi, Girolamo, 15, 37, 48
Furtwängler, Wilhelm, 94–5, 179, 189, 228
Futurist music, 3, 7, 168

Gabrilowitsch, Ossip, 219, 227
Gail, H. R., 211
Galeffi, Carlo, 65
Gallignani, Giuseppe (composer, 1851–1923), 34, 123, 209
Galuppi, Baldassare, 15
Garibaldi, Giuseppe, 5, 207, 233
Gasco, Alberto (music critic, 1879–1938), 24, 168
Gasperini, Guido, 34, 48
Gatti, Carlo, (musicologist, 1876–1965), 86, 88
Gatti, Guido Maria (music critic, 1892–1973), 44, 50, 92, 94, 141, 172
Gatti Casazza, Giulio, 155
Gavazzeni, Gianandrea (conductor, 1909–), 2–3, 42, 52, 91–2, 118, 135, 157–65, 178
Gazzelloni, Severino, 42
Gazette ufficiale, La, 92
General Adminstration for Theatre and Music, 66–70
'Generation of 1880, The', 7, 145, 205
Genoa, 34, 87; Teatro Carlo Felice, 59, 70, 201
Gentile, Giovanni (philosopher, fascist minister, 1875–1944), 19, 34, 43–4, 123–5, 158, 204

Gerarchia, 178
Germani, Fernando, 43
Gershwin, George, 90, 139
Gerster, Ottmar, 189
Ghedini, Giorgio Federico (composer, 1892–1965), 70; *Re Hassan*, 198
Ghinelli, Mario, 215
Ghislanzoni, Alberto, 119, 176–7, 180–1
Giazotto, Remo, 196–7
Gieseking, Walter, 167, 189
Gigli, Beniamino (tenor, 1890–1957), 26, 91, 148–50, 152, 202
Ginzburg, Leone, 51
Giolitti, Giovanni (prime minister, 1842–1928), 7–8, 103–4
Giordano, Umberto (composer, 1867–1948), 47, 70, 81, 83, 101, 110, 120–1, 197, 205, 219; *Andrea Chénier*, 5, 30, 120; *Madame Sans-Gêne*, 56; *Cesare*, 121
Giornale degli Artisti, Il, 238
Giornale d'Italia, Il, 195–6
'Giovinezza', 94, 97, 104, 175, 209–12, 214–16
Giua, Michele, 51, 54
Giuliani, Sandro, 86
Giulini, Carlo Maria, 42
Giuranna, Barbara, 97, 119
Giustizia e Libertà (anti-fascist movement and newspaper), 50–1, 54, 127, 220, 225
Glinka, Mikhail, 56
Gluck, Christoph W. von, 93, 95
Gobbi, Tito, 42, 198
Gobetti, Piero, 49
Godowsky, Leopold, 167
Göbbels, Paul Josef, 161, 180, 189
Goethe, Johann W. von, 47
Gonvierre, Claudio, 43
Göring, Hermann, 149, 161
Gorini, Gino, 93
Gounod, Charles, 56
government, Italian, directives on musical education, 10, 43–8, 145, 164; subsidies to opera houses, 61–4, 67, 78, 84, 129; Mulé Project, 63; theatre censorship, 66; on concert programming, 87, 89; auditorium construction, 98–100; *see also* General Administration for Theatre and Music, Ministry of National Education, and Ministry of Popular Culture
Graener, Paul, 90, 180
Graf, Herbert, 95
Gramatica, Emma, 63
Gramatica, Irma, 63
Granados, Enrique, 14
Grandi, Dino, 152, 213
Grassi, Paolo, 76
Greppi, Antonio, 237, 239
Guarnieri, Antonio, 119, 134
Guastalla, Claudio, 132
Guenther, H. F. K., 190
Guerrini, Guido, 24–5, 47, 90
Gui, Vittorio (conductor, 1885–1975), 53, 60, 68, 72, 88, 91, 93–4, 125, 143–4, 147, 156, 158, 189, 190, 228
Gulli, Franco, 42

Halévy, Jacques, 56
Handel, George Frederick, 95, 187
Haydn, Franz Josef, 94
Heifetz, Jascha, 166, 183, 185
Herriot, Edouard, 225
Hertzka, Emil, 181–2, 188
Hess, Rudolf, 94
Hesse, Hermann, 47
Heyworth, Peter, 174–5
Hindemith, Paul, 38, 89–90, 94–5, 138, 167, 180, 199
Hitler, Adolf, 9–10, 94, 139, 149, 152, 173, 175, 178, 180–1, 190–1, 195, 227–8
Hoare, Sir Samuel, 191
Hofmannsthal, Hugo von, 144, 187
Holl, Karl, 211
Holy Office, 180
Honegger, Arthur, 89, 91, 93, 135, 167, 182, 198
Horowitz, Vladimir, 85, 167
Huberman, Bronisław, 166

Huxley, Aldous, 241

Ibert, Jacques, 90
Illersberg, Antonio, 34
Impero, L', 185
Indy, Vincent d', 177
Israel Philharmonic, 229
Italia letteraria, 160, 162
Italian Institute of Music History, 129, 158
Italian Society of Authors and Publishers, 114–15

Jachino, Carlo, 70, 96
Jadassohn, Salomon, 37
Jaques-Dalcroze, Emile, 44
Jews, *see* anti-semitism *and* racial laws

Kahn, Otto, 156, 178
Karajan, Herbert von, 95, 189
Keiter, Friedrich, 190
Kempff, Wilhelm, 189
Klemperer, Otto, 94, 167, 174–5, 170
Knappertsbusch, Hans, 228
Kodály, Zoltán, 89, 94, 167, 170, 199
Koussevitzky, Serge, 219
Krauss, Clemens, 91, 175
Kreisler, Fritz, 166, 174–5
Křenek, Ernst, 89, 93–4, 171

Labia, Maria, 209
Labroca, Mario (composer and functionary, 1896–1973), 27, 47, 53, 62, 65, 68, 89, 93, 96, 98, 140, 143, 160, 185, 205, 226
La Guardia, Fiorello, 237
Lambert, Constant, 91
Lana, Libero, 42
Lancellotti, Arturo, 119
Landau, Rom, 173
Landowska, Wanda, 166
La Piana, Giorgio, 233, 235
Lattuada, Felice; *La tempesta*, 198
Laski, Neville, 180
Lauri Volpi, Giacomo (tenor, 1892–1979), 150, 152, 189

Lazzari, Marino, 47, 197–8
Leghorn, 87, 111
Lehmann, Lotte, 85
Leo, Leonardo, 37
Leoncavallo, Ruggero, 5, 63, 70, 86
Levi, Renato, 186
Lewis, Sinclair, 55
Liadov, Anatoly, 82
Life (magazine), 234–5
Lipparini, Giuseppe, 213
Liszt, Franz, 37
Littorali della cultura, 96–8
Liuzzi, Alberto, 178
Liuzzi, Ferdinando, 34
Loria, Arturo, 94
Lotta di classe, La, 12
Lualdi, Adriano (composer and functionary, 1885–1971), 21–3, 28, 30, 37, 47, 50, 61–2, 70, 89, 92, 97–8, 141, 144, 158–60, 162, 165, 188–9, 195, 204; *La Grançèola*, 90
Lucca, 18
Lucerne, 229
Luciani, Sebastiano Arturo, 94
Ludwig, Emil, 14–15, 224–5
Lussu, Emilio, 50
Lvov, Yakov Lvovich, 169

Mack Smith, Denis, 8, 17, 20, 123, 194
Maderna, Bruno, 42, 203
Mahler, Gustav, 189
Mainardi Colleoni, Ada, 226
Mainardi, Enrico (cellist, 1897–1976), 85, 126, 156–7, 189, 226
Maine, Basil, 92
Malipiero, Gian Francesco (composer, 1882–1973), 6–7, 16, 25–7, 30, 34, 42, 53, 70, 89, 91, 93–6, 116, 121, 128, 132–4, 137, 141–3, 158–9, 162, 171–2, 205–6; *Pantea*, 90; *La Passione*, 93; *Antonio e Cleopatra*, 94; *Torneo notturno*, 142; *Giulio Cesare*, 145; *I capricci di Callot*, 198; and Mussolini, 128, 132–4, 145
Malipiero, Riccardo, 52, 203
Manchester Guardian, 168

Mancinelli, Luigi, 35, 76–7, 80, 209
manifestos, political: of Italian
   musicians, 23–6, 132; of fascist
   intellectuals ('Gentile Manifesto'),
   124–5; Croce counter-manifesto,
   125–6, 156, 210; of the Race, 182, 193;
   'An Italian Manifesto', 235
Mantelli, Alberto, 198
Manuel, Roland, 94
Marchioro, Edoardo, 118
Marconi, Guglielmo, 110, 230
Marenzio, Luca, 37
Maria José di Savoia, 94, 145, 230, 232
Marinetti, Filippo Tommaso (writer,
   1876–1944), 7, 26, 110, 119, 124, 168,
   208
Marinuzzi, Gino (conductor, 1882–1945),
   30, 47, 65, 72–3, 85, 189, 220
Markevitch, Igor, 93–4, 203
Marotti, Guido, 104
Martini, Arturo, 119, 200
Martucci, Giuseppe, 6, 186, 213–15,
   217–18
Marziali (Milan Prefect), 238
Mascagni, Edoardo, 119
Mascagni, Lina, 110
Mascagni, Pietro (composer, 1863–
   1945), 15, 28, 47, 60, 70, 83, 98, 101,
   106–21, 132, 136, 197, 205; Cavalleria
   rusticana, 5, 63, 71, 106, 111, 136; Il
   piccolo Marat, 56, 107–8; and
   Mussolini, 107–15, 117, 119–20;
   patriotic music, 110; and Vatican, 111,
   201; L'amico Fritz, 111; Nerone, 115–19;
   subsidized, 119–20, 163
Mascheroni, Eduardo, 6
Masetti, Enzo, 96
Massarani, Renzo (composer, 1898–
   1975), 89, 96, 184–6
Massenet, Jules, 6
Mataloni, Jenner, 81–6
Matteotti, Giacomo (socialist leader,
   1885–1924), 126, 152, 209, 213
Mazzini, Giuseppe, 5, 16, 233
Mazzini Society, 232, 234, 237
Mazzoni, Azalea, 151

Mendelssohn, Felix, 184, 189
Menuhin, Yehudi, 167
Mercadante, Giuseppe S., 56
Meridiano di Roma, Il, 55, 162
Messaggero, Il, 199, 233
Metropolitan Opera Company, The,
   155–6, 208
Meyebeer, Giacomo, 56
Michaelis, Meir, 177, 180, 182
Mila, Massimo (musicologist, 1910–),
   2–3, 7, 42, 47–55, 92, 121, 147, 158,
   197, 199
Milan, 5–6, 9, 43, 87–8, 111, 199, 204,
   212, 238; Conservatory, 23, 33–5, 117,
   123, 128, 157, 164, 186–7, 209; School
   of Singing and the Stage, 'M. E. Bossi'
   Music Academy, 43; La Scala, 57–8,
   61, 65, 70–86, 88, 111, 117, 127, 135,
   149, 151–2, 154–5, 160–1, 164, 168,
   186, 189, 198, 201, 219, 222, 227, 234,
   239, and see under Toscanini; Ente
   concerti orchestrali, 88; Teatro del
   Popolo, 88; radio orchestra, 89;
   Teatro Lirico (originally della
   Canobbiana), 98; Teatro Dal Verme,
   99
Milhaud, Darius, 89, 91, 94–5, 140, 171,
   182, 205
Milstein, Nathan, 167
Ministry of National Education
   (originally, of Public Education), 19–
   20, 23, 34–5, 40–4, 46–7, 85, 91, 118,
   123, 130, 158, 197–8
Ministry of Popular Culture (originally,
   of the Press and Propaganda), known
   also as MinCulPop, 19–21, 27, 29, 66–
   70, 87, 119, 128, 140, 142, 156, 162,
   169, 184–5, 198
Ministry of the Interior, 184
Mitropoulos, Dimitri, 167, 185
Mocchi, Walter (impresario, 1880–1955),
   64, 71–2, 108, 153, 188, 239
Modigliani, Amedeo, 177
Modigliani, Ettore, 85
Molinari, Bernardino (conductor, 1880–
   1952), 28, 30, 87, 89, 99, 135, 154–5,
   161, 164, 189

Molinari, Mary, 215
Mondadori, Arnoldo, 158
Mondo, Il, 125, 236
Montanari, Nunzio, 42
Montanelli, Archimede, 12
Montanelli, Indro, 214
Montemezzi, Italo, 56; L'amore dei tre re, 56, 230
Monteux, Pierre, 167
Monteverdi, Claudio, 15, 37, 44, 56, 70, 93, 95
Monti, Augusto, 50–1
Mooser, Aloys, 92, 94
Morini, Mario, 117
Mortari, Virgilio, 90, 95–6
Mozart, Wolfgang A., 47, 93, 189
Mugnone, Leopoldo, 6, 119
Mulè, Giuseppe (composer and functionary, 1885–1951), 21, 24–6, 30, 34, 36, 38, 47, 61, 70, 89, 93, 96, 98, 116, 141, 144, 158–60, 164–5, 204
Müller-Widmann, Oscar (Mrs), 169–70
Munich State Opera, 189
Mursino, Tito Silvio, pseudonym, see V. Mussolini
Musica d'oggi, 12, 16, 34, 43, 46, 96, 99, 178–9, 186–7, 199
Musica e scena, 58, 108, 178
musicians' unions, 10, 21, 23–4, 27–31, 40, 43, 46, 61–2, 67–9, 87, 96, 127–8, 134, 144, 156, 165, 180
music schools, 19; see under cities
Musicista, Il, 180
musique concrète, 7
Mussolini, Benito (fascist dictator, 1883–1945), 5, 7–10, 33, 61, 75, 96, 103, 107–15, 126–7, 131–2, 145–6, 148, 158, 161, 163, 168, 172–5, 194–5, 200–1, 203–4, 208–9, 233, 236; and music, 11–17, 21; and subordinates, 18–20; and musicians, 21–33, 40, 52, 149–57, 197, 202; and lyric theatre, 58; and national opera house, 71, 73; and La Scala, 73–4, 76–9, 81–6, 208; and festivals, 89–90, 92; and Nazis, 94, 178, 180; and Nerone, 117–19; and

Jews, 177–8, 180, 182–4; and composers, see under composers' names; and Toscanini, see Toscanini
Mussolini, Bruno, 15
Mussolini, Vittorio, 15, 153, 199–200, 233
Mussorgsky, Modest, 6, 95
Muzio, Claudio, 72

Naples, 6, 34, 87, 169; Conservatory, 21, 24, 33–4, 121, 164, 204; Teatro San Carlo, 59, 70, 179
Napoli, Gennaro, 24–5, 34
Napoli, Jacopo, 70
Nasi, Giovanni, 49
Nataletti, Giorgio, 179
Nazione, La, 94
Nenni, Pietro, 201, 240
Nettl, Paul, 178
New York, 57; Philharmonic, 111, 183, 212–13; see also Metropolitan Opera Company
Nicolodi, Fiamma, 2–3, 52, 69–70, 89–90, 101, 107, 110, 120, 132, 136, 157
Nielsen, Riccardo, 93
Nordio, Cesare, 34, 47
Noto, Oreste, 237–9
Notte, La, 205
Nuova antologia, La, 128
Nuova Italia musicale, La, 69

Offenbach, Jacques, 95, 189
Ojetti, Ugo, 47, 92, 94, 126, 162, 210
Olivero, Magda, 42
Olschki, Leo, 230
opera houses, 55–86; see under cities; see also under government, Italian
Orff, Carl, 189, 198
Orsini, G., 108, 111, 115
OVRA (secret police), 51

Pacciardi, Randolfo, 233, 235
Paderewski, Ignace J., 167, 172–4
Padua, 34, 87; University of, 133–4
Paganini, Niccolò, 6, 37
Palermo, 6, 19, 70, 87; Conservatory, 22, 34

Palestrina, Giovanni P. da, 15, 37, 44, 122

Panerai, Rolando, 42

Panizza, Ettore, 81

Pannain, Guido, 34, 47, 94, 179

Paone, Remigio, 65, 119, 230

Papini, Giovanni, 26, 123

Paribene, Giulio Cesare, 52, 55

Paris, 50–1, 110, 134, 147, 185

Parma, 6, 87, 122; Conservatory, 33, 122; Teatro Regio, 122

Parri, Ferruccio, 239

Partito popolare, 8

Pasero, Tancredi, 94

Pasquini, Bernardo, 37

Pavese, Cesare, 52, 55

Pavolini, Alessandro, 184

Pavolini, Corrado, 160

Pederzini, Gianna, 18

Pegreffi, Elisa, 42

Pelliccia, Arrigo, 42, 189

Peragallo, Mario, 70

Pergolesi, Giovanni Battista, 56

Perosi, Lorenzo (composer, 1872–1956), 111

Perrachio, Luigi (composer and teacher, 1883–1966), 36–8

Persico, Mario, 70

Pertile, Aureliano (tenor, 1885–1952), 118, 151

Perugia, 87; *Sagra musicale umbra*, 95

Pesaro, 16, 34, 63, 87

Petacci, Clara, 204

Petrassi, Goffredo (composer, 1904–), 2–3, 42, 94, 139–47, 165, 197, 206; *Coro di morti*, 198

Petrella, Clara, 42

Petrella, Errico, 56

Petri, Egon, 166

Peverelli, Carlo, 80

Piacentini, Marcello, 71

Piatigorsky, Gregor, 167, 183

Pick-Mangiagalli, Riccardo, 24, 70, 81, 89

Pierantoni, Gino, 112–14

Pilati, Mario, 90, 96

Pini Corsi, Antonio, 6

Pinzauti, Leonardo (critic, 1926–), 91, 94, 156

Pirandello, Luigi, 26, 110, 124, 168

Pirrotta, Nino, 42

Pisa, 152

Pisacane, Carlo, 55

Pitigrilli (pseudonym of Dino Segre), 51

Pius XI, Pope (Ratti), 111, 182

Pius XII, Pope (Pacelli), 201

Pizzetti, Ildebrando (composer, 1880–1968), 7, 15, 24–6, 30, 34–5, 39, 47, 53, 70, 83, 85, 89, 91, 93, 96–8, 121–32, 141–2, 145, 158, 164, 197–8, 201–2, 205–6; *La rappresentazione di Santa Uliva*, 92; *Orsèolo*, 93; 126–7; *Requiem Mass*, 121; *La nave*, 123; *Fedra*, 123; *Débora e Jaèle*, 126–7; *Scipione l'Africano*, 128; *Epithalamium*, 130; and Mussolini, 126–7, 129–31; and Castelnuovo-Tedesco, 129, 183

Polo, Enrico, 34

Polverelli, Gaetano, 21

Polzinetti, Dagoberto, 86

Ponchielli, Amilcare, 70, 116–17

Porpora, Nicola, 37

Porrino, Ennio, 47

Porro, Carlo, 221

Poulenc, Francis, 90

Prandelli, Giacinto, 42

Pratella, Francesco B., 7, 168

Previtali, Fernando, 42, 93

Prezzolini, Giuseppe, 107, 123

Příhoda, Váša, 167

Principe, Remy, 34

Prokofiev, Sergei, 54, 89, 135, 166–7, 199

Prunières, Henry, 92, 181–2, 188

Puccini, Giacomo (composer, 1858–1924), 15, 24, 59, 70, 101–6, 121, 130, 170, 239; *Manon Lescaut*, 5, 102; *La bohème*, 5, 63, 102; *La fanciulla del West*, 56, 102; the *Trittico*, 56, 102; *La rondine*, 56, 102; *Tosca*, 71, 102; *Madama Butterfly*, 102; *Turandot*, 102, 210–11; 'Hymn to Rome', 102–3; and Mussolini, 104

Purcell, Henry, 95

Rachmaninoff, Sergei, 167
racial laws, 87, 129, 141–2, 146, 171, 177, 183–6, 188, 190–1; see also anti-semitism
Rameau, Jean-Philippe, 93
Ranzato, Virgilio, 14
Rassegna musicale, La (originally Il pianoforte), 16, 36, 44, 46, 49, 50, 92, 127, 141, 158, 172, 178–80, 186–8, 197–9
Ravel, Maurice, 50, 91, 93, 144, 167
Reggio, Emilia, 87
Regime fascista, Il, 46, 231
Reich, Willi, 94, 171
Reiner, Fritz, 90
Remarque, Erich Maria, 158, 227
Resistance, 52
Respighi, Elsa, 132, 215
Respighi, Ottorino (composer, 1879–1936), 7, 24–5, 27–9, 34, 42, 69–70, 83, 89, 96, 111, 121, 128, 130–2, 134, 141, 161, 205, 214; The Fountains of Rome, The Pines of Rome, and Roman Festivals, 131; Belfagor, 198
Resto del Carlino, Il, 218, 221
Rhené-Baton, 166
Ribbentrop, Joachim von, 94, 149
Ribla, Gertrud, 233
Ricordi, G., & Co., 12, 16, 85
Ricordi, Tito (publisher, 1865–1933), 5, 222
Riemann, Hugo, 177
Rieti, 69
Rieti, Vittorio, 90, 96, 185–6
Rimini, 63
Rimsky-Korsakov, Nicolai A., 177
Robeson, Paul, 166
Rocca, Gino, 81, 119
Rocca, Lodovico (composer, 1895–1986), 70, 164; Il Dibuk, 178
Rognoni, Luigi, 42
Roma fascista, 108
Rome, 6–7, 10, 20–1, 29, 34, 96, 99, 140–2, 147, 149, 153, 175, 199, 201, 212, 229; Augusteum, 17, 87–9, 98, 100, 140, 154, 161, 164, 167, 181;

Teatro Costanzi, 18, 71, 98, 106–9, 143, and Teatro Reale references; Conservatory (previously Liceo Musicale), 23, 33, 38, 40, 43, 128, 134, 139–40, 145, 147, 157, 164, 179, 204, 206; Teatro Reale dell' Opera, 28, 59, 65, 70–3, 78, 121, 151, 155–6, 168, 189, 194, 198, 225; Regina Coeli (prison), 50, 55, 153; Contemporary Opera Cycles, 70; Accademia e Teatro Nazionale dell'Arte, 60; First National Exhibition of Contemporary Music, 96; Teatro Adriano, 99, 202; Teatro delle Arti, 145, 198–9; Teatro Argentina, 202
Roncaglia, Gino, 44–6
Ronda, La (movement and monthly), 163
Ronga, Luigi, 94
Roni, Amilcare, 150
Rosbaud, Hans, 92
Rosenberg, Hilding, 93
Rosselli, Carlo, 50–1
Rossi, Franco, 42
Rossi, Mario, 190
Rossi, Michelangelo, 37
Rossi-Doria, Gastone, 158
Rossini, Gioacchino, 56, 82, 92–3, 95, 239
Rossoni, Edmondo, 110
Rota, Nino, 95–6
Roth, Cecil, 177
Roussel, Albert, 89–90, 167, 171
Rubinstein, Artur, 166
Rubinstein, Ida, 94
Ruffo, Titta (baritone, 1877–1953), 6, 152–4, 203
Russolo, Luigi, 7, 168

Saba, Umberto, 177
Salvatori, Fausto, 102
Salvemini, Gaetano (historian, 1873–1957), 9, 48, 123–4, 227–8, 233–6
Salviucci, Giovanni, 165
Salzburg, see under Toscanini
Saminsky, Lazare, 90
San Martino, Enrico di, 40, 172

Santoliquido, Francesco (composer, 1883–1971), 89, 119, 181–2, 188
Sanzogno, Nino, 5, 42, 143
Sapori, Francesco, 15
Saragat, Giuseppe, 201
Sardinia, 7
Sarfatti, Margherita, 13, 178, 185
Sartori, Claudio, 42
Sassoli, Ada, 43
Savagnone, Giuseppe, 70
Scala, La, *see under* Milan *and under* Toscanini
Scandiani, Angelo, 75, 79–80, 84
Scarlatti, Domenico, 15, 37
Scarpini, Pietro, 42
Scenario, 21
Scherchen, Hermann, 91, 93, 166, 172
Scherillo, 35
Schiller, Friedrich, 47
Schinelli, Achille (pedagogue, 1882–1969), 43, 46–7, 163–4
Schipa, Tito, 151
Schleiffer, Yuri, 169
Schnabel, Artur, 167, 179
Schnabl Rossi, Riccardo, 103
Schoenberg, Arnold, 55–6, 92, 106, 135–6, 140, 142, 161, 167, 170–1, 177, 182, 188–9, 198–9
Schopenhauer, Arthur, 55
Schultze, Norbert, 189
Schumann, Robert, 56, 95
Schuricht, Carl, 189
Schuschnigg, Kurt von, 175, 227
Scotti, Antonio, 6
Scotto, Ottavio, 72–3
Scuderi, Gaspare, 30
Secchi, Luigi L., 237
Secolo, Il, 74
Segovia, Andrés, 166
Scriabin, Alexander, 135
Serafin, Tullio, 6, 89, 116, 127, 155–6, 198, 205
Serato, Arrigo, 43, 126
Serkin, Rudolf, 166, 227
Sessions, Roger, 92
Setaccioli, Giacomo, 34

Ševčik, Otakar, 37
Sforza, Carlo, 233–5
Sgambati, Giovanni, 6
Shostakovich, Dmitri, 54, 167, 199–200, 233
Siena, 87; Accademia Musicale Chigiana, 43; *Settimane musicali*, 95
Siepi, Cesare, 42
Simionato, Giulietta, 42
Simoni, Renato, 110
Sinigaglia, Leone (composer, 1868–1944), 53, 202
Smareglia, Antonio, 34
Socialist Party, 8
Soffici, Ardengo, 123
Soldati, Mario, 55
Sonzogno, Giulio C., 70
Sonzogno (music publishers), 58, 108
Sowerby, Leo, 90
Spain, 142, 147, 150, 169, 175
Spalding, Albert, 185
Spani, Hina, 63
Spezzaferri, Giovanni, 30
Spini, Daniele, 131–2
Spontini, Gaspare, 92
squadre, squadrismo, 9, 21, 124, 176
Stabile, Mariano, 13, 189, 239
Staglieno, Marcello, 214
Stampa, La, 23, 25, 47
Starace, Achille, 17, 64, 71, 151, 204, 237
Stefan, Paul, 92
Steiner, Rudolf, 188
Stokowski, Leopold, 167
Storchio, Rosina, 6
Stracciari, Maria, 151–2
Stracciari, Riccardo (baritone, 1875–1955), 151–2
Strakacz, Aniela, 173
Strakacz, Sylwin, 173
Strasser, Otto, 175
Strauss, Richard, 6, 21, 38, 55–6, 82, 87, 91, 95, 144, 157, 166–7, 171, 177, 181
Stravinsky, Igor (composer, 1882–1971), 56, 88–9, 91, 93, 96, 129, 135, 138, 140, 142, 144, 161, 167–9, 182, 198–9, 206
Sturzo, Luigi, 227

Sved, Italo, 177
Szymanowski, Karol, 89, 135

Tacchinardi (music theorist), 48
Taddei, Giuseppe, 42
Tagliavini, Ferruccio, 42
Tajo, Italo, 42
Tamagno, Francesco, 6
Tansman, Alexander, 89
Tarchiani, Alberto, 50, 233–4, 237
Tassinari, Pia, 42
Tasso, Torquato, 95
Tchaikovsky, Pyotr I., 6
Teatro Reale dell'Opera, *see under* Rome
Tebaldi, Renata, 42
Tebaldini, Giovanni, 122
Tegani, Ulderico, 81–2
Telegrafo, Il, 186
Tetrazzini, Luisa, 6, 56
Tevere, Il, 181
Thibaud, Jacques, 166
Thiene, 63
Tintori, Giampiero, 42, 105
Tivoli, 42
Toch, Ernst, 90
Togliatti, Palmiro, 201, 240
Tommasini, Vincenzo, 89, 216, 230
Toni, Alceo (composer and functionary, 1884–1969), 21, 23–8, 30, 47, 82, 90, 96–7, 119, 132, 137, 141, 158–60, 204–5
Torrefranca, Fausto (musicologist, 1883–1955), 6, 47–8, 53, 94, 119, 197
Toscanini, Arturo (conductor, 1867–1957), 1, 6, 59, 88, 111, 142, 149, 151, 161, 164, 179, 183, 185, 188, 207–40; Bologna incident, 18, 213–20, 236; and Gallignani and Cesari, 34–5, 209; and Mussolini, 35, 74–5, 208, 210–13, 215–16, 218–19, 225–6, 230, 232, 235–6; and La Scala, 57, 62, 72, 74–7, 80, 82, 84, 208–11, 218, 237, 239–40; and Puccini, 102; and Mascagni, 111; and Salzburg, 156, 227–9; political police file on, 220–4; and Bayreuth, 227; and Palestine, 229; and BBC

Symphony, 229; and Lucerne, 229–31; declaration 'To the People of America', 234–5
Toscanini, Wally, 236
Toscanini, Walter, 214, 232
Toscanini, Wanda, 214
Thompson, Dorothy, 235
Trent, 7
Treviso, 87
Tribuna, La, 168, 218
Trieste, 7, 34, 70, 87, 169
Turin, 6–7, 34, 47, 50–3, 87, 134, 188, 199, 212; Conservatory, 47, 164, 202; University of, 47, 49; Teatro di, 50, 166; Teatro Regio, 59, 99–100; Experimental Lyric Theatre, 60; radio orchestra, 179, 184

Udine, 87
Umberto di Savoia, Crown Prince (later King Umberto II), 7, 94
Unità, L', 47
UTET (publishers), 49, 52

Valcarenghi, Aldo, 220
Valdengo, Giuseppe, 42
Valisi, Antonio, 42
Valletti, Cesare, 42
Varèse, Edgard, 7
Vatielli, Francesco, 94
Vecsey, Ferenc, 167
Veneziani, Vittore, 186, 237
Venice, 6–7, 16, 34, 47, 87, 128; Teatro la Fenice, 70, 140, 143–4, 172, 175, 198; Biennale, 75, 89–90, 172; *Festival internazionale di musica*, 89–91, 142, 159–60; Conservatory, 134
Venturi, Lionello, 233, 235
Veracini, Antonio, 14
Verdi, Giuseppe, 5, 13, 24, 34, 37, 47, 56–7, 63, 70, 82, 91–4, 130, 143, 149, 153–4, 181, 187, 189, 196, 209, 211, 225, 230, 233, 236, 239
Veretti, Antonio, 70, 90, 94, 96; *La scuola del villaggio*, 198
verismo, 69–70, 122, 159, 205

Verona, 69, 87
Vicenza, 87
Victor Emmanuel III (1869–1947; King of Italy, 1900–46), 9, 16, 40, 73, 106, 130, 150, 182, 197, 200, 234–5
Vienna Philharmonic, 91, 93, 179, 227
Vienna State Opera, 91, 175
Viennese School (Second), 138, 158, 170–2; *see also under composers' names*
Villiers de l'Isle-Adam, Philippe, 203
Visconti di Modrone, Guido, 80, 175–6
Vitale, Edoardo, 63–4, 98
Vittadini, Franco, 30
Vivaldi, Antonio, 14–15
Voce, La, 123
Vogel, Vladimir, 93
Volpi di Misurata, Contessa, 230
Votto, Antonino, 85, 89, 189
Votto, Pariso, 203
Vuillermoz, Emile, 92, 94

Wagner, Richard, 6, 15, 48, 56–7, 82, 108, 134, 194, 230
Wagner, Winifred, 224, 227
Wallek, Oscar, 95
Walter, Bruno, 93–4, 175, 179, 228
Walton, William, 89

Washington, 154, 156
Waterhouse, J. C. G., 3, 185
Webern, Anton, 171
Weill, Kurt, 179, 189
Weingartner, Felix von, 91, 93
Wellesz, Egon, 94
Wieniawski, Henryk, 187
Wolf-Ferrari, Ermanno, 56, 70; *L'amore medico*, 56

Yourcenar, Marguerite, 166

Zagarolo, 139
Zampieri, Giusto, 34
Zandonai, Riccardo (composer, 1883–1944), 7, 24–5, 30, 56, 69–70, 89, 98; *Francesca da Rimini*, 56; *Giulietta e Romeo*, 56
Zanella, Amilcare, 34
Zanettovich, Renato, 42
Zecchi, Adone, 30
Zecchi, Carlo, 85, 157
Zemlinsky, Alexander von, 179
'Zenatello, Giovanni, 6
Zhdanov, A. A., 54
Zuelli, Guglielmo, 34
Zuffellato, Guido, 24
Zweig, Stefan, 191